COMMERCIAL AWARENESS FOR LAWYERS

COMMERCIAL AWARENESS FOR LAWYERS

Andrew Todd, LLB (Hons), Dp Law, MBA
Solicitor, Glasgow

Iain Sim, LLB (Hons), DLP, NP
Solicitor; Company Director; and Visiting Lecturer at the University of Strathclyde

W. GREEN

THOMSON REUTERS

Published in 2016 by Thomson Reuters (Professional) UK Limited trading as W. Green, 21 Alva Street, Edinburgh EH2 4PS (Registered in England & Wales, Company No.1679046. Registered Office and address for service: 2nd floor, 1 Mark Square, Leonard Street, London, EC2A 4EG). For further information on our products and services, visit *www.sweetandmaxwell.co.uk/wgreen*.

Typeset by LBJ Typesetting Ltd.
Printed and bound in the UK by by CPI Group (UK) Ltd, Croydon, CR0 4YY

No natural forests were destroyed to make this product; only farmed timber was used and replanted.

A CIP catalogue record for this title is available from the British Library

ISBN 978-0-414-055971

Thomson Reuters and the Thomson Reuters Logo are trademarks of Thomson Reuters.

CONTENTS

Pour ma marraine Jeanne Morizur,
my parents, my godson Matthew, and Louis.

—Iain Sim

To Mum, Dad, Iain, Lesley and Barney.

—Andrew Todd

FOREWORD

Solicitors help people to make the biggest decisions they'll ever face.

We help people in their personal lives: we help newlyweds buy their first home together; we protect grandparents passing on inheritances to family and friends; we deal with illness and incapacity; savings and investments; and we fight to protect them from prison.

We help people in their business lives: we help directors as companies expand; we protect ideas and property; we act for employees and employers; directors and owners; companies that make money; charities that strive to change the world; we help commerce thrive and economies grow.

Regardless of where your career takes you—whether it be working in a small town for local businesses and families, or for a large city firm on global deals; working in-house for private companies, or the public sector; or, defending the disadvantaged, or prosecuting those who break the law—your advice has consequences and people will rely on you as they make these life changing decisions. Being a solicitor matters.

You should be proud to be a solicitor. I am—because a solicitor has a vital role in the heart of society—and that role starts with understanding what it means to be a solicitor.

Do you know the difference between a lawyer and a solicitor? Solicitors and advocates? Do you know why solicitors have professional standards and the role of the Law Society of Scotland to help protect you and the public? Do you know what skills you need to listen to clients and understand what they want? Can you turn that into relevant advice—and, if you're in private practice, can you do that and make money for you and your firm?

That's why I welcome the publication of *Commercial Awareness for Lawyers*, a book that deals not just with law but with practice, and one that will help students, trainees and new lawyers to answer these questions; understand what it means to be a solicitor; and be part of a profession that is trusted to help people make life changing decisions.

Eilidh Wiseman
President
The Law Society of Scotland

TABLE OF CASES

(All references are to paragraph numbers)

INTRODUCTION

What is commercial awareness?

Job adverts want you to show it. Interviewers question you about it. Employers ask you to demonstrate you have it—but what does "commercial awareness" mean?

Finding a single (or simple) definition isn't easy. To misquote Justice Stewart, "commercial awareness is like pornography—you know it when you see it". But do we? When a lawyer is described as thinking "commercially" what are we *actually* describing? We think commercial awareness causes people problems because the term "commercial awareness" means different things to different people. For some it means knowing the latest news about law firms and lawyers. For others it refers to general business skills like marketing, finance, HR or operations. It has different meanings. There's no single definition that people can turn to and say "this is commercial awareness". Instead, if we want to know what commercial awareness means we need to understand the three main senses in which it's used.

Commercial awareness means knowing what it means to be a lawyer

First, commercial awareness includes understanding what it means to be a lawyer, to be a professional, and how the legal world works. Do you understand your professional standards? Do you know what senior associates do? Do you know why your firm is a partnership? Do you know who the Magic Circle are and why they're called that? In short, do you understand what lawyers and law firms do?

Commercial awareness means knowing your clients

Second, commercial awareness can mean you understand not just how to give legal advice to clients but also the impact it will have on them—both personally and professionally. You're not writing academic essays any more. When you give clients advice it bears real consequences for them. Clients will divorce partners, cut people from wills, buy expensive homes, change their business or even go to jail based on what you tell them. Commercial awareness in this context means understanding that what you do has consequences.

Commercial awareness means knowing how to run a business and make money

Finally, commercial awareness can refer to the general business knowledge and skills that business people have. Can you read a set of financial accounts? Do you know the difference between profit, cash, capital and debt? Can you manage people? Do you have IT skills? Can you sell yourself and bring in business? Are you a businessperson as well as a lawyer?

To make things even more complicated, commercial awareness may not refer to any of these definitions at all—it may refer to a combination of all three. However, if you know all three definitions you'll be prepared for any combination.

Why write a book on commercial awareness?

We believe students, trainees and new lawyers need a book that explores each of the three definitions. One that will help you become commercially aware (however you define it). And, for those looking for their first jobs, whether as a trainee or as a new lawyer, no matter who asks you, you'll be prepared to answer any question about it.

Structure of the book

Commercial awareness means knowing you're a lawyer

In Pt 1 (becoming a lawyer), we examine the current legal market from the point of view of someone just starting his or her career. We explain what lawyers do, who your clients are likely to be, how law firms have developed over the last 200 years, and how they, and you, use reputation to persuade clients to choose you as their lawyer.

During this section we refer to current law firms and some of the work they do. We have tried to refer to firms as we see them in April 2016. However, we realise that the legal market moves fast and firms (and reputations) can quickly change. We had a choice. We could either refer to no firms, as they might change, or we could give you a snapshot of the current market. We thought a snapshot of the current market would be more useful to you. Also, when we refer to firms and we're not quoting a direct source to describe it, we're just talking about our view of those firms. Other people may have a different view. You may have your own view. There's no right or wrong but it'll give you a starting point to agree (or disagree) with what we say.

We also examine some of the technical rules about becoming a lawyer. We look at the professional requirements in Ch.11 (how to be professional) and Ch.12 (how to avoid complaints). While in Ch.21 (how to choose a type of law firm) we look at the different corporate structures used by law firms such as partnerships, limited liability partnerships and limited companies.

Commercial awareness means knowing your clients

In Pt 2 (working as a trainee), we build on the knowledge of Pt 1 (starting as a lawyer) by reviewing the practical skills you need to start advising clients. This involves understanding the effect that your advice can have on clients, not just in a legal sense, but also the business, financial and personal impact it might have. We take a typical transaction and break it down into individual steps, so you can see what you need to do and why. We take you through file opening, issuing an engagement letter, providing written advice, negotiating with others and managing client meetings.

While in Pt 3 (working as a lawyer), we take a look at more advanced skills that you may need as you gain experience, such as managing people, setting goals and how to improve the service you provide to clients.

Commercial awareness means knowing how to run a business and make money

This is about demonstrating your general business knowledge and skills and, in particular, financial skills. In Pt 4 (running a business), we discuss how to give financial advice, how to read financial statements and we give a basic guide to common taxes. We also examine how law firms manage risks and how they manage their intellectual property—an increasingly important area as law firms look to protect their IT and knowledge.

And, assuming you've read Ch.4 (what do law firms sell), Ch.16 (how to delegate work) and Ch.19 (how to improve client service), you'll also have an excellent introduction to marketing, operations and HR.

About our writing style

This is not your usual textbook. It's not aimed at academics. It's written for students, trainees and new lawyers and it's meant to be read as a series of "useful chats" around common events that will happen to you as you start working. Each chapter starts with a snapshot of a typical moment in a lawyer's career. We then examine it more closely. Each chapter is written in a conversational style which we hope you'll find clear, direct and easy to read.

About the book's content

There's so much to cover when you start as a lawyer. Even opening a file for the first time can seem like a huge achievement. We've tried to select the most useful commercial awareness topics for you to know at each stage of your career. Some chapters will not be relevant to you when you are a trainee, but will be invaluable as your career develops. We hope you find all of the content helpful. If you think we've missed anything, covered something in too much detail—or not enough—do let us know. We'd be delighted to hear from you. Future editions can be tailored to cover the topics you want.

Acknowledgements

This book would not have been possible without the help of many people. Eilidh Wiseman and Philip Yelland at the Law Society gave time, support and valuable thoughts during the writing process. However, the Law Society has not seen a draft of the book so any mistakes or omissions are ours, not its.

Lesley-Anne Todd acted as our informal editor, chief comma spotter and formatting queen. Again, any mistakes are ours, not hers. You should have seen what the text was like before she got her red pen to it . . .

A number of people kindly read various chapters in early form. We'd like to thank Madeleine Barratt, Katy Docherty and Mathew Gilhooly for taking the time to read the drafts and providing useful comments.

We'd also like to thank Eileen Patterson and Catherine Hart at the University of Glasgow, Professor Bryan Clark and Professor Charles Hennessy at the University of Strathclyde and Kirsty Swain, Janet Campbell and Simone Hutchinson at W. Green for their support and guidance throughout.

Your comments

This is a first edition. Commercial awareness is a *huge* topic. Some chapters could be expanded to fill their own books. We have tried to select what we think are the most important information students and new lawyers need to know. Please let us know if there's anything you'd like covered and we'll include it in any future editions.

All laws and regulations are intended to be accurate as at April 2016.

Iain NF Sim and Andrew Todd
April 2016

PART 1

Becoming a Lawyer

Chapter 1

WHAT IS A LAWYER?

Introduction

It's Monday. It's the first day of your traineeship. As you walk into your new office you don't know what to expect. After five years of study you're finally a trainee solicitor. But what does that mean? **1–1**

Lawyers are involved in everything from buying homes, writing wills, helping companies grow and expand, prosecuting and defending criminals, to advising governments how to behave. They work just about everywhere: law firms, private businesses, government, court rooms and universities. They advise, strategise, problem solve, write, advocate, negotiate—the list is endless. But what does it mean to be a lawyer and a solicitor? **1–2**

If you're a student just starting your Diploma in Legal Practice (DLP), the answer to this question may be a mystery. You have books and essays, but you've never dealt with clients, courts or fielded calls from other (sometimes irate) solicitors. You don't know what it means to practice law rather than study it. Working as a solicitor means taking your knowledge and using your skill and judgment to *act* on behalf of your clients. That's why new solicitors need to learn a different set of skills.

You have technical knowledge, but you also need the practical skills to use that knowledge on behalf of your clients. You can read every book in the world about hairdressing, but that doesn't mean you can pick up a pair of scissors and just start cutting. You can read the Highway Code, that doesn't mean you can drive. You can read every volume of The Laws of Scotland: Stair Memorial Encyclopaedia, but that doesn't mean you know how to greet clients when they walk into your office.

This section of the book (Chs 1 through 5) is designed for law students. We assume that not everyone who is reading this book is an experienced lawyer. We know many of you are students, trainees or newly qualified. We want these first five chapters to help you adapt from studying the law to practicing the law.

Outcomes

This chapter introduces ideas that we examine in-depth elsewhere in the book. We kick-off with what happens as you start as a trainee. What are the big differences and changes you need to be aware of from studying law at university? As part of this review, we examine how the reputation of the legal profession (and indeed that of your firm) can shape people's perceptions of you. We then look at how you can mould your own reputation to help build your career. By the end of this chapter you'll know the difference between law students, trainees, lawyers and solicitors. **1–3**

Your career: from student to lawyer

Student to trainee

1–4 The difference between studying law and practising is the same as that between reading a book about swimming and jumping in the sea. Reading books and writing essays are useless without practice. You learn to be a solicitor through doing, and your traineeship is your chance to practice, practice and practice some more. You won't write essays. You'll rarely engage in legal debate. Instead you need to speak to clients and other solicitors about more mundane matters. What happens with the keys to the house you're selling? How do you get to court and where should you sit? When you study law you don't need to open files and manage a mountain of paperwork. Nor do you need to choose between twenty emails arriving at the same time and decide which one to answer first. You can't learn all this in a library or a lecture hall. You won't even find the answers in a book; not even this one. You can only do it in an office, at your desk, surrounded by people who have done it before.

1–5 As a trainee, you have a public persona. Whether as an individual, a member of your firm, or as a member of the legal profession, you're expected to live up to the professional standards all lawyers must follow. Your firm will expect you to be an ambassador, and your reputation amongst your colleagues, the profession, clients and the general public will grow. Your traineeship is your first chance to show that you have the skills, experience and judgment to become a great solicitor.

Finally, it's your chance to make mistakes, which is something we don't say often enough. No one is perfect. Mistakes do happen, particularly when you're starting out. Your traineeship gives you an opportunity to gain confidence, improve your existing skills and gain lots of new skills. You will not be the first to make a mistake, nor the last. When it happens, tell your colleagues—they'll have made exactly the same mistakes and they'll know how to fix it.

Trainee to solicitor

1–6 As a solicitor you need to start to build your reputation. If you work in Scotland you tend to find that peers working in the same field quickly come to know you. The profession is small; people know who you are and, if they deal with you, they will quickly form an opinion about you. As a trainee you're protected. Any mistakes are assumed to be a result of inexperience. As a solicitor this protection evaporates quickly. By then you're expected to know (and follow) the professional standards; you're expected to justify your firm's reputation (and indeed your own). Solicitors might gossip about you with colleagues and exchange stories about what you're like to deal with. Are you pleasant? A pedant? Can you be trusted in a courtroom, or on the other side of a boardroom table? All of these things create your reputation and—like your shadow—follow you for the rest of your career.

What is the difference between a lawyer and a solicitor?

1–7 In the rest of the book we'll refer to you as a lawyer. A lawyer has a wider meaning than solicitor. It refers to everyone who practices law. This includes solicitors but also includes judges, sheriffs, advocates and legal academics. In England, it includes barristers too.

A solicitor in Scotland is a lawyer who is a member of the Law Society.[1] An advocate is not a member of the Law Society, however. An advocate is a member of the Faculty of Advocates. While an advocate is a lawyer (and practices law) he or she is not a solicitor (and is not a member of the Law Society). Most of you start as solicitors, as you work for a law firm. As your career develops, however, you can go on to train as an advocate or become a judge, sheriff or academic. In other words, you may not always be a solicitor, but you'll always remain a lawyer.

Your career: applying for traineeships

It's all well and good to talk about your future career as a top notch solicitor, **1–8** a razor sharp advocate, a fair and just sheriff, or a leading academic, but that career has to start with a first step: you need a traineeship. This book is not a guide to finding a traineeship. For that, we recommend you start with the Law Society and the traineeship sections on your university's website. However, we do have a number of general tips to help you.

Start early

If you want to work for one of the larger commercial firms, you need to get **1–9** involved in their summer programmes. Firms recruit most of their trainees from these programmes. If you want to increase your chances of working for them, you need to know not just the dates for traineeship applications (by which time many of the posts could be filled) but also the dates for summer programmes.

Look widely

Commercial firms and public sector traineeships are advertised early, and widely. **1–10** Many high street firms, however, only advertise with the Law Society (if indeed at all). They may also decide to take a trainee at the last minute, when they know they'll definitely need one. If you're looking for a traineeship, you should be proactive. Don't just send a generic CV and covering letter. You should do your research and tell your target firms why you want to work for them. No one wants to feel as if they have received the job seeker equivalent of "you'll do".

Research

This chapter (and Ch.4) should help you to research firms so that you know what **1–11** to look for. Ideally, you should speak to someone who works for the firm but, if that's not possible, use the web, legal directories, the annual legal supplements in *The Herald* and *The Scotsman* (usually published around November), local newspapers and any relevant contacts to garner useful intelligence.

Attend law fairs

Law fairs are the perfect opportunity to speak to people who work in firms, to find **1–12** out first-hand what they're like. Those who attend law fairs on behalf of firms are keen to talk to you, so don't be shy in asking questions. Good questions to ask might include:

---

[1] Membership of the Law Society is governed by the Solicitors (Scotland) Act 1980. We'll look at this in more detail in Ch.11 (how to be professional).

- "How would you describe a typical traineeship at [your firm]?"
- "How would you describe [your firm?]"
- (And, because people like to talk about themselves) "What is your typical day like at [the firm]?"

Be specific

1–13 Tailor your application to each firm you approach. Why are you interested in that firm? Is it because of the type of work it does? Is it because of its name? Maybe it offers opportunities to work in particular offices (whether locally, nationally or internationally)? Tell them why you want to work for them. Firms are interested in students who are interested in them. You have to demonstrate that interest by customising your application.

> "I want to work for [your firm] because I want to pursue a career in civil litigation and [your firm] is ranked as a number one firm in this area. I want the opportunity to work on cases such as [list example you've found in your research]."

Or:

> "I want to work for [your firm] because I want to help families and small businesses in North Ayrshire. I was born and raised in Troon and I want to build my career here by helping the local community."

Be yourself

1–14 Different firms look for different types of people. Some look for legal brains, others for outgoing charmers. You can't be something you're not, nor do you want to spend your traineeship acting. Be yourself during interviews. Some firms will want you, some will not but, if you're yourself, you'll find a firm that suits you best.

Your career options

1–15 You'll take on different roles as your career develops. What follows are a summary of the roles that you would be expected to follow (along with roles required by the Law Society), assuming you tread the traditional path of trainee to partner. We then cover some other roles that don't follow the traditional path.

Traditional roles

Trainee solicitor

1–16 You begin your career as a trainee. A trainee solicitor is someone who's learning to become a solicitor and, in Scotland, has to meet the standards set by the Law Society, before they qualify as an:

Assistant solicitor (or newly qualified solicitor (NQ))

1–17 This is a junior solicitor. You start to gain more client contact and get to tackle increasingly complex work. You will often work with senior solicitors, who will supervise you.

Associate solicitor

Typically this is a junior lawyer with more than three years post-qualifying experience. They have assumed more responsibility and are starting to be the main day-to-day point of contact for clients. **1–18**

Senior Associate

This is a senior solicitor, with strong technical knowledge and experience. They enjoy significant client contact and even have some management responsibility for: supervising a team of junior lawyers, on behalf of a partner, dealing with fees and some firm administration. **1–19**

Partner

Historically, this is someone who owns a share of the firm. A partner is responsible for bringing in new business and keeping existing clients happy. They may do less legal work so they can concentrate on management, finance and client relationships. They are, though, experts in their area of law and take charge of the most complex work. A partner actually might not own a share of the firm. This is a so-called "salaried partner"—a solicitor who, as far as the outside world is concerned, has the authority to bind his/her firm and make decisions on its behalf but, in reality, has no ownership interest in the firm (and is not entitled to share in its profits). A salaried partner is paid a salary, which is subject to National Insurance contributions (just like any other employee). **1–20**

A partner might also take on a number of different roles that are required by the Law Society. These include:

Anti-money laundering (AML) partner

This is a position required by the Law Society. Your AML partner is responsible for compliance with the Money laundering Regulations 2007,[2] the Terrorism Act and the Proceeds of Crime legislation (and the firm's internal policies). We look at these more closely in Ch.6 (how to open files). The AML partner is the first point of contact for any communications from official third parties e.g. the police, the Department for Work and Pensions and HMRC. **1–21**

Cashroom manager/cashroom partner

The Law Society also requires this role. The cashroom manager (also referred to as the cashroom partner) is required to ensure the firm complies with the Law Society's Accounts Rules for dealing with client money. **1–22**

Client relations partner (CRP)

Again, this is a position required by the Law Society. Your CRP is responsible for dealing with complaints. Your CRP keeps a record of all complaints received, investigates them and issues a report to complainers (together with any actions required). We look at this position in some depth in Ch.12 (how to deal with complaints), as the CRP is also the liaison between a firm and both the Scottish Legal Complaints Commission and the Law Society. **1–23**

---

[2] Money Laundering Regulations 2007 (SI 2007/2157).

Training partner

1–24 Once again, this is a position required by the Law Society. Your training partner is responsible for obtaining, maintaining and complying with the firm's licence to provide trainee training.

Managing partner

1–25 This is "The Boss". Your managing partner is elected by his/her fellow partners, to provide strategic direction and to take charge of the management decisions relating to finance, marketing, Human Resources, IT, operations and other business functions. Your managing partner may work with a board of partners to help with specific parts of the business e.g. some firms may have an IT partner or human resources partner to deal with these functions.

Senior partner

1–26 This has two elements. Your firm may view its senior partner as an ambassador. He or she is the firm's public face and is expected to play an important role in dealing with clients, contacts and the press. The senior partner may also deal with the most serious complaints (along with the CRP). In some firms, a senior partner will have another role, too. He or she will chair partner meetings and act as the link between ordinary partners and the board (like a union rep). This is more common in larger firms, where partners may not wish to raise matters directly with the managing partner or board.

Other options

1–27 A number of new roles have been created over the last 30 years. These reflect modern business practices and the need to offer alternative careers for those that don't want to become partners.

Directors

1–28 This is a role that sits above senior associate, but below that of a partner. A director shares many powers and responsibilities with partners, but are paid a salary instead of a share of the profits. In return for being paid a fixed salary (rather than an uncertain share of profits), a director is unlikely to have voting rights and may be excluded from partnership discussions. They tend to have lower targets than a partner (in terms of fees billed and new clients won).

Of counsel

1–29 This is similar to a director, and is a designation preferred by some London (and global) firms. The name "of counsel" originated in the US.

Professional support lawyer/knowledge lawyer (PSL)

1–30 This is a lawyer who specialises in knowledge, legal documents and processes. It is an internal role to help provide lawyers with current information, documents and processes. PSLs are heavily involved in training, IT and (as knowledge specialists) providing support to solicitors on complex legal questions.

Legal engineer

This is similar to a PSL. However, instead of specialising in knowledge, they specialise in reviewing legal processes and devising new, more cost efficient ways of working. A legal engineer often has strong IT skills. **1–31**

Legal project manager

This is a lawyer who manages projects involving large numbers of people, documents and jurisdictions. They make sure that different teams are working effectively by ensuring that everyone knows what they need to do (and when they need to do it). They don't work on deals themselves; they just ensure teams are well managed. We examine project management in Ch.18 (how to be a project manager). **1–32**

Non-lawyer roles

Along with the roles a lawyer may take, there are many other roles and teams needed by law firms in order to be effective businesses. These include: **1–33**

Business development

This is a person (or team) who assists with the work required to win new clients or manage a relationship with clients. **1–34**

Facilities

This team manages the physical things required by a firm, whether it's paper in the print room, a desk in a boardroom, or the office itself. Facilities also deal with health and safety, and may manage the people required to ensure offices work perfectly e.g. receptionists, cleaners or print-room assistants. **1–35**

Finance

This team deals with all the cash coming into and out of your firm. It manages client accounts and assists the managing partner, cashroom partner and board with financial information and budgeting. **1–36**

Human resources (HR)

This team deals with pensions, recruitment, pay, grievances and all aspects of managing employees. It may also assist with training (though this may be a separate department in larger firms). **1–37**

IT

A firm cannot operate without an IT system. Larger firms have their own IT staff, while smaller firms usually need to outsource this to specialist companies that can provide 24-hour support. **1–38**

Legal secretaries/PAs/typists

These are people who act as typists or administrative assistance for one or more lawyers. Many have specialist skills and are as comfortable reading and understanding legal documents as any solicitor. **1–39**

Librarians

1–40 Law firms still have libraries, but the traditional idea of a librarian sitting among dusty books is no more. The majority of legal knowledge is contained in digital libraries and online resources (such as Lexis Nexis or Westlaw). A good librarian ensures that a firm has access to the latest legal journals, textbooks and online sources along with helping with any legal research that is required.

Marketing

1–41 This is a person (or team) who assists with organising events for clients, brochures, online materials and anything that a client might see or hear (see Ch.5 (how do you build your reputation?) for more on marketing).

Paralegals/legal analysts

1–42 This is a person who is not a lawyer, but is qualified (through education or training) to perform legal work that requires knowledge of law and procedure. Paralegals usually specialise in a single area of law. For example, many conveyancing firms use paralegals to deal with settlements, or to deal with repetitive work. Ashurt has established an office in Glasgow and uses paralegals/legal analysts to assist with volume work in the banking and corporate transactions. It has over 180 legal analysts.

Your reputation

1–43 As we said at the start of this chapter, when you start as a trainee or a lawyer you sit at a desk in front of a computer, with a phone, a filing tray and a new pad of paper and you think, "Finally, I'm a lawyer!" What does that mean? The first thing it means is that the general public treats you as a lawyer. Don't think of yourself as a trainee or be under the illusion that being a trainee makes you any less a lawyer. The general public won't make that distinction. You're not just a trainee; you're a trainee *solicitor*.

Professional standards

1–44 If you hire a trainee plumber you expect them to fix your toilet. If you get a junior doctor you expect them to cure you if you're unwell. You may give them some leeway because you know they have less experience than a fully qualified plumber or doctor, but you still expect them to know one end of a pipe (or leg) from another.

In exactly the same way, your clients expect you to be of a certain standard. If they walk into an office in Glasgow or Wick, Inverness or Dumfries, they expect someone who's honest, trustworthy and discreet. They expect a lawyer who puts clients' interests ahead of their own. In other words, they expect you to be professional. As a trainee, on your first day, you automatically share in the reputation (built on professional standards) that all lawyers in fact share.

The reputation of your firm

1–45 The second thing you may notice is that your firm has a reputation, and that reputation applies to you. As a trainee, no one knows who you are. You haven't done anything yet. You haven't spoken to a client or emailed a contact. You've only just arrived. But, while you may be an unknown, your firm is not.

Law firms come in all shapes and sizes. A firm can be large (500+ lawyers), medium (40+ lawyers) or small (2–40 lawyers). You can even choose to work for yourself, as a "sole practitioner". Large law firms with offices in Scotland include CMS, Pinsent Masons, DLA Piper and Eversheds. They each have hundreds of partners, more than a thousand lawyers and offices right around the world. Medium size firms (including the traditional large Scottish firms) include Brodies, Burness Paull, Maclay Murray & Spens, Lindsays, Anderson Strathern, BTO, Harper MacLeod, MacRoberts, Morton Fraser, Thorntons and Blackadders. Medium sized firms include national firms originally based in England, but which have merged with Scottish firms, such as DWF, TLT and Shoosmiths. They also include regional heavyweights like Stronachs, Raeburn Christie Clark & Wallace, Ledingham Chalmers, Brunton Miller, Miller Samuel and Levy & McRae. Smaller firms include specialists (like R & J M Hill Brown & Co Ltd, which specialises in licensing law) and local firms (like McCash & Hunter in Perth, or MacPhee and Partners in Fort William).

Law firms also vary by type. Not all firms cover the same areas of law. They have a large variety of practice areas. They might cover traditional areas like corporate, real estate, banking, trusts and estates, insolvency, immigration, employment, environmental, IP/IT, insurance, intellectual property, criminal, or tax. Alternatively, they might specialise in a limited number of areas (or even just one, if it's boutique).

A firm's size is no indicator of how many areas it covers. A two-partner firm like Wink & McKenzie (based in Elgin, Moray), and which we have picked at random, provides advice about buying and selling homes, wills and trusts, family law, partnership law, litigation, commercial law, powers of attorney, notaries public, statutory declarations, and executries. It covers a full range of services for individuals, families and businesses. In contrast, a firm like Digby Brown (based in Glasgow and Edinburgh) which has 20 partners and around 150 lawyers specialises predominately in one area, namely personal injury claims. It has a number of departments, but these are divided according to the type of accident, injuries sustained and the location or circumstances.

Regardless of a firm's size or the work it does, all firms have a reputation. A reputation based on what they do, what they say about themselves and what others say about them.

Personal reputation

Finally, you have your personal reputation. On day one this will not extend further than your office. Partners will have read your CV, interviewed you, and have an impression about you (what you say about yourself and what they believe you can do). As you walk round the office and start working, people then judge you. Are you fast? Are you accurate? Do you ask smart questions? Do you produce good work? How do you treat people? Your personal reputation evolves (for good or bad) every day until it becomes known alongside your firm (and the profession). Together they make you a lawyer. **1–46**

Your reputation: professional standards

Law Society: Code of Conduct

As a trainee you start with a certain reputation, because every trainee must meet basic professional standards. These include academic standards. After all, you **1–47** need to sit and pass professional exams in the LLB. You need to complete your DLP (and meet the Law Society's learning outcomes) before you can start working for a law firm. You need to complete your traineeship and then be certified as fit and proper to become a lawyer. But why do we have standards?

Historically, the Scottish courts required anyone who appeared in court to meet certain minimum standards. In 1532 an Act of Parliament established the Faculty of Advocates. The Faculty ensured that only advocates could appear before the court after they had completed a process of training and practical instruction known as devilling—a process still followed by advocates today. It was only after the Faculty admitted a person as an advocate that they could represent clients. This ensured that clients and the courts were protected from shysters and charlatans (or "pettifoggers and vipers" as they were referred to in England).

In England, a similar process of professionalism was underway. In 1823, several prominent attorneys formed "The London Law Institution". Its aim was to raise the profession's reputation by setting standards of good practice. It also enforced these standards by disciplining those who did not meet them. The London Law Institution became the Law Society, on 2 June 1825. To be exact, it became "The Society of Attorneys, Solicitors, Proctors and others not being Barristers, practising in the Courts of Law and Equity of the United Kingdom". Not that anyone used this lengthy name. People called it "the Law Society" and, in 1903, this became its official name.

Back in Scotland, the twentieth century saw regulation given a legal basis. While the Faculty of Advocates represented advocates, various associations and faculties of procurators and solicitors represented lawyers. Among those that still exist, the Society of Writers to Her Majesty's Signet (WS Society) was established in 1594 and the Royal Faculty of Procurators, in Glasgow, was incorporated before 1668. This system of self-regulation became more complicated as the number of solicitors in Scotland increased. There was a need to establish one single body that would represent all solicitors. That body was the Law Society of Scotland (LSS) and it was established in 1949 by the Legal Aid and Solicitors (Scotland) Act 1949.

The Law Society doesn't have a monopoly on regulating solicitors. Since 1 October 2008 the Scottish Legal Complaints Commission (SLCC) has carried out part of what formerly was the Law Society's regulatory role. Today, lawyers must comply with standards of conduct, set out in the Legal Services (Scotland) Act 2010 and enforced by the LSS and SLCC. The standards are important. After all, you don't just jump in a car and start driving without reading the Highway Code; equally, you shouldn't start as a solicitor without knowing what rules you need to follow.

In summary, you must be honest, discreet, keep secrets and put your clients' interests before your own. We examine the rules in detail in Ch.11 (how to be professional).

Other standards

1–48 Regulation has increased and, as a profession, we work in many different areas, both geographically and business-wise. Being a lawyer doesn't exempt you from following the same rules as everyone else and, depending on what you do, you may also need to comply with rules of the Financial Conduct Authority, competition authorities and other regulators. For example, perhaps the most challenging of the new regulations has been the anti-money laundering regulations. These require firms to put in place systems and controls to prevent (and detect) money laundering. These include systems to confirm the identity of clients and to assess the risk that they may be involved in money laundering.

Complying with the anti-money laundering regulations can be incredibly time consuming, particularly when dealing with individuals who don't have a lot of paperwork. For example, many spouses have their utility bills in the name of one spouse only. You might complain that the regulations are more appropriate for banks, which after all deal with transfers of money every minute of every day. Yet, you need to follow them, nonetheless.

Along with regulators there's another group that imposes standards on the profession—your clients. Your clients demand that you work in a certain way. This could be as simple as the demanding client who wants you to "always pick up the phone when I call, I won't speak to your secretary", to formal service level agreements which set out targets for you to follow, such as all calls returned the same day or emails acknowledged within two hours. Some clients will even dictate who you may work for so that you don't work for rivals or act for anyone who might raise a court action against them. Client demands can take all forms. We know of one prominent supermarket that requires all of its solicitors to write in plain English. If they don't, they refuse to pay. Another expects its lawyers to work one day a year in their stores so that they understand its business better.

Your reputation: your firm

All law firms have a reputation. It might be for a particular type of work (for **1–49**
example, Digby Brown for personal injury; Turcan Connell for private client and investment; Levy & McRae for litigation; and Dickson Minto for corporate finance). This reputation doesn't mean that this is everything that they do. Each of these firms does more. It simply means it's the first thing that may come to mind when you hear their name.

Reputation may apply to an area as well as a skill. A firm may be known as one of the leading firms in an area: Paull & Willamson (before their merger with Burness) for Aberdeen; Kerr Stirling in Stirling; or McLeod & McCullum in Inverness, to pick three at random. This doesn't mean that they're the best, there are many other good firms in those areas, it just means that those are the first names you may think of when you think of a particular area. Again, you share in this reputation.

On day one at Levy & McRae, for example, your clients will assume you know one end of a courtroom from another. If your firm is good at something, you're assumed to be good at it, too.

Measuring reputation

Legal directories

For larger firms, reputation can be measured. In the UK there are legal directories **1–50**
that rank firms based on quality of service and the reputation of their teams and partners. The two best known directories are *The Legal 500* and *Chambers and Partners*. Both employ researchers to review and rank firms. The research results are published annually. If you check a firm like MacLay Murray & Spens you find, for example, that it's praised for its work with insolvency and corporate recovery. The website of *The Legal 500* says:

> "Maclay Murray & Spens LLP is lauded for its 'friendly and supportive service' and has a 'good depth of insolvency knowledge'"[3]

These directories are the "who's who" of the legal sector, across the UK. They have dedicated sections covering each region and area of expertise. They're compiled from interviews with firms and associated organisations.

Awards

1–51 The Scottish Legal Awards and the Law Awards of Scotland are annual events that celebrate law firms and lawyers. Winning (or even just being nominated) for one of these awards is an achievement. A law firm can use an award to promote itself and you frequently see winners mention the awards in their adverts and PR. In 2015, the big winner of the Scottish Legal Awards was Digby Brown, which collected five awards, including Law Firm of the Year and Managing Partner of the Year. Outside of Scotland each of the main legal press titles holds their own awards ceremonies. *The Lawyer*, *Legal Week* and *Legal Business* each are considered to be important awards to win. In 2015, *The Lawyer* named Osbourne Clark the Law Firm of the Year, for example. At the other end of the scale, local business networks, chambers of commerce and local press all provide opportunities for firms to win awards and promote themselves within their local communities.

Other

1–52 For many firms, their reputation is based on word of mouth. What do people say about them? This is particularly true for high street firms and local firms, which draw clients from a local community.

Clients talk. People recommend one lawyer over another. You want clients to be happy with their service, so they recommend you to others. Conversely, if clients complain then this can quickly build a negative picture of a firm that is best avoided. What you want is for clients to talk like this:

> "[Firm Y] are quick with their advice and don't sit on the fence, which is unusual in a lawyer." (Testimonial posted on website for a national law firm).

Or:

> "I had heard all the horror stories about lawyers charging you for every phone call, letter and email that is sent on your behalf, but I was quoted a figure and that turned out to be the figure charged. This was even with me contacting [them] about nearly everything to do with both the sale and purchase (and a few other things as well), and not once was I made to feel that I was bothering them, and every question I had was met with a clear understandable answer. Thank you." (Testimonial posted on website for a high street firm).

---

3 See: *http://www.legal500.com/firms/2177-maclay-murray-spens-llp/3817-glasgow-scotland* [accessed: 28 June 2016].

Or:

> "[Firm X] has been my lawyer since 1999. I have got off with all trials that [they have] acted for me in. Most recently I was charged with assault to severe injury and permanent disfigurement and I was found not guilty by a unanimous verdict of the jury. [They] seem to always be a step ahead of the rest." (Testimonial posted on website for a law firm specialising in legal aid cases).

Benefits

In the USA, the career resource *Vault.com* has created an annual "Law 100" ranking. This uses the reviews of 17,000 lawyers, who rank firms on a scale of one to 10, according to their perceptions of a firm's "prestige". Respondents are not allowed to rank their own firms and are asked to comment only on those firms with which they're familiar. The ranking provides valuable information about firms and their clients, and the way that reputation links them. For example, the Californian firm, Cooleys, is described by peers as entrepreneurial, tech savvy and a leader in its area. From this you can guess that its clients include Facebook and eBay (which themselves are entrepreneurial, tech savvy and leaders in their fields). **1–53**

A good reputation reinforces why existing clients instruct you and helps persuade new clients to come to you. When Andrew was looking for a firm to help with a large house-building project involving more than 1,000 homes, he used legal directories and other sources to help identify which firms he would invite to bid for that work.

How do law firms develop a reputation?

Let's imagine you meet a client for the first time. You're charming and smart. They're impressed. Within 10 minutes you've worked out what they need and you've helped them decide on a course of action. The next day you write to them with your engagement letter. It's a masterpiece of plain English. It's simple, straight to the point and explains clearly what your client needs to do next. There's only one problem. You have spelled their name wrong. Instead of being their "hero", who knows all the answers, suddenly, you're inattentive. And what does that say about your firm? **1–54**

It doesn't matter what directories say, what awards you win, or word of mouth, sometimes the most important element of any firm's reputation is actually you.

Your career: other options

It's worth remembering that not all lawyers work for law firms. Some work for businesses, the public sector or in universities. **1–55**

In 2014, the Law Society[4] reported that there were 11,000 solicitors in Scotland.

- Nearly a third worked for a "big firm"—a firm with 10 or more partners.
- Over a quarter worked in-house.[5]

---

4 *http://www.lawscot.org.uk/news/2014/11/number-of-scottish-solicitors-reaches-all-time-high/* [Accessed 19 April 2016].

5 There are over 750 different organisations employing Scottish solicitors. Approximately 250 are in England and Wales and almost 100 elsewhere in the world.

- One in twenty worked as sole practitioners.
- The rest (around two out of every five solicitors) worked for a firm with between two or nine partners.

Even though a quarter of the profession works in-house, as a trainee you're more likely to be working for a law firm. Most trainees (nine out of ten)[6] start with law firms, before changing direction after they qualify.

Working in private practice

1–56 If you work for a law firm you might work for a billion-pound business with offices all around the world, like Clifford Chance. You might work for a single partner on a high street in Fife. Both are law firms, but both are different and with different challenges. In general, we can divide firms into different types:

Magic Circle

1–57 This is the name given to five firms that once were the five biggest firms in London (and are still top 10, today). These are Allen & Overy, Clifford Chance, Freshfields Bruckhaus Deringer, Linklaters and Slaughter and May. These are global firms with offices around the world. They specialise in the biggest corporate and financial deals (such as the £12.5 billion sale of mobile operator EE to BT). They don't do wills.

Silver Circle

1–58 These are the next largest firms in London. These include Herbert Smith Freehills, Ashurt, Berwin Leighton Paisner, King & Wood Mallesons, Macfarlanes and Travers Smith.

Global firms

1–59 These include Magic Circle and Silver Circle firms, but also include firms that have global offices. Some, like DLA Piper, are larger than the Magic Circle firms. Again these firms specialise in massive deals, but they may also have regional offices so as to work in Scotland, the Midlands, Manchester and Leeds. They may share some deals and clients with national firms.

National firms

1–60 These are firms with offices throughout the UK. Examples include DWF, TNT and Shoosmiths. They typically work on UK deals that don't require a foreign office. They tend to be strong in local markets.

Scottish firms

1–61 This is exactly what it says: a firm from Scotland such as Brodies, Maclay Murray & Spens or Shepherd & Wedderburn (but can also refer to smaller firms based here too). These are firms that dominate in Scotland and that may have a London or regional office. They work on the largest Scottish deals, act for wealthy individuals and act for medium to large companies.

---

[6] *http://www.lawscot.org.uk/media/431095/Trainee-Statistics-2015.pdf* [Accessed 19 April 2016].

High street firms

Again, this is intuitive. These are firms that traditionally would have an office on the high street (in larger towns and cities across Scotland), but might just deal with individuals, families and small companies. **1–62**

Rural firms

Rural firms traditionally would have an office in smaller towns, in more remote areas. They may be the only firm in town and will cover a wide geographic area, and deal with individuals, families and small companies. They are also usually familiar with agriculture law and practice. **1–63**

Legal aid firms

A legal aid firm is one that deals predominately with clients using legal aid. **1–64**

Working for a business

If you work for a business, you're an in-house lawyer. Typically, you're referred to as "legal counsel". Senior in-house lawyers are typically referred to a "legal directors" or "general counsel". The general counsel is usually the most senior lawyer and has a position advising the board of directors (and may be part of the management team). As a lawyer for a company, the company will be your only client. Your role will include giving business and legal advice, drafting and reviewing contracts, negotiating deals, developing opportunities, helping the business avoid risk, working on investor relations and managing outside law firms that perform legal work for the business. The size of any particular in-house department varies greatly. Some companies may only have one lawyer. The Royal Bank of Scotland, on the other hand, has over 400 lawyers in its group legal team. Some of those lawyers will specialise by working for specific departments within the bank. **1–65**

Working for local or central government: civil

There are lawyers at every level of government: local, Scottish and UK. At local government level you're exposed to a wider variety of work than in the Scottish Government (or indeed the UK Government), where you're more likely to support a particular department. Depending on the department, you might draft legislation, review contracts that the government intends to enter into, and draft, research, provide advice on and enforce laws, rules and regulations. **1–66**

Working for local or central government: criminal

One of the largest legal teams you can join is the Crown Office and Procurator Fiscal Service, to work as a procurator fiscal. As a prosecutor, you represent the Scottish Government in prosecuting crimes. Government lawyers also handle civil cases in which the government is involved. **1–67**

Working as an academic

Lawyers in academia teach, research and publish books and articles on legal issues. They also spend time on administration that may involve tasks such as designing exam questions and answers (and getting these validated through the relevant committees) or dealing with student applications. Typically, an academic **1–68** will start their career by undertaking a masters or a PHD. This may in turn lead to a teaching fellowship with a focus on lecturing, research or a mix of both.

Working as a judge

1–69 An extremely small percentage of lawyers work as judges or tribunal members. The Queen appoints judges (on the First Minister's recommendation). The Judicial Appointments Board for Scotland (JABS) handles applications. The Board makes recommendation for appointment and may assemble a pool of suitable applicants. Judges can then be appointed from this pool as vacancies arise. When a new judge is required, following a request from the Scottish Ministers, JABS makes recommendation to the First Minister. Lawyers don't have the necessary experience and skill to become a judge until many years into their professional careers.

Other options

1–70 A number of new roles have evolved. These include: professional support roles, legal engineering, legal project management and specialist business development roles. Again, these tend to be for lawyers who have worked for a few years and gained the skill and knowledge to understand the legal topics they're dealing with, alongside wider business issues.

Your reputation: personal reputation

1–71 We're back at day one. You're sitting at your desk and you're wondering what will happen next. You may have worked for a law firm as part of a summer placement, but let's assume that this is your first time in a law office.

As a trainee you start with a reputation informed by your CV, application and interview. That is quickly cast aside as people get to know you. In your first week, the people you work with will ask each other "what's he like?" and "what do you make of her?" You're judged not just on the quality of the documents, emails and letters you write, but also on your appearance, your manner and your personality—that's just human nature. You may be the best lawyer in the world, but if you pick your nose (or something worse) at your desk, your colleagues will talk.

Be yourself

1–72 As you meet clients and talk to other lawyers, you develop a reputation that extends beyond the walls of your office. We look closely at how you develop a professional reputation in Ch.5 (how do you build your reputation?). Networking, PR and social media can all help you grow your reputation. As a trainee, however, your first step is to show clients and external lawyers that you're a true professional. There are a number of tips you can follow to help you demonstrate this.

Firstly, remember that as soon as you open your mouth people start forming judgments. You shouldn't try to be someone you're not. Use your personality. You're not a robot. You don't need to be a particular type of person to be a lawyer. Some lawyers are serious, but many are not. Clients (and other lawyers) respond to you as a person, not as a character you play. Be open—be honest. That doesn't mean that you should tell inappropriate jokes, or gossip like you would if you were out with your friends. Showing a personality doesn't mean you need to be an extrovert. Some clients want a Rottweiler. Others want an egghead, with their nose buried in books. Showing your personality—whatever it is—allows clients to choose the lawyer they want. If you're not comfortable snarling, don't pretend to be an attack dog. You don't need to be a lawyer and an actor.

Avoid sharp practice

Don't get us wrong, showing your personality doesn't mean you should be liked. You're not paid to be liked. Rather, you should aim to be respected. If clients don't respect you, they won't trust you, and they won't use you. If other lawyers don't respect you, they may be downright suspicious of you. Being respected in a business context is about treating people fairly. It means avoiding sharp practice—i.e. pushing the boundaries of what is legal or acceptable. If you promise to do something, do it. If you can't do something, don't promise to do it, and then say you've changed your mind or, worse, say nothing. **1–73**

Follow professional standards

We've come full circle. As a trainee you must follow the same professional standards as other lawyers. Not every situation that you encounter can be foreseen. This is especially true when you start, when every day brings new tasks and challenges. Fundamental standards, however, are always present for guidance. If you know that you have to be honest, you then know you can't act for a client who wants to plead "not guilty" when they tell you they have, in fact, committed the crime. If you know that you owe a duty to your fellow lawyers, you then know that you should not mislead them. If you know that you have a duty of confidentiality, you know that you shouldn't divulge information about your clients. **1–74**

Summary

This chapter has introduced ideas that we examine more closely in later chapters. Firstly, professional standards are an essential part of becoming a solicitor. It's those standards that help define how lawyers act. It's your actions, along with your knowledge, that make you a lawyer. Those standards also define how clients view you. We look at clients more closely in the next chapter. **1–75**

Second, your actions are shaped by the firm you join. When you start as a trainee you don't get to choose your reputation to wrap around you like a coat or jacket. Clients, fellow solicitors and others choose it for you based on your firm's action. We'll examine firms more closely in Ch.3 (what are law firms?) and Ch.4 (what do law firms sell?).

Finally, as your career develops, your actions alone will come to define you so that clients will come to you not just because you're a lawyer, or work for a particular firm, but because they want to use you and you alone. We'll examine how you can build your reputation in Ch.5 (how do you build your reputation?).

CHAPTER 2

WHO ARE YOUR CLIENTS?

Introduction

2–1 *It's Tuesday. Day two. You're at your desk and the phone rings. It's reception. A new client (a woman in her early 40s) wants to speak to a lawyer. Your partner is in a meeting and you're the only one available to speak to her. What do you do?*

2–2 The first time you meet a client can be nerve-wracking. You don't know what they might ask. You're scared you won't know the answer. You don't want to look stupid. These thoughts are normal. We've all thought that before our first meeting. We *still* think like that when we meet new clients. It's human nature to worry about the unknown. The same applies to phone calls. It could be a current client, it could be a new client, it could be about something you're dealing with or it could be something new. A ringing phone brings the fear of the unknown just as much as a surprise meeting.

That's why preparation is key. The more you know in advance about clients and the problems they face the easier it becomes to deal with them. But what do you need to know? Knowledge can mean three things:

Technical knowledge

2–3 You know the area of law that applies to your client. You know the ins and outs of the Companies Act 2006 and you can help your client if she's looking to set up a new company.

Commercial knowledge

2–4 You can talk confidently about the issues that matter to your client. If your client is looking to buy a home, you can talk about the local housing market. Are prices rising? Does she need to move quickly to secure the home she wants?

Personal knowledge

2–5 You know what your clients want from you as their lawyer. Some clients want to be consulted on every clause. Others expect you only to highlight "the important ones" i.e. they want you to use your judgment. At the other end of the scale, do you know if they prefer emails to letters? Do they like small talk? Some clients like to chat for a few minutes, whereas others want to get straight down to business. You even need to know if they prefer tea or coffee (a client will remember if you get this wrong).

2–6 Technical and commercial knowledge can be taught. As a trainee, you already have five years of technical knowledge behind you. You may know more about an area of law than your partner who, after all, hasn't spent five years studying the latest developments. Take confidence from that. You may also have a good commercial knowledge from following the news, working part time or simply being engaged in current events.

In short, you're book smart. But book smart is only part of the story. Anyone can make a cup of tea (you just leave a tea bag in hot water). The real skill is making tea for someone else. You need to judge the strength of the tea; you need to know how much milk and sugar to add. You need to turn your knowledge of how to make tea into a cup of tea that someone will drink.

Law is exactly the same. You need to take your knowledge and turn it into advice that your client will understand and can follow. You tailor it based on your personal knowledge of your client. If you don't have experience, you do the same thing you would do if making a cup of tea; you ask them questions.

This chapter aims to help you understand who clients are and what they want from you. We examine different types of clients and provide you with a summary of some of the business and personal knowledge you may need when dealing with them. While this summary won't be true for everyone (every client is different, just as every person is different) it should give you a working structure.

Outcomes

By the end of this chapter you'll know the difference between different types of clients. We'll look at characteristics they share, and the types of people, businesses and other groups who may instruct you. **2–7**

Who are your clients?

Introduction

You're in the boardroom. You've introduced yourself to a prospective client. You've talked about the weather and it's time to discuss why she's here. **2–8**

When you meet your client you need to find out why she wants to speak to you. Does she want to move house? Is she in trouble with the police? Does she run a business and needs help with it? Secondly, you need to talk about what you can do to help. If she's buying a house, does she need help submitting an offer, or with a mortgage, or both? Finally, if instructed, you need to turn your words into action. If she's buying a house you need to draft the offer, order searches, check the title, assist with the mortgage, and complete the purchase. These are the actions you need to take after your meeting. Your meeting may only last 30 minutes, but the actions required thereafter might take weeks (or even months). **2–9**

As a trainee often you feel most comfortable just talking about the actions you plan to take. These are based on your technical knowledge. You know how to draft an initial writ. You can talk for hours about the Ordinary Cause Rules. This is your chance to show off how much you know about the law.

The problem is this—most of what you want to talk about doesn't matter. Your client won't wake up and think, "I'd really love to know the difference between a proof, a debate and a proof before answer." Instead, they're probably thinking, "someone owes me money, how do I get it back?" Clients don't think in terms of initial writs, missives, contracts, case law or summary cause procedure. After all, you don't think about broken carburettors, leaking gaskets or rusty exhaust pipes when you take your car to a garage; you just want someone to fix it. Clients just want their problems fixed painlessly and as quickly as possible. They don't want to know how you plan to accomplish it; they just want it done.

Talking about cases and statutes is fine as a student. You're an academic, after all. You're learning, testing and challenging the law. You're actually expected (and indeed encouraged) to talk about laws and how they apply in your jurisdiction. As a lawyer, however, talking about the law can be too technical a conversation for your clients. Clients are different. You know how to write a 10,000-word dissertation and debate it with your professors, but can you explain it to your mum, your gran, or your first client who has just walked off the street? You'll traumatise them. Clients don't want legal debate. They just want to know that you can fix a problem; they leave the "how" and "why" to your good judgment.

This doesn't mean that an explanation is irrelevant. Some clients do want to know exactly what your plan is, but still that doesn't mean you need to share your knowledge in detail. The best lawyers know what their clients want. They know when to speak to them, and then in a way they understand. They know what to ask so that they get all the relevant information they need. This is what we mean when we talk about client skills, and this is different for each client. Oh—and it takes time to develop (so stay calm).

Before we look at different types of clients, it's worth remembering that clients are just like you. They're not mythical beasts and they're not superhuman. They're no different to your mum, your dad, your brothers, sisters and your best friends. You can deal with people wanting to move home, who want advice when they're made redundant, or who want to divorce but be sure they have access to their children. Alternatively, you can act for companies. That doesn't mean you're not dealing with people too, however. While your file may say you're acting for Scottish Power, a company cannot give you instructions. Companies don't talk, write, email or text. You still deal with people: employees, directors and owners.

Let's look at the types of people you'll meet.

Individuals—civil

2–10 Most folk don't speak to lawyers regularly. If they think of a lawyer, they probably think of someone they've seen on TV. They think of wigs, gowns and gavels (even though they're not used in UK court rooms). They probably know that lawyers have standards but might not be able to define them beyond the basic idea that:

- "they always tell the truth";
- "they can't tell anyone anything you tell them"; and
- "they'll fight for you"

Most importantly, they probably never deal with a lawyer other than at the significant moments in their life. Think about your own life: when have you met a lawyer outside of university or work experience? It may be when a grandparent died and your parents dealt with the estate. Perhaps you have been called as a witness and attended court? Or it may have been when your parents moved house (or you bought your first flat)? All of these are red-letter moments. For individuals, lawyers typically are associated with major life events. These events, when they do happen, can also be years apart.

This means three things when you meet them:

Individuals don't know much about the law

Many clients have no experience of distributing an estate, attending court or selling a house. However, they assume you do and that you can guide them through it. **2–11**

You need to hold their hand

Don't assume that an individual understands everything you tell them. When a mechanic starts talking about fuel pressure do you tell them you don't understand or do you nod your head to pretend that you do? Many clients will nod their heads when you talk. Keep your advice simple and check that they do—in fact—understand. If they don't, your client can become dissatisfied (and you may never know it). **2–12**

Whatever they ask you to do is important to them

Most individuals have a good reason to seek you out. No matter how small the task they ask you to do, you should treat them as if it's important. You might have a five-day proof the following week, but if a client asks you about a simple will, it might be because due to a recent illness they're worried about care costs (and protecting their family). It's important to them, and you should always treat client requests with the respect they deserve. **2–13**

Individuals—criminal

If you're dealing with a client accused of a crime, you might not meet them in your office. Instead, you may have to visit a prison or a police cell. You can be called at short notice. Many firms operate an on-call service, outside normal office hours. You could get a call at 2 am asking you to attend a police station to act for someone who has just been arrested. If so, not only will you have the pressure of picking up their case at short notice, you also have to get to know your client as best you can in a short time (and in a highly pressured situation). **2–14**

You also might well have police officers in attendance. You want to try and find time to speak to your new client privately so that you can work out the best course of action. The heat is definitely on and you won't have long to think. You can't panic. Your client is depending on you to help them, so you must appear to be in control of the situation.

One major difference between civil and criminal clients is that you have to tell people news they don't want to hear. For example, David (a newly qualified lawyer) was asked to go to a local police station to defend a man who'd admitted assaulting a bouncer with a flare. When David met the client he was told the man's wife was pregnant. The baby was due to be born a week later. The man asked David if he'd be released to see the birth. David had to tell him the bad news. A flare was equivalent to a firearm and, because of previous convictions, he would unlikely be released before his sentencing, and any sentence would be at least six years. David was called every name under the sun. It wasn't his fault. He told his client what would happen to him. However, clients facing jail often attack the messenger.

Individuals—families

Many families use the same firm. Parents recommend lawyers to their children. Your firm is seen as the "family lawyer". The same tips apply to families as to **2–15** individuals, but one other factor to consider is that the family may have a relationship with other lawyers in your firm. You're not the first lawyer they've dealt with. It might be unfair, but automatically you're compared with the senior partner who has just retired (and who had dealt with them for 30 years). They assume you know who they are, that you're familiar with all of their files (including that time twenty years ago one of them got a speeding ticket) and they might be offended if you don't know them as well as your senior colleagues do.

When meeting a family for the first time ask colleagues if there's anything you should know, as they can provide all the background information that can help you know what the client wants and how to deal with them.

Individuals—high net worth

2–16 Wealthy individuals often need more specialist advice. Family issues may be more complex, as estates are larger and powers of attorney and trusts are required to protect assets for children (and grandchildren). Often you'll provide advice alongside an accountant, or an independent financial advisor. They also tend to expect a hands-on approach from their lawyer. They're used to good service.

Businesses—types of people

2–17 There are three types of people you may deal with:

- owners—the people who own the business;
- directors—the people who run the business (they may also be owners); and
- employees—the people who work for the business.

Businesses—types of work

2–18 Any business needs two types of work:

Operations

2–19 Basically, this is what a business does (its purpose). WHSmith, for instance, sells newspapers, magazines and books. Its operational business is everything it needs to sell those newspapers, magazines and books. This includes paying suppliers and landlords for premises; preparing advertising and marketing for customers; employing staff; and buying equipment like automated tills that intone loudly that you have an "unexpected item in the bagging area".

Management

2–20 In order to run effectively, a business needs a management tier. WHSmith has about 15,000 employees. It needs HR staff to deal with things like training, dealing with problems, salaries, managing pensions and generally making sure that they're in the shops every day of every week, to help customers. Most large businesses require legal advice just to manage them, before they do anything to make money.

Owners and directors

2–21 You tend to deal directly with the owners or directors of small businesses. As businesses get bigger, the directors and owners take less of a hands-on role and you're more likely to deal with its employees. Just like any individual, an owner or director tends to seek you out when something important has happened. Equally, just like a family, the business may have a long relationship with your firm. Even if they're a new client, they're likely to have used lawyers before. It's worth checking with them what they like and what they don't. There is usually a reason why they have moved firms.

When taking instructions there are two things worth considering:

Instructions

You need to be sure you're taking instructions from the right person. This can be tricky with small companies, as they might be managed by one person and yet owned by a number of people. Many family businesses have one family member who runs it, with the others being shareholders only. Most of the time the person who gives you instructions has authority, but there may also be times when you need the approval of a board of directors or shareholders. Always check. **2–22**

Mistaken identity

Some small business owners don't distinguish between themselves and their company (or companies). It's up to you to make sure that you don't do anything that you shouldn't. Sometimes this may involve reminding your client that the company has its own identity and that you need to ensure that any corporate governance is followed. This could mean that you need to see (or draft) shareholder resolutions or board minutes to confirm actions. **2–23**

Employees

The larger the business the more likely you're to deal with employees (rather than an owner or director). It may be obvious from their job title what an employee does. You may also be able to deduce their seniority. For example, the title "HR Manager" tells you what part of the business that person is in (and also their seniority). To state the obvious, they work in HR and they're a manager, so unlikely to be a senior figure. They probably report to someone more senior, whether in HR or on the board of directors. **2–24**

It's worth checking with a colleague to confirm the position, so that you understand what that person expects of you. A title can only tell you so much. Each person will have a different way of working and expect different things from a lawyer. Andrew once acted for a developer. The main contact was a senior employee who had dealt with many lawyers. Before acting for him, Andrew asked his partner if there was anything he should know. The partner said:

> "Yes. He travels all the time and uses his Blackberry for emails. He hates typing on it so try and write any emails so they can be answered "yes" or "no". If you send him a long email don't expect him to answer it. Phone him instead."

Employees normally report to a boss e.g. an HR director. They might report directly to a board of directors. It's worth knowing the lie of the land, as you may need to change how you provide them with advice. Andrew's client, for example, reported to a board of directors. The board also wanted to know if there were any legal issues that they should be aware of. Andrew would prepare two reports for the client. One was a full report setting out the issues they needed to deal with.

The second was a summary that his client could use as part of the board's papers, rather than having to summarise Andrew's advice.

Large businesses and public limited companies (Plcs)

2–25 Large businesses require a lot of legal work. BP operates in more than 80 countries around the world. It has almost 85,000 employees (more than twice the population of Lichtenstein). It has a turnover of £360 billion (equivalent to South Africa). And, if you run out of petrol, don't worry, it has over 15,000 petrol stations to help you fill up.

How do you provide advice to a company bigger than a country? Most Plcs act through divisions and subsidiaries, and also tend to be split geographically. If your firm acts for BP it may just act for its offshore oil and gas industry, in the UK. Alternatively, it might just provide employment advice. The people you deal with usually are employees and the same advice as dealing with any business applies.

Some firms act for BP across the world. At the start of 2015, there were rumours that BP and Shell might merge. If they did, lawyers would need to do due diligence on each company and deal with the merger documents. This would be a global task. Hundreds of thousands of documents would need to be reviewed. Tens of thousands of documents would be needed to make the merger work in the 80 countries within which BP operates. Only the largest law firms have the people, offices, skills and knowledge to lead a project like this. If you work for them you might feel like a small cog in a big wheel. Remember that your contact might feel the same—they're one employee out of 85,000, after all. In these situations you're not expected to know everything. How could you? Instead, try and obtain clear instructions from your partner or a senior lawyer involved as to your role.

The difference between a private company and a public company

2–26 Along with size, there is another important legal distinction between companies. They can be private companies or public companies. While there are many differences between private and public companies (derived from statute and practice) the general rule is that any company that is not a public company is a private company.

What is a public company? Broadly speaking this is a company that has offered its shares to the public, usually through a recognised stock exchange. To do so, it must satisfy the conditions for listing. A public company uses a recognised stock exchange so it can raise money by its offering shares to the public. This also enables shareholders to buy and sell their shares easily. In return for this benefit (and also to protect investors) public companies are subject to considerably more stringent controls than private companies. Many UK Plcs are, however, not listed on a stock exchange, so the owners should carefully consider whether they're happy to comply with these extra burdens, or whether they should consider re-registering as a private company.

As a lawyer to a Plc you need to be aware of the regulations that might apply. For example, information has to be announced to the exchange before the rest of the world. Breaching these rules, even inadvertently, can have big consequences.

Financial institutions

2–27 A financial institution is a business that conducts financial transactions (for example, a bank). Banks typically take two forms. Commercial banks (like Lloyds Banking Group and the Royal Bank of Scotland) provide savings accounts to individuals and businesses. They provide loans, such as mortgages. They deal in the daily transfer and use of money. You see their names on the high street.

You won't find the second type of banks—investment banks—on the high street. These include Goldman Sachs, Morgan Stanley, Merrill Lynch and Deutsche Bank. They don't offer mortgages or personal loans. Instead they specialise in complex financial transactions. They typically act for companies and governments, either providing advice on transactions, mergers and acquisitions, or arranging (and sometimes providing) finance for these transactions.

Most banks appoint law firms via a formal tender. Firms are asked to bid to provide certain work (for example, securitisation for loans up to £100 million) and the best bids are accepted. Bids contain a number of conditions and may include detailed instructions from the bank about how it'll instruct your firm. For example, it may say that instructions can only be in writing from certain people. As a lawyer you need to be aware of these sorts of instructions.

A bank will be one of your firm's most prestigious clients. You won't deal with them alone. Partners, senior associates and other lawyers are also likely to be doing work for this sort of client (and know its procedures). Again, you should speak to them and ask how they deal with their contacts at the bank; they're best placed to know how such clients operate and what they like from their lawyers.

Other financial institutions include:

Insurance companies

Insurance companies don't just sell insurance. They also invest their customer's **2–28** money into the stock market and other investments.

Private equity firms

Companies such as Blackstone or Terra Firma invest in businesses in order to **2–29** increase their value.

Stockbrokers

These are companies that help individuals and companies invest in the stock **2–30** market by buying and selling shares.

There's cross over between commercial banks, investment banks, private equity **2–31** firms and insurance companies. Different parts of the same bank may have different functions. The Royal Bank of Scotland is a commercial bank, but it also has a part of its business that functions as an investment bank. It also provided insurance through Direct Line (now spun-off). Every part of a bank has different objectives, and the people who work there view their role in different ways. A commercial banker may value building a long-term relationship with a client. An investment banker may only see a short-term gain. Understanding your client can help you work out what you need to do.

Local authorities and public sector bodies

Local authorities

Scotland has 32 local authorities, from Scottish Borders Council in the south to **2–32** Comhairle nan Eilean Siar in the north west. Each council delivers services, including: education, social work, roads and transport, economic development, housing, the environment, libraries, waste management, arts, culture and sport. It also has its own operational issues to deal with. It can employ thousands of staff. It owns hundreds of properties and large tranches of land. All of these matters need to be managed, along with its duty to deliver services to local people. Their official powers and responsibilities are governed by statute. Some services reflect mandatory responsibilities. For example, councils must provide education for five to sixteen year olds. They must also provide fire services and social work services. Some are discretionary, like encouraging economic development. Others, in turn, are regulatory (in order to comply with legislation)—these include trading standards, environmental health, licensing for alcohol and licensing for gambling.

A council governs every authority. A council consists of elected members (councillors) elected directly by local residents, normally every four years. A leader heads up the council. Usually they are the leader of the largest single political grouping in the council. However, not all powers require a decision of the council. Traditionally, a council delegates many of its powers to committees, subcommittees and council officers.

Depending on a local authority's size, the people you deal with may be from an in house legal team, or may be a manager or director of a department. Whoever you deal with, however, take care to ensure that any action is intra vires (that is to say, lawful). Usually this means that the decision you're implementing was taken the correct way by the full council, a committee, sub-committee or officer (as appropriate).

A practical aspect of dealing with local authorities is that you may need to provide advice around any committee or sub-committee's schedule. For example, if you're providing legal advice on a licensing matter, you need to know when the licensing board meets (and from that extract the date it requires papers to be produced, so that members can review them). A practical tip is that you should always check timescales and make diary entries for all the important dates.

Public bodies

2–33 A public body is an organisation that delivers a public service, but is not a government department or local authority. Public bodies come in a variety of shapes and sizes and cover areas like health, social care, economic investment, arts, culture and more. Notable ones include Scottish Enterprise, Scottish Environment Protection Agency (SEPA), Scottish Water, National Museums of Scotland and Revenue Scotland. Just like local authorities, public bodies' official powers and responsibilities are governed by statute or statutory instrument. As Tom Axford, Corporate Secretary and Head of Legal at Scottish Water, has said:

> "We have an unusual legal structure as a public corporation, and we have to comply with both public sector governance and the UK Corporate Governance Code, and benchmark our performance against the private English and Welsh utilities . . . [a] lot of work we do involves explaining to external solicitors our specific legislative environment and statutory powers."[1]

When you act for public bodies you should check not only what legal advice it needs but also how it *should* operate.

[1] T. Axford, "Advice on tap" (17 August 2015), *The Journal of the Law Society of Scotland*, p.42. Available at *http://www.journalonline.co.uk/Magazine/60-8/1020623.aspx* [Accessed 19 April 2016].

Summary

The examples in this chapter are general. Everybody's different. The people you **2–34**
deal with each have their own personality and expectations. However, if you know what they want from a lawyer then you're well on the way to providing them with the right advice. It may seem daunting to deal with all these different types of clients. In practice, however, you tend to deal with just a few. If you work for a big firm, you rarely act for an individual. If you act for a rural firm, you're unlikely to act for a bank. Firms, based on their location and the type of work they do, work for different types of clients. In the next chapter we examine how firms have evolved to deal with different groups of people.

Chapter 3

WHAT ARE LAW FIRMS?

Introduction

3–1 *It's Wednesday. Day three. You have a meeting at another law firm, just one street away. You walk into its reception and you notice that it's very different from yours. It looks like Starbucks; yours looks like a 1980s bus station waiting room. Behind it you see lawyers sitting in a plush, open plan office space. Your office, by contrast, is filled with pokey rooms.*

Even the name is different. They're called "LocalLawyers4U". Your firm is named after its eighteenth-century founding partners. How can two firms that work in almost the same place, for the same people, and do essentially the same work, end up being so different?

3–2 Everyone knows what a lawyers' office should look like. It's wood-panelled. There's a big desk, surrounded by books on statutes and cases. A clock ticks an interminable "tock". It's old, traditional and timeless. Isn't it? Actually, no—the reality is that you probably will never see an office like this in 2016. When you start, you might work for a wide variety of firms. You can work in a high street firm in Peebles or Perth, working for individuals, families or small businesses. You can work for a criminal law practice beside Glasgow High Court, with clients drawn from police cells and accused of crimes they "absolutely didn't do". You can work for estate agencies/legal firms like McEwan Fraser Legal or McVey & Murricane, which operate across Scotland and specialise in residential conveyancing. You can work for national firms with large city centre offices, and clients drawn from the public sector and large Scottish businesses. You can even work for global firms on multi-national deals involving FTSE 100 companies.

As we learned in Ch.1 (what will you do?), nearly 30% of the profession works in house and, for them, giving advice is only part of their role. They work directly for (and often as part of) the board of directors or management teams of local authorities. They're business people as much as they're lawyers. And that's just in Scotland. You also can work around the world. If you go to London, you could join an international firm like Clifford Chance and you could work in offices from Singapore to New York.

Nowadays you have more opportunities than ever before. When you look out the window of your office you might be looking at Edinburgh Castle, Canary Wharf or the Empire State Building. Yet, to most people, there's only one type of law firm, and it has a large desk, a small library and a wood-panelled office. That's where your friends and family imagine you work. Yet, there are hundreds of different types of law firms. This chapter and the next examine how these firms differ and why.

Outcomes

In the last ten years, law firms have undergone big changes. These changes continue to shape both what they do and how they do it. This chapter shows you how changes have led law firms to alter the way in which they work, from simple things (like changing their name, or the location of an office) to more complicated matters (like the way the firm is structured to deal with client matters). We illustrate these types of decision by tracing the history of a single firm, to demonstrate how client demand helped it grow from a single partner to the largest law firm in Scotland and, latterly, to a global firm with over 30 offices worldwide. **3–3**

In Ch.4 (what do law firms sell?) we go on to examine how law firms make decisions (and how these are influenced by clients).

Differences between law firms

Each year the legal press publish comprehensive lists of the UK's biggest and most powerful law firms. As you already know, you find these in *The Lawyer*, *Legal Week* and *Legal Business*. The lists measure and rank firms based on the number of partners they have; the number of lawyers and staff they employ; the profits they make; and their turnover for the previous year. The lists tell you which firms make the most money; which have the most staff; and how they compare year on year. Are firms increasing in size? Are profits rising? How much are partners paid? If you read the list in 2008, you'd have seen that the biggest Scottish firms were: McGrigors, Dundas & Wilson, Burness, Brodies, Maclay Murray & Spens, Shepherd & Wedderburn, Tods Murray, Biggart Baillie and Semple Fraser. **3–4**

If such a list were available a century ago you'd also have found the same names dominating. Firms like McGrigors (then known as McGrigor Donald & Co), Dundas & Wilson and Tods Murray (then known as Tods Murray & Jamieson) were the three biggest law firms in Scotland. For one hundred years the biggest firms in Scotland remained the same. Yet, if you read the lists today, only three survive: Brodies, Maclay Murray & Spens and Shepherd & Wedderburn. McGrigors and Dundas & Wilson merged with global firms to form the Scottish offices of Pinsent Masons and CMS, respectively. Burness merged with the Aberdeen firm Paull & Williamson, to form Burness Paull. Biggart Baillie merged with the UK giant, DWF. Tods Murray and Semple Fraser, however, both collapsed after financial problems.

In just eight years many of the biggest names in the Scottish market (that had been around for centuries) just disappeared. This is not a coincidence. The last eight years have seen unprecedented changes. Some changes are obvious. A few firms have become bigger. In 2000, McGrigor Donald had 40 partners; today, as part of Pinsent Masons, it has over 1,000.

Equally, other firms have become smaller (or disappeared). The smaller firms have more specialisation. Maclay Murray & Spens established Law At Work, in 2001, as a specialist employment, HR and health and safety unit. In 2012, it became an independent law firm. The key to its success is focusing on one small area, and doing it well.

Some changes are perhaps less obvious. Many firms just changed their internal structures so that their management improved. Instead of being run by a partnership (with all partners having an equal say in management) today it's more common to find firms run by a management team, led by one person (a managing partner or chief executive) who makes most of the decisions,

These changes are inevitable and are part of the reason why firms that you might think should be identical are, in fact, radically different. Each firm has responded to change in a unique way. The decisions made over the life of a firm result in the firm you see today. We can demonstrate this best by examining the decisions made by one firm over the last 250 years. Our case study is Dundas & Wilson, once Scotland's biggest law firm, and now part of CMS, the fourth largest law firm in the world. In the following section we'll use its history to examine wider issues and choices for other firms and we'll compare and contrast the two.

The history of a law firm: Dundas & Wilson

3–5 Dundas & Wilson was founded in Edinburgh in 1759. It's been Scotland's leading law firm for most of its history. Partners have included institutional writers like Montgomery Bell, professor of conveyancing at Edinburgh University (and author of *Bell's Lectures on Conveyancing*) and leading Scottish establishment figures. It has acted in some of Scotland's biggest cases and for major household names, like the Bank of Scotland.

Over 250 years it grew from just one partner to having over 1,500 partners, in the early 2000s. It led the way in changing how law firms operate by introducing specialist partners, new technology and new processes. It's the perfect firm to show the choices that law firms can make when responding to change, whether it's choosing an office, choosing a name, selecting partners, making difficult business decisions (like making people redundant), or deciding on a growth strategy.

Choosing an office

3–6 In 1759, if you were walking along Chamber Street in Edinburgh you wouldn't see the National Museum of Scotland or Edinburgh Sheriff Court, as you would today. Instead you'd pass the Duke of Douglas gardens and the new law office of David Erskine, the founder of Dundas & Wilson. You might wonder why Erskine would choose to open his office in Chamber Street. The reasons were simple (and are principles still followed today). Erskine worked in Chamber Street because it was only a few minutes' walk from the courts at Parliament House. He needed an office that was convenient, close to court and which was easy for clients to visit.

We still see lawyers choosing offices that lie near courts, or near clients and contacts. On Bothwell Street, in Glasgow, you find Pinsent Masons and Burness Paull facing each other in the top floors of plush "Grade A" offices (which offices they share with clients like PwC, Barclays Bank, Shell and Knight Frank).

If you cross the River Clyde and walk along Carlton Place, towards Glasgow Sheriff Court, you see numerous signs for criminal lawyers, and you find the police cells where lawyers meet their clients. In Aberdeen we find Brodies, Pinsent Masons and CMS with offices in the west end, next to the offices of the Bank of Scotland, Clydesdale Bank and countless businesses working in the oil and gas sector. While across Scotland, Aberdein Considine, originally based in Aberdeen, has opened offices on busy high streets in places like Stirling, Livingston, Bathgate and Perth, as it tries to buy and sell homes right across the central belt.

Lawyers need clients, and one of the main ways in which they win business from clients is to have offices that are conveniently sited. So, while David Erskine opened an office to be near his clients, even firms as big as Clifford Chance moved their headquarters to Canary Wharf when the banks relocated their London headquarters to the Docklands.

Choosing a type of business

You may have decided on an office, but what type of business do you plan to run? Will you work on your own as a sole practitioner, will you work in a partnership, or will you work as a company (or other corporate entity)? **3–7**

Erskine was a sole practitioner, just like many lawyers are today. At its simplest, being a sole practitioner means exactly that; you're on your own. You own and you run your business. You do everything. You open your office, collect the mail, fix computers, deal with finances, and sort out the admin, answer phones, make the tea and then, once that's all done, carve out the time to carry out the legal work that your clients instruct. Sole practitioners rarely are completely alone. They often employ a secretary or receptionist to staff the office. They may employ a bookkeeper to deal with client funds and finances. They may even have legally trained employees like paralegals, trainees or lawyers who work for them. A sole practitioner is someone who owns 100% of their own business, and that business can range in size from one person to hundreds of people.

Erskine was a good lawyer. He acted for lots of wealthy clients, building a successful legal business before dying in Naples (of gout) in 1791. His will shows that he died a wealthy man. It also shows he left behind 16 children (some illegitimate, and many called David too (including one daughter)). He was rich, and one of the key advantages of being a sole practitioner is that you keep everything you make. You don't share profits with anyone else. If you're successful, then you alone enjoy the fruits of that success.

However, working as a sole practitioner was easier then than it is for lawyers today. Sole practitioners need to comply with more and more regulations. They need to deal with strict financial controls. They may need staff to help them, as they have less time each day to generate fees. It can be a constant balancing act between how much time they spend working for clients and how much time they need to spend just running the business. Sole practitioners need to be a combination of lawyer, businessperson, IT engineer, accountant, marketing expert and more, all of which takes time.

For Erskine, running a business was easier. There were fewer regulations. He didn't need to undertake ID checks to comply with anti-money laundering regulations. Nor did he need to ensure his email server was maintained. One of the biggest advantages Erskine had over modern lawyers was that there was actually less law to follow. The 20th century saw the law of Scotland expand hugely, requiring lawyers to specialise in different areas just so that they could become experts in a particular area. Today, many lawyers prefer to work in a partnership, so they can cover more areas of law for clients.

The pros and cons of partnership

This is the traditional business vehicle, where two or more lawyers go into business together. This was actually the only option open to lawyers who wanted to run a business together, until 2000. Although Erskine was a sole practitioner, he didn't work alone. He had an apprentice, James Robertson, who took control of the firm when Erskine died. Unlike Erskine, Robertson decided that he needed a partner to help him run the business. He approached William Wilson and, when Robertson died, Wilson became partners with James Dundas. The firm changed its name to Wilson & Dundas, and then Dundas & Wilson (though no one knows why, or exactly when, they swapped around). **3–8**

Today, partnerships are created under the Partnership Act 1890. The Act provides that partnerships must involve more than one person (naturally), and that they carry on a business for profit. There is no need to record the partnership in writing but it's recommended that they do so as to avoid any misunderstanding later. A partnership has a "quasi" separate legal personality. The firm can enter into contracts with its partners, can sue and be sued by any partner. The firm can own property in its own name and can be declared bankrupt.

From Erskine, Robertson, Wilson and Dundas we can identify two trends. Firstly, lawyers opened offices where they could source (and then carry out) business. Secondly, some lawyers worked out that it was easier to work together than alone. However, unlike the directors and members of a limited liability partnership (LLP), which we'll cover shortly, partners in a partnership can be held personally liable for the firm's debts. In other words, every partner is responsible for everything the partnership makes and everything it loses.

For William Wilson, this meant that if he made a profit of £100, he would need to share £50 with James Dundas (though in practice, as we see later, they would have agreed a way to divide profits rather than rely on a simple split). However, if James Dundas ran up a debt of £1,000 then William Wilson would need to pay £500 of that debt. What's more, if James Dundas couldn't afford to pay his share of the debt, then William Wilson would need to pay on his behalf; while both shared in the profits, either partner could be 100% responsible for the debts.

This is why partners in a partnership tend to have a unique bond. They need to trust each other, because they're entrusting something precious to each of their partners, namely their bank balance. It also means something else. If you potentially could face a huge bill because of something your partner has done, you probably want a say in every decision that he or she makes. If every decision could affect you adversely, wouldn't you want to know about it?

So why join a partnership?

3–9 The main benefit of being in a partnership is that you can do more. As the 20th century dawned, law libraries grew so big they could no longer be contained on a bookshelf. The big question for many firms was whether lawyers could still do everything. Could every partner cover every area of law?

Choose a specialism

3–10 At the start of the 20th century, Dundas & Wilson had 10 partners. It was one of the largest firms in Scotland. It had an office in Edinburgh beside its main client, the Royal Bank of Scotland. Partners of the firm even sat on the bank's board. It was a success, but one partner knew it had to change to face the challenges the 20th century would bring.

John Richardson was a specialist in banking, agriculture and trusts, and one of the smartest lawyers in the country. The UK Government even had to introduce legislation to try and stop some of his tax schemes as he regularly out-thought the treasury.

Yet, he knew that Dundas & Wilson had to change. In 1911, Richardson called a meeting of his partners and he demanded that each should choose an area of law that would be their speciality. He didn't want partners who were "jack of all trades". He wanted partners who would be experts in just one area. He knew that increased regulation (and a burgeoning volume of law) meant that clients needed lawyers who could give in-depth advice.

He also realised that by specialising in particular areas, the firm would become more than just a collection of individuals. It would be a genuine team that would require its partners to work together. It was this decision that led to the modern careers of banking, corporate, criminal, property and litigation.

Your career

Think about your own career. As a trainee you normally work in a number of different areas of law. Depending on the firm you join, that might include a formal six-month rotation of seats in particular departments. Alternatively, you may just work for a number of partners with different interests over the course of your traineeship. When you qualify, you then need to specialise. This could be in one area. In larger firms, for example, this could involve narrow specialisms. By way of illustration, you might not just work in banking but—instead—work on just one particular financial product. It can be that detailed. **3–11**

In smaller firms you may carry out a wider range of work. On the high street you could deal with conveyancing and corporate work, but it's unlikely you also would do court work too. The days of one person carrying out all the legal work required by any client that walks through their door largely are gone.

Choose a second office (and a third and a fourth. . .)

Between 1980 and 2000, Clifford Chance grew from 12 partners to over 500 partners worldwide. In Scotland, Dundas & Wilson grew from a firm based only in Edinburgh by merging with the Glasgow firm Davidson & Syme in 1972. It opened an office in London in the late 1990s and, in 1997, joined Arthur Andersen's legal network of over 3,000 lawyers. Within two years, revenue shot up by 20%. New partners at the firm would be sent to Andersen's international training centre in Chicago as part of their induction. Every morning they would be woken up by an alarm clock programmed to play Tina Turner's "Simply The Best". The firm was growing bigger and bigger.

How could firms increase in size so rapidly in just 20 years? In essence, they were responding to client demands. As national companies like BP and British Airways dropped the "British" and evolved into multinationals, law firms also expanded to match their clients. The opening of trade borders made it easier for companies to move beyond geographic boundaries and become global businesses. Law firms simply followed. However, even on this larger scale, firms still followed the same instincts they'd always used. Instead of opening on Chamber Street to be near clients, firms were opening in Frankfurt and Hong Kong, in order to capture global clients on the world's biggest stock exchanges.

Growth presented new problems, however. The biggest problem was cash. In order to expand, firms needed money. They needed to pay for more staff, new offices and new equipment. These are costs that any firm needs to pay before they open their doors and start charging fees to clients. Partners had to decide how much they were willing to invest. However, they also had to rely on their partners to "cough up" if things went wrong. Allied to that was the question of trusts—as the number of partners increased, could you trust all your partners, all the time?

Choose your partners wisely

In 2000, Dundas & Wilson was one of the leading firms in Andersen Legal, a network of firms linked to global accountants Arthur Andersen, with **3–12** responsibility not just for Scotland but also for the development of the network worldwide. Though the network was a success, trouble was brewing. In 2001, Arthur Anderson was implicated in a massive fraud at the US energy company Enron. Despite being one of the five biggest accounting firms in the world, in just one year it was gone (along with its legal network). One of the reasons it collapsed so quickly was because it was a partnership.

With over 700 partners, partnerships in accounting had grown so big it was actually no longer possible for one partner to trust all their fellow partners. Indeed, with such a large number (and such a geographical spread) it was likely that they had never met most of their partners.

When Enron collapsed, Anderson faced huge financial claims. It also suffered fatal damage to its reputation. Even though its revenue was nearly $10 billion in 2002, it couldn't survive. One of the effects of Anderson's collapse was that regulators worldwide realised that partnerships were no longer suitable for big global businesses. If one claim could lead to a $10 billion business ceasing to trade, then a replacement would be required to help stop potential losses. A vehicle was required that would facilitate firms taking legitimate risks. Thus LLPs were born.

In 2004, Dundas & Wilson became one of the first firms in Scotland to convert from a partnership to an LLP. The move meant that most partners could limit the losses they would need to contribute to, and it would protect non-negligent partners were the firm sued for damages. In return for this new protection, the firm would publish accounts and release more information publically than a traditional partnership.

An ordinary partnership doesn't need to publish its accounts with any outside body (such as the Companies House). The only people who know how well or how badly a firm is doing are the partners themselves, their accountant, their bank and HMRC. An LLP has to be more open, however, and publish accounts that then are publicly available (via Companies House). The reorganisation meant that Dundas & Wilson was able to successfully relaunch itself as a UK firm. The firm's turnover rose 12%, in 2001/02, to £38 million. By 2004/05 it had grown another 17.1%, to £44.5 million. Its partners regularly were paid over £250,000.

In spite of the new LLP structure, big law firms still faced problems. They had become bloated, and developed bad habits.

Choose unemployment?

3–13 In 2008, a property crash that started in the USA then spread worldwide. Banks became nervous and businesses stopped doing deals. People saved money rather than spend it. The Royal Bank of Scotland's share price dropped from £3.27 (in January 2008) to 50p, by that December. The UK Government had to inject billions of pounds into the economy in order to keep the banks afloat. For the large commercial firms, it was like a tap had been switched off. The banks stopped lending, clients stopped doing deals and no one bought or sold property. The recession was as swift as it was unexpected. One month, offices were busy with lawyers regularly working late and on weekends; the next month everyone was leaving at 5pm because they had nothing to do.

Law firms had to react. The first thing to happen was a series of redundancies. Firms simply didn't need all of the lawyers they employed. While having a speciality is good (because lawyers became experts and expertise sells), if you specialise in an area that has no work, then redundancy swiftly follows. There were no property deals and no banking deals. Couples put divorce on hold because they couldn't sell the house they shared. Lawyers lost their jobs because their firms no longer had any work to give them.

Allen & Overy was the world's fifth-largest law firm in 2008. In December that year it kicked off its restructure with a comprehensive review of its global business, and announced a slew of measures in February 2009. This included a global reduction in its partner headcount by 9%, a proposed 9% cut in the number of associates and other fee earners, a 9% reduction in support staff and pay freezes across the board.

On 1 May 2009, the firm (which has 31 offices worldwide and approximately 5,500 staff) reached the end of its redundancy programme. It resulted in the laying off of around 450 members of staff. The figure comprised 200 associates, 200 support staff, plus a further 47 equity partners. Half of the cuts centred on its London headquarters. An undisclosed number of voluntary redundancies also were agreed.

Choose fixed fees

Clients had less money and were less willing to pay big fees (or fees that were **3–14** not agreed in advance). They started to demand fixed fees. Instead of paying, for example, £100 or £200 per hour, clients would tell firms that they could have £5,000, and not a penny more. Firms had to become smarter. They needed the right people. They needed the cheapest resource to carry out work so they could make a profit on that £5,000. They needed paralegals, IT and project management skills. This is where the great divide started. Innovation, IT and training all cost money and money is the one thing most firms don't have (certainly not in 2008).

Choose the right skills

In Victoria Road, in the south side of Glasgow, there are seven law firms within **3–15** 50m of each other. All are high street firms. Some specialise in conveyancing, others in criminal law or immigration, but most covering a bit of everything. These firms are a mix of sole practitioners and small groups of partners (with one who predominantly specialises in court work, one who deals with conveyancing and one who specialises in family law).

The property partner might bring in £100 an hour, the family law partner slightly more. The court partner however might only earn £485 for a legal aid case at the sheriff court lasting a whole day. That fee covers preparation for (and attending) court. Even if they do no work and just spend eight hours at court, the court partner has brought in £60 an hour. However, no lawyer will turn up and just wing it. The court partner needs to meet the client and prepare. Suddenly, depending on how complex the case may be, they're looking at £30 an hour, £15 per hour, or maybe less—not so lucrative after all. And that's before they pay for rent, for wages, for rates and electricity.

When business is tough, when a recession means individuals have less money to spend, and when government cuts reduce legal aid contributions, what kind of conversations are the partners having in high street firms? Will the property partner and family law partner share their income with a court partner, who may bring in pennies when they bring in pounds? These and other difficult conversations have been taking place across Scotland.

Choose a merger, takeovers or alternative business structures

3–16 The need to make money and reduce costs meant some firms closed. Tods Murray, McClure Naismith and Semple Fraser were the highest profile firms to enter administration. In Tods Murray's case, they'd opened an expensive office in Edinburgh next to their client, the Bank of Scotland. But when the recession hit, the partners could no longer afford the rent and, despite managing to survive until 2014, they had no choice but to close the business when they couldn't generate enough fees to continue paying the bills.[1]

For a number of firms, merging was the solution to reducing costs. Two firms working together offered many benefits. Sometimes the growth brought about by merging opened up new areas of work. Some clients might have wanted larger teams and more back up, and a merger was one way of addressing these concerns before the client left for a rival. The merger also would save costs due to economies of scale (i.e. paying less for goods and supplies, reduced office space and redundancies to obviate duplication).

Finally, a demand for alternative business structures (ABSs) grew. ABSs, as we see later in this chapter, permits non-lawyers to invest in a law firm. Lawyers don't have a monopoly on good ideas. Can you imagine a law firm run by Richard Branson or James Dyson? The latter might hoover up all your business. The problem with ABSs is that non-lawyers don't share your professional standards. They don't owe duties to courts, clients, society or fellow solicitors. Can you imagine Tesco accepting a legal aid case for £15 per hour when they could have a lawyer working on a property transaction for ten times that amount?

Choose . . . the future

3–17 PwC believe that in 10 years there will only be three types of successful firms:

International

3–18 These are firms like DLA, servicing clients who need advice from London to Sydney and from Beijing to New York.

Niche

3–19 These are firms that offer the best service in a particular area, like Dickson Minto for private equity, or Turcan Connell for private client.

Volume

3–20 These are firms like insurance specialists Slater & Gordon, who charge little per transaction and make profits from running thousands of files at once.

3–21 This will affect the high street, criminal practices and national firms alike. Will people walk into a high street firm when there is no high street? If legal advice is a phone call away do you need an office in Victoria Road? As for Dundas & Wilson, does it need an office in Scotland if its clients work in London and Europe? DLA Piper faced a similar decision in 2012 when it asked itself if it needed both a Glasgow and Edinburgh office. In January 2013 it decided it only

---

[1] M. Taylor, "Tods Murrays: Death by real estate", The Lawyer (9 October 2014). Available at: *http://www.thelawyer.com/issues/online-october-2014/tods-murray-death-by-real-estate-2/* [Accessed: 9 June 2016].

needed an office in Edinburgh and so shut its Glasgow office, making many staff redundant. Remember the first thing Erskine did? He opened an office where he could find work. How do lawyers find work? They get work from clients. For Dundas & Wilson, in 2016, those clients are large public limited companies (Plcs), FTSE 100 companies and global businesses. What did their clients tell them after 2008? They said they wanted firms with offices in Singapore, New York and Australia. The wanted more than Dundas & Wilson then could offer. McGrigors' clients were telling them the same thing. The quickest way to grow to a size that the clients wanted was to merge with firms that already had offices in other countries.

Equally, this is also why we think Biggart Baillie merged with DWF. Their clients wanted a firm that had offices in England. Aberdein Considine, similarly, merged with firms in the central belt so that it could expand out of Aberdeen. 2008 changed everything and the firms that were first to react were able to take advantage by growing and changing to reflect what their clients wanted.

Merge or die

Dundas & Wilson merged with CMS on 1 May 2014. One year later, Caryn Penley (former Managing Partner of Dundas & Wilson), was quoted in the *Scottish Legal News* (19 May 2015) praising the success of the merger: **3–22**

> "I'm from the legacy Dundas & Wilson side and from my perspective I think it has gone really well. From a Dundas & Wilson perspective, we had a lot of good clients, but we weren't the right size and we didn't have the reach to service our clients in the way we really wanted to. The combination has allowed us to do that. There are a number of examples where, historically, CMS and Dundas & Wilson would have had contact with similar clients. But the combination has meant we have got more work, have been able to service those clients in a way that those two separate firms could not have done before. For me that really underpins the success."[2]

The future

Law firms have not fully recovered from the recession. Financial results have certainly improved, with many firms reporting healthy profits. However, the attitude and approach of firms has changed because clients have changed. The pressure to reduce fees, to provide better services and to truly understand clients' needs has meant that firms cannot be complacent. Firms cannot assume that their business will stay the same. They need to provide better service; tailored fees and they need to train lawyers who understand what clients want (and who can truly deliver). **3–23**

That's why law firms look different—they're responding to what they think their clients want. It's clients who help shape what law firms will look like and what they offer. However, clients are not the only factor in the future of law firms. There are a number of other trends that we can identify. These are: technology, gender diversity, outsourcing and finance.

---

[2] Caryn Penley quoted in: *http://www.scottishlegal.com/2015/05/19/cms-enters-organic-growth-following-scottish-acquisition/* [Accessed: 14 June 2016].

Technology

3–24 There are firms that send letters rather than emails. There are firms with sophisticated case management systems that automate many common tasks. There are others still working from a paper file. No two firms are the same.

Technology is changing law firms but it doesn't change every law firm at the same pace, because technology requires money and commitment. It requires money because new systems (like case management software) require upfront investment. The benefits of the system are then spread across future work (with costs reduced by lawyers working faster and smarter). If you can't afford the software to begin with, then saving money in the future is just a pipedream. Costs need to fall before all law firms can join the pioneers who invest first. Equally, firms need commitment from staff to use the new technology. We know of one firm that introduced an internal messaging system, yet no one used it. Staff still sent emails to each other. The messaging system was abandoned. For any new system to work it must be used, and that requires training. This takes time, and—yes—even more money.

However, the benefits are clear, as this report from DWF suggests:

> "[We use] optical character recognition technology to scan intercepted mail coming into the firm and route it directly into live matters on the firm's document management system . . . It scans 10,000 items of mail per day to London alone, which translates into a reduction in on-site storage from twelve to five linear metres per fee earner and reduces the cost of floor space—creating flexibility for fee earners and supporting DWF's environmental values.
>
> Building on this, we have implemented printing software that enables fee-earners to print office-specific headed notepaper from an app, regardless of location. This reduces the cost of printing and transporting headed paper to all locations and ensures there is minimal wastage. Clients also have access to the mobile print solutions, and a supported cloud solution enables them to print securely in any DWF office.
>
> Across the business, we have implemented matter-specific scanning, which enables fee-earners to access client documents securely, regardless of their location, and delivers cost and time savings to clients, as work is turned around more efficiently. It also enables our people to work more flexibly—whether on the move, working from home or hot-desking at a client's office—which can deliver benefits to our employees and allows our business to deliver a more responsive service for clients.
>
> In addition, reducing commuting time and allowing employees greater flexibility to work remotely can improve work-life balance, improve stress levels and increase productivity."[3]

It also creates a challenge from clients. As the Law Society identified in its 2015 consultation, *Perceptions and Impacts of Working Patterns within the Legal Profession in Scotland*:

---

[3] W. Lawrence and R. Hodkinson, "The technological edge" (16 November 2015), The Journal of the Law Society of Scotland, p.24. Available at *http://www.journalonline.co.uk/Magazine/60-11/1020978.aspx* [Accessed 19 April 2016].

> "It was . . . widely agreed that new technology had created unrealistic client expectations. Many felt that clients now expect an immediate response to emails, and that the use of computers to draw up forms, documents, etc. means that they also expect tasks to be turned around quickly."[4]

While technology can speed up processes, it also increases expectations. Perhaps it's not a surprise, then, that some firms still send letters if they know it means they won't have to deal instantly with responses. Technology also requires money and staff buy-in. This is why, eight years after the recession, many firms don't look (or act) radically differently than the way they did in 2007. However, the need for change is still growing, not just because of client demand, but also because of the way that the profession is becoming more diverse.

Gender diversity

Historically, people from diverse backgrounds have been underrepresented in the legal profession. Even today, the law school population (as well as the legal profession) does not reflect society. **3–25**

For the last four years, Andrew has delivered a lecture to students on the Diploma of Legal Practice. In it, he asks the students to describe what they imagine when he asks them to think of a lawyer. Nine times out of 10 they describe an old white man, in spite of most of the cohort being young females. This unscientific test shows that the picture of a lawyer as a man with grey hair is ingrained. Try it yourself. Imagine a lawyer. Who do you see?

Yet, if you look at any photo of an admission ceremony for new solicitors for the last five years, you'll see mostly women. Around 70% of all new solicitors are female. For the first time, the Law Society reported in 2015 that the profession had more female than male solicitors. This is a major development. However, the feminisation of the legal profession presents two big challenges. Firstly, although junior lawyers are mostly female, senior lawyers mostly are not. Partners certainly are not, with less than 30% of partners being women. As Christine McLintock (then President of the Law Society) said in December 2015:

> "Although women outnumber men as newly admitted solicitors each year, they continue to be relatively under-represented in senior positions, for example as partners in private practice. What is clear is that employers have to take notice of the increasing numbers of young, ambitious women choosing to enter the legal profession and plan accordingly to avoid losing talented individuals from their business. I have no doubt that we'll continue to see women in the profession rise to the top, but given the results of our own and others' research, it's likely to be many years before we see any kind of equality in terms of the numbers of women in the most senior roles."[5]

This means that male lawyers (typically aged 40 and over) have to adjust to managing a team of female solicitors with career aims and aspirations that they

---

[4] E. Wilson Smith, *Perceptions and Impacts of Working Patterns Within the Legal Profession in Scotland* (research for the Law Society of Scotland, May 2015), p.18. Available at *https://www.lawscot.org.uk/media/519915/Work-patterns-final-.pdf* [Accessed 19 April 2016].

[5] "Scottish solicitors now majority female" (23 December 2015), *Lawscot.org.uk*, *http://www.lawscot.org.uk/news/2015/12/scottish-solicitors-now-majority-female/* [Accessed 19 April 2016].

might not share. Quite simply, that male team leader might not understand the challenges that a female lawyer faces. Men design law firms for men. They may expect long hours that are incompatible with family life. Outside the office, even business development activities might deter female solicitors:

> "Another barrier, that was specific to women in the profession, involved the nature of the work being centred around the traditional 'male' lifestyle/work pattern and not flexible enough to either accommodate 'female' responsibilities or recognise and reward different inputs. i.e. the extensive networking and client entertainment that is required within the profession is typically centred on evening events/activities, making it very difficult for female solicitors who have families to attend/engage in this, certainly with the frequency required to progress their careers within some firms."[6]

Carolyn Fairburn (Director General of the Confederation of British Industry (CBI)) flagged this issue, in November 2015:

> "I've never been a fan of the business dinner. A lot of women aren't. They'd rather go home to their families in the evening. Why not have more early evening events like a panel discussion, a nice glass of wine or two and then everyone off home by 7.30? Maybe the business dinner is a vestige of old business life."[7]

The CBI is taking a lead by phasing out all business dinners it organises, except for its annual dinner.

We're generalising that family life is a concern for female solicitors. We recognise it's a concern for male solicitors, too. However, there's a need for firms to recognise that maternity leave and part-time working are more prevalent among female employees than male. This means that firms need to develop ways of working which are compatible with a family life. This includes encouraging home working, part-time working and a better work life balance. This brings us back to technology. Home working requires firms to have IT systems that allow people to work from home as easily as if they were in the office. It needs electronic files so that people don't need access to filing cabinets and desk drawers. It requires many small changes that, again, cost money. However, unlike the technology trend, this time the need to spend cannot be ignored. If the majority of solicitors are female, then firms will need to make these changes otherwise they'll lose talented staff.

Outsourcing

3–26 London is home to the biggest law firms in the UK. Many global firms like Clifford Chance have traditionally only had an office in London. The problem with London though is that rents are high, salaries need to match, and fees need to

---

6 E. Wilson Smith, *Perceptions and Impacts of Working Patterns Within the Legal Profession in Scotland* (research for the Law Society of Scotland, May 2015), p.29. Available at *https://www.lawscot.org.uk/media/519915/Work-patterns-final-.pdf* [Accessed 19 April 2016].

7 J. Armitage, "Black-tie business dinners should make way for more female-friendly events, says CBI chief" (23 November 2015), *Independent.co.uk*, *http://www.independent.co.uk/news/business/news/black-tie-business-dinners-should-make-way-for-more-female-friendly-events-says-cbi-chief-a6744456.html* [Accessed 19 April 2016].

be even higher to make a profit. However, in recent years, because of the pressure on fees that we've discussed, the biggest firms have had to look at alternative ways to save money. One solution was to move work offshore. In 2007, Clifford Chance launched a Knowledge Centre in New Delhi, to carry out paralegal work and offer support to the firm globally.

This offshoring trend also led to firms looking closer to home to save money as the difference in costs between an office in London and one in Bristol, Leeds, Glasgow or Belfast was considerable. Perhaps not as much as moving work to India, but, having work closer to home meant access to more staff trained in the UK and more staff working in the same time zone as the London offices.

In 2011, Herbert Smith Freehills launched an office in Belfast to offer support services to the firm, focusing mainly on reviewing and analysing large volumes of documents, investigations and due diligence. Ashurt opened a similar office in Glasgow in 2013. It said:

> "We believe the office will help to shape an alternative legal model and career structure in Scotland, benefiting from the high number of exceptional legal graduates."[8]

It employs over 200 people. More and more firms are using offshoring and near-shoring to provide legal advice—and this is a trend that will only increase in subsequent years as lawyers increasingly use their project management skills (see Ch.18 (how to be a legal project manager)) to identify ways to improve legal work and provide it cheaper and faster.

Finance

New technology, better processes and managing workloads all require money. **3–27**
The partnership structure has meant that law firms have been reluctant to invest as partners become personally responsible. Although LLPs have helped, many firms are reluctant to invest because, in practice, while the LLP structure may protect individual partners, a bank lending money may still seek personal guarantees, no matter what the LLP agreement may say.

That's why there has been a push to widen the number of people who can invest in law firms. Large companies, entrepreneurs or investment funds have money to invest in businesses looking to expand. However, until recently, they were banned from doing so as only solicitors could own law firms. This has changed with the introduction of ABSs. ABSs allow non-lawyers to invest and become partners in law firms.

England and Wales

In England and Wales, ABSs were introduced by the Legal Services Act 2007, **3–28**
which came into force between 2008 and 2011. Applications to become an ABS are overseen by the Solicitors Regulation Authority (SRA), which is responsible for judging applications for issuing licences. The first ABS licence was granted in April 2012, and by the end of 2015 it had around 400. Many have gone to existing law firms that want to add a non-lawyer to their partnership or to niche new outfits

---

8 "Ashurt announces opening of new office in Glasgow" (12 June 2013), *Ashurt.com*, *https://www.ashurst.com/media-item.aspx?id_Content=9211* [Accessed 19 April 2016].

in areas like personal injury. For example, among the firms licenced was Lawbridge Solicitors in Kent, a sole practitioner who wanted to add a non-lawyer partner as its practice manager (in this case, his wife).

Other new ABSs are established law firms. Irwin Mitchell was ahead of the pack. It was the first top-50 firm to make the transformation. Since then Gateley, Weightmans, and Knights have followed suit. The last of these is private-equity backed, courtesy of former *Dragons' Den* investor James Caan.

However, the rise of ABSs has not been easy. Among the first licences granted was a licence to Co-Op Law, part of the Co-Operative Group. In 2012 it announced that it had plans to recruit 3,000 lawyers by 2017, to challenge high street firms across the UK. However, despite the backing of a major business it has only about 400 staff (about 100 more than when it started). In April 2015 it announced a loss of approximately £5 million in the first six months of the financial year, and had only edged into the black in the second half (to post a £50,000 profit). In late 2015 there was a high profile failure of an ABS firm. Parabis Law, a personal injury firm, went into administration in November 2015. In 2012, it became the first private equity-backed ABS to be licensed by the SRA, and was seen as one of the forerunners of the new legal landscape. Three years later and with debts of over £70 million, it became insolvent and the business was sold and split between seven firms.

Scotland

3–29 In Scotland, ABS was established by the Legal Services (Scotland) Act 2010. The Act allows non-solicitor partners to work in partnership with other professionals (multi-disciplinary practices (MDPs)), and external ownership through ABS (up to a maximum of 49%). However, five years later it has still not been implemented. One of the main challenges facing ABS is moving from a system where individual solicitors are regulated to instead regulating business entities. At the moment (as we'll see in Ch.11 (how to be professional) and Ch.12 (how to avoid complaints)) it's solicitors and not firms who are regulated by the Law Society). If you do something wrong, only you can be charged with misconduct.

Under the Legal Services (Scotland) Act 2010, it was intended that firms would be regulated, too. This would allow the actions of non-solicitors to be controlled (as non-solicitors wouldn't be caught by existing regulation). However, in order to make this change a new regulatory framework would be required, including specific practice rules, accounts rules and rules in relation to licensing. This change is complex and one that is not yet in place. Until it is, law firms in Scotland cannot use ABS.

This delay has led to complaints. Lorne Crerar, chairman of Harper Macleod, said in November 2015[9]:

> "In Scotland, our failure to grasp a regulatory structure for ABS continues to be a significant disadvantage against English competitors.
>
> The delay in ABS has severely damaged and hampered those firms who viewed it as an opportunity, but we still need it."

---

[9] G. Cameron, "Scottish legal sector expecting further consolidation" (2 January 2015), *Heraldscotland.com, http://www.heraldscotland.com/business/13195526.Scottish_legal_sector_expecting_further_consolidation/* [Accessed 19 April 2016].

Summary

In this chapter you've considered the difficult choices one famous firm made as it grew from a sole practitioner to a global law firm. You've seen how change affects all businesses and that responding to change is the key to success. Firms that don't change simply don't survive. Change needs cash, however. Without cash, law firms like Tods Murray, Semple Fraser and, most recently, McClure Naismith were unable to finance the changes they needed to make. **3–30**

Imagine you could start a law firm from scratch. Imagine you could ignore 250 years of history and build a new law firm. What choices would you make today? How would you respond to the challenges of technology, diversity and investment?

In the next chapter we look at how clients choose law firms and how your firm can react to what your clients want. In other words, we take a look at what happens before a client even walks through the door, picks up the phone or emails you with a new instruction. Why did your client choose your firm on the second day of your traineeship?

CHAPTER 4

WHAT DO LAW FIRMS SELL?

Introduction

4–1 *It's Thursday. Day four. You're in a meeting. It's your second meeting with your new client (from Tuesday) and your partner decides to join you.*

Your client wants to sue her employer for unfair dismissal. Before you start discussing her case, your partner introduces himself and asks why she chose your firm to act on her behalf. She says, "One of my friends told me that your firm always stands up for people and doesn't back down. You're like a dog with a bone and I want a Rottweiler." Your partner says, "You've come to the right place."

And you think, "Am I a Rottweiler now?!"

4–2 Most firms have a reputation. As we saw in Ch.1 (what will you do?), Levy & McRae has a reputation for litigation, Turcan Connell for private client, and Dickson Minto for corporate financing. Along with a reputation for certain types of work, most firms also have a reputation based on its staff, a reputation for "how they carry out that work".

When one of the authors started his traineeship he was told that his firm, a national firm, liked to recruit people who could show they were sociable, as well as knowledgeable about their area of law. The firm wanted lawyers who could talk to clients, not lawyers who'd have their nose in a book. The firm had a reputation at that time not just for corporate law, but also for lawyers who were informal and approachable.

You see a firm's personality more clearly when you start working and you deal with the same firms, again and again. You might hear colleagues refer to one large Scottish firm as pedantic and unhelpful. Another may be referred to as only interested in fees. Others are praised for working hard for their clients, and always pushing for a better deal. Your firm's reputation is more than just pure technical knowledge. It's everything about it. What does it do? How do its lawyers and staff act? What do other people say about it?

Even appearances matter—law firms, like people, are judged on appearances. If your shirt sticks out of your trousers, if your tights have a ladder, if your hair is a mess, if you swear in a boardroom, all of these things change how clients view you: "if they can't dress themselves how can I trust them with my business?" "If they can't control themselves how can I trust them to say the right thing on my behalf?" It's the same for law firms. If your reception is filled with last year's magazines, if your letters are sent on crumpled paper and if your website is still on Geocities, clients might look down upon it: "if they can't send me a letter without spilling tea on it, how do I know their advice is correct?" Knowledge, personality and appearance matter for a firm and, as a trainee, they matter to you. Remember, you don't start with a reputation. You rely on your firm's reputation while you build your own. That's why you need to know what it is, and how you can use it to benefit your career.

Outcomes

When we talk about a firm's knowledge, personality and appearance we're actually starting to talk about marketing and branding. Marketing is not just about adverts and signs. Marketing helps a business identify what clients want. This chapter introduces marketing by examining two techniques. **4–3**

The first is called segmentation. This is a technique to identify what clients want by splitting large groups into smaller groups, based on shared characteristics. For example, if you work for a criminal law practice you might split clients into those that need legal aid and those that don't. You would then treat each group differently as you know you need to undertake extra work to comply with Scottish Legal Aid Board (SLAB) rules, for those clients who need legal aid.

The second technique is called the marketing mix. This is a technique used to identify what you can offer these smaller groups, once you know what they want. For example, if you know some of your clients need legal aid then, instead of explaining what it is each time, you might produce a leaflet explaining what SLAB is and how legal aid works (which you can hand to new clients).

Most people think branding involves a logo. However, it's more than a logo. It's what your client thinks when he or she hears or sees your firm's name. These thoughts might be factual (for example, you have an office in Kirkcaldy with a blue sign above the door) and emotional (that firm's a Rottweiler). Your firm's name exists physically; people can see it. Your brand, however, exists only in someone's mind. Branding helps you to understand what they're thinking.

Introducing marketing

At university you're judged on your knowledge of the law. It's an intellectual exercise, not an emotional one. No university awards first class degrees because they found your dissertation "flirty" or your exam answer "optimistic". You're judged on your intellectual capability, reasoning and rigour. You're judged on your workings, not your conclusion. How you reach your answer is more important to academics than the answer itself. **4–4**

Clients are different. They rarely need the curtain pulled back to see behind the scenes. They want answers, not footnotes. This creates a dilemma. If clients aren't interested in the detail of what a firm does, how does it build a reputation in any area of law? How did Dickson Minto become known for its corporate finance work? How did Levy & McRae become renowned for litigation? This is a difficult question to answer. To help understand how reputations are created and developed, we need to first take a step back. We need to ask a more basic question—what do law firms sell? We say Dickson Minto is excellent at corporate finance, but what does that mean?

What do firms sell?

Law firms are not shops. When David Erskine opened his office in 1759 he didn't sell eggs, clothes or frying pans. He didn't sell anything physical at all, nothing that a client could pick up and touch. Instead he sold something unique, namely the information in his head, and his skill in turning that information into advice clients could follow. **4–5**

Compare Erskine with a shop. If you go into Tesco, you don't buy the store manager's knowledge of stacking shelves or the checkout assistant's expertise in packing bags. You're paying for a tin of beans, a box of cereal or a bottle of coke. You're not buying something unique. These are ordinary items that you can touch and feel. You can buy them in Asda, Waitrose or a corner shop. You're paying for a product, not a service.

What's the difference between a product and a service?

4–6 In simple terms, a product is an object you can touch and hold, like a car, oven, jacket or toaster. It's something you can see, feel, try, taste or otherwise use. It's physical. A service, on the other hand, is an action that you undertake for someone, like a haircut, car repair or medical diagnosis. Unlike a product, a service doesn't physically exist. You can't pick up a haircut—it's an action that you experience, and it's this experience that clients judge.

As Neil Stevenson, Chief Executive of the Scottish Legal Complaints Commission (SLCC) stated in 2015:

> "Rules, guidance, and technical legal knowledge all have a critical role to play in the provision of legal services, but it is also important to step back from those and consider what the client may and may not understand, and how they may be **feeling** [emphasis added] about their situation."[1]

It's how a client feels that is critical to how a firm manages its reputation.

How does a firm manage its reputation?

4–7 Just like you, your firm's reputation is also based on its appearance and personality. You might think it strange to think of a firm as having a personality, but think about other businesses that you know. Apple is cool, Gucci is stylish, Ryanair is cheap; each of these businesses has a personality. Law firms are no different and they're judged on exactly the same criteria as any other business.

When clients walk into your boardroom they don't appear there by magic. The sign above your door influences a new client; as does the look and feel of your reception, how the receptionist treats them and what they think about the boardroom they've been brought into. Before you open your mouth your client will have started to form a view (rightly or wrongly) about your firm. Even a client who phones you for the first time will have read an advert, or at least checked out your firm's website. That client already has formed a view, just as they would if they were walking along a high street before popping into an Apple Store or browsing the web and clicking on *www.apple.com*.

The best law firms—like the best businesses—know that everything it does or says can influence how a client feels. When we say that Dickson Minto has a reputation for corporate finance, what we're actually saying is that Dickson

---

[1] "Correct advice may not be enough, court rules on complaint appeal" (18 August 2015), The Journal of the Law Society of Scotland, *Journalonline.co.uk*, *http://www.journalonline.co.uk/News/1020652.aspx#.VdQ9wvlVhBc* [Accessed 19 April 2016]. Stevenson was speaking about the case of *Walter Scott Sneddon and Sneddon & Son, SSC against a decision of the SLCC* ([2015] CSIH 62). In this case the Inner House ruled that a lawyer's advice to a client could be inadequate even though the advice provided was correct. We'll look at how inadequate advice is judged more closely in Ch.11 (how to be professional) and Ch.12 (how to avoid complaints).

Minto's appearance and personality helps clients think that it has a reputation for corporate finance. The trick is to understand what aspects of appearance or personality (a firm's marketing) influence how a client feels. As Neil Stevenson points out, law firms need to consider feelings because they're providing a service and not a product.

Introducing segmentation: How do firms know what their clients want?

Finding out how clients feel isn't easy. Your firm has to identify its current and prospective clients. If it doesn't know who its clients are, it can hardly make assumptions about how they feel. Identifying clients is not easy. Your firm may have hundreds of clients. It's completely impractical to ask all of them how they're feeling. They would probably think it strange that they were being asked. Instead, your firm has to follow the adage that "you can't be all things to all people" and let that be its guide. Most businesses actually don't try and sell everything to everyone. Gucci sells clothes and accessories to people who want luxury items. Ryanair sells flights to people who want the lowest price. Even Amazon, which arguably does try to sell everything, doesn't sell to everyone. It only sells to people who can access the internet (though admittedly, this is a very large group).

All businesses divide their customers into smaller groups to help sell products and services. This is known as segmentation. Take Tesco, for example. It doesn't just sell one type of tinned tomatoes. It has two. It has Tesco Finest, for customers who are willing to pay more for better ingredients. It has Tesco Everyday Value, for customers who want tomatoes at the lowest price. Tesco has identified two groups of customers and has provided two different tins to help them. Imagine if Tesco hadn't done this. If you want good tomatoes and Tesco only offered Everyday Value, you would shop elsewhere. Equally, if you want the cheapest price but Tesco only stocked Tesco Finest you also would shop elsewhere. Tesco would lose customers by only offering one tin. Separating its customers into two groups helps Tesco sell to all of them.

In the same way, law firms need to segment clients into smaller groups to work out who their clients are likely to be and what they should offer them. We can see this in action when David Erskine decided to open an office in Edinburgh.

Segmentation and David Erskine

Imagine you're opening a new law firm, like David Erskine. Where do you start? **4–8**
Theoretically you can act for anyone in the world, but you know you're never going to act for six billion people. Instead you need to narrow it down to something more manageable. Segmentation can help.

Step 1: As a Scottish lawyer, you probably don't want an office in Alaska, Johannesburg or Beijing. You want clients based in Scotland.

Step 2: Even in Scotland, there are five million people. You need to narrow your choices down and ask yourself what clients in Scotland you want. Do you want to help people in a particular area? Do you want to help people who have a particular problem?

Step 3: If you decide to help people who have been accused of a crime, your choice narrows again. You've divided your clients into two groups: people accused of crimes in Scotland, and everyone else in the world. You can forget about everyone else (they won't need to visit your office) and just concentrate on those who might be accused of a crime.

Step 4: You now have a manageable group of potential clients. When you ask yourself where you should open your office, you can further segment your clients by considering where potential clients would want your office to be. You can assume it's likely they'll want to visit an office that's close to a sheriff court, high court or the Court of Session, or from a local high street.

Step 5: Choose your office. You can choose from a small handful of places that would be perfect for you.

Location

4–9 Erskine could have opened his office anywhere in Scotland. He could have acted for crofters in Ullapool or merchants in Glasgow. Instead, he decided to act for people in Edinburgh. That meant he needed an office in the city, preferably one near the court. This was his first step in segmenting his potential clients. From being able to act for everyone in Scotland, he was separating clients into people who lived in Edinburgh (with access to his office) and those who lived elsewhere. Geography was helping dictate who he would act for.

We see the same thing today. While transport links and communication have made it easier to deal with people across the country, location still matters. Think of the firms you might join: a high street firm in Stranraer is not going to sell a house in Wick; a national firm in Edinburgh is not going to deal with a breach of the peace on Arran. Location matters, and a firm's choice tells you many things about it.

Type of work

4–10 Clients also choose a firm because they believe that firm can help. A law firm won't last long if it doesn't know the answers to the questions clients ask. This was probably not a problem for Erskine, because it was easier to be a generalist in the 17th century. It is an issue today. Ever since Dundas & Wilson decided its partners should specialise, we've seen more lawyers who are experts in just one or two areas. If you're a criminal lawyer, you're unlikely to know corporate finance law. If you're a banking specialist, you're unlikely to know anything about custody hearings. This means that you want clients who need help in the areas you know. You segment potential clients into those you can help and those you can't. For example, when Dundas & Wilson decided that it wanted to act for the Royal Bank of Scotland, it opened an office beside the bank's headquarters.

Other factors

4–11 The location of his office and the work carried out were not the only factors that influenced David Erskine. He also separated potential clients by wealth. He was a smart man, and ambitious. He wanted to be rich and he knew that the quickest way to achieve this was to act for rich men who could afford big fees. The final thing he did was to wine and dine well-known figures like Robert Burns and David Hume, who could introduce him to Edinburgh's wealthiest men.

Location, work and wealth are not the only ways to segment potential clients. In fact, you can split clients by any criteria you wish. Other examples are: nationality; age; sex; and lifestyle choices. For example, if you're a morning person then you may want a gym that opens early. If you like a lie-in, then you want one that opens late. Or you do what Pure Gym does and open 24 hours a day, so that both of you're happy. Your choice of how to separate clients is up to you, and the benefits of doing so are clear.

Benefits

As we saw in Ch.2 (who are your clients?), there are many different types of client. You can act for individuals. You can act for companies. You can act for local authorities. Looking back, can you see that this chapter actually was an exercise in segmentation? What we did was to describe a number of smaller groups and the things we assumed they would want from their lawyer. **4–12**

For clients, segmentation means that they get a lawyer who understands what they want and need, without them having to explain everything. If you're looking for a divorce you want to speak to a lawyer who understands family law. If you're looking to move house you want a lawyer who knows the area you're moving to. Segmentation helps clients pick the right firm.

The marketing mix

When Ledingham Chalmers opened an office in Stirling we could say it was acting on segmentation.[2] Ledingham Chalmers is a medium sized firm with 10 partners. It originally was based in Aberdeen, but today it has offices in Edinburgh and Inverness. It has a reputation for agricultural law (among other areas) and has been described by Chambers & Partners 2015 as having a "sizeable offering covering all issues affecting both rural business and private clients in the agricultural sphere". **4–13**

In 2012 it decided to open a new office, but where would it choose? Many of Ledingham Chalmers' clients are farmers and estate owners. When it came to opening a new office in the central belt, it would have asked itself where those farmers and estate owners would want that office to be; they chose Stirling Auction Mart. This was a radical choice. The Auction Mart is based outside of Stirling. It's a standalone building in the middle of fields. It's off a main road, so no one visited it that didn't mean to be there. However, it's a building that potential agriculture clients would visit. Ledingham Chalmers didn't need to open in the center of Stirling to attract families, individuals and companies. It would be more convenient for clients to see them at the Auction Mart.

Ledingham Chalmers considered what its potential clients wanted and it opened an office to suit. However, opening an office is not the end of the decisions a law firm can make. Everything a firm does can be viewed in terms of what its clients want. Let's take Ledingham Chalmers, again. It has a reputation for agricultural law. Its clients are farmers and estate owners. You might assume that farmers and estate owners need conveyancing advice, as they own land. They may also need family law advice to ensure that land is passed to future generations, intact. They may need tax advice to deal with faming subsidies, and company law advice if they own the farm through a company or trust. Provided Ledingham Chalmers have lawyers who know these areas of law, their clients will be happy. Problems develop, however, when clients' needs change.

What might happen if a farmer needs advice on how to develop wind farms? If you want to keep this client you either need to learn about renewables law (fast) or find someone in your firm who can help. If you can't, the client will move to a firm that can help him. Knowing what your clients want is much more than just

---

[2] We have used Ledingham Chalmers as an example for this section based on our interpretation of how they acted. We have not interviewed anyone at the firm. We use this as an example of how a real decision may have been made.

knowing what they want currently. It's a constant process to check your assumptions about what they want now, and in the future. The marketing mix helps firms decide what assumptions are important.

What is the marketing mix?

4–14 If you walk down a high street, every shop is different. HMV is piled high with DVDs and CDs. The Apple Store is bright and clean, and filled with iPhones and iPads. Poundland contains a bit of everything. They all look different, but they're all based on similar ideas. They're the result of decisions made about: product, price, place and promotion.

Product

4–15 Every store has to decide what to stock. What should it sell? Is it phones, music or £1 bottles of Fairy washing up liquid?

Price

4–16 Every store has to decide how much it will charge. Is it £1 for everything or different prices for different products?

Place

4–17 Every store has to decide where it will be located. Should it be based on the high street, at a retail park, in a city or in small town?

Promotion

4–18 How does it tell customers what it sells? Does it need a logo? Does it need advertising? If so, what should it say or show?

4–19 These four categories (product, price, place and promotion) are known as "the four P's" and, when they're combined, form the ingredients of a marketing mix. The marketing mix is the combined effect on a customer of all the decisions a business makes about product, price, place and promotion. Let's look at an example of this in action by examining one of the world's largest companies, Apple.

How does the marketing mix work?

4–20 Steve Jobs, Steve Wozniak and Ronald Wayne founded Apple on 1 April 1976, to develop and sell personal computers. It's the 12th largest company in the world (according to Forbes' "World Biggest Public Companies" list 2015)[3] and everyone knows its products: the iPod, iPhone, iPad, iMac and iWatch.

Over a million people visit an Apple Store every day. It holds the credit card details of more than half a billion people, which is more than any other company. It brings in more money than Hewlett-Packard, Google, Intel and Cisco combined. It has twice the cash of the US. It managed to achieve all that by starting from nothing; just three men in a garage who followed three goals.

[3] Available at *http://www.forbes.com/global2000/list* [Accessed 19 April 2016].

- It would understand its customers. It would know you as well as you know yourself.
- It would keep things simple. It would get rid of junk so that everything it did was needed.
- It wouldn't listen to the phrase "never judge a book by its cover". It would *always* judge a book by its cover. If something looks good, people think it is good.

It still follows these three rules today.

Product

Unlike other tech companies, Apple only sells a limited number of products. Compare that with Sony, which produces and sells a Sony version of almost all forms of electronic equipment, from bedside clocks to televisions, car radios, games consoles, cameras and Blu-ray players. Apple has fulfilled its second goal not just by producing products that are easy to use, but also only producing a small range. Its products are simple to use. They don't even come with instructions—Apple believes that its products should be that easy to use. **4–21**

Price

Apple is an expensive product. It charges among the highest prices for a mobile phone or tablet. In return, it promises simplicity and quality. Its high price is one way to reinforce that quality: "my iPad must be better than a Windows Tablet—look at how much more expensive it is." **4–22**

Place

Apple shops are simple, clean, and modern and designed to look better than any other shop on the high street. The stores are located on the most expensive streets: Buchanan Street (Glasgow) and Covent Garden (London). This reaffirms the idea that Apple products are better than those of competitors. Even staff are trained to live Apple's philosophy. If you want to become an Apple Genius you have to follow a book that tells you how to look, what to say (it warns you to avoid big words) and—even—how to stand. The Apple Genius employee guide tells staff that "touching" and "moving in closer" indicates acceptance and should be used to help clinch a sale. **4–23**

Promotion

Apple spends millions of pounds creating classic ads to let you know what they sell and what makes them different. An advert like the white headphones and black dancing silhouettes is used to advertise iPods. It tells you everything you need to know about the iPod. It's music in your hand. And it's got white headphones. And it does that by living up to the three values Apple set itself in 1979. It's simple, it looks good, and it gives customers what they want—all of their music in a small white box. **4–24**

When taken together, the four ingredients of product, price, promotion and place all tell the same story. If you buy an Apple product you may pay a lot for it but you'll receive a phone, tablet or watch that is better, more stylish and easier to use than any other.

How does this use of marketing mix compare for a law firm?

4–25 Let's look again at Ledingham Chalmers. We can see that choice of location is just one element of Ledingham Chalmers decision to open in Stirling. Other factors that might have been relevant include:

Price

4–26 An office in Stirling is more expensive than one located out of town. By choosing an office in a cheaper location, Ledingham Chalmers could charge clients less than its rivals.

Promotion

4–27 With an office in the Auction Mart, Ledingham Chalmers would have signs that visitors would see every time they visit. When eventually they need a lawyer, which name will they first think of? An office in the Auction Mart may avoid the need for Ledingham Chalmers to advertise.

What is the most important factor about the marketing mix?

4–28 Since companies' products define them, they must do their best to back up their claims. For example, if Apple were to state that an iPod could hold your entire music library, but in fact it could only store one album, it would need to repackage the product.

Secondly, the price of a product must reflect the budget of a company's intended customers. A company must not charge inflated prices for low-end ingredients contained within a product. If the iPhone screen were made of cheap plastic and easily scratched, and not toughened gorilla glass, Apple would find it hard to justify sky-high prices.

Thirdly, a company's marketing mix must include accurate product placement to ensure that its product reaches its target customers. This includes advertising in the right publications and placing the product in stores that a company's target audience shops in. That's why you don't find Gucci in Matalan. Gucci only want its products sold in its own stores, high-end fashion shops and the best department stores (like Harvey Nichols and Selfridges).

Finally, a company's marketing mix includes product packaging, public relations and branding, as well as the sponsorship of well-respected people who attest to the product's claims and benefits. Though this can go wrong, as Apple found out when it gave away a free U2 album and tens of thousands complained about receiving an album they didn't want on their iPhone. In short, the marketing mix must be consistent. This is where law firms struggle. They don't sell a product; they sell a service (their knowledge, personality and experience).

Law firms and the marketing mix

4–29 You may have spotted that the four P's start with "product", and you might ask how this applies to law firms, which sell services. A product is something you can touch and feel, sell and buy. A law firm doesn't sell products. We don't make anything. We don't work in factories. We don't produce anything that clients might pick up and touch. Law is a service and services are intangible. As we've seen, services are more about how a client feels than what they can see. A GP doesn't produce pills, they provide reassurance and advice. A travel agent doesn't make two weeks in Magaluf, they provide advice on when to go and where to stay. A service happens in the "here and now". It can't be repeated and it can't be replicated.

Further, a service depends entirely on the person providing it. If we asked you for advice, what you say and how you say it will be completely different from any other person we ask. If law is not a product, then how do we apply the four P's? A service is judged by three other factors: physical evidence, process and people. The four P's become seven, when dealing with services. It is the seven P's that define what law firms can offer to clients.

What are the seven P's?

A product is simple. You can pick it up and you can touch it. A service is more complicated. We need to look at more than just product, price, place and promotion, when we consider a service. We also need to examine how the service is performed (the process), we need to check if it's intangible or whether it leaves a physical trace (the physical evidence). Let's examine David Erskine, again, and reflect on the seven P's. Imagine you're sitting in his consulting room, watching as he puts pen to paper. Remember, Erskine has decided to open an office in Edinburgh, aimed at rich lords and merchants. How does the marketing mix help him? **4–30**

Product

Erskine is not making a product. He is offering a service. We can't look at a box, or tin or plastic cover to judge his service. We need to look at the physical evidence, process and people involved. As we'll see in Ch.5 (how do you build your reputation?) some firms are starting to offer products but, for the moment, we'll keep it simple by assuming all firms only provide a service. **4–31**

Physical evidence

The second P is physical evidence. Just like a snail, services leave a trace behind them. As lawyers, you speak to clients to give them advice. You meet them in boardrooms. You call them on the phone. But that's not all that you do. You also produce letters, emails, contracts, advice notes, text messages and hand written notes. All of these extra documents are the physical evidence that a service has been performed and they can be just as important as the service itself. **4–32**

Let's imagine Erskine meets a client for the first time. He's charming and smart, and within 10 minutes he's worked out what they need. The next day he writes a letter to them confirming what he said. This time, his letter is long, dull and filled with obscure legal jargon. It even has a passage in Latin. Now, instead of being charming and smart, the client has no idea what he's been sent or what it might mean. Erskine is no longer the right lawyer for him.

Today, with the increased use of email to provide advice it's even more important that your writing is easy to read. You're judged more and more on how you write. Equally, as well as getting the content right, the physical evidence you leave behind should look good. Remember Apple? Appearances do matter. Even simple things like the font in your letters say a lot about your firm.

- Is Times New Roman too boring?
- Is Comic Sans too childish?
- Is Arial Black too aggressive?

Everything your client sees and hears from your firm should be brilliant. Everything your client should see or touch should reinforce the reasons they have chosen you.

Process

4–33 As a lawyer you follow set processes. Sometimes these are formal. Your firm may have case management software that breaks down a transaction step by step, or it may follow checklists. Even if your firm doesn't, you'll soon find that you tend to do the same thing each time you deal with a similar transaction. If you're buying a house, for example, you'll ask the seller for titles, you'll prepare an offer, have follow up questions on the title, prepare a report for your client, conclude a missive and prepare a disposition for settlement, before dealing with cash and keys. It's the same process from A to B, each time.

Much of this process is hidden from a client's view. Your client won't see you pick up a title, read it, make notes on it, and report back on what it says. The decisions a firm makes about how it approaches these types of process can affect clients. A good example of how processes can affect a customer's view of a business is telephone banking. If you want to pay a bill from your account, banks have decided that—rather than phoning a branch direct—you need to phone a helpline. Banks also have decided that a real person doesn't need to deal with your request, and you can do it automatically via the helpline. On the one hand, banks argue that they have streamlined a process. On the other hand, how does that process make you feel? Do you like not having to queue? Or, do you hate having to constantly read out your account details to a computer?

Think about law firms. How do they deal with calls? Traditionally, if you called a law firm you either would speak to a receptionist or a secretary, before they put you through to a lawyer. Today, many firms list their lawyer's direct dial number on their websites. You can phone them directly. Law firms assume that clients value being able to speak to lawyers, as easily and quickly as possible.

Dundas & Wilson has also used process as part of its promotion strategy. In 2012, it set up a paralegal team to cover high volume, routine work. It promoted that team in the press, with articles carried on BBC Scotland and other news sites. As a firm it was saying that its process would save clients' money (they would be paying for paralegals, not lawyers). For cost conscious clients, that's a great message to hear.

Place

4–34 This is your firm's "shop", the place you and your customers meet. For most of us this will be an office. Your office is your firm's chance to impress your clients. We've looked at location, already, but your office is more than just a location. It's also where you meet your clients, and they form a view of your firm based on what they see.

Brodies, one of Scotland's biggest firms, opened a new office in Glasgow in 2015. It is located on the top two floors of a brand new building in Queen St. It's surrounded by shops including Ralph Lauren, Mulberry and Hugo Boss. Other tenants include Grant Thornton and Deloitte. It is one of the most impressive offices in Glasgow. As a client, if you walk into the reception area you might think: "this firm must be the best, to afford an office like this." Brodies have looked at location. Many of their clients are large corporates, so they need this office in Glasgow. They're in the city centre, where most of the biggest businesses are, so this office is the right one for them.

However, what if you're accused of a crime? Would you be impressed with this office or would you be too intimidated to go in? Or, if you were a small business that worries about costs, would you use a firm with an office like this? Decisions go back to what your clients want. The choice made should reflect the assumptions firms have made about their clients. We can see this clearly on the high street. Here you'll find that lawyers have offices on the busiest shopping streets. On the high street, law firms tend to be part of the community and so they want to be somewhere that you can pop into easily when you go into town. Many also have estate agents, so they'll have their property boards out so that people can see the homes (a product) for sale.

However, "place" isn't just about offices. It's wherever you meet clients. Macleod & McCallum, a firm based in Inverness, also runs road shows throughout the Highlands, using local halls and hotels to meet clients. By using local locations, we believe it's sending a message to clients that they don't need to come to Inverness to see a lawyer; the lawyers will come to them. Finally, "place" also covers a firm's virtual reception. Your website and social media can all be used to host your online office.

Promotion

Promotion covers everything you might say or do to raise awareness of who you are and what you do. This includes sponsorship (like Harper Macleod sponsoring the 2014 Commonwealth Games in Glasgow), advertising in newspapers, PR and writing for the press, appearing on TV, winning awards, or attending events and meeting clients for coffee. It even covers adverts on the side of a double decker bus, like an advert CMS Cameron McKenna took in London to promote itself and a charity it supported. **4–35**

Price

We're not going to say a lot about price at this stage as we cover that in Ch.13 (how to set fees). What we'll say is that one of the main debates about pricing for law firms is between charging a fixed price and hourly rates. Some clients hate hourly rates because they don't know what they'll end up having to pay. On the other hand, some clients hate fixed fees because the work may change, the fee may no longer apply, and the fee needs to be renegotiated to cover what the firm actually did. **4–36**

If you're listening to your clients—and you are because of segmentation—most of them will tell you they want a fixed fee. If you're creating a law firm, what kind of price should you offer? Ultimately it comes back to your client. Some clients are happy to pay more; some only want to pay the cheapest price. People don't change just because they're "shopping" in a law firm, and not for tomatoes in Tesco.

People

For law firm's this is the biggest factor. We've said a law firm is nothing without its clients. It's also nothing without people. If a client walks into a boardroom and there is no one to speak to them, nothing else matters. An office cannot provide advice. A letter doesn't write itself. Law firm's need people. They need you. We'll look at what you can do in the next chapter. **4–37**

Marketing mix summary

There are no right or wrong answers when considering the marketing mix. Each ingredient must be considered in light of the assumptions you've made about your **4–38** clients. Equally, no one ingredient can influence a client, on its own. You may be the greatest lawyer in the world but if your website is on Myspace, no one will phone you. All of the ingredients of the marketing mix need to work together. Imagine a firm with an advert in the Cumbernauld News saying it's your local firm, but which only has an office in Abu Dhabi. That wouldn't make sense. It's the combination of all the factors—its brand—that make a firm's reputation, and yours.

Your firm's reputation

4–39 You've seen how segmentation works and how different firms have approached the marketing mix—now try two exercises. Firstly, pick a law firm (your own or another) and try and carry out your own segmentation of its clients. Once you've thought of who they're and what they may want, imagine you're opening a new law firm. What would you offer those clients? Would you have an office? If so, where would it be? What kind of work would you cover? How would you deal with your clients? Would you have a secretary? Direct dial numbers? Would you make every lawyer be on Twitter? What kind of advertising would you have, if any?

Once you've thought of a few examples and you have an image of this new firm in your mind, carry out a second exercise and compare those with the real firm you've picked. Does your new firm match your firm? We bet it doesn't.

What you'll find is that most firms don't currently offer what their clients want. Firms with offices on the high street are finding their clients shop in huge supermarkets, on the edge of town. The high streets are dying and passing trade is falling away. Large corporates have expensive offices but clients want to pay lower fees, because of the recession. You'll find numerous examples where expectation and reality doesn't match and that's because most firms need time and money to change.

Segmentation and marketing mix is fine in theory, but in practice it can be a long, hard process to change around a firm to match what clients want. Tods Murray opened an expensive office in Edinburgh, with views of the castle. It wanted to emphasise it was a major corporate firm. Unfortunately, it paid a rent it couldn't afford and, as it was tied into the lease, it couldn't change. Its options were limited. It badly wanted to be a corporate firm, but when the corporate work dried up, it was fatally exposed.

Let's look at Dickson Minto. At the start of this chapter we said that it has a reputation for corporate finance work, built over a long period. We can see how they did this and how they maintain that reputation, by analysing the seven P's.

Place

4–40 They opened an office in Charlotte Square in Edinburgh, the traditional heart of Edinburgh's financial district (and now the home of the First Minister). It is one of the most prestigious addresses in Scotland. Opening an office here told prospective clients that this firm was aiming to be the best.

Promotion

4–41 Dickson Minto doesn't talk to the press. It doesn't advertise. This is typical of corporate finance clients (like private equity houses, which don't court publicity). By not promoting itself, Dickson Minto highlighted its discretion and confidentiality. These are attributes its clients value.

People

Alistair Dickson and Bruce Minto founded the firm. Both were corporate partners in Dundas & Wilson. They already were considered to be among the best corporate lawyers in Scotland. The firm didn't start with a blank canvas. It started with their names and reputation. Most firms start this way and most take the names of their founding partners. Examples include: (William) Slaughter & (William) May, (George) Allen & (Thomas) Overy, (James) Dundas & (William) Wilson and (Alistair) Dickson (Bruce) Minto. **4–42**

It's this final "P" that becomes the most important element of how firms gain (and maintain) a reputation. As we said, you don't start with a reputation. You rely on your firm's reputation while you build your own. But this transfer is not just in one direction. Your firm needs your reputation, just as much as you need its reputation.

In the next chapter we look at the actions you can take as a trainee (or lawyer) to help your firm and your clients. As US author Maya Angelou said:

> "I've learned that people will forget what you said, people will forget what you did, but people will never forget how you made them feel."

Summary

All law firms work with the same ingredients and largely follow the same recipe. A firm that deals in personal injury needs to know the same laws as any other, and the same processes for dealing with clients' injuries. Despite these similarities, firms nonetheless appear vastly different. At one end of the scale you have a firm like Slater & Gordon that has offices around the world and advertises on TV for new clients.[4] On the other, you have your local high street firm that deals with claims as and when they come through the door. **4–43**

Knowing how those firms differ is an essential part of commercial awareness, as it shows how the legal market has developed based on how law firms react to clients (segmentation) and how it will develop to respond to client demands (marketing mix). Knowing segmentation and marketing mix is a critical element of the first definition of commercial awareness, namely knowing the legal market.

---

[4] As we finish writing the book, Slater & Gordon are reported to face financial problems and have taken action to close offices and reduce the number of people it employs.

CHAPTER 5

HOW DO YOU BUILD YOUR REPUTATION?

Introduction

5–1 *It's Friday. Day five. It's the end of your first week and you need to find your partner to sign a letter that has to be posted that very night. It's only 14.00 but, when you speak to his secretary, she says, "he's on a course . . . a golf course that is. He'll be back on Monday. He always plays golf on a Friday with clients." And you think: "what an easy job. He's playing golf while I'm stuck in here doing his work. How do I get to do his job?"*

5–2 One of the biggest misconceptions that students and new lawyers have about their career is that the best lawyers must have the best legal knowledge. Many do. They wouldn't be partners if they didn't. But many don't. They have other skills that help bring in clients. They know how to sell themselves and their firms and, without clients, law firms have no business. Winning clients is the most important thing a partner does. They can't impress anyone with their legal knowledge until someone walks through their door and instructs them. That's why if you're serious about your career, an ability to bring in work is essential. It's a skill that will become more and more important as the legal market becomes more competitive.

In this chapter we look at a number of ways in which you can build your reputation, to help you win business. We look at the traditional skills required to network, and wine and dine contacts. We look at the impact of PR and the press to help you become known to peers and to the public. We look at social media, and how it has created a platform for lawyers to connect to other people. It's business development and marketing skills that set smart trainees and junior lawyers apart. If you embrace this early, you can develop the skills that suit you best and start building the confidence you'll need for the remainder of your career.

Outcomes

5–3 This chapter should be read alongside Ch.4 (what do law firms sell?). As you build a reputation you're also representing your firm. If your firm is a traditional law firm that still sends letters instead of emails, it's harder for you to gain a reputation as being the cutting edge of social media. Equally, if you write an article for the *Daily Star* when you act for FTSE 100 companies that are more likely to read the *Financial Times*, your firm might not be happy. You need to align your work with your firm's reputation.

In this chapter, we examine the steps you can take to create and build a reputation. We don't intend that you do all of the actions we suggest. Some people are great at networking; some hate it (even when they know what to do). Instead, they might love writing articles. This chapter is about opening the possibilities that you have so you can select the best way for you (and your firm) to build your (and its) reputation.

Your reputation

Day one

As we've said before, on day one, your reputation won't extend further than your desk. Colleagues may have an idea of what you're like from your CV and interview, but it's up to you to show them what you're capable of. This means that in your first few months people judge you. **5–4**

Back in 2000, Andrew was a trainee for McGrigor Donald (which became McGrigors and then Pinsent Masons). He started in its corporate department. It was fantastic experience. The first thing he was asked to do was to buy a football club. His first task was to research the current shareholders, for his head of department. He thought he'd done a good job and that was confirmed when one of the other partners showed him an email he'd just be sent from the head of corporate to all the other partners in the department. He wrote: "Use Andy Todd. He's really good." The next day another partner asked Andrew if he could help with a share purchase agreement to buy a chain of shops. He said that even though Andrew was "just in the door" he could have a stab at drafting it. Andrew spent a week on that document, labouring day and night. It was going to be the best share purchase agreement the world had ever seen. It would be so good that not only would the partner email the rest of the team, he'd be high fiving strangers on the bus.

Andrew was so proud when he handed it over. However, the partner took one look at it before giving it back, saying, "you do know it's the seller and not the purchaser we act for? You'll need to change everything." How quickly reputations change (and that was even before Andrew had met a client).

Changing reputation—you

At university you're judged on your knowledge of the law. You write essays and answer exam questions that test your ability to understand and interpret the law. It's an intellectual exercise, not an emotional one. Clients want something different, however. They want results, not reasons. **5–5**

Think of a meal. Does the chef show you how he cooks your lamb chops, cuts your carrots, fries your chips and scoops your ice cream? No. You judge your chef on the plate that you eat. Just as they don't show you how the ingredients are transformed into a meal, so you're not expected to show every case, statute and textbook. A family that buys a house wants to know when it will get the keys. A man accused of a crime wants to know if he's going to jail. A banker wants to know if the money she lends to a small business will be paid back. They don't want missives, court rules, or the finer details of the Companies Act. Clients don't want to see inside your kitchen—they just want fed.

Before they even meet you, as we have seen in Ch.4 (what do law firms sell?), your client has started to form a view (rightly or wrongly) about you and your firm. Even a client who phones you for the first time has likely read an advert or checked out your firm's website. Again, before even a word is spoken, your client has formed a view. Perhaps the biggest influence on them is that you're a lawyer: lawyers are trusted; lawyers are honest; lawyers keep secrets and put their clients' interests ahead of their own, because they follow professional standards.

All of these things—your professional reputation and the reputation of your firm—can be enhanced by your reputation. Once a client speaks to you they're no longer judging you on how they expect a lawyer to behave, or what an advert about your firm may have led them to expect. They're judging you on your actions, words, advice and personality. It is up to you to protect and build your reputation, because it's the one thing you carry throughout your entire career.

Changing reputation—your career

5–6 There are different stages to building your reputation. As a trainee, your reputation is more about your technical knowledge and the people you work with. As a newly qualified lawyer, however, you should start to look at extending a reputation outside the firm to existing contacts and clients. As you become more senior you're expected to build a reputation among your local community or the business markets you work in. Think of your reputation as a stone falling in a river. At first the ripples are gradual and small but as time passes they gradually extend further and wider until one small action stretches from bank to bank. A small stone can create a big splash if you build your reputation through networking, PR, promotion and social media.

Networking—new contacts

5–7 Andrew once acted for the chief executive of a large property company. He was three years qualified and was buying a large office block. The transaction was a nightmare. Andrew would speak to the chief executive every hour, for days on end. He thought he was building a good relationship with him. However, when the deal was done and Andrew phoned him and asked if he would like to meet for a coffee, the chief executive said: "No, why would I want to do that? You're just a lawyer."

Rejection is brutal. It doesn't matter if you're 16 and asking someone to the school prom, or 26 and asking a contact for a meeting. It's difficult not to take it personally. Yet, as trainees and new lawyers you're often asked to go to business events and, afterwards, asked if you're going to meet anyone that you met there. It can seem intimidating. If you go to a drinks reception or a local networking group, it can seem that everyone is much older than you and that they all know each other already. It's easy to hide and to only speak to people you know (usually some colleagues who have come with you). It's easy also to latch onto that lovely first person who gives you the time of day and never let him/her out of your sight because otherwise you'd have to say "hello" to someone else. We've all been there.

That's the thing. We have all been there because most people feel exactly the same way as you. When you go to an event most people don't actually know each other. They're in the same position as you. If they're talking to someone, it's usually a colleague from their office. They would welcome someone else to speak to—they've already covered all the office gossip. Just approach them. However, saying that is a lot easier than doing it. That's why we've set out some tips on how you can make networking easier.

What is networking?

5–8 We don't like the term "networking". It suggests something formal and fixed, like telecom masts and underground cables. We prefer to think of it as something softer. Networking is simply meeting people, having a conversation and, if appropriate, keeping in touch afterwards. When people say they can't network, they're saying they can't talk, which is daft.

Meeting people takes many forms. It can be a cup of coffee, a drink after work, a round of golf, a formal lunch with a local chamber of commerce, even a lavish awards ceremony with everyone in black tie. However, at its heart, it's any place or time that you have a conversation with someone else.

Networking benefits

Law firms need clients. We can't repeat this enough. Clients want lawyers who know them and can help them. As we saw in Ch.2 (who are your clients?), this means lawyers who have the personality to relate to (and understand) clients. Meeting people is your chance to practice those skills with lots of different people, with lots of different personalities. You won't connect with everyone, no more than you're friends with everyone in your university class or law firm. However, the more you do it the easier it becomes, as you share knowledge, identify opportunities, build connections and grow your confidence and reputation. **5–9**

Share knowledge

Meeting new people is great for sharing ideas and knowledge. Ask questions of the people you meet. They'll be delighted to talk about themselves and their businesses. What are they currently working on? What are the current challenges? What are their recent successes? People like talking about themselves so, if you ask the right questions, you find out lots of information about them and you might see things from another perspective. **5–10**

Let's assume you work for a high street firm. You go to a local business chambers lunch. If you talk to business owners you can find out which of them are busy, what they do, whether they have any problems they need help with, and whether your firm might be able to support them.

Opportunities

It's natural that meeting people eventually will result in opportunities. The thing you won't know is when or how they'll materialise. It's rare that someone will say, "I need a lawyer" or will look to instruct you straight away. However, if you spot an opportunity, that's the time to say, "would you like to meet to discuss this?" or to make a mental note to follow up with them afterwards. **5–11**

Connections

There is a lot of truth in the saying "if you scratch my back, I'll scratch yours". As a lawyer you meet lots of people with lots of different skills and knowledge. If someone you meet has a problem that you think one of your contacts can help resolve, suggest putting them in touch. If you do someone a favour, generally they feel obliged to return it in the future. When they meet someone who may need a lawyer it will be you they recommend. **5–12**

Increased confidence

Meeting people, and pushing yourself to engage with them, actually helps to increase your confidence. This is important, because your firm depends on you to make connections. The sooner you learn, the easier it will be to use these skills (especially as you become more senior). **5–13**

Raising your profile

Being visible and getting noticed is a tangible by-product of meeting people. By attending business and social events, people begin to recognise you. This can help you to build your reputation as a knowledgeable, reliable and supportive person by offering useful information or tips to people who need it. You're also more **5–14** likely to get more clients, as you'll be the one that pops into their heads when they need what you offer.

Networking tips

Select the right events

5–15 You don't need to be out every night meeting people. In fact, you don't have to be out at all if your strengths lie with PR and social media. But, if you do need to "wine and dine" then make sure you pick the right events for you, whether this is a cup of coffee or hosting a table at an event.

Attend events with a clear goal. That may be to find an opportunity to win some business, it may be to publicise you or your firm, or it may be to ingather information from attendees. It's important that you know why you're going to an event. If you don't know, why go? Networking isn't compulsory. You have many other things you could be doing. Always have a plan and know why you're going to a particular event. For example, if you work in corporate insolvency you may want to join the R3 group. This is a networking group dedicated to people who work in insolvency, such as administrators, accountants, bankers and lawyers. Alternatively, if you work in renewables, you may want to attend the Scottish Renewable Awards, because many of the big players in that industry attend. Going to random events is not smart. You might as well walk into any pub or restaurant and hope for the best. You want to go to events that you know will help you and make the best use of your time.

A good place to start with identifying the right events is to ask your supervisor or partner (since they might be going, too). Once you have identified an event you should prepare for it, just like you would any client meeting.

Event preparation

5–16 The first thing to think about is whether you should discuss "the law". We say no—at least, not unless you're asked. Conversations are more effective if you look to build a relationship with the people you meet. A casual drink at an evening reception is not the place to discuss the Companies Act, land reform or changes to sheriff court fees. Mechanics wouldn't talk about carburettors when they meet (at least we hope not). Lawyers don't need to talk about statutes. Remember, potential clients (for that's what the people you meet are) won't be interested in the nuts and bolts of what you do.

Instead, look to build a relationship by using small talk and asking general questions about them. Show that you're interested in their work. Remember that you're building a professional relationship, and not looking for a friend or partner. Some business relationships may evolve into that, but this is not speed dating for business people. In other words, approach it like you would any business task.

Make a list

5–17 Before you go to any event, try and see if there's a list of guests. Check the list and try to identify the people you might want to speak to. These could be people who you already know, and who would expect you to introduce yourself. They may be clients of the firm who would expect you (as the firm's representative) to say "hello". It may be people who you don't know but would like to know. If you act for a lot of small businesses, then you may wish to speak to the directors of other businesses. If you deal with employment matters, you may want to speak to people in HR. In other words, be sensible. When compiling your initial list, try not to underestimate anyone's potential to be a knowledgeable resource. Don't be discouraged if you have only a few people on your list at first; each contact will direct you to more people and your numbers will soon multiply.

Conversation topics

You should always attend every event fully prepared, so that you don't waste anyone's time by asking him/her to explain basic details you could learn easily on your own. You wouldn't approach a doctor and ask him what he does, would you? You might ask instead if he specialises in a particular type of medicine or whether he is a GP, surgeon or anaesthetist. Equally, you would think someone silly if they asked you what a lawyer is. This doesn't mean you need to stalk people over the internet. You don't want to casually mention that you enjoyed the photos of their holiday in Magaluf in July 2007. A simple Google search, or a search of LinkedIn, usually is enough to get started. It's worth checking with colleagues if they know anyone on your list. The chances are that some of the people who plan to be there will have been at events before, with your senior colleagues. You may also wish to check the news and sport, for topics. But only do this if you're comfortable talking about a particular subject. You don't need to know the latest scores on *Match of the Day* to have a conversation. Sometimes saying "I don't know much about football" (or indeed any other sport or topic) is a good way to change the subject into something that you're comfortable with. Most people are polite and will help change the subject too. **5–18**

At the start

You may want to start by talking to people who you're comfortable with, such as colleagues or even contacts that you already know. This is fine. Everyone needs to warm up and relax. But don't stick with the same people all night. No one will take offence if you say, "it's been nice to talk to you and it's time to start mingling again." You can be subtle and say, "I need to go the toilet, it's been nice to talk to you." When you come back you start a conversation with someone else. This isn't a party. People expect everyone to move on and speak to others. **5–19**

Introduce yourself

When you meet someone new, introduce yourself by making eye contact, smiling, stating your first and last name, and giving a firm but brief handshake. Listen for the other person's name (believe us, it's easy to miss when you're nervous). Try and use it two times while you're speaking. This helps you to remember it. If you're not sure of their name, it's better to ask them to repeat it than to use it wrongly. No one minds repeating his or her name. In fact, they probably want you to repeat your name too as they won't have remembered it either. **5–20**

Listen first

Let the other person speak, especially if you have approached them. No one wants to be approached by someone who only talks about him or herself. Ask questions, listen carefully to the answers, and ask more intelligent questions about what you have just been told. Even if you're just asking about the weather it's flattering to be asked a question that seeks an opinion. Flatter the people you meet. Of course, there does come a point when too many questions will make you less a flatterer and more the Spanish Inquisition. Let the conversation develop naturally, and if it comes to an end then finish it politely and move on. **5–21**

Follow up

5–22 The end of the event is not the end. It's the start. You should have met a number of people. You should have learnt something about them or their business. If you think it's appropriate you can drop them an email or give them a call after the event with anything that you think they may find helpful. If they've mentioned they've a problem with their landlord, you might have a useful note that they can read that explains the legal issues. If they mentioned that they're having problems with their tax return, you might recommend an accountant. If there is nothing immediate and the contact is someone that you just want to keep in touch with, just look for other events that they may attend and make a note of some of the things they said so that next time you can show you remember them. The worst thing you can do is to do nothing. If you're doing nothing, then someone else (a rival) is contacting them instead.

Have realistic expectations

5–23 It's unlikely that someone will instruct you or your firm the first time they meet you. Relationships take time to build. It may be the third, fifth or even 10th time you meet someone before they think of something you can do to help. It may be never. But the more people you meet, the more you show a sincere interest in them, the more chance you give yourself to turn contacts into clients.

Be yourself

5–24 There's no ideal personality for networking. Being loud and gregarious may get you noticed but equally it drives many people away, who prefer quiet conversation. Some people want to talk to someone witty, some might want a serious conversation, others may look for thoughtfulness. That's why it's easier to be yourself and not think that you need to be a particular type of personality. You find people who will want to talk to you because of who you naturally are and not who you pretend to be.

Networking—existing clients

5–25 The same tips apply for existing clients. The advantage of dealing with existing clients is that a lot of the hard work is already done. Your partner and colleagues should know a lot more about them and be able to recommend how to deal with them. For example, some clients hate black tie events, so don't invite them to a formal dinner. Others like an early morning coffee, before being caught by meetings and emails. Many public sector contacts, meanwhile, will have strict guidelines based on the Bribery Act 2010 about what they can accept as hospitality. They may need to pay, also, which may make them think twice about accepting your invitation to Andrew Fairlie at Gleneagles.

As a trainee and new lawyer, the best way to meet existing clients is to piggyback a senior lawyer as they meet their contacts. You can learn from them how they network, and you can build your confidence knowing they're right beside you.

PR—advertising and promotion

5–26 Advertising is an effective way of telling people about your firm. We include it within this chapter because, if you're involved in advertising, you should know that there are Law Society rules that you must follow. The three main elements of those rules are that:

- you shouldn't try and steal another solicitor's client;
- any advert or promotion must not be inaccurate, defamatory, illegal or likely to bring the profession into dispute; and
- it should not mention any client without permission.[1]

This means that you can't tout business from someone who you know is represented by another solicitor. This can be tricky. Most companies have a solicitor that they use. Does this mean you can't have any adverts in case someone reads them, who already has an existing solicitor? No; there is an exception for general advertising. What this rule is getting at is targeting directly another lawyer's client.

The rules also mean that solicitors need to be mindful of not bringing the profession into disrepute. This has led to adverts for a law firm on beer mats, distributed to local pubs, being banned. A late night advert featuring lawyers in motorbike leathers and riding Harley-Davidson bikes has been banned, also. However, the Law Society relaxed its approach in one recent advert that featured a man, a fan and a bucket of excrement (with a tag line based on a well-known phrase). However, most firms still are conservative with their advertising and simply market their name, the areas of law that they deal with and how to contact them.

PR—media, updates and websites

A good way to keep in touch with clients and contacts is to send them updates on **5–27** the law that affect them. You can do this by writing articles for your website, a legal update or by writing for the local, national or business press. Identify where you want to be published. If it's your website, then you have full control over what you say and how you say it. If it's a third party website or the local, national or business press then you normally prepare a pitch before writing a full article. The pitch will be a short summary of your idea and why it's relevant to readers. For example, if you were writing an article for *Personnel Today*, a specialist employment magazine read by HR professionals, you would need to explain why your idea would interest an HR manager. It would not be enough to say that, for example, pensions law would be changing as a result of auto-enrolment, you would need to explain that auto-enrolment affects all businesses and that HR managers need to ensure their systems are updated to cover all their employees.

This is an example of a pitch Andrew wrote for an article in the February 2016 edition of *The Journal of the Law Society of Scotland*:

> "The Lands Tribunal of Scotland published a decision today on a long running dispute about factoring common areas in Scotland. It examines how companies like the Greenbelt Company charge residents for maintaining open spaces like play areas, community parks and grass strips beside roadways. The case looks at whether such arrangements are legal, whether they can be changed and whether residents can challenge their factor and change them. It would be of interest to all residential conveyancers dealing with

---

[1] The Law Society of Scotland Practice Rules 2011 r.B3: Advertising and Promotion. Available at *http://www.lawscot.org.uk/rules-and-guidance/section-b/rule-b3-advertising-and-promotion/rules/b3-advertising-and-promotion/* [Accessed 19 April 2016].

homes in housing developments and lawyers acting for housebuilders. I'd be happy to write an article on it if it would be of interest to The Journal."[2]

If you're targeting local or national press, you have to show why your idea is topical. The press is interested in current news, so your ideas need to reflect the latest developments. If, for example, the Court of Session issued an important judgment, you would need to contact a paper the same day with your idea so that it can appear in the next day's edition.

Finally, if you're ambitious, you may want to write an academic textbook about a particular area of law. This is a serious statement that you're an expert in that area. It's a major undertaking, though, and maybe not one for your traineeship given the amount of work involved. You may want to wait until you have gained more practical experience as a lawyer.

PR—speaking

5–28 Many people don't like public speaking but it's an effective way of gaining a reputation. If you stand up and speak then people assume you must be confident and that you know what you're talking about. They look up to you and, if they're interested in the topic, may seek you out for your opinion. There are a number of ways to find speaking opportunities. One is to organise your own seminar and invite clients and contacts to it. This could be on a hot topic, or a subject that you think they would benefit from hearing about. For example, the Consumer Act 2015 came into force on 1 October 2015. It affects most businesses that sell to the public. You might want to organise a seminar that tells people what the main changes are and how it affects them.

Alternatively, you might want to showcase your reputation for an area of law by taking part in seminars to the legal profession. Companies like CLT Scotland and the events team at the Law Society are always looking for ideas for events. While you may not be talking directly to potential clients, speaking at such events is a powerful way to win over potential clients when you mention it to them. If you're teaching fellow lawyers about an area of law, then you must be a leading expert in that area.

The important thing is that you know what your audience comprises. Your talk about the Consumer Act 2015 will be completely different if given to business owners than it would be if given to fellow lawyers. You can be more technical with lawyers. You need to limit yourself to potential impacts, when dealing with non-lawyers.

Social media

5–29 We love social media, but it's a difficult subject for many law firms given the risks that go with it. What if someone writes something objectionable? It's easy to do on a platform like Twitter given the 140 character limit that largely inhibits subtlety. Law is nuanced, Twitter is not. Equally, Instagram allows you to publish photos instantly, but it's difficult to take a photo in a law firm. Confidentiality rules mean that you must be careful not to reveal any information which could be

---

[2] A. Todd, "The end of deeds of conditions?" The Journal of the Law Society of Scotland (18 January 2016) Available at: *http://www.journalonline.co.uk/Magazine/61-1/1021197.aspx* [Accessed: 10 June 2016].

linked to a client. Even a computer screen in the background of your image could reveal information, were someone to zoom in. Think of the politicians caught out by long-range lenses, carrying papers into Downing Street. Facebook tends to be more personal. What you post is intended for friends and families, and the way you behave towards them is different to how you behave with a client.

Even LinkedIn, a platform for business contacts, can be misused, as the Charlotte Proudman incident demonstrated. Ms Proudman is a barrister. In September 2015 she received a message from a partner in a law firm praising her "striking image". She believed the message to be sexist and "called the partner out" by publishing the message on Twitter. In response to incidents like these, the Law Society has published guidance on how solicitors should use social media, responsibly.[3] We have printed excerpts below—we can't phrase it better ourselves:

> "Participating in social media can present significant personal and business benefits, and members of the legal profession should seek to engage with social media in a positive way.
>
> Two key pieces of advice can be given:
>
> 1. To remember that all professional responsibilities apply regardless of the medium of communication.
> 2. For law firms and in-house legal teams to have a social media policy in place for partners and staff."

And:

> "The use of social media is subject to the same ethical and professional standards as all other conduct of a member of the legal profession. Individual solicitors must ensure they abide by the professional practice rules and maintain professional relationships with clients and other members of the profession."

It also highlights issues around connecting with people online:

> "One of the key characteristics of most social media sites is the ability to link to other users, for example by becoming a 'friend' or 'follower'. The links between different users are often publicly visible. The impact of suggesting a relationship or interest though creating links through social media should be carefully considered. Issues such as conflict of interest may arise, with the possibility that a perception of conflict may be created even if the individual does not consider a conflict to exist. This may happen, for example, if a client notices that his or her solicitor is 'friends' with a solicitor acting for the opposing party to a case or with a judge or tribunal members involved in a case. Creating a link with clients through accepting them as friends on a social media site should be approached with caution. Members of the legal profession should

---

[3] The Law Society of Scotland Practice Rules 2011, Section E, Division B: Social Media—Advice and Information for the Legal Profession. Available at *http://www.lawscot.org.uk/rules-and-guidance/section-e-general-guidance/division-b-the-management-of-files,-papers-and-information/advice-and-information/social-media-%E2%80%93-advice-and-information-for-the-legal-profession/* [Accessed 19 April 2016].

> take care to consider the nature of their activity on that site—including whether it is a business or personal account—and how the client might view the solicitor's online activities and relationships, visible through the site.

Some social media platforms will show content from friends and contacts within your own 'stream'—consideration should be given to how this external content could be perceived by employers and clients, and consideration given to settings to ensure all linked information within your pages is appropriate. Linking to other members of the legal profession should likewise be treated with common sense, and care should be taken to avoid inappropriate online communication, such as discussing a case or posting any other confidential information, and any potential or perceived conflict of interest. It is worth remembering that even 'direct messaging' (private communication between two individuals) is not necessarily secure. It should also be noted that the internet allows information to be linked together, and that issues have arisen for professionals from that. For example, a passing comment about a 'difficult client' on Twitter might be linked with the time of the tweet, and information from a public court hearing to specifically identify the client in question (as happened recently in an English disciplinary case)."

For those of you who aren't into social media, we summarise the main platforms below (and give examples of how lawyers might use them).

Facebook

5–30 Facebook is the most popular social media service, with around three-quarters of people in the UK using it on a regular basis. Facebook is great for local firms that are looking to advertise and target local users. Check out the Facebook page of Scullion Law, a Hamilton based firm. Its Facebook page is an excellent showcase both of the firm's staff and the work the firm does. Larger firms also use Facebook for graduate recruitment. HR teams have a Facebook page to communicate with prospective traineeships. Check out the DWF Graduate Recruitment as an example of how a firm keeps graduates up to date with opportunities.

We don't recommend that you use your own Facebook page for business. As the Law Society warns:

> "Members of the legal profession should take care to consider the nature of their activity on that site—including whether it is a business or personal account—and how the client might view the solicitor's online activities and relationships, visible through the site."[4]

You should check your security settings to see if the content you post is visible to third parties. Remember clients and contacts can "Google" you too.

Twitter

5–31 If you use Twitter for business, then you want to focus on showing authority in your area of expertise. Share links to information and give your own unique opinions too. The best lawyers on Twitter use it to comment on recent development and provide commentary. For example, David Allen Green (an English lawyer

---

[4] See: *http://www.warrenknight.co.uk/2016/01/04/the-demographics-of-social-media-users-in-2016/* (4 January 2016) [Accessed: 14 June 2016].

and writer) uses Twitter to provide commentary on areas of law that interest him, including human rights and rights of free speech. In Scotland, Burness Paull's David Morgan provides employment tips, in a single tweet. Others, like Inksters' founder, Brian Inkster, discuss the latest ideas for improving how lawyers work. Scotland has a strong academic presence on Twitter, with Professor James Chalmers, *regius* Professor of Law at the University of Glasgow, for example, being particularly active on criminal law issues.

Firms use Twitter to respond to client queries or to publicise legal news. CMS has different accounts to allow you to follow the latest news on employment or insolvency, for example. High street firms, like McReevy & Co, also provide regular updates, on criminal and legal aid matters.

As with every other social network, the most important thing you can do is to be yourself. Think about posting opinions, news, and messages around your areas of interest. If you're looking to build your reputation as an agricultural lawyer, you want to follow organisations such as Scottish Land Action and land reform activists (such as Green MSP Andy Wightman). Share information that is valuable to the people you want to talk to and they'll find you. It's also worth remembering that networking on Twitter is no different from meeting people face to face. Just as you wouldn't shout in someone's face at a drinks reception, so you shouldn't immediately tweet "FOLLOW ME, DAVID MORGAN, FOLLOW ME PLEAZ!" Just as you would if you meet someone in real life, you should find out what the person you want to talk to is interested in, be polite and then start a discussion with them. The only difference is that everybody can see your tweets. Quite often someone who is a follower of a "friend's friend" will see your tweet and respond "out of the blue." Serendipity can lead to all kinds of unexpected opportunities.

LinkedIn

LinkedIn is different. It's designed specifically for professional networking **5–32** (finding a job, connecting with potential business partners) rather than simply making friends or sharing photos, videos and music. To us, this makes it boring. What's the point of a social network that removes all the fun of being social? However, as young lawyers, LinkedIn does provide a useful way to keep in touch with contacts, as they change jobs and roles. In your 20s your peers will change jobs frequently and it's easy to lose track of them. LinkedIn provides a good way to track changes as they're updated, and for you to get in touch and congratulate them (or offer support). It also provides a good way to contact recruitment agents, discreetly . . .

The main thing to remember is that LinkedIn is one of the first places a business contact may look to find out more about you. Keep your profile up to date and make sure it has all the relevant information about you that you would want them to read.

YouTube (and other video sharing sites)

Firms have been slow to embrace video. The reasons are twofold. People are **5–33** reluctant to appear on camera, and you need a certain level of skill to make good videos. However, with technology becoming cheaper and video editing simpler, it's a great time to experiment. Our only warning is that your video should look good—videos are visual, after all. Use proper lighting. Be engaging. Watch some "how to" guides to "vlogging" to pick up the basics. For examples, check out the

Law Society's videos on Vimeo. In particular, its guides for first time buyers and starting a business show how effective a video can be when dealing with complicated subjects. For examples of law firms using videos, check out Pinsent Masons' award winning HR Network TV, a news bulletin dedicated to employment law news.

These are all good examples of how firms use YouTube for their own purposes, but you should also be wary of appearing on it accidently. Building a reputation takes time, losing a reputation can take seconds. In 2013 a Clifford Chance trainee was filmed in Oxford, for a documentary video. He said, "I'm a City lad and I f******g love the ladness. I love the City." When he was asked what he meant by "ladness" he said, "the ladness is just basically f******g people over for money." He was drunk and he wasn't at work. However, when Clifford Chance watched the video it released a statement:

> "The comments made are inappropriate and they're at odds with our principles and the professional standards we espouse as a firm. One of our trainee lawyers is the subject of our formal disciplinary procedures which may result in termination of the training contract with the firm."[5]

This trainee was probably playing up for the camera. However, when it comes to his leaving speech, do you think they'll mention his wonderful research skills, or his YouTube appearance?

This isn't just a problem for people caught talking about business. In 2015, US Law firm Goldberg Segalla sacked Clive O'Connell (a corporate partner in its London office) after he referred to Liverpool fans in a YouTube rant as, among other things, "scum scouse idiots."[6]

It didn't matter that he wasn't representing the firm, talking about clients, business or the law, when his comments were publicised.

Blogs

5–34 Blogs allow you to discuss in detail particular aspects of law or practice. Given there is no restriction what (or how much) you can write your only challenge is to write engagingly so that people enjoy reading it. A regular blog can help build a readership that then will see you as an expert in your field. Again we refer you to David Allen Green's blog, "Jack of Kent" and Brian Inksters' "Times Law Blawg".

Pinterest/Instagram/Snapchat (and other photo sharing sites)

5–35 A photo is worth a 1,000 words. The rise of Pinterest, Instagram and Snapchat evidence that we want to share photos of the things we like. While photo sharing sites may not be the first thing that pops into your head when you think of a law firm, they do allow firms to share photos of their people and offices to give you a glimpse of what it's like to work for them. Check out Urban Lawyers (which covers events for law students) and Tunde Okewale's musings on human rights. Have a look at Aberdeen Considine, also. It uses Pinterest to sell homes.

---

[5] *Quoted in http://www.rollonfriday.co.uk/TheNews/EuropeNews/tabid/58/Id/2909/fromTab/36/currentIndex/1/Default.aspx* [Accessed: 10 June 2016].

[6] Quoted in *http://www.theguardian.com/commentisfree/2015/Nov/14/should-you-be-sacked-for-off-duty-behaviour-clive-o-connell-chelsea-scouse-scum* [Accessed: 10 June 2016].

Personal reputation: a warning

The legal world in Scotland is small. Even within the UK, lawyers working in the same areas of work know each other and gossip about one another. All the while, working as a lawyer gives you a position of respect in a community. If you work in a small town you're "the lawyer", whether you're writing a will or shopping in the local Tesco. Your personal reputation always impacts your professional reputation. We have a simple scenario to show you how this works. If the comedian Frankie Boyle were a lawyer, would you ask him to defend you in court? **5–36**

We're going to answer this by turning it around. Why wouldn't you use Frankie Boyle? Frankie is a solicitor. That means he will act honestly, promptly and with integrity. He won't tell jokes about you behind your back because he'll keep your secrets confidential. You reasonably can assume all of these things precisely because he is a solicitor.

Let's assume Frankie works for McGreevy & Co, a firm with an excellent reputation for court work. You know you're in good hands; a firm like McGreevy & Co wouldn't employ Frankie if he weren't good at his job. So, why wouldn't you use Frankie Boyle? Here's a conclusion you probably don't want to hear. Many people wouldn't use him because they just don't like his jokes. His personal reputation would be too much for some. Just like the Clifford Chance trainee, sometimes—no matter how unreasonable it may seem—what you do in your personal life affects your professional reputation.

Summary

Business development and marketing skills set smart trainees and junior lawyers apart from your peers. Most lawyers will have the technical skills to do the same work as you—so, what sets you apart, is your ability to bring in, work with and understand clients. If you start developing these skills early in your career, you'll become indispensable to your firm. **5–37**

PART 2

Working as a Trainee

CHAPTER 6

HOW TO OPEN FILES

Introduction

It's a new week. Your partner is keen that you start working for your new client and asks if you've opened a file. You tell him that you've asked your secretary to do the necessary, but you don't yet have a passport or utility bill. Your partner says, "that's okay, the paper work can wait till later." Is he right? 6–1

We hope that we convinced you in Pt 1 that working as a lawyer is all about creating a good relationship with your clients. If you know about them (what they need, how they wish to be treated etc.) you'll be a better lawyer because you can tailor your advice to suit their needs. A hairdresser checks how you want your hair to look before they start cutting. Similarly, you should check exactly what your client wants before offering advice. 6–2

Simple things do matter. Clients shouldn't be left waiting in your reception. Boardrooms should be comfortable and designed to help clients feel at ease. You shouldn't have spelling mistakes in letters or emails. The difference between an average lawyer and an exceptional one is ensuring that everything a client sees, hears and feels assures them that you're doing your best for them. This starts the first time a client hears about your firm, visits your office, browses your website or discusses you with family, friends or colleagues. However, their first proper exposure to you comes when they instruct you. One of the first things you need to do at that point is to ask your client to comply with anti-money laundering regulations.

The regulations require new clients to confirm their identity and they require you to consider whether what a client has asked you to do could create a risk of money laundering. Money laundering is a criminal offence. It's the act of creating a fake source for money obtained from crime. Some lawyers view the regulations as a bureaucratic exercise. We don't. Instead, we see it as a vital step in building your knowledge about your client and what they're trying to achieve. If you start to act for a company, do you know what it does? Who owns it? What influence do they have on the decisions the board makes? What do the directors do? Are you dealing with them directly or via an employee? By asking the right questions you not only comply with the regulations, you also find out valuable information about your client.

Let's assume that a company makes electronic gadgets. It wants to buy all the shares of another company that makes batteries. Let's assume, also, your instruction comes from an employee. You need to comply with the anti-money laundering regulations to confirm the company's identity and whether there's a risk that this share purchase could involve money laundering. From a regulatory point of view, you need documents to confirm your client's identity. These could be 6–3 incorporation documents, the company's latest annual report and the passport of one of its directors. However, to judge whether a transaction might create a risk of money laundering, you need to know more. Why is the company doing this particular deal? Is it part of its normal business to buy other companies? How is it paying for the shares?

By asking these questions you not only can judge the risk of money laundering, you also gather information about the company and how it works. If this is the first time that it has ever bought another company, you'll know your client likely will need "hand holding" throughout the transaction. If it buys companies regularly then you can reasonably be assured your client won't need detailed explanations; it will know the lie of the land from the previous deals.

Outcomes

6–4 We'll examine the statutory framework and regulations required to comply with anti-money laundering rules. There's no escaping that you need to know the legal framework of this area of law. However, we'll show you how you use that knowledge to help you understand your clients (and their aspirations) better. By the end of the chapter you should know not only the regulations, but also how their application can enhance your client relationships.

A note on practice

6–5 Before examining the regulations, it's worth noting that there can be significant differences in practice, depending on the firm you work for. For example, in-house departments are not subject to anti-money laundering (AML) requirements. Some firms also have staff and software to carry out many of the tasks. For example, the Law Society endorsed the use of the "AML Compliance Solution" in June 2015, as an online software solution.

Notwithstanding the additional help that a compliance team (and software) can provide, you need to be familiar with the rules. Ultimately you remain responsible for AML and your reputation (and even your practicing certificate) is at stake if you don't comply. We also hope that we can convince you that understanding your client also helps you to provide better advice.

Money laundering basics

Background

What is money laundering?

6–6 Money laundering creates a fake source for money obtained from crime, so that you can spend it without the Government finding out its provenance. It's the act of disguising the source (or true nature) of money obtained through illegal means. For example, if you make £20 million in cash selling drugs, you can't walk into a bank and deposit it into your account. The bank will want to know where the money has come from. It will notify the police if it believes it has been obtained illegally. The cash might be considered to be "dirty". That's the nub of money laundering. Criminals need to have evidence that their money is "clean"; i.e. some financial records showing where the money has come from. Their dirty cash has to be "cleaned", by passing it through a number of legitimate businesses before depositing it in the bank (hence the term "money laundering"). Be under no illusion, laundering criminal assets is illegal.

What are the consequences of money laundering?

If you're involved with money laundering, then you're committing a crime. It doesn't matter if you don't know that you're taking part in money laundering. There is no requirement to show motive. 6–7

How does it work?

Money laundering usually involves three steps: 6–8

1. placement—illegal funds are introduced into a financial system;
2. layering—a number of transactions are carried out to hide the source of the funds; and
3. integration—any profit generated by the transactions (as well as the original illegal funds) are withdrawn.

For example, when you make £20 million in cash selling drugs, you can't tell the bank the truth. Instead, you set up a car wash and tell the bank that you made your fortune valeting cars (lots and lots of them). The bank accepts your explanation and opens an account for you. This is the placement stage. You then move your money to make it harder for the police to find the original source. This could be as simple as bank-to-bank transfers, changing currency, or buying expensive goods like cars, jewellery or property. Each time you move your cash you obscure the original source. This is the layering stage. The final stage is integration. You sell the cars, jewellery and property, and you deposit your newly cleaned cash in your bank. You no longer have dirty money. You have clean cash and an explanation that (ironically) will wash.

How do you stop money laundering?

Most countries have AML regulations. It's regarded as a global issue and there has been a concerted effort to ensure that countries adopt minimum standards to stop criminals exploiting a weakness in any one country (and use it to access the global financial market). 6–9

Global

Although regulations are similar across the world, different regulations do create practical difficulties if you deal with companies registered abroad. Foreign companies may have different standards than those required in the UK. For example, US companies have more stringent rules. This may mean that if you deal with an American company (such as a US bank) it may require more information than required under the UK system. For example, in America you need to identify if someone involved in a transaction is a relative of a Supreme Court judge. It may be unlikely that a client in Scotland has a cousin on the Supreme Court bench, but the bank needs to show it has asked the question in order to pass its audit checks. This is unusual though and, in 99% of cases, you should only need to follow the UK regulations. 6–10

UK regulations

In the UK the main regulations are contained in: 6–11

- the Terrorism Act 2000;
- the Anti-terrorism, Crime and Security Act 2001;

- the Proceeds of Crime Act 2002;
- the Serious Organised Crime and Police Act 2005; and
- the Money Laundering Regulations 2007 (as amended).

The regulations apply to all those who act in the course of business, including legal professionals, and they set out requirements to identify customers/clients, the source of funds and the risk of money laundering.

Practice notes

6–12 The Law Society is currently developing a Money Laundering Guidance Note for Scottish solicitors. In the meantime, it has adopted Pt 1 of The Joint Money Laundering Steering Group Guidance.[1] The Law Society of England and Wales has published an excellent practice note to help lawyers understand the regulations. That, also, is available from the Law Society's website and is updated regularly.

What do you need to do?

6–13 Money laundering is a crime that is always changing. There are many checks within the financial system to identify money-laundering risks, so criminals need to be smart if they want to hide the true source of funds. As one scheme is uncovered, a new scheme is dreamt up. It's important to start by pointing out that you're not being asked to stop money launderers. You're not the police. Instead you're being asked to help reduce the risk of money laundering by having systems in place to spot suspicious activities and report those so that they can be investigated further.

Your systems should do two things. Firstly, the identity of your client needs to be verified, so you can confirm that they're who they say they are. Secondly, any risks involved in the work that you plan to do (that could lead to money laundering) are explored and analysed.

When do you assess the risk?

6–14 Risk assessment is an ongoing process that starts when:

- you open a file for a new client; or
- you open a file for an existing client for who you do not act for regularly.

Are there any other times you should assess the risk?

6–15 You must also assess the risk of money laundering if you:

- suspect money laundering at all;
- have doubts about information previously obtained about an existing client; or
- believe that any information needs to updated.

[1] Available at http://www.jmlsg.org.uk [Accessed 19 April 2016].

Confirming identity

How do you confirm a client's identity?

Confirming a client's identify is known as Client Due Diligence (CDD). CDD has two elements: **6–16**

1. If your client is an individual, you identify and verify his/her identity using documents and information obtained from a reliable, independent source. This could be from a passport or photo-driving licence.
2. If your client is not an individual, you need to identify the ownership structure. For example, you could identify the shareholders and directors of a company.

How do you identify and verify an individual, owner or person who controls the client?

It's unlikely that a money launderer will tell you his or her real name. You must check that what your clients have told you is true, so as to make it harder for money launderers to fool you. You do that by obtaining evidence that supports their claim. This includes documents, data or information that comes from reliable and independent sources: **6–17**

- original documents (such as a passport or driving licence);
- electronic verification (through third party software); or
- information from a reliable third party (such as another solicitor).

In practice you're always best obtaining original documents so that you can confirm your client's identity yourself.

Going back to our scenario, you have a client who is an individual. She is a new client, so you need to ask her to confirm her identity. To that end, you would ask to see an original passport or photographic driving licence. You also would ask to see a recent utility bill, to confirm her address.

What happens if you don't complete CDD?

If your new client is evasive or acts suspiciously (for example, by forgetting to bring the documents), you must stop acting and should consider whether you need to report them. It may be that your client is just forgetful. However, there may be a more sinister motive and that she is not who she claims to be. **6–18**

Can you act for a client before you've checked their identity?

Yes. ID verification can be completed while you establish a business relationship, where it's necessary not to interrupt the normal conduct of business and where you assess there is little risk of money laundering. You must, though, complete the verification as soon as practicable after initial contact. Your partner was right; you can start acting for your client straightaway. However, you must get her ID information as soon as possible, and certainly before any actions involving money occur. Do not permit funds or property to be transferred, or final agreements to be signed, before completion of full verification. **6–19**

What happens once you complete CDD?

6–20 CDD is not a one off process. You must conduct ongoing monitoring, on a risk appropriate basis, including:

- scrutiny of transactions, to ensure that they're consistent with your knowledge of your client, their business and risk profile; and
- keeping your CDD documents up to date.

What if clients are unable to produce standard documentation?

6–21 Some clients are unable to provide standard verification documents, for entirely legitimate reasons. An elderly client may not have a passport, for example. A homeless person clearly won't be able to confirm an address. If you decide that your client has a good reason, you can accept a letter from an appropriate person who knows him or her (e.g. social services).

Enhanced due diligence

6–22 You need to conduct enhanced due diligence where:

- your client is not dealt with face-to-face;
- your client is a politically exposed person; and
- there is a situation that presents a higher risk of money laundering.

This involves further verification of identity, more detail on the ownership and control structure of a corporate client, further information both on the purpose of your retainer and the source of funds, and, lastly, enhanced ongoing monitoring.

Using CDD to build your relationship with your client

6–23 CDD can be invaluable when finding out information about clients who aren't individuals. When you explore the ownership structure of a company, you're checking how the client is run. Does it have a single shareholder or is it a public limited company (Plc)? Who are the trustees of a trust? Who is the beneficiary of the trust? The questions you ask help shape your advice.

Assessing risks

General risks

6–24 You also need to assess if your client's transaction brings with it the opportunity of money laundering. In some cases, it will be obvious that it won't. If your client is pursuing an employment claim, she is unlikely to have any opportunity to launder money, because little money is involved in bringing a claim. If you're providing legal advice to someone accused of assault, it's also unlikely to offer any scope for money laundering.

However, there are many transactions where there is a risk of money laundering. These include:

- complicated financial or property transactions;
- providing assistance in setting up trusts or company structures, which could be used to obscure the ownership of property;

- payments that are made to, or received from, third parties;
- payments made in cash; or
- transactions with a cross-border element.

General signs of risk

Signs that you should look out for include: **6–25**

- Instructions in niche areas in which your firm has no background, but in which the client claims to be an expert. If a client says, "it's okay, I know what I'm doing, and I'll keep you right", you need to ask why they picked you. Why choose a lawyer who doesn't know anything?
- If your client is based a long way from your office, consider why you have been instructed. Why did they not use someone closer?
- Instructions that change unexpectedly might be suspicious, if there seems to be no logical reason (especially if the instructions involve money).
- Be aware if your client:

  — deposits funds into your client account but then ends the transaction, for no apparent reason;
  — tells you that funds are coming from one source and, at the last minute, that source changes;
  — unexpectedly asks that you send money received in your client account back to source (either to the client or a third party).

- Be wary of disputes that are settled too easily, as this may indicate sham litigation.
- Be aware of:

  — loss-making transactions, where the loss is avoidable;
  — settlements paid in cash, or paid directly between parties;
  — complex or unusually large transactions;
  — unusual patterns of transactions, which have no apparent economic purpose.

Specific risks

The following situations may provide signs of risk in specific transactions. **6–26**

Charities

If you're acting for a charity, consider its purpose and the organisations it's aligned with. If you're receiving money on a charity's behalf, be alert to unusual circumstances (for example, excessive sums of money). **6–27**

Commercial work

Company structures make them attractive to money launderers, because it's possible to obscure true ownership for relatively little expense. **6–28**

Estates

There is no requirement that you should be satisfied about the history of all of the funds that make up an estate. However, be aware: **6–29**

- where assets have been earned in a foreign jurisdiction;
- where assets have been earned (or are located in) a so-called suspect territory; or
- if you discover (or suspect) that beneficiaries are intending not to pay the correct amount of inheritance tax.

Forming a new company

6–30 If you help form a new company, be alert to any signs that it might be misused. Do you know who the shareholders and directors will be? What is their relationship to the person who is instructing you? What is the company intended to do? How will it be financed?

Powers of attorney

6–31 If you're acting as an attorney for someone you may uncover financial information, for example, regarding non-payment of tax or the wrongful receipt of benefits.

Property work: ownership issues

6–32 Be alert to unexplained changes in ownership.

Property work: funding

6–33 Transactions that don't involve a mortgage have a higher risk of being fraudulent. Look out for large payments from private funds (especially if your client has a low income) and be wary of multiple payments from a number of sources.

Property work: funds from a third party

6–34 Third parties (for example, relatives) often assist with purchases. However, you may be asked to receive funds directly from these third parties and you need to decide whether (and to what extent) you need to undertake CDD in relation to them.

Property work: direct payments between buyers and sellers

6–35 You may discover (or suspect) that cash has changed hands directly, between a seller and a buyer. If you're then asked to bank that cash in your client account, this presents a problem—the source of the cash is not your client.

Property work: valuing

6–36 If you become aware of a significant discrepancy between the sale price and what you reasonably would expect such a property to fetch, ask questions.

Property work: lenders

6–37 You may discover that your client is attempting to mislead a lender in order to inflate a mortgage advance (for example, by misrepresenting his/her income). However, until the improperly obtained mortgage advance is received, there is no criminal property for the purposes of the disclosure obligations under the Proceeds of Crime Act 2002.

Tax

Tax evasion, whether committed by your client or another party to a transaction, can result in you committing a Proceeds of Crime Act 2002 s.328 arrangement offence (we'll cover this in the offences and penalties section below). **6–38**

Trusts

The key risk period for a trust is during set-up, when a donor is divesting money and/or assets. Information about the purpose of the trust can help allay concerns. Similarly, information both about the donor and those who have control of the trust's assets is required. **6–39**

Using CDD to build your relationship with your client

Again, reviewing a transaction with your client is a vital part of finding out what they're trying to achieve. Your client may want to buy land for various reasons. They may want to buy it as an investment, to sell on in 10 years. They may buy it to develop it. They may buy it to use themselves, or to lease or sell to others. Knowing what they're doing (and why) helps you not only to assess the risk of money laundering, but also to tailor your advice and build a relationship with your client. **6–40**

Record keeping requirements

What do you keep?

You need to keep a record of everything you have done, including copies of any identification documents you've obtained. This is crucial. If there's ever an investigation into one of your clients, or the Law Society investigates your firm, you can prove that you complied with the regulations. **6–41**

How long do you keep records?

You must keep your records for five years beginning from: **6–42**

- the date a business relationship ends; or
- the date a transaction is completed.

Offences and penalties

There are consequences for failing to carry out AML checks. All references are to sections of the Proceeds of Crime Act 2002. **6–43**

Section 327—concealing

You commit an offence if you conceal, disguise, convert or transfer criminal property, or remove criminal property. This includes concealing or disguising its nature, source, location, disposition, movement, ownership or any rights connected with it. **6–44**

Section 328—arrangements

You commit an offence if you enter into, or become concerned in an arrangement, which you know or suspect facilitates the acquisition, retention, use or control of criminal property by or on behalf of another person. To become concerned in an arrangement suggests a practical involvement, such as taking steps to put the arrangement into effect. **6–45**

Section 329—acquisition, use or possession

6–46 You commit an offence if you acquire, use or have possession of criminal property.

Sections 330–332

6–47 Finally, the Proceeds of Crime Act 2002 requires you to report suspicions of money laundering. A failure to report carries a maximum penalty of five years' imprisonment. There are three elements that each determines if you have to make a report.

Knowledge

6–48 Knowledge means actual knowledge. There is a suggestion that shutting your eyes to the truth may amount to knowledge.

Suspicion

6–49 *Da Silva* argues that for "suspicion":

> "It seems to us that the essential element in the word 'suspect' . . . is that the defendant must think that there is a possibility, which is more than fanciful, that the relevant facts exist. A vague feeling of unease would not suffice".[2]

The test is subjective.

Reasonable grounds to suspect

6–50 This is an objective test. Were there factual circumstances from which a reasonable person should have inferred knowledge, or formed the suspicion that another is engaged in money laundering?

Tipping-off

6–51 There are two tipping-off offences:

1. Section 333A(1)—it's an offence to disclose that a report has been made to the Serious Organised Crime Agency (SOCA), if that might prejudice any investigation.
2. Section 333A(3)—it's an offence to disclose that an investigation into money laundering is being contemplated or carried out, if that's likely to prejudice the investigation.

Defences

6–52 Section 338 allows for authorised disclosure regarding suspicion of money laundering as a defence:

- before money laundering occurs;
- while it's occurring, but as soon as you suspect it;

---

[2] *R v Da Silva* [2006] EWCA Crim 1654.

- after it has occurred, if you had good reason for not disclosing earlier and you make the disclosure as soon as practicable.

If your firm has a money laundering reporting officer, you should make any disclosures to him/her. If your firm doesn't, you should make your disclosure directly to the National Crime Agency (NCA).

What if you suspect part way through?

Section 338(2A) provides that you may make an authorised disclosure in these **6–53** circumstances if:

- at the time the initial steps were taken, they weren't a money laundering offence because you didn't have good reason to know or suspect that the property was criminal property; and
- you make a disclosure of your own initiative as soon as practicable after you first know or suspect that criminal property is involved.

Exceptions to failure to disclose offences

There are other situations in which you'll not have committed an offence for **6–54** failing to disclose:

- you have a reasonable excuse[3]; or
- you're a professional legal adviser and the information came to you in privileged circumstances.

Summary

The anti-money laundering regulations are an unavoidable part of opening files **6–55** and working with clients. However, they can be a useful reminder of the importance of knowing who your client is and what they're trying to achieve. They can help you become a better lawyer. Remember, the best lawyers know their clients and that starts the moment you open a file.

---

3 There's no judicial guidance on what might constitute a reasonable excuse.

CHAPTER 7

HOW TO WRITE ENGAGEMENT LETTERS

Introduction

7–1 *Same day. Minutes later. After asking if you've opened a file, your partner asks if you've sent the engagement letter to confirm what you'll do and how much the firm will charge. You say "no"—you've never had to write an engagement letter, after all. "What do I need to cover in the letter?", you ask.*

7–2 In February 1999,[1] Grant McCulloch, a past Law Society president, wrote an article for *The Journal of the Law Society of Scotland*. In it, he suggested clients who complained about solicitors mainly did so because of poor communication (not because of mistakes). He suggested that if solicitors were clear about what they were doing for clients, clients would know what to expect and many complaints could be avoided. McCulloch was right, and it's a Law Society requirement that all clients are told what you'll do for them.

Would you buy a new coat if you didn't know what type of coat you were buying or how much it would cost? No. Yet, clients use solicitors without knowing exactly what the solicitor will do or what the final bill might be. The more information you give clients at the start of transactions the more informed they become. This doesn't mean that you have to give them definitive answers. Some areas of law (like litigation) are fraught with uncertainties. What might seem a simple case may end up requiring hundreds of boxes of evidence, numerous witnesses and days in court. Your client, with no experience of court work, may have thought they'd have an answer in three months, and yet three years later the case still hasn't been decided. If you can warn them of the twists and turns that litigation can take, then they won't be surprised if it takes longer than anticipated. Nor should clients expect a bill based on just three months' work; you'll have warned them that your fee will be based on the time you actually spend on the case. An engagement letter is a vital first step to helping your client understand what will happen next. It's more than a contract. It's your first chance to demonstrate what you can do and how you'll do it.

Outcome

7–3 By the end of the chapter you'll understand the Law Society requirements for issuing engagement letters and you'll know the main terms that should be contained within. We examine some common business terms that usually are

[1] G. McCulloch, "Who wants a happy client?" (1 February 1999), The Journal of the Law Society of Scotland, *Journalonline.co.uk*, *http://www.journalonline.co.uk/Magazine/44-2/1001136.aspx* [Accessed 19 April 2016].

included. These are terms that are not required by the Law Society but which are useful to help your client understand more about the work you'll do.

Basic structure of engagement letters

Law Society

At its simplest, an engagement letter is a letter (or email) that sets out: **7–4**

- what you'll do;
- how much it will cost;
- whether there is any contribution towards legal advice and assistance or legal aid;
- who'll do the work; and
- who the client can contact if they have any concerns.[2]

Template

Though every transaction is different, there is a basic template you can follow **7–5** which can be tailored for each client. McCulloch provided a starting point, in 1999. He suggested the following:

> "I refer to our meeting today when you instructed me to proceed with investigations regarding your accident. There are a few matters that we discussed, but would, I think, be helpful to bring to your attention. I will be dealing with your case myself, although on occasion I will be assisted by my assistant, Mr Jones. I will undertake the necessary investigations into the cause of your accident, to establish if there is someone responsible for it, and thereafter try to negotiate a settlement on your behalf. I will report regularly to you on developments as they arise.
>
> As you know, my charges will be based upon the Law Society General Table of fees which allows for an hourly time rate to be charged, and specific charges for letters and the like. At the present time my hourly charge-out rate is £90 per hour, and that of my assistant is £60 per hour. As agreed, I will send you an invoice at the end of every three months indicating the amount of work I have done on your behalf, and what outlays have been paid by me, on your behalf, to other persons. As you know, if you're successful in your case I may be able to recover some expenses from the other side, so the final costs cannot be known at this stage. In the event that you have any dissatisfaction in respect of the work that has been done for you, then please raise it with me at the earliest opportunity in the hope that it can be resolved. If, however, you wish to take the matter further then feel free to contact Mr Smith at this office, as he is the partner responsible for client relations.
>
> I hope this sets out the position. Please do not hesitate to contact me if you have any matter of concern. I shall be in touch as matters unfold."[3]

---

[2] The Law Society of Scotland Practice Rules 2011 r.B4: Client Communication, Guidance related to Rule B4: Client Communication Generally. Available at *http://www.lawscot.org.uk/rules-and-guidance/section-b/rule-b4-client-communication/guidance/b4-client-communication-generally/* [Accessed 19 April 2016].

[3] G. McCulloch, "Who wants a happy client?" (1 February 1999), The Journal of the Law Society of Scotland, *Journalonline.co.uk*, *http://www.journalonline.co.uk/Magazine/44-2/1001136.aspx* [Accessed 19 April 2016].

As you can see it contains many of the essential elements of an engagement letter. It confirms the work, the fee (though the Law Society Table of Fees is no more, so isn't appropriate today) and the person who'll deal with it. While it doesn't cover legal aid or complaints, it's still a good starting point. If you examine engagement letters from firms today, the first thing you notice is that they have become much longer. It's rare to find an engagement letter that's three paragraphs long. This is because many firms use engagement letters to cover not only the Law Society's requirements but also to inform clients of the firm's full business terms and conditions (in other words, its full contractual terms). For example, you find information about jurisdiction (for disputes), limits to potential claims and other standard clauses. We think this is an unfortunate trend; an engagement letter is meant to help clients. Turning engagement letters into quasi-contracts only makes them less readable and client-friendly. Many clients don't want to read contracts. That's why they use a lawyer. If so, sending them a contract to read is not a good start to your relationship.

In the next two sections we summarise the main terms of an engagement letter (as required by the Law Society) and standard commercial terms and conditions separately, so you know what is essential to include in your letter.

Law society requirements

7–6 Let's say you've been instructed by a new client to help her sue her former employer for unfair dismissal. You've met the client and she's impressed both with your partner and your firm; she wants you to act for her. This is your chance to impress her and show her that she has made the right choice. You know the Law Society requires you to issue an engagement letter but what does that involve? There are a number of steps, which we examine now.[4]

When should a client receive the engagement letter?

7–7 Your client must receive her engagement letter at the earliest practicable opportunity after instructing you. This doesn't mean that you need to send it straight after your first meeting. You may not know at that stage exactly what you'll do. If a client asks you to help them, it may take time to work out what they need and how you can help. However, as soon as you know what is required you should issue her engagement letter.

Are there any exceptions?

Repeat work

7–8 If your client regularly instructs you in the same type of work, you don't need to keep sending them the same engagement letter. Instead it should be provided the first time, and you only send a second or third letter if you need to update the original instructions (for example, if your price has changed or the scope is different).

[4] The Law Society's rules can be found in r.B4: Client Communication, and the corresponding guidance notes for it. Available at *http://www.lawscot.org.uk/rules-and-guidance/section-b/rule-b4-client-communication/* [Accessed 19 April 2016].

Impracticable

If work is urgent and there's no practical opportunity to provide an engagement letter before it's done, you don't need to send it. This may occur if you have an interim interdict that requires you to go to court immediately, or if you do work which is completed at a single meeting. The Law Society itself gives the example of a client who may be about to go on holiday and wants to make a will. They may have instructions implemented immediately and just sign the will at the first meeting. **7–9**

Children under the age of 12

Although you don't have to provide children under the age of 12 with an engagement letter, you still need to provide one to a parent or guardian if they're providing instructions for the child. You also need to be careful that you still communicate effectively with the child so that they understand what is happening. **7–10**

What should the engagement letter contain?

Engagement letters set out: **7–11**

- what you'll do;
- how much it will cost (usually an estimate, including VAT and outlays, or details of how a fee will be worked out, e.g. on hourly rates);
- whether there's any contribution towards legal advice and assistance or legal aid;
- who'll do the work; and
- who the client can contact if they have concerns.[5]

What you'll do

Put yourself in your client's shoes. Some clients may know exactly what you'll do for them if you write, "We'll raise an unfair dismissal action against your employer." However, most clients require more information. They want to know what the steps will be and how long they might take. For example, you may want to write: **7–12**

> "Firstly we'll prepare and raise a claim on your behalf. There then will be a period when we prepare for a tribunal hearing. This may involve preparing evidence and taking statements from people who may be able to help your claim. While we do this, your employer will be taking similar steps. We'll need to respond to them. Finally, we may need to attend an employment tribunal. The tribunal may take a number of days and this will depend on the amount of evidence it has to deal with. We would estimate this will take three days but this may change as we prepare for it due to additional evidence that may be required."

What you're trying to do is to avoid any risk of misunderstanding or confusion. The client should know exactly what you're doing for them. While you don't need

---

[5] The Law Society of Scotland Practice Rules 2011 r.B4: Client Communication, Guidance related to Rule B4: Client Communication Generally. Available at *http://www.lawscot.org.uk/rules-and-guidance/section-b/rule-b4-client-communication/guidance/b4-client-communication-generally/* [Accessed 19 April 2016].

to go into step-by-step detail, you should cover all the significant elements. It's also important that you tell your client what you won't do. A common exclusion that commercial firms include in their engagement letters is that they won't provide tax advice. It's assumed that corporate clients will have had independent advice from an accountant, and firms want to be clear that tax is only covered if instructed.

Fees

7–13 McCulloch's template referred to the Law Society Table of Fees. This is no longer used and the Law Society believes it's not appropriate to refer to fees recommended by the Society. Instead you need to set out:

- your best estimate of how much the work will cost and how it will be calculated;
- a fixed fee; or
- a mechanism for calculating a fee once the work is complete (for example, based on hourly rates or a percentage of a price).

When you send your engagement letter to your client you may want to say:

> "Based on the work that we outlined above, we estimate that the final fee will be £10,000 excluding VAT and costs. Our final fee though will be based on our hourly rate of £250 for a partner and £100 for a trainee."

Or

> "Based on the work that we have outlined above, we'll charge £10,000 excluding VAT and costs. This fee is fixed so that if the work takes longer than we have estimated you'll not be charged any more."

Or

> "Our final fee will be charged based on the time spent on this work by our staff. Our hourly rate for this work will be £250 for a partner and £100 for a trainee. VAT and costs will also be payable."

Or

> "Our final fee will be 1% of the selling price for your home. We'll charge VAT on the fee. If your home sells for £200,000, then our fee will be £4,000 plus VAT and costs."

Estimates—a word of warning

7–14 If you provide a client with an estimate, then you must be clear that the figure quoted is not a fixed fee. If you're not (and your client accepts it in writing) then your "estimate" might be considered to be a fixed fee and you won't be able to charge your client a different price. Also, to protect clients, you need to keep them updated if your estimate changes significantly. If you tell your client that you estimate her fee for the unfair dismissal claim at £10,000 and then you try and charge her £50,000, you could be in breach of professional standards. The Law

Society recommends that you write to your client to let them know that his/her estimate may change, as soon as you know:

- you're approaching the limit of your original estimate; or
- that the cost of work will materially exceed your estimate.

Additional costs

Many transactions incur additional costs. If you sell a property, then you need to pay for property reports and searches. If you buy property, then Land and Buildings Transaction Tax (LBTT) and registration dues need to be paid. If you go to court, you may need to pay for an advocate or an expert witness. Closer to home, some transactions use a lot of paper and you may want to charge for excessive photocopying and printing. All of these costs should be raised with the client so that they're not hit with an unexpected bill. You should also tell them when costs might be charged. The cost of LBTT can run into thousands of pounds (if not more for expensive properties). If a client doesn't pay LBTT within 30 days of buying a property, he/she could face penalties and interest payments. You need to tell them as soon as possible when payments are due so that they can plan for it. **7–15**

Payments to account

Law firms are not banks. You don't provide clients with loans. Yet, that's exactly what you do when you pay costs in advance and then charge them back to clients at a later date. This may be okay if your costs are small (for example, under £100 for a court fee). However, if a QC charges £500 an hour, you want to make sure that your client pays that cost. A payment to account (whether to cover costs or fees) is fine. However, you do need to cover this in the engagement letter. Equally, you need to tell the client what will happen if they don't pay. For example, you may need to withdraw from acting if costs haven't been paid. If so, this could leave your client in a difficult position, especially if you withdraw at a late stage and they need to find another lawyer quickly. If you've told them in advance that this could happen, you'll be okay. **7–16**

Third party paying fees or costs

If your client's costs are to be paid by a third party (such as a trade union, insurer or lender) then you don't need to set out any specific details, but any part of the fee which your client might be asked to pay should be included (such as a success fee in a speculative action). **7–17**

Third party fees

The Law Society recommends that you explain to your client if there is any potential liability for other people's costs. This could include paying expenses if they're unsuccessful in a court action. For example, you may wish to say to your client: **7–18**

> "Along with our fee and costs, you may be required to pay the legal fees of your former employer if they successfully defend your claim. These expenses will be decided by the court."

Legal aid

7–19 Legal aid is the term for schemes available to help people with the costs of legal advice or representation. The Scottish Legal Aid Board (SLAB) administers the various schemes.

There are four types of legal aid:

- advice and assistance;
- civil legal aid;
- legal aid for children's hearings or court hearings connected to a children's hearing; and
- criminal legal aid.

You're not required to explain the legal aid system to clients. Instead, you can comply with this requirement by sending clients copies of guides and leaflets provided by SLAB. This doesn't mean that you can't provide advice if you want. You still can and, if so, the Law Society is happy that this be sent by a separate letter.

Who'll do the work?

7–20 Your client has met you and your partner. However, there may be other people who might work on her claim. You might have a paralegal to manage the cataloguing and processing of evidence. An assistant might appear at some of the procedural hearings, where a lawyer is required to be present but the court will only consider a minor or insignificant matter. The engagement letter is your chance to confirm to your client who they'll speak to and who will deal with their work. This is particularly important if your client expects a particular person to deal with their work. For example, they may expect your partner to do everything. Your partner, however, knows that you should do some of the work as it doesn't require their knowledge and skill and it will be a lot cheaper. You need to tell your client this upfront so that they know why you're speaking to them.

A typical letter from a partner might say:

> "I will be in charge of your claim and you should call me if you have any questions. I will also be assisted by [my assistant] and [my trainee] who'll help with some of the routine work required with cases of this type. They'll help ensure that legal fees are kept to a minimum as work will be carried out by the right people for it."

Who the client can contact if they have any concerns

7–21 Every firm in Scotland must have a "client relations partner" (CRP) to handle client complaints. Your CRP will be the first point of contact for clients who want to complain and they'll keep a record of each complaint received and follow its own written procedure for dealing with the complaint. Your engagement letter should tell clients what to do, who to contact, and how to set out the complaint. It should also notify clients that they can contact the Scottish Legal Complaints Commission (SLCC) and that time limits may apply. We look at the complaints process and the SLCC more closely in Ch.10 (how to avoid complaints).

A typical engagement letter may say:

"If at any time you're dissatisfied with our service, you can raise this with me, or if you would prefer to speak to our client relations partner you can raise it with them. Our client relations partner is [name of partner] and you can contact them by phone, email or write to them at this address. You're also entitled to complain to the Scottish Legal Complaints Commission (SLCC). The SLCC operates strict time limits for accepting complaints, which require complaints to be made within one year of the service ending or the conduct occurring. However, the SLCC will disregard any time it considers that the complainer was unaware of their concern. Full details for raising a complaint can be found at *http://www.scottishlegalcomplaints.com*."

What happens if you don't send an engagement letter?

You should always send an engagement letter; at the least it helps to build your **7–22** relationship with your clients. However, there are also penalties if you don't. If you don't send a letter you could be in breach of professional standards. While Law Society guidance does indicate that an occasional failure will not be a serious breach, regular failures could lead to a charge of professional misconduct that, in turn could lead to your practicing certificate being suspended or even removed.

Business terms

Along with Law Society requirements, your firm will also want to include business **7–23** terms to govern your relationship with your client. These terms include many of the typical contractual terms you'd expect to see in a business contract. These include:

- confidentiality clauses;
- clauses dealing with ownership of any intellectual property produced during the course of the work (i.e. does your firm own the advice it provides?);
- data protection;
- freedom of information (to the extent it may apply);
- early termination;
- third party rights, and
- choice of law.

There are three that we'll look at more closely. These are anti-money laundering (AML), dealing with client money and limiting liability.

Anti–money laundering

If you're dealing with a new client, then you need to comply with the AML regu- **7–24** lations as discussed in Ch.6 (how to open files). Even with an existing client you may need to reassess, update and verify your client due diligence and make a fresh assessment of any risk of money laundering that a new transaction may bring. Often your firm's standard terms will include a description of activities required by the laws and regulations related to AML. A typical clause might say:

"We'll not be ready to start for you until we have completed all regulatory checks required by the Proceeds of Crime Act 2002, the Money Laundering Regulations 2007 and the Terrorism Act 2000. This may include carrying out customer due diligence and ongoing monitoring. We may need to ask for information from you including information as to identity and ownership.

Until we receive this information and confirm that we're satisfied with it we may not be able to start acting for you."

Dealing with client money

7–25 Clients trust you to deal with their money. You'll receive mortgage funds to buy homes, a purchase price to buy a business, loan funds and compensation. You'll also manage executory funds until they're passed to a beneficiary. Your firm can deal in everything from tens of pounds to hundreds of millions (if not billions for the largest corporate deals). You need to reassure clients that their money is safe in your hands. While the Law Society account rules help to reassure clients that solicitors will follow a set procedure to keep their cash safe, it can also be worthwhile setting out in your business terms how you'll do that. A client may not know that you'll keep their money separately from the firm. They may also not know how you'll invest that money while you keep it. You want to confirm how it will be kept so that there is no argument later as to whether it should have received a higher interest rate, or been invested elsewhere.

A typical clause might say:

> "Any money we hold or receive on your behalf will be held by us in a separate bank account known as a client account. The client account will be held separately from the firm's money. We'll keep in touch to let you know how the money is invested and we'll account for any interest in accordance with the then current Solicitors (Scotland) Account Rules."

Limiting liability

7–26 There is a risk with every transaction that something might go wrong. It wouldn't be fair if your firm were potentially open to a limitless claim. Firms would stop taking clients if that were the case. Instead, to allow for a fair risk, firms can use their business terms to limit what might happen if something goes wrong. These limits tend to take two forms: a liability cap and/or disclaimers.

Liability cap

7–27 A liability cap limits the amount a firm will pay to its client if something goes wrong. The cap might be a fixed sum (e.g. £10 million); a percentage of the fee; fixed by reference to the firm's professional indemnity insurance so that it cannot pay out more than it's insured for; or by some other formula. A cap will be justified provided it has been agreed by the client and it's reasonable in the circumstance. This will depend on the level of the cap and transaction it applies to.

A typical clause is:

> "You acknowledge that any claim against this firm will be limited to the level of professional indemnity insurance cover held from time to time by us. We currently hold professional indemnity insurance cover for TEN MILLION POUNDS (£10,000,000)."

Disclaimers

7–28 A disclaimer doesn't just limit any amount a firm may need to pay. Rather, it excludes it altogether. As with a liability cap, to be effective, a disclaimer must be brought to the attention of the client and must be expressed in clear and unambiguous terms.

A typical disclaimer to limit losses to direct losses only is:

> "We do not accept responsibility for indirect, special or consequential losses."

Disengagement and non–engagement letters

Just as you write to a client to tell them what you'll do for them, it's important to also write to them to let them know when you're stopping acting for them. Disengagement and non-engagement letters refer to the situation where either you need to stop acting for a client (disengagement) or you decline to act for a client who has approached you (non-engagement). **7–29**

Disengagement letter

You may have a number of reasons why you need to bring a piece of business to an end. You may need to withdraw due to a conflict of interest or other professional obligation. You may want to stop acting if you've not been paid or you've not received money to pay other costs. Or you may simply have not received any further instructions to proceed and you want to close the file so you can move on. The Law Society advises that you should write to clients if you intend to close their file.[6] You should ask for instructions within a set period of time (if that's what you need) or advise the client that you intend to close the file. **7–30**

If you don't write to them then you may be left in a situation where the client thinks that you're still acting for them and then subsequently blames you if nothing else happens. A disengagement letter helps ensure that both you and the client are clear as to the current position of their work.

Non–engagement

Just as you want to tell a client that you're no longer acting for them so you'll want to tell potential clients if you can't act for them. Again there may be good reasons for this (for example, you may be conflicted). By politely telling them that you can't act, you're helping them find someone who can help. **7–31**

Summary

The law involves many complicated ideas and concepts. Taking an employer to court; buying a house; funding a business; writing a will; or trying to gain custody of children all involve laws, processes, people and places that clients are not familiar with. The engagement letter is their map. It's the starting point to guide clients through everything that could happen. As with the money laundering regulations, don't consider it another piece of mundane admin. It's more important than that. Driving a fast car is exciting but no one wants to be trapped in the passenger seat, not knowing where they're going. Help your clients by explaining what you'll do and how you'll do it by being smart with engagement letters. Give them a map and let them know where they're going and how they'll get there. **7–32**

[6] The Law Society of Scotland Practice Rules 2011 r.B4: Client Communication, Guidance related to Rule B4: Closing of Files. Available at *http://www.lawscot.org.uk/rules-and-guidance/section-b/rule-b4-client-communication/guidance/b4-closing-of-files/* [Accessed 19 April 2016].

Chapter 8

HOW TO WRITE TO CLIENTS

Introduction

8–1 *After writing an engagement letter, you give it to your partner to review. A couple of hours later and it's covered in red ink. Your partner explains that he's rewritten the letter in plain English, to make it easier for the client to read. "Clients don't like legal terms or long explanations", he explains, "you need to keep things simple, so she understands exactly what we're going to do for her. It's not an essay."*

8–2 Words matter. As a lawyer, you know this more than most. Not only do words have a dictionary meaning, they may also have a meaning derived from statute, case law or both. Your choice of words in some way defines you, because the majority of your work as a lawyer is spent writing emails, letters, contracts, initial writs, wills and other documents. Yet, it's the one skill that isn't taught at university. Furthermore, you won't find any guidance in the Law Society's rules and regulations beyond a nugget that says you must communicate appropriately with clients. What does "appropriate" mean? Does it cover *how* you write as well as *what* you write?

This is an important question. As we saw in the last chapter, Grant McCulloch believes that most client complaints stem from poor communication, rather than sub-standard service. This is reinforced by recent statistics. The Scottish Legal Complaints Commission (SLCC) has identified that almost 60% of service complaints (between 2009 and 2014) were due to poor communication.[1] If this is so, then improving your communication has to be one of the most important things you do. Clients want (and need) you to communicate effectively. Statistics demonstrate that you need to do all you can to avoid miscommunication. Clients want solicitors to help them, not put up linguistic barriers.

Remember, every time you write to a client you (clearly) know what you're talking about, but does your client? Has she spent four years at university? Does she know which laws apply to her? Or, do you need to explain even the basic concepts? Even if your client is a lawyer, she'll still appreciate a simple explanation more than one replete with legalese. As an experiment, we asked the in-house team of a large public limited company (Plc) for examples of poor communication, from their external lawyers. They sent us this:

> "The defender's agent advised the Court that the defender's position is that the Answers to the Counterclaim do not present a substantive defence to the counterclaim. The defender is maintaining his criticisms of our principal

[1] SLCC, *Five years on—facts and figures* (SLCC, 2013), available at *https://www.scottishlegalcomplaints.org.uk/media/47440/five_years_on_-_facts_and_figures.pdf* [Accessed 19 April 2016].

> claim and indeed the answers to the counterclaim, all as outlined in the defender's Note of Basis of Preliminary Plea and Supplementary Note of Basis of Preliminary Plea already forwarded to you."

They'd instructed a firm to recover money. The particular lawyer who received this missive isn't a litigator. They had no idea what it meant. What are "answers to the counterclaim"? Why don't they amount to a "susbstantive defence to the counterclaim"? What is the "counterclaim"? Do you think that this firm would be instructed again, given that no one knew what it had done?

This is why we cover off some basic tips to help you improve your writing. This is not intended to be a comprehensive guide to construction and grammar. We assume you know the basics. Instead, examine perhaps the main techniques used to make your writing easier to read, more direct and, most importantly, accessible to the greatest number of people. If you follow these steps you should never have a client phone you and complain: "I got your letter, but what does it mean?"

Outcomes

By the end of this chapter you'll have learned four tips to improve your writing, **8–3** including structuring your writing to make it easier for clients to understand what you're trying to say to them.

Readable writing

The Blah Story by Nigel Tomm is a 23-volume novel. It's notable for having the **8–4** longest sentence (and the longest word) in the English language, some 2,087,214 letters long. Here's an extract:

> "Blah intimidated, they blah to blah blah, where blah and blah passed a blah blah. Blah little blah that blah blah one blah surprised to blah what blah their blah were blah. . . [and on for over one million more words]".[2]

All in all, it has almost 12 million words, 70 million characters and 18 thousand pages. It was never a bestseller. However, for everyone who thinks *The Blah Story* is one of the worst books ever written, someone else praises its attempt to challenge our perceptions of literature, by making the reader fill in the blanks, or the "blahs". One person's great work of art is another person's kindling, because writing is subjective. Everyone has different styles and different tastes. Some only read 19th century French literature, others only read Batman.

That's why this chapter isn't going to teach you about good (or bad) writing. Instead, what we'll do is share four techniques to make your writing more readable. Readable is different from "good". Regardless of what you think about the literary qualities of *50 Shades of Grey*, or the latest Jack Reacher, you can't deny that they're easy to read. Here's the authors' favourite extract from "50 Shades" (as we call it): "I scowl with frustration at myself in the mirror. Damn my hair—it just won't behave".[3] It's easy to read, and readable writing is the reason why millions bought it, while *The Blah Book* is only printed to order. But why learn readable writing? What has readable writing got to do with being a lawyer? The

---

[2] N. Tomm, *The Blah Story* (BookSurge LLC, 2007), Vol.10, p.1.
[3] E.L. James, *50 Shades of Grey* (2011), p.1.

answer is simple. 90% of your life as a lawyer is spent writing on a computer. You meet clients, you make calls, you go to court and—for sure—you speak to colleagues, but the emails, letters and reports you prepare define your job. If you want to be good at your job you need to be able to write in a manner that the majority of your clients understand. Your hard work is meaningless if no one reads it. Or, worse still, it's read but without any understanding (i.e. it's regarded as "legal mumbo jumbo" or just "blah blah blah").

Take this extract from a client bulletin issued by a Magic Circle firm. The bulletin sets out to explain the difference between two common legal concepts, "reasonable endeavours" and "best endeavours":

> "Some important distinctions arise throughout the delineation of these two terms, yet equally, courts have often been reluctant to affix unqualified criterion, rendering some such distinctions imprecise."

We challenge anyone to understand this sentence without a clear head and a strong cup of coffee. Yet, this is a bulletin sent to clients, published on its website and—supposedly—meant to be helpful. It might be good legal writing and it might well be precise, but it sure isn't readable.

Tip one: write shorter sentences

8–5 This is perhaps the greatest opening sentence of all time. It's by Charles Dickens and it comes from *A Tale of Two Cities*:

> "It was the best of times, it was the worst of times, it was the age of wisdom, it was the age of foolishness, it was the epoch of belief, it was the epoch of incredulity, it was the season of Light, it was the season of Darkness, it was the spring of hope, it was the winter of despair, we had everything before us, we had nothing before us, we were all going direct to Heaven, we were all going direct the other way—in short, the period was so far like the present period, that some of its noisiest authorities insisted on its being received, for good or for evil, in the superlative degree of comparison only."

That's pretty good, isn't it? There's only one problem. It does go on a bit. It's over one hundred words long. We were bored by line three. We know it's considered a classic, but couldn't it just be a little shorter? How about: "Good times, bad times, just like today!" We're not saying that this is better than Dickens, but it does have a certain energy and directness that Dickens lacks. Arguably it's more readable, also, because you get the point without having to think about it as much. Some of the nuance and elegance is lost, but subtlety is what great literature is all about.

You, on the other hand, are writing to a client. You're not writing great literature. You don't need allegories, symbolism or a thesaurus (and your work should definitely be non-fiction). Instead, you need your work to be readable so that your clients understand you. The first lesson is a simple one. Short sentences are more readable than long sentences. How do you know if a sentence is too long? The trick is not to write with your hands. Instead, write with your ears. The simplest test of good writing is to read it out loud. If you're sitting in an office, perhaps do this under your breath so as not to disturb your secretary. You don't want to give her a fright when you start reciting:

> "It was the best of times, it was the worst of times, it was the age of wisdom, it was the age of foolishness, it was the epoch of belief, it was the epoch of incredulity, it was the season of Light, it was the season of Darkness, it was the spring of hope—[*BIG INHALE*]."

If you read what you write then you know immediately if any sentence is too long, because you'll run out of puff. How do you make your sentences shorter? The easiest way to write shorter sentence is take out all the "ands" and replace them with full stops. You'll make your work easier to say out loud, and to read.

Tip two: use short words

This leads to our second tip. Use one short word instead of three longer words. **8–6**
You might think you sound smart when you use big words. That's drummed into you since childhood. The more words you know the smarter you must be (like Stephen Fry). However, according to a study published in Applied Cognitive Psychology, the answer is an emphatic "no". Ironically, the title of the study was *Consequences of Erudite Vernacular Utilised Irrespective of Necessity: Problems with Using Long Words Needlessly.*

To be smart, you must stop *trying* to sound smart. Use short sentences and use small words like these[4]:

Long	**Short**
At that point in time	Then
By means of	By
By reason of	Because of
By virtue of	By/under
For the purpose of	To
For the reason that	Because
From the point of view of	From/for
In accordance with	By/under
In as much as	Since
In connection with	With/about/concerning
In favour of	For
In order to	To
In relation to	About/concerning
In terms of	In
In the event that	If
In the nature of	Like
On the basis that	By/from
Prior to	Before
Subsequent to	After
With a view to	To
With reference to	About/concerning
With regard to	About/concerning
With respect to	On/about

[4] This list was suggested by Richard C. Wydick in his excellent 1978 article "Plain English for Lawyers" (1978) 66 California Law Review 4, Article 3, p.731, available at *http://scholarship.law.berkeley.edu/cgi/viewcontent.cgi?article=2362&context=californialawreview* [Accessed 19 April 2016].

For more examples read any article or book that discusses plain English. We also recommend the *Guardian* and the *Financial Times* style guides. These set out how these publications use language.

Tip three: get to the point

8–7 Lawyers are bad at answering questions. It's not how we think. We prefer to set out arguments, a logical progression of thought and, finally, reach a conclusion. That's great for an essay, but awful in real life. Clients don't want to wade through your thought processes to get to the answer. They're shouting, "get to the point!" If you're "guilty", you don't want 10 pages telling you what happened. If your contract is unenforceable, you don't want 20 pages debating it. This doesn't mean you can't include some detail. Just be smarter about telling people what they want to know, first, and then tell them what they need to know (if they wish to read more).

Take Oscar Pistorius, the Paralympian athlete. He was accused of murdering his girlfriend. As you probably know, he was found guilty of culpable homicide, instead. If you remember the trial, this decision took two days to reach. If you face life imprisonment, would you want to wait two whole days before being told what will happen? Instead, the judge could say, "I have found you guilty of culpable homicide and here's the reasons why." Journalists don't think like lawyers. In fact, they think in the opposite way, and they give their readers all the information they need first. This is a technique known as the "inverted pyramid".

What is the inverted pyramid?

8–8 The inverted pyramid (also known as "front-loading") is a style of writing where you include the most important details in the first paragraph. This is particularly important for web writing, where readers have short attention spans and more often just scan articles. Pick any website, particularly news sites like the *Guardian, TMZ* and *Daily Mail Online*. Read the headline and first paragraph of any story. Then ask yourself if you know everything you need to know about the story? We bet the answer is "yes". The inverted pyramid has its roots in traditional media, dating back to the time of the telegraph and the early days of the newswire. One historian cites the reporting of the death of Abraham Lincoln in 1865 as one of the first examples of the inverted pyramid. *Associated Press* sent the following telegraph to all newspapers: "The President was shot in a theatre tonight and perhaps mortally wounded."

Contrast this with the *Daily Mail Online* story about the rapper, Kanye West (August 2015):

> "Kim for First Lady? Kanye West announces he's running for president in 2020 during epic MTV VMAs acceptance speech (but admitted he smoked a joint before going on stage)".

We've given you examples of two stories. They're completely different, but each tells you everything you need to know in just its first line. Abraham Lincoln was shot and mortally wounded in a theatre. Kanye may run for president (but he might have been high).

Let's pick another article. This story, about Ukraine, comes from *BBC News* (August 2015). The headline: "Russia sends 'aid mission' to Ukraine".

The first paragraph:

> "Around 300 lorries of humanitarian aid have left the Moscow area bound for eastern Ukraine, Russia has said."

The first paragraph gives us more information. 300 tonnes of aid had left Moscow, bound for Eastern Ukraine. Then come some critical words: "Russia has said". This is a story about Russia telling the world it's sending aid to Ukraine.

The second paragraph:

> "Russian media said the cargo, including hundreds of tonnes of grain, baby food, power generators and medicine, will go to the civilians trapped by fighting in the area held by pro-Russia rebels."

The second paragraph expands on the first. We now know that it's the Russian media that has made the claim that the cargo is aid for Eastern Ukraine. We know more detail about the aid; it's hundreds of tonnes of grain, baby food and generators. It also fills in detail about who is receiving the aid: civilians trapped in areas held by pro-Russia forces.

As you can see, each paragraph adds more detail. It expands on the snappy headline. It doesn't build to a conclusion like a legal essay or a judicial decision. Ask yourself, what do your clients read? Do they read websites, newspapers, magazines and books? Or, do they read case reports from the Supreme Court and legal textbooks by academics? Then reflect on whether you should write like a Supreme Court judge, or like a journalist writing an article.

What's the benefit of the inverted pyramid?

The main benefit is that the readers of a paper can glean the gist of an article by **8–9** reading only the first paragraph. This helps them to decide whether they want to read further. If they stop reading, they still have the key details of the article. From a writer's perspective, this style lets you engage your audience quickly and also to maintain their attention. In this age of short attention spans, readers are impatient, you need to get to your point quickly.

How do I write using the inverted pyramid?

This is easy to aspire to, but hard to achieve. If it were easy, we'd all do it natu- **8–10** rally. Before starting any writing ask yourself who your reader will be. Is it a single person or a group of people? What do they want to know? Do you have something to tell them? Do you need information from them? Whatever it is that you need them to know, make sure you get that message out in the first paragraph. Use as many of the five "w's" as you can (who, what, where, when, why), and also one "h" (how). By addressing these points, you probably have summarised the article as a whole, in a few sentences. If not, go back and rewrite your introduction so that it does.

When writing to a client, start with the most important information first. Then go on to include more detail, until you finish with the least important information. In other words, get to the point.

Examples of readable legal writing

Shorter sentences and smaller words

This is an extract from an article carried in *The Journal of the Law Society* **8–11** *of Scotland*. The first sentence is over 100 words long. What's more, the words "ratified" and "treaty" could puzzle some readers, as could the use of Latin phrases.

> "On the 300th anniversary of the 1707 Union the late David Walker, Regius Professor Emeritus of Law in the University of Glasgow, wrote in this Journal (June 2007, 14) an authoritative article in which he noted 'the continuing failure of the Westminster Parliament, and its advisers and draftsmen, to appreciate that the Union was made by a treaty within international law and merely ratified by the parliaments of the two uniting states under their domestic laws, so as to put themselves out of existence and create a new sovereign state in lieu' ".[5]

This sentence is difficult to digest.[6] However, remember, this isn't about good or bad writing, and indeed many international law experts would find this article perfectly okay. Andrew studied international law, and he can't wait to read the second paragraph, but even he realises it's not going to be an easy read.

Let's look at another example. This one is even more specialist: an article on tax rules for limited liability partnerships (LLPs). Here's the second paragraph:

> "This [consultation] focused on two perceived misuses of the existing partnership tax regime: first, removing the presumption of self-employment for those LLP members who are 'salaried members' in order to tackle the disguising of employment through LLPs; and secondly, counteracting the tax-motivated allocation of business profits or losses in mixed membership partnerships (typically a mixture of individuals and corporates)".

Let's apply our first two tips to this passage. Shorter sentences and smaller words would give us this:

> "The Government's consultation did two things. It removed a presumption that some LLP members were self-employed. It revised rules for allocating business profits or losses in mixed membership partnerships".

The longest sentence is 13 words, the shortest is five words long. It's not interesting, but this isn't about being interesting. Rather, it's about readability. We could go further:

> "OMG! OMG! OMG! You won't believe what the taxman's done to LLPs—he's ripped up the rulebook. You need to watch out. Don't tell him you're self-employed when we all know you're fibbing. Don't fiddle with your profits—you'll only get caught. He's on the war path."

Clients expect you to keep things professional, so perhaps this isn't the style you should use. However, it does demonstrate that it's possible to make even the driest subjects into something that can be read by anyone.

---

5 Iain Campbell, "The Union and the law revisited" (14 July 2014), The Journal of the Law Society of Scotland, *Journalonline.co.uk*, *http://www.journalonline.co.uk/Magazine/59-7/1014185.aspx* [Accessed 19 April 2016].

6 Of course, this article was written for a legal audience so it can be assumed to be more academic than a BuzzFeed article.

Get to the point

Let's look again at Slaughter & May's article. You need to explain to a client the difference between "reasonable endeavours" and "best endeavours". This is a fairly common question, when looking at a contract. This is how Andrew described it (in a contract with a landowner). He said: **8–12**

> "I recommend we (*who*) use 'reasonable endeavours' (*what*) to get planning permission for X houses by January 2016 (*when*). This is because (*why*):
>
> 'Reasonable endeavours' is the weakest of the weak. All we need to do is to show we've done something—anything—to get planning. Doesn't need to be much, it just needs to be relevant.
>
> 'Best endeavours' is homemade hooch. Avoid. You'll go blind. It says we'll do everything we can just short of bankrupting ourselves to get planning."

As you can see, the second and third paragraphs expand on the first. There is no need to explain what "reasonable" and "best endeavours" are before you recommend one. The developer may accept your recommendation without reading further. If they want to know more, they can read on.

Why you should use readable writing

It's just bad business to write badly. It's in everyone's interests that you communicate clearly so that your clients know what you're doing and what they need to do. If you don't, misunderstandings may occur, your client then is disappointed and you may lose business (or, worse, receive a complaint). **8–13**

You can even test this scientifically. Readability tests assess the reading age someone needs to be to understand your writing, on a first reading. You can find free tests online. Just search for "readability tests". They work in a similar fashion, by counting the variables that have the biggest impact on readers: sentence length, number of syllables per words, and the number of passive sentences. Each formula works things out in a slightly different way, but most allow you to copy and paste a bit of text. A typical magazine has a reading age of 10 (or secondary school), a typical legal bulletin has a reading age of 24 (or post-graduate study). If you want your writing to be universal, then you want to be nearer to 10 than 24.

File management

After writing to your clients you need to update your file. Your file, whether kept in a paper folder or stored electronically (on file management software like iManage or FileSite) is your record of everything that has happened. Although the Law Society has guidelines on how long you should keep your files once your work is complete, it doesn't have any practice rules setting out what you should do on a daily basis. We suspect this partly is because good file management depends on the work you do and the systems your firm uses. Some firms have IT systems that save all documents automatically, provided you include a file reference. Others still rely on paper files. Litigators may need files that store more than paper. Conveyancers need files for title documents. Projects lawyers need a system that doesn't require them to print their 200+ page contract every time a change is made. What works for one lawyer or firm may not work for another. **8–14**

Instead, we think that that advice given by Alistair Sim in 2000, in *The Journal of the Law Society of Scotland*, still best encapsulates it. He said that file management is "as much about good housekeeping and good management as it is about good legal advice". If files are being well managed:

- every file should be readily locatable;
- correspondence and documents should be neatly filed;
- time limits should be clearly noted and diarised; and
- all work should be regularly reviewed.

If all of that is being done, you're in control of your files and in a better position to cope with the more complex, technical aspects of client work. If these things aren't being done, you're not in complete control of your files. There then is a greater risk that:

- instructions will be overlooked;
- by relying on your memory, wrong assumptions will be made; and
- delays will occur and critical dates will be missed.

When you're in control of your files, your work is likely to be completed more efficiently and with less panic. Further, it is more likely that your clients will be kept updated regularly. What does "staying in control" mean in practice? It means nothing more than being disciplined about systems and procedures for opening, tracking, maintaining, reviewing and closing files.

Summary

8–15 Good writing is a joy, but we know it's a challenge. Five years of university is poor preparation for clear, direct writing. At university you're asked to write to a word count, and this can encourage padding. If you have 900 words written down, but a word count of 1000, you won't just leave in all the "ands", you may even add a few more. These are habits that you need to break. You're not writing for an academic, you're writing for a business woman who only reads the news on her iPad, a young father who left school at 16, a pensioner with poor eyesight—everyone, in fact, except that academic.

That's why we encourage you to apply our four tips to your emails and letters. Try writing an opening sentence that tells your client everything he or she needs to know. Check those words and phrases that can be shortened. Your clients will thank you and you'll avoid the sort of miscommunication that leads to client complaints.

Chapter 9

HOW TO SPEAK TO CLIENTS

Introduction

You re-write your engagement letter and your partner signs it without any changes. "It's good", he says, "you've covered everything the client needs to know in a way that she'll understand. The next thing you need to do is talk to her to get the instructions we need to move her claim along. You need to find out all the relevant information and also to guide her through the questions she'll need to consider, so that we can present her best possible case to the tribunal. Can you arrange to meet her?" 9–1

As we said in the last chapter, words matter. They matter not just when you write them but also when you speak. If you say the wrong thing, you can start wars. If you say the right thing you can make someone fall in love with you, and, while you shouldn't be starting wars or seducing people in the office, your words can have an equally powerful effect. Clients make life-changing decisions based on what you tell them. They'll change their plea and go to jail, they'll divorce partners, they'll cut family members out of wills, they'll sue for millions and change everything about their business based on what you say. That's why, in this chapter, we're going to help you work out what you should say to your clients (and others) and how you should say it. 9–2

Outcome

Speaking to clients involves a range of knowledge and soft skills. What follows is a mixture of theory, business advice and practical exercises, all of which are focused on helping you to develop an understanding of what you need to do to become better at speaking to clients, and managing and leading meetings. We look at the practical steps you should take before arranging meetings. We then look at how you should start meetings, listen and ask sensible questions, how to end meetings effectively and how to take the right actions afterwards. 9–3

Starting out

How do you start speaking to clients? It's easy. Just open your mouth and start talking. However, you're a professional, you have a reputation and you don't want to open your mouth and say just anything. Where do you start? 9–4

What is a client?

In this chapter we talk about speaking to (and meeting) "clients". However, our advice actually applies generally, for example to agents, intermediaries or other solicitors. We refer to clients only for simplicity's sake. 9–5

What is a meeting?

9–6 When we say "meeting", what do you think of? You probably think of two or more people sitting around a boardroom table. However, many meetings take place by telephone, conference call, video call, Skype and Facetime. The nature of meetings has changed. Equally, you might think that a meeting takes hours. This also has changed. Most modern meetings happen quickly. People don't want to sit or speak for hours. They've got other things to do and places to be. When we refer to meetings, we're referring to anything from a 30 second call to just one person, to all day meetings with 20 or more people in a boardroom.

Whatever type of meeting you have, you should prepare in the same way. You can make just as good or as bad an impression in 30 seconds as you can in a day. If you phone someone and get his or her name wrong, ask a stupid question or give them wrong information, you damage your reputation just as much as if you turn up at court without your papers.

How do you prepare for meetings?

9–7 You need to prepare. You need to know what you want to say before you walk into the boardroom, pick up the phone or connect to a video call. You should know why you're speaking to a particular client or contact, what you hope to achieve, what they want to achieve and how you wish to present yourself. There are some simple, practical steps you can take so that you don't make basic mistakes. For example, go to the right place at the right time; make sure you phone the right number; speak to the right person, and so on. These steps (and many others) are set out in the following table, and should be your starting point for all meetings.

Practical steps checklist

9–8

Confirm people	This may seem obvious, especially if you're only speaking to (or meeting) one person. However, as your meetings grow larger it's easy to miss people out. If you do, they may feel miffed and might become difficult, even if they agree with you.
Confirm time	For formal meetings and calls, confirm a date and time. Send a meeting appointment if you can, so that they can be added to diaries.
Confirm location	Confirm the location (whether physical, online or on the phone). Some law firms have more than one office in the same city (for example, Brodies has two offices in Edinburgh) so it's worth double-checking where you'll be.
Confirm meeting arrangements	If appropriate, provide map directions to your attendees, or instructions as to how to join your conference (or video) call. If you're driving, make sure you know when you need to leave to get to your meeting early. Most sat navs let you look up traffic problems and congestion, prior to starting your journey. If you don't have a sat nav then check Google maps for traffic information.

	If you don't know about parking arrangements, check to see where the nearest car park will be.
Prepare	Regardless of where your meeting is, review your notes, file and any legal aspects that might be relevant (we'll look at this in more detail, a little later).
Research	Do some basic research on the people you're going to meet, especially if this is a first appointment. Try and know the basics about everyone who's going to be there (right down to the PA). There are loads of resources to trawl, including Google, Twitter, Facebook and LinkedIn. Ask your colleagues, if you're meeting an existing client. We know of one property lawyer who invited a blind man to view a property. If only he had asked a colleague, he would have avoided an awkward faux pas.
Get ready	Pack everything you need to take with you well before you leave, to ensure you don't forget anything. Do this the night before if you've got a morning meeting, or first thing in the morning if it's an afternoon meeting.
Last minute check	Scan the news before you leave, to see if there's anything happening that might relate to your client's business/ industry. If there is, then you'll come across as sharp and savvy. If not, you'll still come across as sharp and savvy.
Be a good host	On the day itself, if you're meeting in your office, make available some refreshments e.g. tea, coffee, water and biscuits.
Don't be late	Most importantly, start on time. Clients can be late—you can't.

This checklist may seem overkill if you're just phoning a client. Do you need to confirm when you're going to speak and how you'll do it? We argue "yes". A former colleague started all his calls with, "are you free to speak?" and, while most times the client could speak straight away, the question would often be followed by, "when would be a good time to call you?" Equally, if you're making a call, you may only intend to ask your client one question. However, your client doesn't know that. He or she might take the opportunity to ask you about other matters. Having your client's file available (whether a paper copy or on screen), means you have the answers to hand.

Using our checklist (even for the simplest of calls) will help you develop good habits when meetings become longer, more complicated and involve more people.

What should you think about before a meeting?

Along with the various practical steps we've outlined, you should also think about **9–9**
what you want to get out of the meeting, what your guests want to achieve, and how you intend to carry yourself.

What's your purpose for speaking to the client?

Be clear in your mind why you're speaking to your client. If something ancillary **9–10**
comes out of it, that's fantastic, but have a clear objective. If you're meeting a client

for the first time, your main objective may be to get information from them. If you're phoning them to discuss a particular issue with a case, your objective may be to get instructions. More likely, your conversation will have multiple objectives (for example, to progress a particular business issue and also to develop your relationship with them). Consider how you might further both agendas in the one meeting.

What's in it for them?

9–11 We examine some possible benefits you can offer clients later, but for the moment just keep this in mind. Every client (existing or prospective) has an agenda. Spend as much time thinking about what your client will say, as you do in thinking about what you'll say. Consider the different ways your client might react to the information you're going to give them. Try and consider the business and/or personal pressures the client might be under.

How are you going to help them? You might be looking for instructions but they may want reassurance that they've done the right thing in even raising a claim, for example. They're often less interested in what you plan to do than in how confident you're about their prospects. A meeting that consists of, "well, we could do this or we could do that or we could do this other thing, what do you think?" won't reassure a client as much as, "you have two options. I will discuss both but I think the second will really raise the stakes for your employer and make them more likely to make you a cash offer."

How are you going to present yourself?

9–12 This links you back to your reputation (see Ch.5 (how do you build your reputation?)). How do you want a client to see you? Will you be happy and chatty, or serious and to the point? What is your personality and will it suit the meeting? A discussion about adoption is likely to require sympathy and empathy. A call to ask for money laundering information may require humour to point out the absurdity of asking a client who's been with the firm for 30 years to confirm his or her identity.[1] Equally, it's easy to be a nodding dog and agree with everything a client tells you, but are you prepared to act as devil's advocate and challenge their views? Are you willing to question assumptions? This can be the hardest part of taking meetings as a new lawyer.

Remember, you have a duty to offer independent advice and to act in your client's best interests. This sometimes means giving them bad news or disagreeing with what they tell you. This can difficult, at first, especially when you're trying to tell someone who may be a lot older than you that they're wrong. In these cases, a good way to approach this is to phrase your response in hypothetical language: "have you considered what will happen if that is not the case?" and, "let's assume for the sake of argument that you can't do that, we would then need to consider . . ." etc. Thinking not only about what you'll say but how you might say it, will make your meetings more effective.

Why you should meet clients

9–13 As a new lawyer, you might wonder why you need to meet clients at all. It can seem a distraction from getting on with the important contracts, cases and paperwork that "absolutely must go out this afternoon." This thought is short-sighted.

[1] Not that the money laundering regulations are absurd—but you'll find that many clients find them to be when asked for ID.

No one gets promoted because they can draft a contract without spelling mistakes. People get promoted because of their reputation, and that comes from what your clients say about you after meeting you and speaking to you.

Your benefits

You should see the benefits of meetings as: **9–14**

Enhanced confidence

Often new lawyers feel anxious. However, by regularly leading client meetings, you'll overcome (or at least control) your nerves. **9–15**

Develop your leadership and team working

When you take a client meeting, you are acting as a leader. You're leading a meeting by keeping to an agenda; shaping the meeting's structure and outcomes; asking questions; and bringing it to a conclusion. By taking meetings, you build up your leadership skills. **9–16**

Meetings also encourage teamwork. If you're working with a colleague (for example, a year one trainee) you're actually building and managing a small team in your meeting. After your meeting, you might have that trainee do some work. You'll certainly be asking your secretary to type up letters etc. In other words, you'll be delegating, which is a key management skill.

Networking

Every client meeting is a window to a potentially influential person. It's your chance to shine. You never know where your career might lead you. You're not just gaining exposure to your own network, you're also building connections with your network's network. If your client knows a third party who has a need that matches what you can offer, assuming you've made a good impression then you may get an introduction. **9–17**

Enhances your reputation

If you can upsell (and cross-sell) (see next section) you'll create a good impression in the eyes of your partner. You'll be seen as someone who can leverage increased business from existing clients and generate business from new clients. **9–18**

Meet targets

This is a related point. If you upsell, you generate more business for yourself and so you can more easily meet your billing targets. As young lawyers, this is a serious measurement of your performance. **9–19**

Firm benefits

There are also business benefits for your firm: **9–20**

Information sharing

This is a key advantage. It can be as simple as your client sharing updates about their business financials, new deals they're involved with, new start-up projects, and so on. With this information you can better judge if your clients are going to be **9–21** good prospects. Your firm might be able to get involved with their new projects. You might also get an early warning of any problems they're facing which might impact on them paying any outstanding fees (which, in turn, helps inform a decision whether to take on new work). They might inadvertently leak information about your competitors; you might get nuggets about the services they offer, their charge out rates, their relationship with clients and so on. If a client recently has used another firm, it's also your chance to ask them why. Why did they not come to you?

Upselling

9–22 Upselling is where you identify additional needs that your client might have and then you provide a service that fulfils them. For example, your client might ask you to draft a lease for a new rental property. What else might you ask them? What other services could you sell? He or she might need you to review the planning history of the property or check the property tax position. If you convince them that they need to cover these areas too, your £1,000 fee might just have trebled. But you can't really unlock that potential by email; you have to meet them to discuss what they need.

Cross-selling

9–23 Cross-selling is where you identify a client's additional needs and then you bring in someone else from another team within your firm to provide the service. You even, at a push, bring in an acquaintance from another firm altogether (for example, for specialist tax advice). It's basically upselling, but done horizontally as opposed to vertically. In other words, you don't get the extra business yourself. However, it still improves your firm's gross profit (either because it's getting to do the additional work or has charged a commission, if the work has been sub-contracted). It also helps to future proof your firm, because your client is tied in via multiple strands.

Let's assume that your client wants to lease a new property. However, you know that she wants the property in order to set up a new business. You persuade her that it would be safer for her to set up a new company to operate the business and take the lease. You can bring in a corporate colleague to help set up the company.

Downsides

9–24 While all this talk of new business sounds good, there are some downsides to taking loads of meetings, especially with potential clients. How so? Not every meeting leads to work and nor is every meeting even productive. Some clients like to talk, and if you phone them to ask a simple question you can still be on the phone 30 minutes later. Andrew had one client who he knew would take 45 minutes per phone call no matter the subject. If you're working on a fixed fee basis, you can appreciate how meetings like that eat into your time (and profit). On a related point, if you're meeting a potential client, you might be giving up (or deferring) meeting another potential client. If the meeting you take transpires to be a time waster, then you've missed an opportunity. This is an opportunity cost, and unfortunately it's impossible to value "what might have been".

Finally, just as your client might reveal a competitor's information in a way that benefits you, this can work both ways. That same client might be indiscreet about you. Again, it's a risk you need to weigh up.

Step one: prepare an agenda

You know the benefits. You've considered the checklist and you know what you want to say, how you want to say it and how a client might react. Let's consider in more detail the practical steps you can take to make your meetings more effective. A good first step is to prepare an agenda. An agenda is incredibly important because it lets you communicate important information about your meeting to stakeholders beforehand. **9–25**

In particular, an agenda:

- can be used as a checklist to ensure that all the required points are covered;
- can be used as a tool to help deal with disgruntled clients who complain, in the aftermath of a meeting, that certain points weren't discussed;
- lets clients know what's going to be discussed, giving them the opportunity to come prepared and better informed, which makes for more efficient meetings;
- provides a focus for your meeting; and
- gives you the opportunity to impose controls (especially relating to time, if you have other commitments that you can't change).

What should an agenda contain?

You understand how important an agenda is to the effectiveness of your meeting, but lots of lawyers don't know how to create one. Here are our eight top tips: **9–26**

- Send an email confirming your meeting, its goal (or goals) and all the administrative details (when, where etc.).
- Ask those invited to accept or decline the meeting. You can use free online applications, like Doodle, to help.
- Consider the agenda items you want to include.
- Ask everyone who's coming to contact you (say no later than two days before) with any agenda items they want to add.
- Once all agenda requests have been submitted to you, summarise them in a table format with suitable headings:

    a. agenda item;
    b. presenter (who'll lead the discussion on the point); and
    c. time allocated.

- Ensure each agenda item relates to the goals of your meeting. If an inappropriate request is made, suggest that this be discussed at another meeting.
- Be realistic. Don't cram too much into a one-hour meeting. When people (especially colleagues) accept a meeting, generally they expect to be finished on schedule. It's better to under-play the time available, leaving a small amount of time (say 10 minutes) to spare.
- Send your agenda to all participants the day before, with a reminder of the goals (also location, time and duration). At this point, check with the presenters (if there are any) that they're happy with the order in which they'll be speaking, and the amount of time they have been allocated.

Do you always need an agenda?

9–27 Yes. While you may not need to follow all eight steps to prepare for a simple meeting, it's still worth working through them, each time. You may not prepare a full agenda but you may want to write a couple of notes on your note pad as a reminder of what you'll say, what you need to cover and who you need to speak to. You can then refer to the note, to make sure that you get everything you need.

Working with colleagues

9–28 Don't forget to send your agenda to any colleagues if they're going to join your meeting. This is important because, not only will they want to know what you're going to talk about, it also helps:

- establish clear roles for each person—this avoids duplication and also the embarrassment of both of you talking over each other on the same points;
- identify someone to observe and take notes—this may be you in your first meetings as a trainee, and, if so, use this opportunity to observe how others act in meetings;
- consider whether the mix of your team members will provide a suitable range of knowledge and skills; and
- consider if everyone needs to be there—a common mistake is to invite everyone to a meeting when some people may only be needed for part.

Step two: starting meetings

9–29 Let's assume you've followed our suggestions thus far. You've arranged a meeting and you've thought about what you want say (and how you plan to say it). You've drafted an agenda and circulated it. You've turned up on time (ready and raring to go).

The next issue is, simply, how best to start. Take it as read that you need to smile and shake your client's hand. What we're getting at is what you should do once your client is ready to talk. Basically, your client wants to know two things. Firstly, why am I here? Secondly, why should I care?

Meeting steps

9–30 To help you answer these questions, there are four steps you can take. You should:

- inform;
- excite;
- empower; and
- involve.

Inform

9–31 This is where you let your client know the purpose of the meeting and the expected outcomes. An agenda really helps here. You can run through it and ask your client to confirm they're happy with it. If you don't have an agenda, you might say: "the purpose of this meeting is . . . when we're finished, we'll have achieved . . .".

Excite

9–32 You may have your client in the room, more in body rather than in soul. How do you excite them and get them really buzzed? You make statements that answer the question, "what's in it for me/why should I care?" Compare these two openings. Which does the better job of "exciting"?

Example 1:

> "Good morning, it's a pleasure to meet you. Let me start by reviewing why we're here. The purpose of this meeting is to sort out a draft will and power of attorney. I suppose you have to do these things, don't you?"

Example 2:

> "Good morning, it's nice to meet you. Let me start by reviewing why we're here. The purpose of this meeting is to sort out your new will and power of attorney. It's really important to do this because various tax rules have changed, and as a high net worth individual it's important you understand how these might impact on the distribution of your estate. It's also important that your loved ones can make decisions on your behalf when you're no longer able to. By the end of the meeting we'll have all the information we need to prepare the documents which will help protect you and your family."

The second is by far the better statement. It does a much neater job of describing various benefits to your client. Notice another thing: excite statements tend to contain a greater number of the words "you" or "your". They serve to tie a client into a meeting; they get the client excited about being there. In other words, the key to getting your clients excited about participating in a meeting is to explain clearly what's in it for them.

Empower

You describe to your client the role he or she will play during the meeting. The goal is to ensure that your client (or potential client) is clear on the power that they have. You see, when people feel empowered they tend to be much less hesitant about participating and are much more willing to open up and be collaborative. Remember, when a client starts talking you might also pick up information about your competitors. **9–33**

Often, a single empowering statement is sufficient. Other times you might find that multiple statements are needed to empower a client who is used to being told what to do (especially if it's a corporate client).

Examples:

> "Just stop me if you want me to go over anything, or explain anything."
>
> "You have a choice between court and arbitration. As I explained, a court could be costly but it will provide a definitive answer. Arbitration is cheaper but there's no guarantee it will work. Which option do you prefer?"

Involve

Get your client involved immediately using a so-called "engagement question" that furthers the meeting purpose. Why? This engages them and helps achieve "buy-in". There are a few different ways you can do this. **9–34**

- Key topics approach: you think about the purpose of your meeting and build a list of key topics with your client. You might say, "if we're going to be successful today, what do we need to talk about? Let's make a list first so we have a checklist of what we'll need to cover today."

- Personal outcomes approach: you visualise how a successful meeting would go. You might say, "given your objectives, what are the outcomes you personally would like to see come out of today's meeting?"
- One-minute check approach: this works well if you meet a client regularly. You could say, "it's been several days since we were all together. Let's start with each person giving a quick update from the last time we met." While another option might be, "we were last together on 1 December. Since then, there probably have been some significant events that have occurred. Can you update me?"

Step three: listen and ask questions

9–35 Once you've started a meeting you should be using your listening and questioning skills to help you get the information you want.

Listening skills

9–36 The following exercise (for which you'll need a friend to volunteer to help you) demonstrates just how critical it is to listen.

Get your friend to go away and prepare a short, three-minute talk. He or she will speak to you about something that has interested them recently (be it an experience, their last holiday etc.). While they speak, every time something interesting arises (that makes you want to ask a question or makes you tempted to react in some way), raise your hand for five seconds and then put it back down. Do this throughout the entire conversation. You're not allowed to interact with your friend. You can't ask questions, nor can you affirm your understanding. You must remain totally silent. As well as raising your hand, try deliberately to lose focus. You can do this by staring out the window, or by becoming transfixed with a detail on their jacket. The aim is to create a distraction to your listening.

Once the three minutes are up, ask your friend how they felt talking to you. What emotions were evoked? You can expect answers to include statements like, "I didn't feel listened too", "I didn't understand why you were putting you hand up", or "you distracted me." Try repeating this exercise a few times with different people. You'll come to appreciate why active listening is important.

Questioning skills

9–37 This next exercise demonstrates why good, open questions are essential if you're going to elicit information. In fact, developing a list of possible questions is something you can (and should) do as part of your pre-meeting preparation.

Firstly, think of a famous person (but clearly don't tell your friends who it is). Start a timer. Each of your friends then asks closed questions, in turn (for example, "are you a man?" or "are you an actor?"). Their aim is to work out who you're. Gradually, they'll narrow the possibilities and eventually arrive at the correct answer. This illustrates a point: closed questions get you nowhere (fast) if you want to gain information.

The second part of the exercise is to put your friends into pairs. Each of you then has 60 seconds (in your pairs) to take turns in asking open questions of each other. The aim is to find out five things about the other person, in the time available. Make sure you write them down.

What you'll tend to find with these short exercises is that if you ask open questions you get lots of information, in a short period of time, compared to the amount of time it takes to find out just one piece of information using closed questions.

What are close-ended questions?

Close-ended questions are those that can be answered by a simple "yes" or "no". "Did you get here by car?" "Would you like a cup of tea?" These can be answered with a yes or no. If your client arrived by train and would prefer a coffee, your conversation will seem curt if they keep saying "no". **9–38**

What are open questions?

Open-ended questions are those that require more thought, and certainly more than a simple one-word answer. "How did you get here today?" "What do you like to drink?" Your client can give you more information. "I got the train from Edinburgh as the roads were gridlocked" or "could I get a coffee, no milk or sugar?" **9–39**

These are simple examples, but the distinction becomes important when you're trying to get information from a client. You want to start by asking open questions, such as "how can I help you today?" and "is there anything else I should know?", so that you can find out as much information as you can. You only ask closed questions if you want to confirm something specific. Here's an example:

> "How can I help you today?"
>
> "I've recently been made redundant by my employer and I don't understand why they've done this."
>
> "Who is your employer?" (Asking for specific information.)
>
> "Company X."
>
> "And what do you think they've done wrong?" (Opening up the conversation again to try and understand how the client thinks.)

Step four: non-verbal communication

This is an incredibly important aspect of your behaviour. We communicate non-verbally all the time. Non-verbal communication includes: eye contact, body language, facial expressions, mirroring, approach, face to face (proximity), senses and silence. Let's run through each of these. **9–40**

Eye contact

It's really important for sincere communication that you give your client your complete attention. For this you need lots of appropriate eye contact. This shows not only respect but also helps you connect to that person. **9–41**

Body language/facial expressions

When we communicate with people, they derive information in the following proportions: **9–42**

- 7%—words;
- 38%—vocal characteristics (tone, volume, inflection); and
- 55%—body language and facial expressions.

Does your face match your words? When you aren't speaking, what does your face say to those around you? You have to match your body language with your intent. Know that your client is always watching you, albeit he or she might be speaking.

Approach/proximity

9–43 Both are forms of communication. Clearly, you should approach everyone from the front and be aware of just how close you are when speaking, especially when someone is seated. Applying that to meetings, don't ambush your client and make sure that the meeting space is set up appropriately.

Senses

9–44 Again, just be aware that you can communicate with other senses: smell, sight and taste. What do you think we mean by smell and sight? Keep stocked up on soap and shampoo, and make sure you're well turned out. This might sound like something your mum would say but she says it because she's right—and it's just as true in the office.[2]

Silence

9–45 Silence is unsettling. You might have seen psychological research that shows that people tend to jump in to fill silences. If you're trying to get information out of a client during a meeting this can be a useful tool, but its best avoided in other circumstances as it can make people feel uncomfortable. It's also worth using sparingly otherwise people will just think you have nothing to say if you fall silent every five minutes.

Step five: ending meetings

9–46 Earlier we said that an agenda is a really useful tool to help you to end your meetings on time. After all, you've got other things to deal with. You are busy people. Ending a meeting on time also educates your client that your time is valuable. How do you do it without appearing to be rude? When you feel that all the business aspects have been dealt with, consider these different approaches to end on a positive note:

Verbal cues:

- reassure your client they're on the right track;
- perhaps congratulate them on their decision;
- explain the next steps;
- mention each agenda item and review the decisions made, or actions required; or
- make a defined closing statement, like "I've got one final question before you leave . . .".

---

[2] Just read this question to Ask Ash in The Journal of the Law Society of Scotland: "Ask Ash" (19 March 2012), *Journalonline.co.uk*, *http://www.journalonline.co.uk/Magazine/57-3/1010933.aspx* [Accessed 19 April 2016].

Give physical cues:

- close your file and move it off to the side;
- extend your hand for a handshake, giving a verbal cue (like "thank you for coming in today");
- change the subject to something generic, like the weather; or
- as a last resort, stand up and your client (should) follow your lead.

Step six: after the meeting

Arguably this is the most important step. If you don't do what you say you'll do, you undo all your good work. Imagine meeting a lawyer who is charming, smart and knows exactly what you need to do. Imagine that lawyer not doing anything for six months. What do you think of them now? **9–47**

After the meeting may be the final step yet it's so often forgotten. It includes:

- dictating the minutes of your meeting (or write a file note);
- working out your next actions;
- working out any actions that your client needs to take;
- reviewing any deadlines;
- writing to your client, setting out the agreed next steps (with timelines);
- putting key dates in your diary (e.g. intimation dates etc.);
- allocating work across your team (if necessary); and
- arranging your next meeting.

Minutes/file note

You need to record the discussions that take place in every meeting, as well as all the decisions reached. It's important to detail, also, any disagreements (especially if you have recommended a course of action that your client has overruled). It's important to set down tasks that need to be actioned. This should include what the task is and can also include what the outcome of that task will be (e.g. a document, a report etc.). It's essential to record the name of the person who is assigned to a particular task. **9–48**

But a word of advice—there should only ever be one person responsible for actioning an item. A date for the completion of each task should be recorded. This will remind the task owner that it has to be finished by a set date. It also allows you, as the owner of the legal project, to check on progress.

Delegation

Delegation is a managerial skill. We deal with it in depth in Ch.16 (how to delegate work), so we're going to limit ourselves to a few basic words of advice. If you're going to delegate tasks that arise in the course of a client meeting, you need to think about your team member's suitability. Think about whether he or she has the knowledge, skill and experience to do what you're asking of them. If not, consider whether there is time to put in place appropriate training. If not, it ought instead to be completed by someone that already has experience. Delegation, if done properly, is an excellent way to motivate your team and give people a sense of responsibility. When we say "properly", you need to remember that what **9–49** you're delegating is the authority to do something. You're not delegating your responsibility; you remain accountable for what they do.

Summary

9–50 Meeting clients (and contacts and other solicitors) is an essential part of being a lawyer. Every case has at least two people. Every house sale has a seller and a buyer. Every lawyer has a client. You'll always need to speak to someone—and the more you prepare the better you'll be.

CHAPTER 10

HOW TO NEGOTIATE

Introduction

You've met your client. You've raised her claim and immediately received some good news. Her former employer is prepared to settle and pay compensation. Their lawyer sends you a compromise agreement, to confirm the terms and compensation. However, your partner takes one look at it and shouts, "completely unacceptable!" He tells you to, "arrange a meeting with their lawyer and negotiate better terms. Our client can do much better than this." **10–1**

Over the course of your career, you'll be asked to negotiate lots of agreements and documents. It might be a settlement offer; a contract; financial matters following a divorce; a commercial deal; a personal injury claim; or a lease for a new property. Whatever it is, you'll be asked by clients to negotiate on their behalf. **10–2**

In many ways a negotiation is just like any meeting: it could take place in the formal setting of your boardroom, or it could be a 30 second telephone call. Just like in the last chapter, while the format can change, the principles remain the same. You'll either be trying to persuade someone to accept what you say, or you'll be trying to reach an acceptable compromise.

In our scenario, your client has been offered £20,000 by way of compensation, but has been asked to sign a restrictive covenant that will prevent her working for a rival firm for five years. Your client is happy to accept £5,000 in compensation (as she has raised her claim as a point of principle), but wants to start work after six months. You have parameters in which to negotiate and, while you know where you want to end up, it's up to you how you get there. Do you offer £5,000 straight away? Do you ask for more (say £10,000) and see how they respond before moving to your actual position? Tactics matter and, depending on what tactics you use, they could mean the difference between reaching agreement, accepting less or, ultimately everyone walking away. As a new lawyer, negotiations can be daunting, but if you follow the principles set out in this chapter you'll know how to prepare and how to handle yourself, so that you can achieve the best results for your client.

Outcomes

This chapter looks at the theory and practice of negotiation. We explain what we mean by negotiation and we look at the tactics and skills required to negotiate successfully. **10–3**

Negotiations basics

Those new to negotiation are often anxious about a lack of experience. If that's you, relax. In actual fact, everyone has some experience of negotiation: **10–4**

- when you buying something from Gumtree ("I'll give you £90 instead of £100, and I can come round tonight and pick it up");
- when you haggle over a bill with friends ("I should pay less as I didn't have any cocktails");
- when you were young and wanted to stay out late ("If I can stay out until 11pm I promise to keep my mobile switched on at all times");
- when you're older and married, and still want to stay out late ("If I can stay out until 11pm I promise to keep my mobile switched on at all times"—this never changes);
- when on holiday, bartering in a street market; or
- negotiating your new mobile phone contract when you need to decide between different options.

In other words, the fact that you might never have led a formal negotiation is not something to worry about. You already know how to negotiate. You do it all the time. But what is negotiation?

What is negotiation?

10–5 Negotiation is what happens when people who disagree try and agree something together. If you prefer a formal definition then negotiation is the process by which you seek to achieve a mutually beneficial agreement on a matter (or a number of matters) with someone else (your opponent, if you will). This other person will have different needs and goals to you and negotiation is the process by which a compromise is reached. Every negotiation is unique. Each differs in terms of its subject matter, the number of participants and your approach. One day it's Gumtree, the next it's a multi-party compromise agreement. Regardless, your approach should be the same.

Why negotiate?

10–6 Good negotiations contribute to your success in any business (not just the law). Firstly, they help to create enduring, mutually respectful relationships and, secondly, they enhance existing relationships. In other words, if you get your negotiation right, your opponent will be much more inclined to do business with you in the future. It's worth remembering that Scotland has a small legal profession, so if you're a nightmare to deal with or if you use underhand tactics other lawyers will talk about you. You want to be someone who, when named, others lawyers say, "they're good to deal with" and not, "oh no, not them."

Where do you start?

10–7 In terms of procedure, negotiations are incredibly flexible. You're free to shape them in accordance with your needs and those of your opponents. You and the other parties may want a formal meeting, or you may just want a phone call. It's entirely up to you to agree. What you'll find is that formal meetings happen less and less. A lot of documents are negotiated by phone or email before any meetings take place. We've assumed in this section that you're preparing for a meeting, but the tips are just as relevant for email and phone calls. You may not go into as much detail, but the process is a good one to know. Better to know too much and to cut down what you need, than to know too little and miss something.

In terms of representing clients, you need to be clear about your mandate to lead any negotiation and also about your opponent's authority. Do you have the power, either within your firm or from your client? Always be wary of negotiations involving companies and their agents. Your opponent needs to have express or implied authority from the company he or she claims to represent. In other words, do they have the power to broker a deal, or not?

What do you need to watch out for?

No negotiation can guarantee the good faith or trustworthiness of its participants, **10–8**
though you can reasonably expect every lawyer to act in good faith (if they're to meet professional standards). Some clients however may say "black is white" and "white is black" to get a deal done (and then completely ignore everything you've agreed). If you have clients like that, you need to make sure that you maintain your own standards by remaining objective. You'll have many clients but you only have one reputation.

An example of bad faith would be to use a negotiation as a stalling tactic, either to delay you or your client from moving forward with, for example, litigation. Usually this becomes apparent, as meetings will rehash the same issues again and again. If this happens, you either call the other side on it by asking, "do you actually want to do a deal?" or you revert to your Plan B and continue with your client's claim.

Finally, you need to understand that some issues simply are unable to be negotiated. There is little chance of an agreement if, for example, you and your opponent are divided by diametrically opposed beliefs which leave no room for concessions. It's possible that from time to time your negotiations might just break down. The absence of a neutral third party as arbiter sometimes results in parties being unable to reach an agreement, because quite simply they might not be able to work co-operatively. What's more, that lack of an arbiter might actually encourage your opponent to be overly aggressive, in an attempt to take advantage of you.

Successful negotiation

It's fair to say that a successful negotiation is one that: **10–9**

- generates the best possible deal in the circumstances;
- avoids litigation;
- achieves a workable, lasting agreement;
- establishes or maintains a client relationship; and
- maintains professional standards and ethics.

Interests v positions

A key point when working towards a successful outcome is to understand the **10–10**
difference between interests and positions.

Many commentators believe that negotiations stand a much greater chance of success when parties adopt an interests based approach. If you focus on mutual needs and interests, and use objective standards (as opposed to subjective standards), there is a greater chance of reaching an agreement that meets the needs of both you and your opponent. This is sometimes called a "win-win" approach.

What's the difference between interests and positions? Interests tend to be long-term. They relate to your overall situation, and might develop and change over time. Positions, by contrast, tend to be short-term and focused more specifically (indeed, narrowly) on a particular issue. Let's look at a simple example. A plumber is needed to do a job in a hotel. The plumber wants a minimum of £100 to put down his remote control on a wild and windy night; the hotel is willing to pay a maximum of £100. In this case the positions are the same and a deal can be struck. What if the hotel has a policy of paying only £80 in call out charges? If this negotiation were purely positional (specifically cash positions), there could be no agreement. The plumber would simply say no. However, the plumber has a wider interest, namely developing his business. If the hotel were to take the plumber's interests into account it could offer, for example, to put him on its approved suppliers list. This would cost the hotel nothing but might allow it to fulfil its interests too i.e. having its premises maintained in good order.

Let's look at our example. Your client is young and she has a long career ahead. She doesn't mind taking a short break, as long as she receives some compensation. Equally, she doesn't want her employment restricted for five years as that would affect her career prospects. Her long-term interest is to win her case, but not have it affect her career. A short-term position (to win £20,000 at all costs) will not help her achieve that. While she might get £20,000, she may live to regret it. However, were your client in her 60s and not bothered about another job, her interest would be to get as much money as possible to help her retirement. She would be willing to sign anything to get £20,000.

Understanding your client's interests helps you judge whether their stance is likely to be helpful. When advising them you can say, "I think this is a good offer because it will give you a good nest egg for retirement and you won't have to give up anything important in return" or "I think this is a bad offer because while it's a big amount now, think about what will happen in two or three years. You still won't be able to work in a similar job—and £20,000 doesn't stretch that far."

Ethics

10–11 We've touched on professional standards and ethics. Remember, as a solicitor you have ethical obligations that include, for example, an obligation not to mislead fellow solicitors. You must bear this in mind, if negotiating with another solicitor on behalf of a client.

Turning to corporate bodies, since the inception of the Companies Act 2006 s.172, directors must promote the interests of their companies in good faith. This includes having regard to:

- the likely consequences of any decision in the long term;
- the interests of the company's employees;
- the need to foster the company's business relationships with suppliers, customers and others;
- the impact of the company's operations on the community and the environment;
- the desirability of the company maintaining a reputation for high standards of business conduct; and
- the need to act fairly as between members of the company.

These arguably can be said to be a form of corporate "ethics". It may be that your firm is a limited company, in which case you're bound by the terms of s.172. Corporate clients, almost certainly, won't be impressed if you behave unethically acting on their behalf. We repeat again, clients may be unethical—but you can't be.

Style

You can be two main types of negotiator. The first is a co-operative (interest based) negotiator who: **10–12**

- tends to be friendly;
- tries to avoid conflict; and
- makes concessions to reach an agreement.

Is this you?

The co–operative negotiator

This sort of negotiator always starts from the premise that negotiations need not be "zero sum" (i.e. the gains of one party shouldn't be at the expense of the other party). Mutual interests are identified and objective standards are used. The goal is to reach an agreement acceptable to all participants. **10–13**

You know that your client's employer doesn't want her to start working immediately for a competitor. You know that your client is happy to take a short break. When you propose a one-year break (and they propose three) you might ask questions about which competitors they don't want her to work for. From this, you can identify that they're only concerned about her working for their main rivals. Perhaps, then, your client might indicate that she has no intention of working for those firms and is happy to accept a longer restriction for those two, provided she can work for other firms after one year.

If you adopt this approach, it has the advantage of creating joint benefits. However, some disadvantages are: your concessions might not generate agreement; you might be vulnerable to exploitation and might not recognise it when it happens; your opponent may think you're not "fighting their corner" and regard you as weak; or you might react emotionally to your opponent's competitiveness and "lose face". Allied to this is the concept of the principled negotiation. Those who favour principled bargaining believe that being positional can lead to situations where parties will be stubborn ("hard bargaining") or accept big, unilateral losses ("soft bargaining") in order to reach agreement. Principled bargaining attempts to reconcile the interests underlying the positions. This form of negotiation is increasingly popular. It could be called co-operative "plus".

The competitive negotiator

The second type of negotiator is the competitive negotiator. This type of negotiator: **10–14**

- treats opponents as adversaries and they play to win;
- keeps the pressure on;
- can be perceived as quite threatening; and
- demands concessions, yet makes no concessions.

Is this you?

If you adopt this approach, you try to maximise your advantage at the expense of your opponent. Mutual interests are eschewed, in favour of a positional stance. The advantage of this approach is that it minimises the risk of exploitation. The main disadvantage, however, is that increased tension (caused by brinkmanship) inhibits the mutual trust that is required to unlock joint gain. This tends to cause a breakdown of negotiations.

Let's go back to our example. Let's say you insist that your client wants £20,000 and a one-year restriction, or else you'll take her claim to the employment tribunal (which will be public and could be bad PR for her employer). Even if the employer responds with—say—£10,000 and a one-year restriction, you still push for more, and that's when they walk away.

A further disadvantage is that, over time, your reputation for being competitive precedes you and you tend to conclude fewer deals. Why? Past opponents are less inclined to do business, as they don't see any advantage in negotiating with you.

The steps to negotiation

10–15 A great negotiation involves lots of preparation and planning, both on your own and with your team. You need to marshal all your facts and arguments. During a negotiation you'll need to question your opponent, listen, think and even discuss various matters with your team (and client).

Step one: process v act

10–16 Firstly, you should treat negotiation as a process rather than an act. Processes can take place over a period of time, or last just a single session. They're inherently flexible. If you view negotiation as an act you'll tend to consider it a "one off" and immediately be time-bound, putting yourself under pressure to conclude an agreement in one session. That, in turn, can encourage you to be positional. Positions, after all, can be accepted or rejected quite quickly. Interests, on the other hand, can take time to be fully articulated, explored and aligned.

Think about Prime Minister David Cameron's re-negotiation of Britain's EU membership, in February 2016. This was not a one off process. He'd met repeatedly the other European leaders in the run up to the final meetings. He'd spent time speaking to every interested party to test what he would offer and what they would accept in return. The final meetings themselves took three days to complete (with offers and counteroffers). Whether you think the outcome was successful is a matter for your own personal politics. However, in terms of process, Cameron treated the negotiation as a process lasting several months and not just a single meeting in February 2016. You can learn a similar lesson in even the simplest of negotiations.

Don't assume that one meeting will deal with all points that might need to be negotiated. You and your client (and the other party and their solicitor) may need to reflect on what was said and what was offered. You may want to change your position based on what you learn.

Step two: assessment

10–17 Your negotiation begins with a communication (either from you or your opponent) indicating a willingness to bargain. Since negotiation is a voluntary process, the first step has to be to assess whether your opponent is serious.

Factors that might help you make that assessment are:

- whether a negotiated solution is in their interests;
- their credibility (perhaps elicited from previous dealings);
- whether there's a disparity such that it would be impossible to negotiate equally; and

- whether that person has the authority to enter into negotiations and to conclude an agreement (especially if they're representing a company).

Step three: practical steps

Once you've green-lit a negotiation, you need to start preparing. **10–18**

- Agree the purpose of your meeting. What are you intending to achieve? What is the scope of the negotiation? Is this a preliminary meeting, or is it being held with a view to concluding an agreement?
- Agree an agenda. This brings a structure to your negotiation. It also helps you exercise control. You don't want to be taken by surprise and forced into a bargaining situation where you feel you need more time or information.
- Agree a timetable. Remember, a negotiation is a process (not an act). What will the frequency of your negotiations be, and how long will they last?
- Work out who will be present at the sessions.
- Choose a venue (preferably a neutral location).

Getting the preparation right is not only good business practice, but also helps to reinforce your credibility (and thus contributes to establishing confidence and trust).

Step four: preparation

The next step is to plan your strategy. Thorough preparation is the key. In no particular order, you need to: **10–19**

- marshal your arguments;
- find out as much as possible about your opponent (including any information about how they have conducted negotiations in the past);
- ensure that everyone in your team is on the same page (internal disagreements work against you by undermining your authority);
- work out what questions you might ask;
- anticipate the questions you'll be asked and work out how you'll handle difficult questions;
- decide how your negotiation will be handled—will it be just you talking, or will your colleagues contribute?;
- consider when and how you'll call a private team meeting (a "time out") that will interrupt the negotiation (this might be appropriate if a new issue emerges);
- consider how best to play to your strengths and to exploit your opponent's weaknesses;
- remember that your opponent will have "monkeys on his or her back" i.e. the external pressures that are on a person to reach an agreement; and
- check if there are any critical dates you will need to know.

Step five: consider your BATNA

You need to give consideration to your best alternative to a negotiated agreement (your so-called "BATNA"). BATNA is a benchmark that protects you from accepting terms that are too unfavorable, but also from rejecting terms that would be in your interest to accept. **10–20**

Quite simply:

- if a proposed agreement is better than your BATNA, you should accept it;
- if a proposed agreement is worse than your BATNA, you should continue your negotiations; and
- if you cannot improve the proposed agreement, you should consider withdrawing from negotiations and pursuing your BATNA.

Having a well worked out BATNA increases your negotiating power. If you know that you have a really strong, viable alternative, you don't need to concede as much and—in fact—can push your opponent harder. Why? You simply won't care to the same degree as you would if you didn't have that great alternative.

If your BATNA isn't strong, however (or if it's non-existent), your opponent will be able to make demands that you'll likely have to accept, because you don't have a better option. Let's assume your client is broke. She owes £5,000 on credit cards, £2,000 on her overdraft and is three months behind on her mortgage. This example also shows the importance of timescales and key dates. If your client has a mortgage to pay and no money to pay it, this limits your tactics.

The opposite is true, too. Your BATNA may make it easy to negotiate. Your client may be a millionaire. She's not suing for the money, but instead for principle's sake: employers should not get away with treating people unfairly. While not her first option, she might be happy to see the case go to a tribunal and have it heard in public, so that people can find out how her employer has acted. Her BATNA means that if she's offered an unattractive deal, she's able to reject it, even if it risks a breakdown of the process.

It's important to improve your BATNA wherever possible. If your BATNA is strong then it's worth revealing it to your opponent, early on in the negotiation. If it's weak, it's much better to keep it quiet. Always try and work out what your opponent's BATNA might be.

Step six: the negotiation

10–21 What follows are our top tips for the negotiation, itself.

- Agree the facts. This helps to foster a spirit of co-operation and also ensures that you're not working at cross-purposes.
- Agree common interests. The objective here is to make everyone feel that they're striving towards a common goal (that is, if you're being a co-operative negotiator).
- Question and listen. Negotiation requires great questioning and listening skills. Using them effectively helps you obtain extra information and also lets you assess how your opponent is approaching the negotiation. Listen for clues as to what your opponent's interests are, and to what they might be prepared to agree. Often, if you just listen, people give away more than they intend to.
- Before you amend your position on any point, consider why you're doing so. Try not to move unless you're sure there is a positive benefit.
- If you're negotiating several terms, think of them as a package, like "juggling balls" in the air. There is a benefit in playing different terms off against each other. However, if you let your opponent negotiate each term

individually and sequentially, you can't revisit them later (without looking unprofessional).

- Summarise and recap regularly. This helps you to slow the pace down and take back control (which is useful if you need some breathing space and/or thinking time).
- Record your agreement. This seems obvious, but a note summarising the points that have been agreed is always worthwhile.
- After the event, analyse your negotiation. Think about what you thought would happen and what actually happened. Why did things perhaps turn out differently (whether or not in your favour) and how could you manage the process better the next time?

Step seven: the offer

This is the big one. At some point in your negotiation, someone is going to have to make an offer. The timing of that offer, and the question of which party should make it, is often determined by the overall dynamic of a particular situation. However, if you end up breaking the ice, always give your reasons first and then make your offer. If you do it the other way round it weakens your position, because it appears apologetic. It then seems to your opponent that you're justifying yourself (or making an excuse). In response to your offer, you should always be able to answer the question "why?", or "how did you arrive at that figure?" To be credible, it's best to be able to refer to objective criteria. For example, you could refer to similar products, previous agreements your firm (or your client) has entered into, current market practices and so on. **10–22**

It's also worth considering making a hypothetical (rather than a real) offer. This means if you make a proposal you should be able to retract it, if it's rejected, without revealing your true position (or having to reveal you were bluffing). The following two examples demonstrate the difference.

Example one

You tell the employer's solicitor that your client is prepared to accept a two-year restriction and £10,000 compensation. You've told your opponent two things: the length of the restriction and the amount of compensation that your client is willing to accept. They could say, "we'll accept a two-year restriction but we can only offer £5,000." But when you say you'll accept £5,000 in return for a one-year restriction, they'll likely say, "you've already admitted that your client can accept two years, so we're only negotiating on price now." **10–23**

Example two

You tell the employer's solicitor that *if* the employer were to offer a two-year restriction *and* £10,000, *then* your client would consider it. If they offer £5,000 and try to hold you to two years, this time you can ask for one-year. You can justify it because you've linked your position to a hypothetical offer, and you said only that your client would *consider* it, not accept it. **10–24**

Finally . . .

Throughout your negotiation, remember to remain within the limits of your authority (or your client mandate). Ensure that there's constant communication with your client (if applicable). You must be certain that you've specific **10–25** instructions as to whether to conclude a proposed agreement. At the end of the day, it may become necessary to end negotiations, having carefully examined your BATNA and concluded that this is the best course of action.

Troubleshooting

10–26 There are some common issues that crop up in negotiations that are worth considering. These are teamwork and standard negotiating tactics.

Teamwork

10–27 If you're working with others in a team, always resolve disputes well away from the negotiating table. You must avoid revealing any hint of disharmony to your opponent through body language. Brief your team to keep their poker faces on, at all times.

This can also apply to your client. You don't want your client looking at you in surprise when you make your latest offer or, worse, saying something along the lines of, "I said I didn't want that much" or "why are you asking for that?" Make sure they know how you want them to react. An unpredictable client can work in your favour. Andrew had one meeting with a client who threatened to throw himself out of a top floor window unless the lawyers "got a bloody move on." What was turning into an all-day meeting was then wrapped up in 30 minutes. We don't recommend this as your standard tactic though.

Standard negotiating tactics

10–28 Your opponent may try to use a variety of tactics to obtain an advantage. These might include pressure tactics (attempting to force you to accept specific terms), intimidation (implicit or explicit), ambiguity about the scope of their mandate, and even unethical behaviour (e.g. misleading you), though they shouldn't, as this would be a breach of professional standards. Preparation is the key to responding effectively. Previous experience of your opponent can yield useful information. Good communication techniques and, specifically, strategies on how to communicate with difficult people can also be helpful.

Ultimately, how to respond is a question of your personal judgment. What may be an appropriate response in one situation may, in contrast, be a bit heavy handed in other circumstances. Below we give you a range of common mistakes and problems, along with our suggested strategies/responses.

Tactic	Possible responses
"Take it or leave it"	• avoid and move on to another issue; • ask to justify the statement; • call their bluff.
Silence	• meet with silence; don't be intimidated; • ask a pre-planned question to fill the silence; • don't start talking to fill the silence (a natural tendency).
Don't drop "floppies"	• don't say "about X or Y" as it reveals latitude in what you might settle for.
Sun in your eyes	• move seat; • draw it to the attention of the other party; • don't be intimidated.
Travel plans	• think about keeping your return travel plans a secret as your opponent may "run the clock down" to put you under pressure to conclude.
Large demands	• ask to justify the demand; • counter with similar demand; • call their bluff.
Lack of authority	• question the extent of opponent's authority; • seek to reconvene.
Feigned surprise	• stick to your guns.
Anger/threats/ personal attacks	• defuse the situation if you can; • don't be drawn in to a fight; • remain professional; • move debate on; • if necessary, end the session.

Summary

Negotiation is a skill, and one that requires you to change your tactics and approach each time you do it. The more you practice, the better you'll get. By following the processes set out in this chapter, you'll develop into a good negotiator who can—more often than not—get the results your clients want. **10–29**

CHAPTER 11

HOW TO BE PROFESSIONAL

Introduction

11–1 *Before you meet the employer's lawyer, your client phones you. One of her friends has told her that she will get more money if she makes a claim for sexual discrimination. Nothing of the sort happened but, if it might help you negotiate a better deal, she's happy to make the allegation. What do you do?*

11–2 This is an extreme example that highlights the need for you to think not just about the legal advice that you give, but also how you conduct yourself. As a solicitor you have a duty to your client, but that isn't the only duty you have. You also have a duty to other solicitors, to the court and general public to maintain professional standards. These include: trust and integrity; independence; acting in the best interests of your client (which doesn't mean blindly doing what they ask); avoiding conflicts of interest; observing confidentiality and maintaining a relationship with the courts. How do you balance all of these interests? In practice, if you understand how standards are set and followed, it soon becomes a natural process. A useful tip to remember when starting out is this one, given by a senior partner of a large corporate firm. He would say, "if it feels wrong, it probably is wrong, so don't do it!"

In this chapter we look at how solicitors are regulated by the Law Society Practice Rules 2011, standards of conduct, detailed rules on particular topics and best practice guidance. When you start working for clients, the rules and guidance help you write engagement letters (as we saw in Ch.7 (how to write an engagement letter)). If a client tries to make you lie, the rules and guidance also help you work out how to respond. We also mention two additional sets of rules that might apply to you. If you do criminal work, you need to know about the Code of Conduct for Criminal Work and Scottish Legal Aid Board Code of Practice. If you intend to become an advocate, you need to know about the Faculty of Advocate's Guide to the Professional Conduct of Advocates. We do not cover these in detail and simply highlight that they exist. Finally, we look at the rules and guidance in practice. What happens if a client (or even a colleague) asks you to do something that simply doesn't comply with professional standards?

Outcome

11–3 By the end of this chapter you'll understand the main practice rules and practice guidance set out by the Law Society. You'll also have an overview of the standards of service and guidance that are relevant to you. You'll know where to look for help if you find yourself in a difficult situation.

Professional standards

What is a "professional"?

You may have heard the phrase "the professions". Traditionally, these were regarded as including architecture, the clergy, engineering, law and medicine (though the list has expanded as modern jobs have evolved). These professions had a different status to other jobs because they had requirements that set them apart. These were: **11–4**

- a specialised training or education;
- a statutory qualification;
- formal apprenticeship;
- code of ethics;
- regulatory oversight by the government (or self-regulating); and
- membership of a professional body in order to practice.

Let's look at each in turn.

Training

Section 5 of the Solicitors (Scotland) Act 1980 states that the Law Society can set regulations to control how students are trained, where they're trained, and the minimum requirements for passing exams (before a student can become a solicitor). Before a university can teach solicitors it must meet the Law Society's standards and be certified by it. There are currently 10 universities certified to teach law. They're: the University of Aberdeen, the University of Abertay, the University of Dundee, the University of Edinburgh, Edinburgh Napier University, the University of Glasgow, Glasgow Caledonian University, Robert Gordon University, the University of Stirling and the University of Strathclyde. **11–5**

A statutory qualification

All lawyers must first complete the LLB and Diploma in Legal Practice (DLP). Both the LLB and DLP contain courses set by the Law Society to ensure that every solicitor has the knowledge and skills required to be a solicitor. The Law Society stipulates the content of courses to ensure that all students are taught to the same syllabus. For example, every DLP student is taught courses based on the Professional Education and Training 1 (PEAT 1) requirements. **11–6**

A formal apprenticeship

Before you can become a lawyer you must complete a traineeship. Again, the Law Society stipulates the learning outcomes that all trainees must achieve over the course of their two-year traineeship. These are the Professional Education and Training 2 (PEAT 2) requirements and they relate to: **11–7**

- professionalism;
- professional communication;
- professional ethics and standards; and
- business, commercial, financial and practice awareness.

Code of ethics

11–8 As a lawyer you must observe the Law Society Practice Rules 2011 and associated guidance. If not, you might face disciplinary action and even lose your right to practice. We examine the rules and guidance later.

Regulatory oversight

11–9 Lawyers are regulated by the Scottish Legal Complaints Commission (SLCC) and the Law Society (or Faculty of Advocates). We examine each of these in Ch.11 (how to avoid complaints). For the moment, it's enough to know that these regulators can take action if you fail to meet the professional standards required of you.

Membership of a professional body

11–10 You can't work as a solicitor if you're not a member of the Law Society. In order to become a member, you must have been taught at a university certified by the Law Society, passed your LLB (Hons) and the DLP, completed your traineeship and (on top of all that) you must be a "fit and proper person to be a solicitor."[1] "Fitness" means that you have fulfilled all of the requirements to become a solicitor and that you have the necessary knowledge and skill. Your training partner will be asked to confirm this as part of your application to become a solicitor, at the end of your traineeship. "Proper" means that you have the right character to become a solicitor. For example, as a lawyer, you're expected to be able to manage a business, so if you have been bankrupt or been involved with an insolvent company, this casts doubt on that ability. Equally, you're expected to uphold the rule of law. The Law Society may take a dim view of past criminal convictions and even being involved in serious civil matters. Finally, you must act honestly and demonstrate an understanding of the requirements to avoid conflicts of interest or breaking confidentialities. The Law Society will review all the relevant facts before admitting you as a solicitor.

How do you show that you're "professional"?

11–11 Clients expect you to be professional. As we saw in Ch.1 (what will you do?), this is built on the reputation that solicitors have developed over centuries. In order to show that you're professional you must understand (and follow) the standards expected of solicitors.

What are the professional standards of a solicitor?

11–12 You need to comply with standards of conduct, set out within the Legal Services (Scotland) Act 2010 and enforced by the SLCC and the Law Society. These standards are contained in practice rules, supported by practice guidelines.

Practice rules

11–13 Solicitors are important. As we saw in Ch.2 (who are your clients?), you're involved in the biggest events of your clients' lives. You'll help clients buy their first home, you'll deal with the death of parents and grandparents, you can help them when they marry, you'll be involved if they divorce, you'll protect children,

---

[1] Solicitors (Scotland) Act 1980 s.6.

you'll save innocent people accused of crime, you'll ensure that the guilty are treated fairly, you'll help businesses grow, you'll help people make fortunes (and protect them if deals turn sour), you'll stand in court and you'll hold your clients' hands. Throughout, you're expected to show you're a professional and justify the trust they place in you.

The practice rules have been with us (in one form or another) since the Law Society was established, in 1949. The Law Society has the power to make practice rules (which are mandatory for all solicitors). This is set out in the Solicitors (Scotland) Act 1980. The current rules are the Professional Practice Rules 2011. The Professional Practice Rules 2011 contain rules about qualifying as a lawyer, becoming a partner, setting up law firms, the roles required by people in your firm (such as a client relations manager), alongside rules about how to deal with clients' money and more specialist subjects such as professional indemnity insurance. As a new lawyer, we think the most important rules to know are those relating to the standards of conduct; the rules that show you how you should behave as a lawyer.

Standards of conduct

The standards of conduct are designed to set out clearly how you should act, not just **11–14**
to your clients but also to the court, the public and to others in the legal profession. The main code is the Standards of Conduct, approved by the Law Society in 2008 (and revised by the Professional Practice Rules 2011). You can find the standards of conduct in their original form in r.B1 of the 2011 Rules. However, we've set them out below in a different order. When the standards were first approved, the Law Society prepared a guide for clients to help explain what they were and what they meant. This was based on the importance that clients place on each of the standards. That is the order we've followed.

What are the standards of conduct?

There are 15 standards to help ensure that you put a client's interest first, you keep **11–15**
their secrets, and that you act honestly and with integrity at all times. We examine each one below.

1. You must act with trust and personal integrity

You must always act honestly and with integrity. This means you must not know- **11–16**
ingly lie to anyone (whether clients, other solicitors or the court). You must behave in a way that demonstrates that you have personal integrity and are fit to carry out the duties of a solicitor.

Lying can take a number of forms. At one extreme a solicitor who told his client that they were divorced and then forged a divorce certificate, clearly lied. However, not all lies are so flagrant. Let's say your client phones you at 3pm to ask if you've sent out a contract. You've actually forgotten all about it. You can either tell them the truth, or you can tell them that it's "in typing" and that it will be sent later that day. What do you do? It's just a little white lie, isn't it?

Acting honestly also means that you shouldn't act recklessly. It would be reckless to tell your client that the contract has been sent out because—let's say—you think a colleague has sent it. After all, you could check and find out for certain. You may not have intended to mislead your client, but that's what you've done by failing to check. Trust and personal integrity is the most important standard demanded by clients. It is vital that you always try and act honestly, even if that means admitting your faults.

2. You must maintain confidentiality

11–17 Clients expect you to keep their secrets. Whatever they tell you should not be repeated (unless a court orders you to, or they intend to commit a crime). It can be hard to keep secrets. Sometimes you want to talk about your work to friends, flat mates, relatives and colleagues. You might be acting in an exciting court case, or on transactions that are making front page (or back page). When Andrew started as a trainee, he worked for a world famous football club. However, he couldn't tell anyone about it even though he knew the inside track on a number of big sporting stories. Even one slip can destroy your reputation.

Take the case of Christopher Gossage, a lawyer with Russells. He told his wife's best friend that one of his clients (an author, Robert Galbraith) was, in fact, JK Rowling. This best friend revealed all on Twitter and soon the whole word knew. Gossage said he believed he was speaking "in confidence to someone he trusted implicitly"[2] but the lesson here is that you shouldn't share confidential information with anyone. The rules don't have an exception for people you trust implicitly. In fact, r.B1.6 says: "[o]nly the client, Acts of the legislature, subordinate legislation or the court can waive or override the duty of confidentiality." This doesn't include your mum, dad or best friends.

3. You must act in the best interests of your clients subject to preserving your independence and complying with the law and the principles of good professional conduct

11–18 You mustn't blindly follow a client's instructions. If your client asks you to argue sexual discrimination when you know that she's inventing it to leverage more money, you need to tell her that you can't do that, and that it would be in her best interests to avoid any arguments that could involve her (and you) lying to a court.

Rule B1.4 is explicit about your need to provide independent advice:

> "You must also remember that your client's best interests require you to give honest advice however unwelcome that advice may be to the client and that your duty to your client is only one of several duties which you must strive to reconcile."

This standard is difficult for trainees and new lawyers, because you may not know what the best interests of a client might be. It may not be as clear-cut as our scenario. Equally, you may have a supervisor or colleague giving you instructions that you don't agree with, but you press on regardless. It must surely be okay, otherwise they wouldn't have told you to do it?

A good example is page swapping. This is the practice of swapping a page in a signed document, to change a word or phrase. Usually this happens if someone spots a mistake. Perhaps there is a typo and, rather than have the entire document re-signed, it seems easier just to swap the page with a corrected version. Let's say your partner tells you to do it because it'll take a week to get everyone to sign it again and it'll annoy the client. So far, this seems entirely trivial. However, what happens if your client changes firm and has a copy of the original document that

[2] Quoted in M. Kennedy, "Lawyer who uncovered JK Rowling's Robert Galbraith alter ego fined £1,000" (31 December 2013), *Guardian.com*, *http://www.theguardian.com/books/2013/dec/31/lawyer-uncovered-jk-rowling-robert-galbraith-fined-cuckoos-calling* [Accessed 19 April 2016].

they then refer to in a court action? That document is lodged with a court and questions are raised as to why their version is different from the version you sent. Have you acted with personal integrity?

Later in this chapter we look at other steps you can take when confronted with issues where a client or a colleague asks you to act in a way that makes you think you may be in breach of the standards of conduct. Ultimately, you may need to refuse to do what a client asks of you. If your client insists that you raise a claim of sex discrimination you may even need to stop acting for her. Your reputation and professionalism is more important than being your client's unthinking mouthpiece. You're a lawyer and you know that you have standards. You have a reputation and a career that will last far longer than your relationship with any client. It's too important to risk for anyone.

4. Any fees you charge must be fair and reasonable

Remember, when you start acting for a client you must tell them how much they're going to pay for your service (or how you'll calculate the cost). Your engagement letter will set this out (as discussed in Ch.7 (how to write an engagement letter)). If you don't tell them this, then any fee must be fair and reasonable. If your fee is based on an hourly rate, you must tell the client what that rate is (and of any changes to it). This is particularly important for any long running transactions, as your firm will probably increase its rates each year to take account of inflation and other factors. If it does, you need to tell your clients. If you don't, they can argue that they shouldn't pay the new amount and you could find that you have breached the standards of conduct by not charging a fee that is fair and reasonable. **11–19**

5. You must have proper instructions

Think about how we talk about legal work. We take "instructions" from clients. We give "advice". We're our client's "legal agent". You give clients options, you tell them about risks, you may even recommend a particular course of action, but, ultimately, you need a client to tell you what to do. You can't stand up in court and say your client is guilty without speaking to them first. Equally, you won't draft a contract without knowing what your client wants it to say or do. **11–20**

For some clients this may involve issuing instructions about everything. Let's say you're asked to draft a lease for a client who wants to lease a property to Starbucks. Your client may want to know what every clause says as they've never leased a property before. They need to know what the process involves and how it'll affect them. Another client, a big property company like Land Securities, knows exactly what leases say and may only need to know that the rent will increase every five years. Different clients require different approaches. The ultimate goal is the same; you need to have your client's instructions before you can do anything. Knowing how to take instructions is a skill that you develop as you deal with clients. At all stages it's important that you record your instructions. Then, if you're ever asked to justify an action you have an email, letter or file note to cover it.

Linda Moir, Senior Claims Technician for RSA Professional & Financial Risks Claims, writing in *The Journal of the Law Society of Scotland* (December 2015) sets out three useful tips to follow to ensure you have a record of instructions[3]:

[3] L. Moir, "Magic bullets" (14 December 2015), The Journal of the Law Society of Scotland, *Journalonline.co.uk, http://www.journalonline.co.uk/Magazine/60-12/1021099.aspx* [Accessed 19 April 2016].

> "A brief handwritten note is good; a detailed typed one is better—outline the advice given."

And:

> "Ideally, issue a letter [authors note—or email] to the client to confirm the advice given —not only that advice was provided, but exactly what was said ... Make sure the file tells as full a story as possible of the transaction, including clear notes of discussions with clients and of any instructions provided. Remember: memories fade, file notes do not."

While it's useful to know how a court will look at your files,

> "be aware that in any dispute as to what was said, a court will generally assume that the client—for whom the transaction is probably more significant—is likely to have a clearer recollection than the solicitor, for whom it was only one of many similar transactions in a career. The client file is the single best weapon available to those who seek to defend the claim."

You should ensure that you have proper instructions and keep a clear and accurate record of it in your client file.

6. You must have the relevant legal knowledge and skills to provide a competent and professional service

11–21 Former US Vice President, Donald Rumsfeld, once spoke of the "known knowns", "known unknowns" and the "unknown unknowns". What he was trying to say was that there are some things you don't know that you don't know, and that these are the most dangerous of all. How can you avoid something completely unexpected? The "unknown unknowns" can be a problem for lawyers. You may think you know an area of law, like contract law. Let's say you're asked by a client to draft a £2 million contract between a construction company and a plant hire company, to hire JCB diggers. The plant hire company is to be paid monthly for the next two years. You draft this and, six months later, your client comes in and tells you that they've just received a demand for the remaining £1.5 million because they'd not paid last month's payment on time. It's only then, after asking a colleague, that you find that there's an Act of Parliament that deals with this issue. If you don't follow set instructions, they have the power to demand instant payment. You didn't know about this law. You didn't even suspect such a law existed. You have an "unknown unknown". Situations as extreme as this are uncommon, but it's easy to stray into territory where you think you know everything. That's why you need to be careful to avoid "dabbling" and only give advice on the areas you're comfortable with. Not everyone is a polymath. This doesn't mean that you can't research new areas. Many lawyers are generalists who know a wide number of areas. However, as the number of laws increase, it's harder to keep up to date with everything.

Along with the knowledge to advise on a particular area, you should also have the time to deal with it. If you have all the time in the world, you can advise on anything. You would have the time to research the answer and check that there are no unknowns. You'll rarely have time, though, to do everything as thoroughly as you might like. A client may phone you at 5pm and need an answer by 9am the next day.

A client may be due in court in two hours and you've only just spoken to them. You need to act fast and that means you need to be comfortable with what you're doing, so that you can give the client the best advice in the circumstances.

We know that this standard can be intimidating. You may think that if you fail, your partner or colleagues will think less of you. They won't. They've all been in the same position. They know what it's like and they'd all much rather you asked for help than if you tried (and failed) to do something they asked. Trust us, if you find yourself in a situation where you're unsure what to do, ask for help.

7. You must communicate effectively

We've covered this in Chs 8 and 9, but we repeat it here: it's not what you say or write, it's what your client understands. Write and speak clearly. Make sure your client understands what you're telling them so that they can make informed decisions. **11–22**

8. You must deal with other lawyers in a manner consistent with persons having mutual trust and confidence in each other

You'll deal with other lawyers every day. They might be on the other side of a transaction, you might face them in court, but you mustn't forget that they're bound by the same professional standards and should be treated in the same way you would wish to be treated. It can be hard to remember this, particularly in court when (in the heat of the moment) you view everything as "them v us". It doesn't matter, though, how hard you fight; you still must treat other lawyers with respect. This means that you stand by the promises you make and you don't knowingly (or recklessly) mislead them. It also means that you don't speak to their clients directly, without their permission. Once a client instructs a lawyer, he or she is their spokesperson and you're not showing them respect if you try and circumvent them. **11–23**

9. You must provide independent advice

Your client expects you to provide advice free of external influences. This includes any influence from your firm. Your firm might want to benefit from the fees associated with a five-week hearing in the Court of Session. However, if you know that your client wants to avoid confrontation, mediation may be a better option for them and you have to advise them accordingly. **11–24**

10. You must disclose personal interests

If your client asks you to do something that you have a personal interest in, you must tell them. This lets the client decide if they want to use you. A good example is if a client asks you to recommend a mortgage broker or financial advisor. You might receive a fee for referring clients to other service providers. If so (and assuming the fee is legitimate) you need to tell your client so they can consider whether that fee might influence your opinion. **11–25**

11. You mustn't draft wills where you, or someone close to you, is a beneficiary

This is self-explanatory. If a client intends to include you (or someone close to you, such as family member) in their will, you should refer them to another solicitor. **11–26**

12. You must show respect to the court and deal with it honestly and accurately

11–27 Courts operate on the basis that they have the full facts needed to reach a fair judgment. Witnesses need to give honest statements (as far as they can remember) and solicitors need to provide information and legal arguments that cover everything a court needs to know. This means you don't hide evidence from your opponents (or the court) just because it doesn't support your case. Nor do you do anything that might affect the information a court receives from witnesses.

This duty frequently can conflict with your duty to act in the best interests of your client. You may think that it's in your client's best interests that a witness statement is not shared with the crown. However, if the court finds out, your actions will be far more damaging to your client than if you had made a disclosure. Now, you're not only dealing with evidence that supports the case against your client, you're viewed unfavourably because you've tried to hide it.

13. You must avoid conflicts of interest

11–28 Solicitors can't work for two or more clients who have conflicting interests. A good test is to ask whether, if both clients were sitting in front of you, you would give them the same advice. If not, you have a potential conflict of interest and you must inform the clients before you can act further, for either party. In some circumstances you can continue to act provided you have told them about the conflict and they agree that you can continue. However, just because you have consent doesn't mean that you avoid all conflict. If something then unfolds and the clients are unable to agree, you may still need to withdraw from acting for one (or both).

In some cases, you might not have a legal conflict but rather a commercial conflict. Some supermarkets, for instance, won't want you to work for a competitor, to obviate the risk that the information they share with you might be passed to that competitor. Many large companies stop their lawyers acting for anyone who sues them. That's why, in London, some law firms specialise in banking litigation because the Magic Circle (and indeed other global firms) are prevented by their clients from taking on banks.

14. You must provide reasons if you withdraw from acting for a client

11–29 Once you start acting for a client you must give them fair warning if you intend to stop, along with the reasons why. We suspect the most common reason is because a client has failed to pay fees.

15. You must not discriminate against anyone

11–30 As well as being the law, the Law Society's Standards of Conduct state that you must not discriminate against anyone based on race, sex, marital status, disability, sexuality, religion, belief or age.

Are the Standards of Conduct mandatory?

11–31 Yes. Unlike practice guidelines and standards of service (which we review, next) the Standards of Conduct are mandatory. If you don't adhere to them, you might face a professional misconduct charge. We look at professional misconduct in the next chapter.

Are there other codes of conduct?

Yes. For example, there is a Code of Conduct for Criminal Work. However, according to Paterson and Ritchie it's not clear if it's mandatory for solicitors undertaking criminal work, or whether it's merely taken into account if there is a complaint.[4] There are also codes of conduct and guidance for immigration, insolvency and mental health work. You should refer to these if you intend to work in these areas. **11–32**

The account rules

What are the Accounts Rules?

These are contained in r.B6 of the Practice Rules 2011. As a lawyer you have to deal with money, and lots of it. At a basic level this might be the funds sent to you to settle your fee, but it can also include: **11–33**

- money from clients to pay costs (such as the cost of a report, search or even an advocate's opinion);
- settlement monies (such as loan funds to buy a house or purchase funds to buy shares in a business);
- executory funds (to be distributed to beneficiaries);
- compensation, following a court case;
- money in a trust; or
- money on deposit (to be paid when certain events occur).

This money is not your money, or your firm's money. It belongs to someone else and you have a responsibility to use it only for a specific purpose.

At any time, your firm could be dealing with hundreds of thousands of pounds (think of any average house) or even millions of pounds (think of any large corporate or banking deal). It's vital that there are rules in place to ensure that clients' funds are safe. This is what the Accounts Rules set out to achieve.

What rules are most relevant for trainees and new lawyers?

The cashroom manager of your firm is responsible for ensuring compliance with the Accounts Rules. The Accounts Rules include rules about how to handle cash from clients and third parties, and more advanced rules about how to operate and monitor client accounts. **11–34**

For new lawyers, your first exposure to the rules will be when dealing with cash, cheques and bank transfers. Your firm should have processes in place that you can follow. However, you should remember the following 10 tips.

1. If a client gives you more than £50, you must lodge it into a client bank account without delay. This normally means the same day.
2. Every client must have a separate account.
3. You must keep all of a client's money in a designated account at all times. This means that if all of your clients walk into your office and demand their money, you can oblige. This is different from a bank. A bank is only required to be able to repay 10% of its clients' money, at any one time.

---

4 A. Paterson and B. Ritchie, *Law, Practice & Conduct for Solicitors*, 2nd edn, (Edinburgh: W. Green, 2014), p.14.

4. There is an exception to this rule. If you hold a lot of money for a client, you should lodge it in an account that yields a decent rate of interest. You're allowed to invest funds in an account that requires up to a month's notice for withdrawals.
5. If you make a mistake, fix it as soon as possible. Sometimes you might pay money into the wrong account, for example. You won't be punished for your mistakes provided you fix them as soon as possible.
6. With permission (such as in an engagement letter), you can use a client's funds to make a payment on their behalf, or to meet any costs you've incurred.
7. With permission (such as in an engagement letter), you can use a client's funds to pay your fees.
8. You cannot use a client's money to make a payment on behalf of another client, without their written permission.
9. You must pay back any money as soon as there is no longer a reason to keep it.
10. You must pay promptly any money received on behalf of a client, to that client, as soon as you can.

Practice guidelines

11–35 These are guidelines published by the Law Society to flesh out its Practice Rules and to set out what it considers to be best practice in specific situations. The guidelines can cover general matters, such as how to deal with files. For example, there are specific guidelines about what files should contain, how long they should be kept for and what you should do if you lose them (you inform the Law Society's Registrar Department, within a reasonable length of time). There are specific guidelines to help with different areas of work. For example, if you work in conveyancing, there are guidelines dealing with Home Reports.

As the introduction to the guidance on the Law Society's website states:

> "The purpose of Guidance is to assist solicitors and others providing legal services to meet the standards of good professional and ethical practice. Some of the Guidance explains or illustrates the ways in which the Practice Rules are applied or interpreted. Some of the Guidance is not specific to a particular Rule or Rules but relates to the carrying out of a particular type of service or applies to particular circumstances only."

How do you know which guidelines apply to you?

11–36 The Law Society's website is fantastic. It contains all of the practice rules and guidelines, and is updated regularly. It allows you to search the site in a number of ways, including by your area of work, so you can easily find which rules and guidelines apply to you. We suggest that you speak to your colleagues when you start, and ask if there are any specific guidelines that you should know about.

Other guidance

Standards of service

11–37 Standing alongside the Standards of Conduct, the Law Society has standards of service. If the Standards of Conduct tell you how to behave, the Standards of Service refer to the quality of work that a client should receive from you. The Standards were approved by the Law Society in 2008 and came into force in 2009. They're not mandatory. However, you're expected to follow them unless, in the event of a complaint, you can show you had good reason not to. As you'll see, the Standards of Service often are similar to the Standards of Conduct. That's because both often have a service and conduct element, making it impossible to separate them out.

The Standards of Service align with four principles. At the core lie the interests and needs of clients. The principles are:

- competence;
- diligence;
- communication; and
- respect.

Let's look at each, in turn.

Competence

- You must know (and apply) the relevant law when giving advice. **11–38**
- You must keep up to date with legal developments.
- You must ensure that anyone you delegate work to is properly trained and supervised.

Diligence

- You must deliver on commitments (you must do as you promise) whether **11–39** to a client, another solicitor, the court or a member of the public.
- You must act in the best interests of each client.
- You must regularly look at ways in which technology can support client service. By way of example, this may include client reporting systems, file and data management systems and knowledge management systems.
- You must fee any file promptly and use transparent fee arrangements so that clients know what they're being charged, and why.

Communication

- You must use clear language and your advice must be capable of being **11–40** easily understood by your client.
- You should agree the means and frequency of communication with your client.
- Any engagement letters (or equivalent) must clearly explain and define the service to be carried out, how that work will be carried out, who is responsible and the cost associated with the service.
- You must tell your clients how complaints will be handled if they're dissatisfied with your service.

Respect

- You must treat each person (whether a client, other solicitor or third **11–41** party) as an individual and recognise diversity, different cultures and values.

Summary

11–42 As the Law Society states in the introduction:

> "Lawyers interact with a wide cross section of our society and fulfill a critical role in meeting the interests of that society. Their clients are entitled to expect a good level of professional service from their solicitor. This means the solicitor must demonstrate the appropriate legal knowledge and skill to address the needs of the client, must communicate effectively in a clear and understandable way with their clients and others, must do what they say they're going to do, and must treat their clients and all others with respect and courtesy at all times."[5]

Scottish Legal Aid Board (SLAB)

Code of Practice

11–43 All firms and solicitors providing legal aid services must follow the SLAB Code of Practice. The Code sets out the standards required by the Board including:

- firms and individual solicitors must act in accordance with the standards of professional conduct, defined in the Code;
- services provided by firms and solicitors (and materials submitted to the Board) must be of the standard defined in the Code; and
- firms must operate systems of management and administration that meet the requirements of the Code.

We won't cover the code in detail, as SLAB plans to implement a new framework. However fundamental aspects will remain.

- Standards for the minimum knowledge, skills and competencies required by solicitors.
- Standards for business systems required to deliver criminal legal assistance.
- Standards of service to clients, taking into account duties to the court and funder.

The Code helps SLAB and solicitors deliver publicly funded criminal legal assistance that is cost-effective and of quality, to the people of Scotland.

Handbooks

11–44 Alongside its Code of Practice, SLAB publishes handbooks containing its current guidance. The latest editions are available, free of charge, from its website (*http://www.slab.org.uk*).

SLAB states that:

[5] The Law Society of Scotland Practice Rules 2011, Section E, Division A: Standards of Service. Available at *http://www.lawscot.org.uk/rules-and-guidance/section-e-general-guidance/division-a-standards-of-service/guidance/standards-of-service/* [Accessed 19 April 2016].

"Each handbook includes:

- information about registering to provide different types of legal assistance and quality assurance
- all our policies on applications, and practical advice covering all stages of a case, including
    - applying for, and providing, advice and assistance and ABWOR [assistance by way of representation], and our approach to different types of case
    - applying for, and providing, legal aid, and our approach to different types of case
    - procedures after legal aid is granted—for example, the requirements for sanction for certain types of work, reporting procedures, amendments to grants or changes in circumstances
    - clawback and expenses in civil cases
- a section on legal aid for contempt of court
- guidance on accounts
- all current legal aid legislation, as amended, relating to that type of legal assistance
- an easy-to-use contents list and search service."[6]

Council of Mortgage Lenders (CML)

The CML is the main trade body representing UK mortgage lenders. It includes **11–45** banks, building societies, and other lenders who, together, account for around 95% of the nation's residential lending. All solicitors involved in residential lending should be aware of the CML Handbook. It provides comprehensive instructions for solicitors and licensed conveyancers acting on behalf of lenders in conveyancing transactions. The CML Handbook covers general instructions that apply to all lenders, and specific instructions from specific lenders. If you're acting for the Bank of Scotland, you should check the CML Handbook to find out what general instructions apply and if the Bank of Scotland has any specific instructions you need to follow.

Client requirements under contract law

Individual clients may require you to adopt standards, too. Large companies, for **11–46** example, may have a service level agreement that contains targets, such as returning calls the same day or acknowledging emails within two hours. At the other end of the spectrum, a client may ask you only to phone them in the afternoon. However, whatever they ask you to do you must comply with the professional standards set by the Law Society. If a client asks you to do something that would cause you to breach the standards, you should refuse, explain why and, if they persist, withdraw from acting for them.

---

6 SLAB, "Legal assistance handbooks", *Slab.org.uk*, *http://www.slab.org.uk/providers/handbooks/* [Accessed 19 April 2016].

What to do when you find yourself in a difficult position

11–47 Remember, professional standards are like the Highway Code. They'll tell you what to do and how to behave, but it's up to you, ultimately, to comply. The Highway Code tells you how to drive on a motorway, but it's up to you to work out how to drive on the M8 through Glasgow at 5pm, in a three-mile tailback, with impatient cars darting from lane to lane. The professional standards are no different. They may tell you not to act in a conflict of interest scenario, but what happens when a client who has used your firm for 30 years asks you to act for both him and his wife in a "simple transaction", and gets angry when you say you can't? Life can't be lived by paper rules. You'll have times when you don't know what to do. In those situations, you can turn to:

- colleagues;
- friends;
- the Law Society; or
- LawCare.

Colleagues and friends

11–48 If you find yourself in a difficult position you should always tell your colleagues. This is easier in larger firms, as there are more people to speak to who can give you an independent view. You may even wish to speak to your client relations partner; he or she will be keen to help, to deal with any issues as soon as possible. You may be nervous about talking to others. You want to appear as if you know what you're doing. It's hard to admit you've made a mistake. That's only natural. What you'll find, though, is that your colleagues will have been in the same sort of position themselves. They'll know how you're feeling, they'll have a good idea what to do next, and they won't look down on you for bringing it up. In fact, they'll be pleased that you've raised it and that you haven't tried to hide it.

If you work in a smaller firm it can be a bit harder to speak to colleagues. If so, speak to your friends in other firms. You must abide by confidentiality rules, but you can still speak to them generally. "A problem shared is a problem halved" is a cliché, because it's true.[7] If you need independent advice, you can speak to the Law Society.

Professional practice at the Law Society

11–49 If you have a query relating to solicitor rules or are looking for guidance, you can call the Law Society's team of solicitors on the professional practice helpline on 0131 226 8896. The Law Society helpline provides confidential support and advice, with two exceptions. The exceptions are where a solicitor making an inquiry states that he/she has or may have dealt dishonestly with client's money or

[7] In fact the *Daily Mail* reported in 2014 that researchers from California have proved that the best way to beat stress is to share your feelings—and sharing with someone in the same situation yields the best results: V. Woollaston, "A problem shared, really IS a problem halved: Discussing problems with people in similar situations reduces stress levels" (30 January 2014), *Dailymail.co.uk*, *http://www.dailymail.co.uk/sciencetech/article-2548917/A-problem-shared-really-IS-problem-halved-Study-finds-discussing-problems-people-situation-reduces-stress-levels.html#ixzz3xVIttsTe* [Accessed 19 April 2016].

where there is either knowledge or suspicion that a solicitor (rather than their client) is engaged in money laundering. You don't need to give your name when your call and the advice can be anonymous. However, if you do speak to the Society, we recommend that you keep a note of what was discussed so that you can refer back to it later. You can even ask the Law Society to write or email you their advice (though, naturally, this obviates any anonymity).

LawCare

If you're dealing with a difficult situation, you may be stressed or depressed. You may feel you're relying on alcohol or drugs to help you cope. If so, you can speak to LawCare, a specialist charity that deals with lawyers who are experiencing personal issues. LawCare can be contacted by email or, anonymously, by phone via its helpline (0800 279 6888). **11–50**

Legal Defence Union (LDU)

The LDU is an independent organisation, set up to promote and protect solicitors' welfare in Scotland. It provides prompt, expert and confidential advice on problems that may affect solicitors, including: **11–51**

- problems of conflict, conduct, confidentiality;
- threat of contempt of court;
- police contacts with the office (production orders, specifications etc.);
- Law Society or Guarantee Fund inspections; and
- a citation to appear before the Discipline Tribunal.

As part of membership rights, LDU members have access to a telephone help line (01356 648480). You can find more information on the LDU website at *http://www.ldu.org.uk*.

Example of professional standards in practice

Trying to live up to professional standards can be difficult. Different standards may infer different actions, and you're stuck in the middle, trying your best to reconcile them. We can see this in the following scenario. Imagine you're in your second year and you're still helping your client with her employment claim. **11–52**

Background

One day, you're reviewing the file when you notice there have been several developments, including a settlement offer from her former employer and an email from the QC acting for you recommending your client take it. **11–53**

There doesn't appear to be any contact with your client for several months and it's not clear whether she's aware of these developments. You raise this with your partner. He tells you that there was no need to bring these points to her attention because, from previous experience, he knows the client tends to be slow reaching decisions, and it's easier to keep her involvement to a minimum. This strategy has worked well and the partner has achieved good results for her before. In the partner's view, the QC is being cautious. He feels that the client's case is stronger than the QC suggests and he doesn't agree that she should settle. He's satisfied that he can negotiate a better settlement. He tells you to let the defender's solicitor know that the offer is rejected. What do you do?

What professional standards could apply?

11–54 This example raises questions about communication and whether you're acting in your client's best interests. You'd check the Practice Rules 2011 and you'd find that r.B1.9 (effective communication) states:

> "You must communicate effectively with your clients and others. This includes providing clients with any relevant information which you have and which is necessary to allow informed decisions to be made by clients."

The rule then goes on:

> "You must advise your client of any significant development in relation to their case or transaction and explain matters to the extent reasonably necessary to permit informed decisions by clients regarding the instructions which require to be given by them."

You know there's been several developments which have not been passed on to your client. There has been a settlement offer and a recommendation from the QC. Both of these are significant and your client should have been informed under r.B1.9. Also, if there's been no communication at all for several months, this also could be a breach of the duty of effective communication too. Your partner might argue that he is applying r.B1.4 to act in the best interests of the client (by getting a higher settlement). Rule B1.4 states:

> "You must at all times do, and be seen to do, your best for your client and must be fearless in defending your client's interests, regardless of the consequences to yourself".

However, it also says, "your duty to your client is only one of several duties which you must strive to reconcile." In this situation, even if your partner believes he is acting in the client's best interests, he should have informed the client about the offer (and the QC's opinion), given his own opinion and then allowed the client to choose what to do next.

What should you do in this situation?

11–55 As a trainee, we know it's difficult to challenge the view of a partner. If you don't want to speak to him, we'd suggest you seek advice from another colleague, perhaps a senior associate or partner in the same team or even from the firm's client relationship manager. If you don't feel comfortable talking to a colleague or the client relationship manager, you can contact the Law Society. You can even do this anonymously. You're never alone and you should always feel like someone, whether in your firm or at the Society, can help you.

Summary

11–56 As your career develops from trainee through solicitor to, perhaps one day, becoming a partner, your professional reputation goes with you. That reputation is built on professional standards and it's up to you to live up to those standards. It may not be easy but if you know what they are (and who to turn to when you need help) you'll go a long way to achieving that.

Chapter 12

HOW TO AVOID COMPLAINTS

Introduction

Your client has asked you to lie for her. You tell your partner; he says he'll try and persuade her to change her mind. 12–1

One week later, you receive a letter from your client (copied to your partner). She denies ever asking you to lie and demands an apology within seven days. If you don't, she threatens to report you to the Scottish Legal Complaints Commission. Your partner tells you not to worry, but how can you not? You've heard lawyers can lose their practicing certificate if a client complains. Do you need to look for a new job?

The Law Society's Standards of Conduct define you as a solicitor. The standards reassure clients that they can trust you. They help set solicitors apart from other professions. They are both your platform and your shield. They are your platform because they raise your actions to a level that inspires trust both in the general public and those that instruct you. They are your shield because they protect you, if clients complain. 12–2

The standards we outlined in Ch.11 (how to be professional) define not only how you should (and shouldn't) behave. Remember, you're not expected to be perfect. From time to time you might do things that disappoint your clients, but that doesn't mean that you've failed them. If a court finds your client guilty, they may blame you even if you have done nothing wrong. He may believe another lawyer might have saved them. However, if you adhere to the standards, you can demonstrate that you did everything that you could (and should) to help. However, for the standards to matter there must be consequences for failing to comply. Otherwise they're just words. In the first section of the book we looked at the reputational benefit of meeting the standards. However, less positive consequences flow from any failure to adhere to the standards. These include damage to your reputation, that of your firm, but also that of the profession as a whole.

Outcomes

Courts and local faculties originally upheld the profession's standards. Today, the Scottish Legal Complaints Commission (SLCC), the Law Society and the Faculty of Advocates are the bodies that police compliance. The SLCC deals with service matters. The Law Society and the Faculty deal with conduct matters. In this chapter we examine how service and conduct issues are dealt with, by tracing a complaint from start to finish. We describe the role of each party involved in the complaint and their responsibilities. What is the SLCC and what does it do? How does the Law Society deal with a complaint? By the end of this chapter you'll 12–3 know everything you need to know to deal with complaints and, better still, how to avoid them in the first place.

Who deals with complaints against lawyers?

12–4 The current model of regulation focuses on individual solicitors, not firms. That means if a complaint is received it's you (not your firm) who will be investigated. Three main "enforcers" carry out any investigation: the SLCC, the Law Society and the Faculty of Advocates. Each has it owns remit and procedures. Though, as we'll see, the SLCC has an overarching role to ensure that clients are treated fairly and complaints are resolved, no matter which body deals with them.

Scottish Legal Complaints Commission (SLCC)

12–5 The SLCC was established in 2007. Its main powers are set out in the Legal Profession and Legal Aid (Scotland) Act 2007. The SLCC is the first point of contact for all complaints against lawyers, in Scotland (including solicitors and advocates).

The SLCC operates independently of the Scottish Government, the Law Society and the Faculty of Advocates. On its website (*http://www.scottishlegalcomplaints.org.uk*) it proclaims its independence:

> "We appreciate our position of independence is valued by our service users by providing a greater sense of impartiality and objectivity to reviewing complaints".

The SLCC has two main jobs. One is to decide whether a complaint has merit. The second is to act as a filter as to which body should investigate the complaint, and how should it be resolved. If a complaint relates to service, the SLCC will attempt to resolve it. However, if a complaint relates to conduct, it will refer it to the Law Society or the Faculty of Advocates. The SLCC's role is then to oversee the investigations by the Law Society or the Faculty. Sometimes, a complaint will involve a mix of service and conduct. If so, the SLCC will review the service element after the Law Society (or Faculty) has investigated the conduct element.

The Law Society

SLCC complaints

12–6 The Law Society was established in 1949. It's independent of the UK and Scottish Government and is funded entirely by its members. Its main powers are set out in the Solicitors (Scotland) Act 1980. The Law Society has a dual role to promote both the interests of the profession and the interests of the public.

If the SLCC refers a conduct complaint to the Law Society, the Law Society appoints a case manager to investigate. The investigation involves corresponding with the complainer (and the solicitor in question) to find out what happened. At the end of its investigation, the case manager reports to the Law Society's Client Relations Committee, which then decides whether to uphold the complaint, and, potentially, then to refer it to the Scottish Solicitors' Discipline Tribunal. The Law Society's Client Relations Committee has an equal balance of solicitor and lay members. If a complainer is unhappy with the way in which the Law Society handles their complaint, they can ask the SLCC to review the decision.

Other complaints

Along with complaints referred from the SLCC, the Law Society also operates a compensation scheme, called the Guarantee Fund. This is to reimburse clients in the event of a solicitor's dishonesty. It operates a separate scheme to deal with complaints about fees (we look at this at the end of the chapter). **12–7**

Scottish Solicitors' Discipline Tribunal (SSDT)

If the Law Society finds that a complaint involves misconduct, it refers the most serious cases to the SSDT to decide on a course of action against the solicitor in question. The SSDT also was established by the Solicitors (Scotland) Act 1980. It is governed by the Scottish Solicitors Discipline Tribunal Procedure Rules 2008. The Tribunal is an independent body that generally sits with two solicitor members and two non-solicitor members. It has the power to censure, fine, restrict, suspend or strike a solicitor from the Roll of Solicitors, removing a practicing certificate so that they no longer can work as a solicitor. A decision of the SSDT can be appealed to the Court of Session. **12–8**

The Faculty of Advocates

Faculty of Advocates' Complaints Committee

The Faculty of Advocates is a body of independent lawyers, admitted to practice as advocates before the Scottish courts. The Faculty is a democratic body led by a dean who is elected by the whole membership and is assisted by four office bearers. The Faculty is self-regulating and controls its own admissions and discipline. The Faculty's current rules are set out in the Faculty of Advocates Disciplinary Rules 2015. The Complaints Committee deals with any matters referred by the SLCC. The Committee comprises an equal number of professional and lay members. If a complaint about conduct is upheld (after careful consideration of representations from both parties) a range of penalties may be imposed, including a fine or an award of compensation. **12–9**

Faculty of Advocates' Disciplinary Tribunal

More serious complaints may be referred to the Faculty of Advocates' Disciplinary Tribunal, which also is composed of an equal number of professional and lay members. The range of penalties available extends further, to include suspension or expulsion. **12–10**

Dealing with a complaint

You'll almost certainly deal with a complaint at some point in your career, even if you provide a great service. You really can't keep all of the people happy, all of the time. You won't win every case, not every transaction will run smoothly and not every piece of advice will be what a client wants to hear. Instead, a client might complain that you didn't do something you should have done, or that you didn't deal with their work as well as you might have. If they're guilty, they'll still have expected you to clear them. If they're fined, they'll still have expected that fine to be less. If there's a delay in the sale of their house because the bank didn't send you the money on time, you're to blame. What should you do? In our example, your client is unhappy. What happens next? **12–11**

Who can complain?

12–12 Clients (clearly) can make complaints and, as you might imagine, tend to lodge the majority. Third parties also can complain, if they're directly affected by your actions. However, only a relatively small number are able to demonstrate this.

Stage 1: contact the Client Relationship Partner (CRP)

12–13 In Ch.7 we discussed engagement letters. You'll recall that a key requirement is that you tell your clients who the CRP is. This is so that clients know who a complaint should be made to, in the first instance. Every firm has to have a partner designated as CRP and they must tell the Law Society who that person is. This is so that clients can find out who the CRP is by phoning the Law Society—and for the Law Society to refer any complaints it receives to the CRP too. For sole practitioners, the CRP may be a partner from another firm, a contact in the local faculty, or other colleague.

If the CRP receives a complaint they must act quickly to acknowledge it. They'll contact the client to confirm they've received it and they'll set out the steps they intend to take to investigate it and report back. The CRP will then try to resolve the complaint before it's escalated to the SLCC or to the Law Society. The complaint may just be a result of a misunderstanding or miscommunication. The client may be satisfied knowing that the CRP will put in place steps to avoid any such misunderstandings in the future. For example, when your client complains that they don't hear from you, the CRP may promise that you'll update them regularly and will check with you to make sure you're doing that.

If a client's not happy with the CRP's response they can escalate their complaint to the SLCC. As we'll see, this starts a process that can take years to resolve and involve many hours of work, even if the complaint is rejected. That's why you'll find CRPs will try and do everything they can to resolve complaints without having to involve the SLCC. Dealing with complaints quickly is a sign of good service and will likely lead to clients staying with you and using you again. Letting it continue will only drag out the client's complaint and will make it less likely that they'll stay with you or give you more instructions. It makes good business sense to deal with complaints properly and promptly—even if you think you're in the right and the client is wrong.

A Newly Qualified (NQ) at a major firm worked for a housebuilder. They were passed a file dealing with a request from a customer of the housebuilder that their garden was smaller than it should have been and they'd asked the housebuilder to correct it. The NQ checked with the housebuilder who said they would be happy to fix it. The NQ confirmed with the customer that the housebuilder would fix it then the family said . . . nothing. For two years. The client was a national housebuilder. It had more important projects to do than move a garden fence so it did nothing too until, one day, two years later, a woman phoned and complained that the NQ had done nothing for two years. She's bought the house from the customer and had expected the garden to be fixed. So, she complained and that complaint was passed to the CRP. The CRP said, "I'm very sorry to hear this, we can fix this now and would you like £500 as compensation?" It didn't matter that the NQ had done nothing wrong. They'd contacted the customer and confirmed that the client would move the fence and the client had simply not done it. The firm still paid £500 and said sorry. Why? If the CRP can't solve the problem at this stage, he has to inform the complainer that they should go to the SLCC. That's where things get complicated—and time consuming.

Stage 2: SLCC

Not all complaints can be dealt with by the CRP. Let's assume in our example that you'd not only failed to contact your client but you'd also failed to mention that her employer had offered to settle her case. You thought she wanted more so had rejected it without telling her. She's found out about the offer and would have accepted it. She has a new job and just wanted to put this case behind her. She complains to the SLCC that you rejected the offer without telling her and she faces a lengthy employment tribunal with no guarantee of success. **12–14**

How do clients complain to the SLCC?

There are two types of complaint: **12–15**

- service; and
- conduct.

A service complaint is generally one about the quality of work that a lawyer has carried out. This covers level and frequency of communication and any delay. When you read about someone taking five years to complete an executory of a will, that would probably be a service complaint. A solicitor not phoning back? That could be a service complaint. Not sorting out a garden on time? Service complaint. The SLCC handles all service complaints.

A conduct complaint is an action that potentially breaches one of the standards set out in the Standards of Conduct. For example, a solicitor should not lie nor should they act in a conflict of interest, anything which is a conduct complaint is passed to the Law Society (or Faculty) to deal with.

It's not often clear whether something is a conduct or service issue. It could be both. If it is, then the Law Society will look at it first before passing it back to the SLCC. If a lawyer told their client they had fixed the garden when they hadn't, that could potentially be a service complaint, and, as it took two years to complete, it would also be a conduct issue because they'd lied. The SLCC's initial role when dealing with complaints is to act as a gatekeeper. It must decide whether a complaint is a service or conduct complaint—or a hybrid. This is a function that can take months. Imagine you're a solicitor facing a complaint, that's a long time to have it hanging over your head, and we haven't even started to look at the complaint yet, we're just selecting the right category for it.

In our example, is your lack of communication a service or conduct issue? You could argue it's a service issue. It's about the quality of our work. You should have communicated more. However, the fact that you've not passed on relevant information about the case—potentially information that could have brought it to an end—could be a conduct issues as you've not just failed to pass on information, you've potentially breached one of the standards of conduct. The standards on effective communication state:

> "Solicitors must communicate effectively with their clients and others. This includes providing clients with any relevant information which the solicitor has and which is necessary to allow informed decisions to be made by clients . . . solicitors must advise their clients of any significant development in relation to their case transaction and explain matters to the extent reasonably necessary to permit informed decisions by clients regarding the instructions which require to be given by them."

If the complaint is about conduct or if it's a hybrid that potentially involves both service and conduct, then it'll be passed to the Law Society or Faculty of Advocates to deal with first.

This is where the complaints system becomes "creaky". Imagine you're a client. You've complained about a solicitor not returning your calls. You just want someone to deal with it and you're told that two people will deal with it. And not only that, the first person you've complained to (the SLCC) is no longer looking at it at all. Instead you're back at square one as the Law Society writes to you to say that they're dealing with this. Months have passed and yet you don't appear any closer to a resolution.

Additional tests

12–16 The SLCC filter the complaints in two other ways to check its eligibility. It checks the complaint has been submitted on time and it checks that it's a serious complaint.

Time: First, it'll decide if the complaint has been raised within one year of the date when the complainer should have known the service or conduct was unacceptable.[1] In exceptional circumstances this can be extended but it would be rare for the SLCC to accept a late complaint without a good reason. For example, a serious illness that prevented the complainer raising it earlier.

Seriousness: Complaints which are described in the Legal Profession and Legal Aid (Scotland) Act 2007 as "frivolous, vexatious or totally without merit" are rejected by the SLCC. The SLCC on its website describes these complaints as:

> "Frivolous could be applied to a complaint that has little merit or is of a trivial nature, or where to investigate it would be out of all proportion to the seriousness of the issues complained about.
>
> A vexatious complaint could be one made with the intention of causing annoyance or trouble for the person or firm complained about. Totally without merit could be applied to a complaint that could not amount to a breach of service or conduct standards, is insupportable in law or has no substance whatsoever to it."[2]

Stage 3: reviewing conduct complaints

The Law Society

12–17 This is where the real work begins and there's still a long road to go. From a regulatory perspective, the Law Society is only interested in poor or inadequate service. As we've seen in the last chapter, the Society enforces standards to avoid inadequate conduct or misconduct. If you provide an adequate service or better, then you should never have to deal with the Law Society.

If inadequate service or misconduct is alleged, and the SLCC refers the complaint to it, then the Law Society will appoint a case manager to investigate

---

[1] The SLCC has announced, just before publication, that this time limit may be extended to three years. See "SLCC set to approve time limit changes" (25 March 2016), The Journal of the Law Society of Scotland, *Journalonline.co.uk*, *http://www.journalonline.co.uk/News/1021542.aspx#.Vvo74eIrJD8* [Accessed 19 April 2016].

[2] *http://www.scottishlegalcomplaints.com* [Accessed 19 April 2016].

the complaint. At this stage it's up to the complainer to provide evidence of the complaint. There is an assumption that the solicitor is "innocent unless proven guilty". However, as a complainer this can be a difficult concept to grasp because the complainer will be asked to provide evidence that confirms the solicitor has not complied with the standards of conduct. In effect, the complainer becomes the prosecutor, which can be tough.

The complaints process is based on statute. It's a legal process with legal terms and definitions. And, as we've seen in Ch.11 (how to be professional), it can involve many grey areas. A solicitor's response can refer to cases and decisions that may show the complaint has no merit. However a complainer, without legal help, may not know the importance of what they read. There is perhaps no way to avoid this but it does mean that in practice a complainer may face a disadvantage compared to a solicitor. Complainers may be on the back foot simply because they may not have the expertise to deal with the concepts required.

The case manager, though, will try and help while remaining neutral. They'll look for two things: evidence of misconduct and evidence of unsatisfactory conduct. This investigation may also take months depending on the complexity of the complaint and the need to give both the complainer and the solicitor time to respond to each other's response to the investigator's question.

Once the investigation is complete, the case manager will compare the facts to the relevant standards and decide whether a case of misconduct or inadequate professional service has been established. They issue a report and both the complainer and the lawyer have 21 days to review before it's passed to the Client Relations Committee of the Law Society for a final decision. By this point a year or more may have passed since the original complaint. The committee will either approve or amend the report. If a complaint is upheld they may pass it to the SSDT. If the complaint is rejected it's sent back to the SLCC (though the complainer can appeal to the SSDT).

Scottish Solicitors' Discipline Tribunal

The SSDT is made up of both lawyers and lay members. If a complaint is upheld **12–18**
and referred to it, then it can:

- take away your practicing certificate so you never work as a solicitor again;
- suspend you;
- restrict how you practice, such as imposing a condition that you must be supervised or you're not to appear before a court;
- fine you;
- publish your name in *The Journal of the Law Society of Scotland* along with a report of the complaint.

Appeal to the SLCC

If a complainer is not happy with the way the Law Society has dealt with the **12–19**
complaint then it can appeal to the SLCC. This appeal is purely about process, e.g. was it fair? Did it follow proper procedures etc.? It's not an appeal to challenge the Law Society's decision or a decision of the SSDT. That requires an appeal to the Court of Session.

Appeal to Court of Session

12–20 The Court of Session (and ultimately the Supreme Court) can hear appeals from the SSDT in order to challenge its decision.

Stage 4: service complaints

12–21 If the complaint is a service complaint or involves a service then it'll be dealt with by the SLCC. Similar to the Law Society, the SLCC will appoint an investigator to investigate the complaint. As you may imagine, this means that we could, yet again, be back at square one if the complaint is a hybrid complaint. The Law Society's investigation is ignored. A new investigator is appointed and the process begins again.

At any point during the investigation the parties can agree to settle the complaint but, if it's not settled, then it's referred for "determination". A determination is a binding decision by the Determination Committee of the SLCC based on the evidence investigated. By this point, months may have passed. Is it any wonder why CRP's might pay £500 and say "sorry" rather than face months or years dealing with a complaint?

Other sources of protection for clients

The Client Protection Fund

12–22 Every law firm is insured by the Master Policy. The Master Policy is an insurance policy managed by the Law Society. If your firm is sued, then the Master Policy can help pay compensation or damages. However, the policy is not comprehensive. It doesn't apply if a claim is based on dishonesty, as you can't insure against your own dishonesty.

The Client Protection Fund (formerly known as the Guarantee Fund) is a statutory fund that was created by the Solicitors (Scotland) Act 1980. It's paid for by all solicitors who pay an annual subscription to the fund. If a client has lost money because of the dishonesty of a solicitor—or a member of his or her staff—and they're unable to obtain redress from any other source, then they can apply to the fund. Any claims for compensation are investigated by the Law Society before a decision is taken on any compensation paid. Even then, awards are discretionary.

Taxation

12–23 The SLCC does not review whether a firm has charged a reasonable fee. If a client is unhappy with a fee it can request the firm to provide a breakdown to show how it was calculated. If they're still unhappy after receiving a breakdown they can ask for the account to be independently checked. This process is known as "taxation" and is carried out by an Auditor of Court.

The Auditor examines all the relevant paperwork and decides what the correct fee should be. Its starting point will be your engagement letter (as discussed in Ch.6). This shows the importance of setting out your fee up front. If you have raised an invoice and it follows the procedure set out in your engagement letter, then the Auditor should have no problem confirming your fee. Problems only develop if you have changed how the fee will be calculated or how much it is without the client's approval. The Auditor will normally hold a hearing to which the parties are invited to attend. Its decision is binding and it can approve or reduce the proposed fee. In return, it'll charge 4% of the fee as a charge for its service. This charge is normally levied on whoever "loses" the taxation: the firm, if the fee was excessive, or the complainer, if the fee was justified.

Other regulations: England and Wales

If your firm has an office in England and Wales, it'll be regulated by the Solicitors Regulation Authority (SRA). The SRA is an independent body that regulates all solicitors and law firms in England and Wales. It was set up in 2007 under the Legal Services Act 2007. The Act required one independent body to regulate solicitors. The Law Society of England and Wales would no longer regulate the profession. Instead the SRA sets outcomes and it deals with all complaints against solicitors. **12–24**

Other than its complete independence from the Law Society, the main difference between it and the SLCC is that it sets outcomes not standards. In Scotland, a standard is prescriptive. It tells you to do something e.g. issue an engagement letter. Provided you issue the letter the standard has been met. In England, outcomes are not prescriptive, they don't tell you how to do something, they only set out a goal. Instead of asking you to issue an engagement letter the outcome tells you to inform your client what you'll do for them and how much it'll cost. How you do that is up to you. You could phone them and make a file note, you could write an engagement letter or you could do something else—a text message even—provided the client knows what you'll do for them.

For more information on the SRA we recommend their website (*http://www.sra.org.uk*).

Other regulation: financial services

Some solicitors specialise in providing clients with independent financial advice. If you're providing financial advice then you'll find that that this advice is regulated by the Financial Conduct Authority (FCA). The FCA is the successor of the Financial Services Authority. It began operating on 1 April 2013. It sets standards or policies that it expects firms (including law firms) to meet. **12–25**

Other financial service regulations

In Ch.20 (how to talk to client about finance) we look at how financial markets work in more detail. For the moment, if you're dealing with financial service regulation we would point you in the direction of the Financial Services Act 2012 and the Financial Services and Markets Act 2000. While the main regulators are: **12–26**

- HM Treasury—responsible for the legislation we operate under and the general framework of regulation.
- The Bank of England—the central bank of the UK.
- The Department for Work and Pensions—responsible for public policy on pensions and for the Occupational Pensions Regulatory Authority.
- The Prudential Regulation Authority—regulates major banks and financial companies.
- The Pensions Regulator—regulates occupational pension schemes.
- The Financial Ombudsman Service—independent body that settles complaints about financial services firms.
- The Financial Services Compensation Scheme—an independent body that handles claims for compensation from consumers when regulated firms become insolvent.

- The Pensions Ombudsman Service—set up by law to investigate complaints about pension administration.
- The Pensions Advisory Service—provides independent information and guidance about pensions and retirement plans.

SLCC guide to avoiding complaints

12–27 The SLCC has published 12 tips for solicitors to help avoid complaints.[3] These are good practical suggestions and include:

Tip one: taking on work you can't do

12–28 This should be obvious but it can be hard to admit to a client that you don't know how to do the work they ask you to do. You may also not want them to use another lawyer so you take on work that's outside your comfort zone. The SLCC recommends that you don't take on work in an area of law in which you're not confident, or to take on more work than you can realistically manage.

Tip two: use clear engagement terms

12–29 Although engagement letters are compulsory, the SLCC still deals with complaints where an engagement letter hasn't been issued. A good engagement letter prevents complaints by setting out clearly what you'll do, when you'll do it and how much the work will cost. If you don't have an engagement letter, or its terms are unclear, then clients can argue that you've not done what you said, when you said you would do it, or charged more than they thought.

Tip three: manage clients' expectations

12–30 This is connected to tip two. But managing clients' expectations doesn't stop when the engagement letter is issued. Keep your client "in the loop" about timescales, particularly where those change, or look likely to change. Ultimately there should be no nasty surprises.

Tip four: use file notes

12–31 Clients will instruct you by phone and at meetings along with letters and emails. They won't write down what they say. You should though as, if there's a complaint, you need to show you have a record of what you were asked to do or what happened. Accurate and clear file notes of meetings and telephone conversations mean that you'll have a permanent record of what you were doing and why you were doing it.

Tip five: keep a good file

12–32 One of the SLCC's first steps when investigating a complaint is to ask for your file. If you have good file notes and a copy of all emails, letters and other documents (whether printed out or stored electronically) this will help ensure you have a record of all of the client's advice and instructions.

---

[3] SLCC, *Preventing Complaints* (2013). Available at *https://www.scottishlegalcomplaints.org.uk/media/46745/preventing_complaints_v1.00.pdf* [Accessed 19 April 2016].

Top six: use clear language

We can't say this enough—and Ch.8 (how to write to clients) covers this in detail—write clearly, write simply and avoid legal jargon. Make sure your client understands what you're telling them. **12–33**

Tip seven: quality control

Clients can demand immediate responses. You'll be under pressure to reply or to send out documents. You'll rarely have enough time to do everything you want, but this doesn't mean that you shouldn't try and have systems in place to check things as you go. As a trainee you may need to check every document with a colleague before they're sent. As a new lawyer, you may have more freedom but complicated work may still need checked. You may think this will delay sending out documents—which can be stressful as deadlines approach—but better to have them checked than to have them sent back, or worse rejected, if they contain mistakes. **12–34**

Tip eight: keep track of dates and time limits

This may be as simple as a diary, an Outlook Calendar or a case management system, however as many transactions are time-critical you need a system to keep track of dates and time limits. A good tip is to check what your colleagues do in the same team. If it works for them, it can work for you too. **12–35**

Tip nine: deal swiftly with delays

Legal work can be subject to delays which are not in your control e.g. a witness may have to go to hospital and a hearing needs to be delayed. If this happens, make sure that you let your client know—don't keep quiet in the hope that things will naturally correct themselves and that you'll somehow catch up. Clients don't mind delays if they know why the delay has happened and what you'll do to sort it out (if anything). Clients hate being kept in the dark. Remember tip two: manage their expectations. **12–36**

Tip ten: don't be afraid to pass on bad news

Continuing on from delays, you may have worse news to give to a client. A witness may change their statement. A purchaser may walk away before you conclude missives to sell a house. There is nothing you can do in these circumstances except tell the client as soon as you can. **12–37**

Tip eleven: supervision

Although this tip applies more to senior lawyers who are likely to delegate more work, it also applies to any work you might give to a secretary, paralegal, or, when you become a new lawyer, a trainee. Make sure the person doing the work knows what they're doing. If they don't, then mistakes will happen. It's your responsibility to ensure that they know what to do. It's not their mistake if you give them something they can't do—it's yours. **12–38**

Tip twelve: it's not just about your clients

We mentioned this earlier in the chapter—third parties can raise complaints too. It may be harder for them to do, but you should be conscious that when you're dealing with third parties—and other lawyers in particular—that they can raise **12–39** complaints too. What this means is that no matter how good the service you have given to your own client, the other side can raise a complaint against you. You should bear this in mind when dealing with third parties.

Tip thirteen: admit your mistakes

12–40 This time, thirteen is not unlucky for some. It's an additional tip that we have learnt to our cost and relief throughout our careers. If you make a mistake, tell someone. All mistakes are fixable if caught in time. The earlier you admit your mistakes the easier it is to fix. It's only the cover up or ignoring mistakes that leads to problems. As a trainee and new lawyer, you'll make mistakes, we all have. Don't be afraid to share yours, you'll find that your colleagues will be happy to help you as they'll have made the same mistakes too.

Summary

12–41 The complaints process is rigorous. It's only fair to both the complainer and the solicitor involved that any allegations are checked thoroughly, investigated, and judged based on a full and frank report. However, what this means in practice is that there is a great deal of duplication. If a complaint is a mixed complaint—one containing both service and conduct issues—then two or more investigators are required. Two or more investigations are required. Two or more reports are required, and complaints take longer to deal with.

If enforcing standards requires complaints to be dealt with swiftly then the system may need reviewed. This has been identified by Neil Stevenson, the Chief Executive of the SLCC. He has said:

> "We . . . investigate, try to settle, and determine the case. The professional body separately investigates, determines at committee, then maybe sends to a fiscal for a view, a committee considers it again, then the fiscal prosecutes at the Discipline Tribunal but on behalf of the professional body. Meantime, the consumer is not happy how their case was dealt with, so they raise a handling complaint under the statute with us. We then investigate the professional body investigation, but in the meantime the unhappy solicitor appeals the SSDT decision and it's off we all go on a jolly holiday to the Court of Session. Confused? We have to explain this to complainers every day.
>
> On top of this, there are at least four different legal and evidential standards applied at different stages, and many stages are utterly fixed in statute. When you see the process, as a customer experience for the lawyers and the consumers involved, it looks like madness. I am not criticising any particular element or role, but there has to be a debate on whether that is the model that really delivers best for lawyers and the public."[4]

[4] Quoted in P. Nicholson, "Balance in redress" (15 February 2016), The Journal of the Law Society of Scotland, *Journalonline.co.uk*, *http://www.journalonline.co.uk/Magazine/61-2/1021326.aspx* [Accessed 19 April 2016].

PART 3

Working as a Lawyer

CHAPTER 13

HOW TO SET FEES

Introduction

After two years of hard work you've qualified as a lawyer. Congratulations. You're about to take the first steps to show that you have the knowledge, skills and ability to be a lawyer in your own right. It's a big change. **13–1**

One of the first things you notice is that your partner wants to talk to you about fees. "While you were a trainee", he says, "I didn't want you to think about fees. However, as a lawyer, you need to start bringing in money. That means that you need to agree appropriate fees with clients so that they get value for money and we make a profit. I want you to start by sending out an engagement letter to this new client, a small business that wants to lease a shop on the local high street. How much do you think we should charge them?"

Every business needs to make money. If it doesn't, it'll soon be out of business. **13–2** Law firms are no different. They have bills to pay every month. They may pay rent for an office, money for office supplies, and they definitely pay wages to staff. All of this costs money, and this money comes from charging clients a fee for carrying out legal work.

Charging fees used to be simple. However, as the economic landscape has evolved, as clients have come to expect greater value for money and as competitors have become—well—more competitive, so the fees lawyers charge also have changed. Traditionally, lawyers charged by time. You would be charged by how long it took your lawyer to carry out the work. If it took 10 hours, and they charged £200 per hour, your fee would be £2,000. Simple.

Today, clients want more nuanced options. They want to know how much they'll be charged in advance, so they can budget with greater certainty. In response, firms offer fixed prices or other alternative fees. If they don't their clients choose firms that do. Imagine you go to a restaurant and the waiter tells you that the establishment charges £5 per minute for every minute you eat. Would you eat there? Or would you pop down to your local McDonald's where you know a Big Mac will cost you £2.69 and, for that, you can sit-in for as long as you like? We know which one we'd choose.

In this chapter, we examine the main ways you can fee clients and why clients might choose one option over another.

Outcome

By the end of this chapter, you'll understand the difference between hourly rates, **13–3** fixed fees and other alternative fee arrangements. We examine the link between what you do and how much you fee, and we look at how the way you work influences the final fee paid by clients.

"How much is a pint of law?"

13–4 If you walk into your local Tesco, you know exactly how much everything costs. If you want a four pack of Granny Smiths you pay £1.99. If you want a bag of satsumas, you pay £2.99. What's more, if you want to compare apples and oranges, the prices are on the shelf, in big letters, making it easy to judge.

Try walking into a law firm. Do you see any prices? Do you know how much it costs to speak to a lawyer? Let's go back to your first week as a trainee; all the way back to Ch.2 (who are your clients?). This time, imagine you're a client. You walk through the door, you sit in a boardroom and you meet a young lawyer who tells you exactly how to raise a claim against your former employer. At the end of the meeting, you ask perhaps the most important question for you: "how much will this all cost me?"

As a lawyer, how do you answer? Tribunals can be complex. Depending on the evidence involved, the witnesses called and the time required preparing, you could be talking 50 hours, or you could be talking 200 hours. That's before you know how the employer will respond. Will they be fast or slow? Will they keep to the main issues or will they try and introduce new ones? You want to give your client a rough estimate, but how can you when there are so many variables? All the time you're thinking "what will this cost?" your client is also thinking "I only have £2,000—I wonder if that will be enough?"

What is a price?

13–5 Before we examine how you set a price, let's answer a simple question first. What is a price? A price is the amount of money expected, required, or given in payment for something. In your case, your "fee" is the money you expect to be paid for your legal advice.

How do we set a price?

13–6 This is where things become more complicated. Prices can be set in a number of ways. We'll look at three: cost, by competitor and value.

Pricing by cost

13–7 This is one of the simplest ways to price something. You set your price based on how much something costs. Let's say you sell milk and every two litres you produce costs 79p; this covers milking your cows, packaging and transport to your local Tesco. Tesco then will charge more than 79p in order to make a profit.

It's the same with a television. If all the components of a television cost £100 and it costs £50 for fixed costs (like premises and staff) then, again, the retailer has to charge more than £150 in order to make a profit. In each case, shops look at how much it costs to sell something and then charges more, to make money.

You might well be thinking that it must cost more than 79p to produce two litres of milk? In fact, doesn't it cost more than 99p? There have been newspaper reports suggesting that it costs more to make milk than the price paid by Tesco for it.[1] That's true, but the principle is the same. In this case, Tesco pay farmers 79p (Tesco's cost) so that they're not the ones losing money. Why might they do that, though?

---

[1] "Q&A, Milk prices row and how the system works" (11 August 2015), *BBC.co.uk*, *http://www.bbc.co.uk/news/business-18951422* [Accessed 19 April 2016].

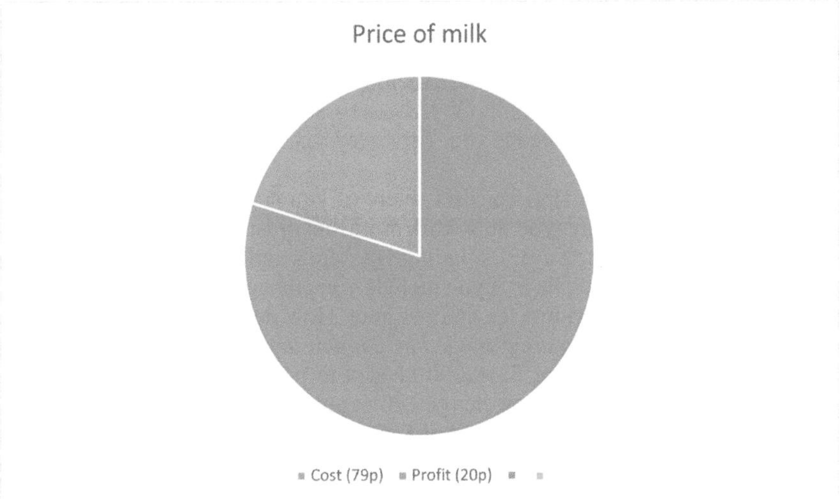

Pricing by competitor

Tesco is in the midst of a price war. Asda, Morrisons, Sainsbury's and others all charge 99p for milk. If Tesco charges more, its customers would switch to a rival. Tesco's prices are dictated by what its competitors are doing. In other words, it's not looking at cost any more. Instead, it's competing on the prices set by others. This is a dangerous path because you might not be able to sell at the same price as a competitor. **13–8**

Let's assume you're a small newsagent, selling milk at £1.29. Tesco opens next door, selling milk at 99p. You know you need to drop your price, but how can you? Tesco can buy in bulk and, in consequence, pay less under the economies of scale. You have to buy a single crate. You can't save money; it costs you £1.20 for each bottle of milk, and that's that. If you try and compete, you'll lose money. What can you do?

Pricing by value

Pricing by value might save your business. Pricing by value means charging a price based on what your customer is willing to pay. If you have a newsagent, you may have customers who don't want to stand in line at a self-service check-out. Instead, they want someone who can help them shop and they're willing to pay more for that help. Pricing by value is much harder than pricing either by cost or competitor. Pricing by cost is the easiest. You just need to sit down and work out how much something costs you to make or do, and then charge a higher figure. Pricing by competitor is easy, too. How much do your competitors charge for the same thing? Pricing by value, however, means you need to understand who your customers are, what they want, and what they're willing to pay. Chapter 5 (how do you build your reputation?) can help but, as you know, there's a lot of guesswork involved in understanding customers (and clients). It's more of an art than a science. **13–9**

How do law firms set prices?

Let's look at how law firms might use each of these options. **13–10**

Law firms setting price by cost

13–11 Part of the reason for using hourly rates is that these are based on cost. A law firm should review its costs regularly. These include rent, bills and other costs and can be worked out for a week, month or year. Let's say for your firm the figure is £250,000 per annum. That means your firm needs to fee at least £250,000 before it makes any profit.

Let's assume that your firm consists solely of you and a partner. Each of you can work eight hours a day (you may work more, but most hourly rate calculations assume a normal working day). Excluding weekends and holidays, in 2016 there are 253 working days (506 days if you include you and your partner). That means that you and your partner must fee £62 per hour. How do we know this?

£250,000 divided by 506 days divided by 8 hours in each day = £62 per hour

£62 per hour generates the £250,000 needed to pay all your costs. However, you want to make money, so you charge £70 per hour. This means that you make £283,360 per annum, creating a profit of £36,360.

£70 multiplied by 8 hours multiplied by 506 days = £283, 360 per annum

This is a simple example. In real life, a client wouldn't expect to pay the same for a partner as for a trainee. A partner can charge more to reflect skill and experience. However, this example does illustrate the problems with hourly rates. These are:

Maximum profit

13–12 There are only 24 hours in a day. If you charge an hourly rate then the most you can ever charge is 24 times your hourly rate (assuming you're working all night and don't go home, have lunch, dinner or even a toilet break).

Limited time

13–13 To be realistic, you need to assume that you're not actually going to be working on client matters every minute of the day. You might have gossip with your secretary, check the news, catch up on social media, and, more seriously, have admin to deal with.

You also can't charge clients for everything. You might start drafting a contract only to realise that you're using the wrong template. You might want to read a case in full, even though you know it, just to check you have it right. That's why most firms that use hourly rates also have another target such as utilisation (or realisation). This is the percentage of time each day that your firm reasonably assumes can be charged to clients. Your utilisation target might be 75%, with 25% of each day accepted to be time that you cannot charge to clients. In an eight-hour day, only six hours will be chargeable.

Client time

13–14 Your firm also assumes that not every client will pay for every hour you spend on their work. Some files may take longer than expected, but that doesn't mean a client will pay for the privilege. If you expect a contract negotiation to take five hours and you tell the client in their engagement letter that you'll charge them five hours, you'll find it difficult to go back and charge for 20 hours.

Utilisation includes an element of downtime and non-payments. A law firm can assume that not every hour of otherwise chargeable time will be charged. Instead of 75% of your time being chargeable, your firm might assume that only 60% eventually will be charged. In addition to 25% of your time being spent on admin, perhaps another 15% either can't be charged (or your client will refuse to pay).

Going back to your average day (eight hours) you're losing almost half that to work that you can't charge for. In our example, you're only charging 4.8 hours to clients. That's part of the reason why firms have looked at alternatives, such as billing by value. Firms want to make money and not be limited by the number of hours in the day that their lawyers can bill.

Billing by value

You don't expect to walk into your local Tesco, pick up your weekly shopping, take it to the checkout and only then find out how much it costs. Naturally, you prefer to know the prices up front. Clients are no different. They want to know how much it'll cost to hire you. You might say that your fee will be calculated by reference to hourly rates, inevitably the next question is still: "can't you tell me how much in total I will pay?" **13–15**

Billing by value means setting a price that a client is willing to pay. For many clients, especially since the 2008 recession, that means a fixed price. In other words, you (and they) agree a price for your work before you start. Your fixed price might be based on cost. One way to fix a price is to work out how long it'll take you to do the work and then base your price on that. For example, if a client asks you to prepare a lease, you might assume (from your previous lease work), that it'll take you 10 hours. You can then tell the client that it'll cost £550 (i.e. 10 hours at £55 per hour). If you complete the work in nine hours, you make a £55 profit. If you take 11 hours, you make a £55 loss. The faster you complete the lease, the more profit you make. The longer it takes, the more you lose.

Your fixed fee doesn't need to be priced on cost, however. You could price it on the value the work has to your client. For example, if you're client is caught speeding and they face losing their driving licence, you might consider how much that licence is worth to them. If the client is a travelling salesman, then he may well be willing to pay a premium, if you can help him retain his licence. Even if the actual work takes just five hours, you could charge £5,000, because you know how vital the matter is.

No win/no fee is partly based on this principle. If you don't get a result for your client then you haven't done anything valuable for them, so why should you be paid? If you're paid by cost, then you should be paid a fee for the work you've done.

Billing by competitor

It's easy to compare different types of milk. It's not so easy to compare law firms, because clients are not comparing "like with like". You're not the same lawyer as the trainee in the firm down the road. Your partner is not the same as other partners. You both might charge £55 per hour, but are clients buying the same thing? **13–16**

This is why you need to know who your competitors are and how clients choose between firms. Your knowledge of clients (see Chs 2 and 5) should help you to identify who your clients are, and what firms make up the competition. You can then identify the prices they charge. Do they offer a fixed fee of £199 for conveyancing? If so, it's going to be difficult for you to charge £200 per hour without good reason. You need to understand what your competitors' prices mean, also. It might be the £199 only applies to homes that are on the Land Register and worth less than £200,000. You, on the other hand, might specialise in commercial leases, and so this fee doesn't apply to you. You're not comparing "like with like".

Pricing options

13–17 Setting a price clearly requires information. If you're setting a price based on cost, then you need to know the cost of what you're providing. If you're setting a price by value, you need to know what your clients value and what they might pay for it. Finally, if you set a price based on what your competitors charge, you need to know what their prices are and what they offer for it.

Can you spot the problem? You need information to set a price, and a good deal of that comes from third parties, clients and competitors. That's part of the reason why charging by the hour has been popular. You work out your price (and your potential profit) based on information that you control (as your firm should know its own costs). However, basing a price just on costs isn't necessarily what clients want. They may want a fixed fee. They may want you to offer a no win/no fee arrangement, as they won't have any money to pay you unless they're successful.

When you're asked to prepare an engagement letter and put in place a fee, you have to decide what information you have (on which to base your judgment) and what you can offer (relative to your competitors). We can see this clearly, below, when we examine each of the options. These are broken down into hourly rate, capped fees, blended rates, fixed fees and success fees.

Hourly rate

What is it?

13–18 You charge clients by the amount of time that you work on their files. This is charged in six-minute intervals.

Advantages

It's simple to implement and easy for clients to understand.

Disadvantages

It rewards inefficiency; the longer you spend the more you can charge. There is no incentive to finish work quickly.

Capped rate

What is it?

13–19 This is a variation of the hourly rate. It caps the rate so that fees are not unlimited. This cap could be daily, so that you can't charge more than eight hours in a single day or so you can't charge, for example, more than 20 hours in a week, no matter how long you actually work on a file. To take it a step further, the cap might be a total figure that you can't charge above. For example, you might agree an hourly rate of £150 per hour, with a total cap of £20,000 to cover all work.

Advantages

Your clients can set limits so that they know what the highest likely cost will be.

Disadvantages

Your cap needs to be one that still lets your firm make a profit. If you agree a daily cap of two hours a day, but it regularly takes you four hours of work each day, you're giving a client two free hours (and you're not able to use that time to do work for another client who would pay).

Blended rate

What is it?

This is a variation of the hourly rate. Normally, every lawyer has a different rate. **13–20**
A trainee may be charged at £90 an hour, an assistant at £120, a senior associate at £150 and a partner at £200. A blended rate gives a client one rate for all fee earners (for example, everyone is charged out at £140 per hour). This means a client receives a discount if senior lawyers are involved, as they don't need to pay £200 for a partner. However, if junior lawyers do the bulk of the work, the firm clearly is paid more.

Advantages

The big advantage is simplicity; your client receives one rate for everyone.

Disadvantages

There is a conflict between the firm's interest in making sure junior lawyers are profitable and a client's desire to see senior lawyers working on their file (giving them a real terms discount). It can be difficult to reconcile this conflict and not have the client say: "why didn't the partner just do all the work as they knew what they were doing? I'm paying the same price for them, after all!"

Fixed fees

What is it?

This does what it says on the tin, as the advert goes. You set a fixed price for all **13–21**
(or part) of your work. For example, if a client asks you to help them with an employment tribunal, you could offer to do it all for £9,000 regardless of how long it might take.

Advantages

Your client knows exactly what they must pay.

Disadvantages

Your client may not know exactly what they're paying *for*. In your engagement letter you list all the assumptions that apply, in order that you might offer a fixed fee. For example, for an employment tribunal you can assume that there will be less than three witnesses. If there turns out to be 300 witnesses, you need to change your fee because you're doing 100 times more work. Your client may not appreciate that because the underlying assumption has changed, their fee also must change. They still believe they're paying £9,000 when, in fact, you need to charge £90,000 to cover all the extra work. A fixed fee requires you to calculate exactly what you've got to do for a client. This may not be easy.

Fixed fees (weekly, monthly, annual)

What is it?

13–22 Most fixed fees are based on individual pieces of work, like a lease or a contract. However, a number of firms offer clients the option of paying a fixed fee to cover all of their legal work for a fixed length of time. For example, Tyco pays Eversheds an annual fee to provide legal advice. Many employment firms offer a hotline service where HR managers pay an annual fee and then can phone as often as they need to, without incurring any additional fees.

Advantages

Your client knows exactly what they're paying for and your firm knows it has a guaranteed fee for the year. It doesn't need to rely on winning each piece of work, individually.

Disadvantages

Your firm needs a lot—and we mean *a lot*—of information before it can set a fee. It needs to know exactly what legal advice a client might need during the period. This information might be based on historic legal costs, but it also needs to predict what might come up. It also needs to make a large number of assumptions. For example, Court of Session actions can torpedo any budget. As you can imagine, these assumptions create the same problems as for normal fixed fees, a client may not appreciate that assumptions sometimes have to change and then dispute changes to their fees.

Contingent fees—success fees

What is it?

13–23 A contingent fee is linked to the successful conclusion of a piece of work. If a client is suing for compensation, you might agree that you'll only fee their file if you're successful. On the flip side, there are also abort fees. These are fees that are agreed if your client is unsuccessful. For example, if your client doesn't succeed in buying a business, you might agree that you only get 20% of the fee you otherwise would have charged

Advantages

A lot of legal work is risky. There's no guarantee that a client will win a case, get their house, sell their business or complete a deal. This risk has to be at the front of your minds. Many clients won't have the money to pay for a court case, even if they have a good legal reason for raising it. That's why, for individuals, no win/no fee arrangements are attractive. They allow the client to take a risk.

For corporates, a success fee also is attractive. They see the lawyer sharing in their risk. If corporate clients only make money if their deals are a success, they won't like a law firm that renders fees regardless. It's much easier for you to ask the question: "can you pay this bill?" when your client is ecstatic that a deal has been done (especially if they're richer for having done it).

Disadvantages

This is the same as for fixed fees or hourly rates (depending which you're using). You need to make sure that any success fee is profitable and that an abort doesn't lose you too much. You need information about your client to know what success actually means to them. You don't want to be saying that your success fee kicks in as soon as an employment tribunal gives its decision, if your client believes success is only demonstrated once they know that the decision isn't going to be appealed.

Don't forget about costs

Regardless of whether you're setting a price based on value or competitors, never forget that you need to recover the cost of your work. You can match a competitor's price, or you can charge a price your client is willing to pay. However, if that price does not exceed your costs, you lose money. This is why (regardless of the fee option) your firm needs you to record your time accurately (as we see in the next chapter). Your firm can use that information to work out if it's making money. **13–24**

For example, you may have quoted a fixed fee of £500 to complete a small claim, but it ends up taking you £1,000 worth of time to do it. Your firm needs to know this so that either it can increase its price the next time, or it can streamline its workflow to ensure that a similar job is completed within a £500 budget (for example, by having someone more senior doing that piece of work).

Don't forget about professional standards

Remember that you have a professional obligation to tell clients in their engagement letters what you intend to charge (or how you calculate fees). You also have an obligation to tell them if any assumptions change and that you plan to propose a change in their fee. We recommend that you're always open with your clients about fees; don't put off a discussion until the last minute. Your clients have budgets and definitely won't appreciate you changing a fee late in the day. They may not have the money to pay it or may need to obtain fresh board approval (if a corporate client). The sooner you discuss fees, the easier it is to agree changes. **13–25**

Summary

Setting a price is not easy. It requires information, informed guesses and an ability to see the big picture. However, as a new lawyer, it's worth spending time examining the various options and how they might apply to your clients. You may be able to offer a different option that is more appropriate (and better for your firm) than just hourly rates. **13–26**

CHAPTER 14

HOW TO RECORD TIME

Introduction

14–1 *After reviewing the fee, you agree a fixed fee of £1,500 (excluding VAT and costs) for the lease of the high street shop. Your hourly rate is £150 per hour but, after one week, you've spent five hours working on the lease. By the end of the second week, you've spent 10 hours, and, by the time you've finished, you've spent 20 hours.*

However, you've not recorded your time anywhere. Your partner checks your time sheet and asks how long it took and you say "10 hours"—you don't want to appear slow. Your partner is happy: "That fee was spot on—if we get another, we can charge the same amount and now we'll make a profit". Is he right, considering you've spent twice as long on it as he thought?

14–2 As we saw in the last chapter, setting a fee requires robust information. If your firm uses hourly rates, then it has to set a rate that recovers its costs and generates a profit. Equally, once a piece of work is done, the firm will want to charge for all the time that you and others have spent on it. If you don't record your time accurately then your firm simply won't have the right information to work out whether your fee is profitable. We know recording time is a chore. No one enjoys it, but it's critical. If you don't know how long something takes then you won't know if you're making money, or losing money. That's why your firm has to know how you spend your time. It's checking to see if it's making a profit.

Different firms have different ways to record time. Some depend on you writing notes on files, some have electronic systems, others even do it automatically by monitoring how long it takes to write emails or letters. Regardless of how sophisticated a system is, the principle behind time recording remains the same. How long does it take you to complete a particular piece of work? As the saying goes, "time is money" and, for many law firms, "money is time".

Outcome

14–3 By the end of this chapter, you'll understand the concept of and business rationale for time recording. You'll be able to impress your partner with your knowledge of fee recovery, common time-recording errors and the different processes of time recording. We'll also throw in some hints and tips to help you develop yourself as good time recorders.

Benefits of time recording

14–4 Time recording is the act of logging all of the time you spend on a particular client's file, together with a short description of what you have done. Why do you need to time record at all? It seems a bit laborious. Isn't time recording a thing of the past, especially when so many lawyers are moving towards charging fixed fees? If the answers were "no—we don't need time recording", we could wrap up the chapter. That would be too easy. It'll come as no surprise that there are a number of sound business reasons to record time.

Evidence

Let's forget about your firm for the moment. We know from the last chapter that your firm needs information to set fees. But why does it need this information? Time recording provides essential financial information. It's the one tool that shows you just how much time you've spent on a client matter and also provides you with a summary of what you've done. As we saw in the last chapter, your time recording is directly linked to your hourly charge out rate. It helps you know (at a glance) how much work you've done. This work that you've done is known as your work in progress (your WIP). Most firms expect you to meet an annual WIP target. This might be anything between 1,000–1,500 hours. If you meet your targets you increase your chance of a pay rise, a bonus and promotion. **14–5**

Accurate time recording also helps clients. Some solicitors send clients a breakdown of the time they've spent, so that the clients can see what they've done. This is useful if you spend more time than you expect; you might want to let a client know that he or she is getting a discount if you've agreed a fixed fee and your actual time is more than the price agreed. This can help with repeat clients who'll then be more willing to pay more next time, knowing how hard you worked. Some clients will ask for a breakdown of your time. Accurate time recording (with a good narrative) enables you to respond to the sort of client queries that start: "why am I paying so much for . . .".

Lastly, if your client decides to exercise any contractual right to send their file for external taxation (i.e. an external audit) as we looked at in Ch.11 (how to avoid complaints) then—clearly—the information that time recording yields helps the auditor reach an informed decision and, hopefully, one in your favour.

Complaints

This flows naturally from our first point. Time recording shows the time you have incurred on a job, which (in turn) forms the basis of your fee note. Fees that can be linked to objective time recording data are, by their nature, transparent. This helps reduce the number of potential client complaints (which is good risk management) and, if they do arise, to deal with them effectively. On that note, dealing with complaints is good for business. It's an example of customer relationship management in action. A lot of research has shown that disgruntled clients who present issues that are resolved quickly become loyal clients. **14–6**

Accuracy

Time recording is the basis of your WIP (Work in Progress) figure. WIP, however, is not cash. You can't spend WIP. It won't pay the rent. It's not profit. It's only potential profit, which might then become cash. It does not become cash until you convert it into a fee that is—in turn—paid. **14–7**

An example might help demonstrate the difference between WIP, profit and cash. Let's assume you've worked 10 hours for a client. Your charge out rate is £100/hour. Based on the time you've spent, your WIP is £1,000. However, this is not yet profit, because you haven't fee'd your file. You suggest to your partner that the file be charged at £1,000 to cover all the time you have spent on it. However, your partner knows the client won't pay more than £500, no matter how complicated the work might have been. Your potential profit is based on the £500 actually billed, rather than the time you spent on it. Now, let's assume the client takes three months to pay your bill. Your WIP is £1,000. Your potential profit is based on a £500 invoice—and your cash is only received when the client pays three months later. Good time recording always gives you an accurate WIP figure that, in turn, lets you assess whether you need to render interim fees (see below for more in interim fees).

Increases profits

14–8 Brian Inkster (Inkster LLP) says:

> "The more profitable fee earners at Inksters are definitely those that time record the best . . . by improving time recording all around we improve profitability".[1]

This is true—accurate recording does increase your firm's profits. How? In a bid to secure work in a competitive market, fee earners sometimes underestimate their time when issuing an estimate or a quote. It's easy to understand why; you don't want your existing clients to leave you for another firm. You also want to be super-competitive in order to tempt new clients to come to you.

However, it's a bit of a trap and it can lead you into situations where you end up working lots of extra hours you haven't quoted for, meaning you end up with a much smaller profit margin. By recording your time, you can see exactly how long the same (or similar) piece of work took, previously. If you know how long a job will take, you can quote much more accurately. To put it another way, you can't price for profit if you don't know how much the work is costing your firm to do.

Time recording ensures that no unit of time is forgotten about; all of your time is available to you (or your line-manager) when assessing a fee note. Even picking up one extra six-minute unit of time a day, over a year, significantly increases your profits.

True cost of time

14–9 If all your time is recorded (including time you spend on client admin) then a calculation can be made of the true cost to your firm of any piece of work that you do. This is especially important when you're working for fixed fees. Your hourly cost rate includes a nominal allocation of rent, other fixed costs, heat/light and—of course—wages. If you render fees that don't make back the hourly cost rate, then your firm won't stay in business very long.

Trends and future planning

14–10 Good time recording helps to spot trends and highlight work that you shouldn't be doing using fixed fees. Let's say, for example, that you price a particular service at £499. Your charge out rate is £100 per hour (to make it simple). Over a financial quarter your time recording routinely shows that you take six or seven hours to complete that type of work. What does this trend tell you? It tells you that each time you take on this work you'll lose £100 to £200 for your firm. Unless you're registered as a charity, you want to try to avoid providing free work to clients

---

[1] Quote from Brian Inkster obtained by the authors.

You can also use trend information to look at sophisticated pricing policies, like fixed fee bands. With fixed fee bands, as a client matter becomes more complicated, it moves up to the next fee band. In other words, you can use time recording information to pick the most appropriate cases for fixed fees, or to make your fixed fee structures more sophisticated. You can plan better for the future. However, you can't undertake any trend analysis without data.

Performance

You can use time recording data to assess how long a fee earner takes to complete a piece of work. If necessary, your firm can make an appropriate intervention with further training to improve his/her performance. **14–11**

Imagine we have two lawyers. Both do the same type of work. Iain always fees 10 hours and Andrew always fees 20 hours. Your partner might want to speak to both to explore why there's such a difference. Perhaps Iain doesn't record his time accurately and he should be recording 20 hours? Perhaps Andrew needs extra training to help him understand the contracts involved so that he can become faster. Accurate time recording allows you and your firm to ask the right questions and then look for ways to improve.

Understanding fee recovery

We talked in the last chapter about how a fee deals with two chunks of money. The first chunk is to pay for your firm's costs (including you and your time). **14–12**

Full cost recovery is where you recover the total cost of your services. That is to say the cost of your time (your salary etc.) and also your share of costs that are not directly related to delivering a service, but which nonetheless are necessary to run your firm (office rent, heating, lighting etc.). The aim is to avoid running at a loss because the true cost of providing your service hasn't been met. This requires some mathematics. You need to work out what your hourly cost rate is and then make sure you render fees that at least cover these costs or, better still, exceed them. You only make a profit (otherwise known as a margin) if your fees exceed costs.

You should always render your fee notes promptly after a transaction concludes. Bear in mind the "gratitude curve". This states that a client's willingness to pay fees diminishes as time passes, no matter how happy they're with the quality of your service at the time.

Recovery

Your recovery (or realisation) rate is the percentage of your fees that are paid. Clearly, your target is to recover as many of your fees as possible (and at full value). How do you achieve that? **14–13**

Interim fees

You don't need to wait until the end of your work before issuing a fee. Many legal tasks last months, if not years, and clients may prefer you to issue smaller regular bills than to receive one large bill at the end. **14–14**

Interim fees:

- boost cash flow (so you can pay office rent, staff salaries and other bills);
- reduce the risk of your clients trying to negotiate you down (or even refusing to pay) a single, large fee at the end of a long transaction; and

- deal with real-world market volatility. If one of your clients runs into financial difficulties, then you'll struggle to get back anything like the amount you're owed. Instead, you'll be writing-off your unpaid fees as bad debts. Bad debts are bad, hence the name.

Shedding clients

14–15 This might sound a little counter-intuitive but it can be effective. Often the time spent in fee disputes is just not worth the aggravation. You can spend a lot of time and money to recover only a little bit more than you spend. Always consider the cost of recovering money as well as the sum you'll actually receive if successful.

The idea behind shedding is to identify and remove the worst performing 1% to 5% of your clients every year. In year one this makes little difference but over a five-year period you'll dramatically change your client base. What you're looking at is how much money they bring in to your firm and how long they take to pay their fees (indeed if they pay at all). This only works if you have good quality new clients coming in. This is why networking is important even if you're busy.

Referrals

14–16 Ask your good clients (i.e. regular payers) for referrals. People deal with people who are like them. If you ask your best clients for referrals, then they're likely to introduce you to people who will appreciate you. Similarly, fee resistant clients are likely to refer you only because you're perceived as "cheap", or a "push-over".

Elasticity

14–17 If you increase your prices by 10%, what percentage of your clients do you think will leave? The answer for most firms is almost none. Generally, the demand for professional services is inelastic for two reasons. Firstly, clients want to deal with you because they trust you and it takes time to build that trust. Secondly, even with a 5% to 10% increase, the size of your fee is often just not enough for them to worry about. Just bear in mind that there is a "glass ceiling" above which the client drop off rate increases dramatically. The point, here, is that by increasing your fees a little, your good payers will—to an extent—help to cancel out those who either don't pay or who want to negotiate.

Staff training

14–18 Your firm will have procedures in place to recover fees. Make sure you know what those are and, if not, ask for training.

Costs

14–19 In a 2012 article for *LegalTechnology.com*, Stewart Hadley noted that a decade ago, 97% of firms billed clients for photocopying and almost all of those bills were paid. By 2012, only 87% of firms were billing for photocopying. Nowadays, scanning is common (and there are associated costs e.g. cloud data storage). Lots of documents are also printed to a network printer. However, only 51% of law firms recover printing and only 36% recover scanning. Basically, the disbursement (costs) landscape (i.e. what is incurred for clients and what is charged back to them) has changed.[2]

Profitability is king. Your fee recovery needs to include the recovery of client costs. These must be passed as far as is possible (and prudent) back to the relevant clients. To recover these costs, however, you need to record them accurately. Modern systems of any sophistication will let you capture this data. Some points for you to ponder: how many sheets of printing are being charged to "firm expenses" rather than to your clients? Are you even tracking your printing? Are you charging for scans (to take account of server space)? Are you capturing other "hard costs" such as taxis and couriers? Which teams are systematically charging disbursements and which are not? Which of your team has the highest write-off percentages? We've said it before and we'll say it again—you can't manage what you don't measure.

Financial leakage

Not recouping otherwise recoverable legal fees and client costs is called "financial leakage". At one end of the spectrum it can be down to you as a fee earner simply not taking care in assigning a correct matter number, when doing time recording. At the other end, however, it can be indicative of a general resistance to recovery (e.g. because you charge fixed-fees). You know enough to appreciate that a recoverable fee and/or a recoverable cost that isn't clawed back is, quite simply, lost profit. **14–20**

Common time recording errors

There are classic errors in time recording that the authors see cropping up again and again. **14–21**

Failure to record

Some solicitors don't time record at all. A common excuse is that they just don't have the time. For all the reasons outlined in this chapter, however, you should appreciate why you must time record, whether you work for fixed fees, even if only to obtain management data. **14–22**

Human error

The best example of human error is using the wrong matter number. To get all the data you need to correctly set fixed fees (or to adjust your hourly billing rates), you need to allocate your time (and all client disbursements) against the correct matter number. It's just a case of taking care. **14–23**

Narrative

Remember, more and more clients want an objective justification for their fees. A common error is that solicitors either don't provide a narrative at all, or only input a partial narrative. It's so important, from an evidential perspective, to make sure you write down what you actually do for your clients. **14–24**

A warning, though—make sure what you write is appropriate. You shouldn't write anything in a fee narrative that you wouldn't write in an email. Clients

[2] See: *http://www.legaltechnology.com/latest-news/the-changing-face/* (17 October 2012) [Accessed 15 June 2016].

can—and will—read the narratives to see what they're paying for. One trainee, after a week of photocopying evidence for an important case, wrote as their narrative for the day, "eight hours of ****." The client read it, demanded both an apology and discount, and got both.

Double write–off

14–25 This is where fee earners try and reduce their billable time in order to maintain an image of efficiency, in the eyes of their partner, by allocating otherwise chargeable time inappropriately to firm admin. This frequently happens if bonuses are based on hitting targets such as 85% realisation across all files. If recording time means missing targets, then a fee earner may think to record it wrongly. This is a so-called DNA factor; an in-built reluctance to be transparent if a person feels that doing so would be damaging to him or her.

You have to record all your time as either billable time or client admin. Firstly, it helps your firm to decide whether to get you additional admin support. Secondly, if you don't do it, you effectively are writing down your time before you even draft your fee note. If your partner caps your fee further, you have a double write-off.

Timing

14–26 Often solicitors wait several days to record their time. We know you're busy people, but you need to record either as you go or at the end of your working day. If you wait too long inevitably you forget what you did, when you did it and why you did it.

Forgotten time

14–27 This flows from the previous point. If you don't record your time regularly, you forget what you did. You might then under-record. If your partner then discounts what you have recorded then, again, you have just given your client a double discount.

Time recording processes

14–28 There is a whole host of ways that you can time record (so you have no excuses not to do it). They all have different pros and cons. Whatever you choose, however, it has to be applied and used consistently.

Back of a napkin

14–29 We're only half joking when we suggest this. It may be basic and it's probably inappropriate, but at least it's better than not recording your time at all.

Paper

14–30 With this method you keep a template at your side, filling it out as you move from one project to the next.

Pros

The only plus, in this day and age, is that you can use paper recording when your IT goes down. At the end of a day, if you've shut your PC down and a client calls, you can also make a quick paper entry (to save time re-booting).

Cons

There are several: solicitors often forget to fill out paper timesheets, or they try and play catch-up at the end of a day. If you don't use this method in real-time it becomes difficult to use accurately, with each passing hour. It's hard to track time on paper accurately if you're jumping around from file to file. Paper timesheets also can only account for so many matters. There will be days (we hope) when you'll deal with more projects than you can physically fit on a sheet, leaving you using multiple sheets (one of which, according to sod's law, ends up being lost). Lastly, your data is useless unless entered into software that can run reports.

Excel spreadsheets

With this method you use a PC based spreadsheet. **14–31**

Pros

Using spreadsheets overcomes most of the drawbacks of paper entries. In addition, you easily can run reports with Excel spreadsheets. As they're digital files, they can be backed up and archived more effectively than your paper timesheets. Excel is universal so your learning curve, if you haven't used it, will be small.

Cons

There are a few drawbacks with Excel. If you use it, you'll be entering lots of data into spreadsheets every week, eating up a few hours of your time. If you need more sophisticated add-ons, you'll spend a significant number of hours customising your templates. You'll still need paper timesheets as a backup.

Software/apps

This is where you do your time recording on your PC using an off-the shelf software package (or a bespoke package) or using an online, cloud based tool. **14–32**

Pros

Using software (and mobile apps) overcomes most of the drawbacks of using paper time recording sheets. It retains the benefits of Excel based time recording, but also deals with the downsides associated with spreadsheets. Some firms have increased their profits after incorporating software time recording into their workflow. Why? They start to pick-up time that just wasn't tracked, before. Software lets you keep track of multiple client matters at once, making it easier to switch between them without losing time. Packages also make generating detailed reports easier. Lastly, since data is tracked in real-time, you can record at the click of a button. No more daily or weekly data entry.

Cons

The only real drawback is cost. Packages with multi-user licences definitely put a dent in your wallet. Cloud based packages (or PC based packages with cloud back-up) should keep your data secure in the event of IT failure, but you may still need to keep a hard copy.

Improving time recording

Culture

14–34 Culture does play a part. Your firm needs to encourage a culture of time recording. Often fee earners will say that time recording is tedious; your firm needs to ensure that its system is user friendly and ergonomic from a workflow point of view.

Incentives

14–35 Incentives work; ask your firm to reward those who time-record on a daily basis (e.g. a monthly prize). You can also set-up your system to stop time sheets being submitted until all your target hours are accounted for.

Quick improvements

14–36 Quick improvements with time recording are easy. Your homework from this chapter is to identify the top three things you'll change about your time recording. It could be as simple as this:

- record one extra unit of time per day (that otherwise would be allocated to client admin or firm admin);
- time record at the end of each day; and
- provide a better narrative.

As with all changes in human behaviour, you should never try to alter more than three things at any one time.

Once you have your top three priorities, commit to introducing one of them each week. Write your commitment down and stick it to your office wall. A written commitment is much more potent and you'll be more likely to stick to it. After three months, print off your reports and look to see just how much you have improved. You'll be surprised the difference that small changes make.

Summary

14–33 Becoming a good time recorder requires training and a consistent approach. It's about forming good habits. If you record time after each piece of work, it becomes a natural part of your work.

CHAPTER 15

HOW TO MANAGE YOUR TIME

Introduction

Six months after qualifying you have 10 files on your desk, another hundred in your cabinets, 20 unanswered emails in your inbox, and your Outlook calendar is reminding you that you have a half-day holiday today to meet your mum for lunch. Yet, your partner keeps giving you more work. The senior associate wants you to take a document to the sheriff court this morning and your secretary is refusing to do photocopying, because she's too busy with your partner's dictation. You don't have any choice; you need to cancel lunch. You're not going to be leaving the office anytime soon. 15–1

Your contract may say that you'll work from 9am to 5pm. However, we don't 15–2
want to lie to you: you won't. More often than not you'll work late. You may even work weekends. As you gain responsibility, you'll find that bringing work home helps you feel like you have a head start on the week. It's simply a fact of life that if you act for clients then you don't work regular hours. On the high street, a client can phone at 4:55pm with an urgent question and you need to deal with it. In legal aid firms, your clients are not just accused of crimes during working hours. In corporate firms, your clients may not even be on the same time zone, if you deal with people across the world. Your "home time" could be your Asian client's start of the day.

This doesn't mean that you've signed up to be a solicitor 24/7. It just means that you need to understand that events can dictate what you'll do in a day. That's why it's important that you plan your time effectively. You have limited time and you don't want to spend every waking hour at your desk. You need skills to decide what to do and when. Just because a client emails you, it doesn't mean they need an answer straight away. Some just need you to acknowledge that you have received their message. However, it's up to you to decide how to deal with every demand made of you. This is time management, and it makes you a much more effective solicitor.

If you don't believe us, we have the stats to back this up. A 2007 survey by Proudfoot Consulting (covering 2,500 businesses over four years, in 38 countries) revealed that wasted time costs UK businesses £80 billion per year. That's equivalent to 7% of GDP, to put it in context.[1] Good time management is good business, especially when your fees are based on time.

[1] Quoted from the "2007 Proudfoot Productivity Report", as reported in the news article on *http://www.reliableplant.com/Read/8753/cost-of-poor-productivity-in-uk-put-at-%C2%A380-billion* [Accessed 15 June 2016].

Outcomes

15–3 By the end of this chapter, you'll know what time management is and how you can take practical steps to work more efficiently. We set out the key steps required to identify the reasons why you might not be using your time effectively. We then suggest ways in which you can tackle these issues.

What is time management?

15–4 Have you ever wondered how some people always seem to have the time to do everything that they need to do? Are you perhaps one of the many who feels that you're rushing around, always struggling to meet deadlines? Ever wondered why that might be? The reason, simply, is that these people have become good both at using time effectively and in deploying good time management skills.

Time management is not difficult to understand as a concept, but it can be quite hard to achieve in practice. Why? It requires you to invest time (which you may not have a lot of already) and effort, to prioritise and get organised. However, with a little application, two things happen:

- the process becomes a habit; and
- your time management quickly improves.

Afterwards, with only light-touch monitoring, your days become more structured. This leaves you with bags of time to deal with everything you need to do: answering emails, drafting contracts that your assistant gave you two weeks ago, and your own filing. As you pick up new time management skills, you'll gain much more control over your working (and personal) life.

Effective time management

15–5 The key to effective time management is to understand the difference between those tasks that are *urgent* and those that are *important*.

Urgent or important?

15–6 An urgent task is one that can be classed as requiring immediate attention and action. However, whether you actually give it that immediate attention may (or may not) matter. An important task, however, is one that always matters. Not doing it'll have big consequences for you and/or your firm. Let's look at some examples. Reflect on whether you think each is urgent, important or neither.

Answering the phone—urgent or important?

15–7 If you don't answer your phone your caller will ring off. You won't know why they called. It might be a new client wanting to give you the retainer of a lifetime. It might also just be a call to tell you that you could claim back PPI. Arguably, answering your phone is urgent but perhaps not important.

Going to the dentist—urgent or important?

15–8 If you don't go to your dentist you might suffer dental problems. On that basis, this arguably is urgent. If you start to get tooth decay, then does that change it to important? That seems reasonable also. In other words, something that is urgent—but not yet important—can change to something that is important.

Checking Facebook—urgent or important?

Do you check Facebook at the start of each day? Do you check it regularly during the working day? Perhaps checking social media is neither urgent nor important? Understanding the distinction between tasks that are urgent and important is the key to prioritising your time and managing your workload. That, in turn, comes down to: **15–9**

- using time management tools, like a priority matrix (we look at this next);
- a good time management mind-set; and
- controlling your environment (again, we look at some practical strategies, later in this chapter).

Time management tools

A priority matrix

A priority matrix is an easy to use, intuitive grid that lets you organise your tasks into four categories: **15–10**

- do first;
- do next;
- do later; and
- don't do.

It has scales for "urgency" and "importance". At a glance, you can see which tasks are both important and urgent, and those that are neither important nor urgent. An example of the form is included in the Schedule.

You can use a matrix for your daily tasks and—zooming out—for weekly (and even monthly) tasks. Its application is limitless and it only takes a couple of seconds to draw a grid on a piece of paper, and then update it as necessary.

We issue one health warning. "Urgency" and "importance" are not set in stone. Remember the example we gave you about answering the phone? Things can gradually (or suddenly) change from being urgent to important (and vice-versa). A client phoning just once might be urgent. The same client phoning you three times in 10 minutes is probably both urgent and important. You have to review your matrix regularly to decide if something requires to be moved because it has become more (or less) important. Then it can be dealt with accordingly.

Mindset

The next aspect of effective time management is for you to develop the right mindset. Let's examine a few different factors: **15–11**

Owl or lark?

You have a time of day during which you tend to work best. Are you a morning person or a night person? In other words, are you an owl or a lark? Whatever you are, make sure you schedule your most difficult tasks for that time. Andrew prefers drafting long documents first thing in the morning before starting any other work so as not to get distracted. Iain, on the other hand, prefers working in the evening once all the smaller tasks have been completed. **15–12**

Multi-tasking

15–13 Generally, people are not good at multi-tasking, because it causes the brain's processing capacity to be split across two or three things, to the detriment of each individual task. From a time management point of view, it's better to finish one job before moving onto another. Remember, you can only do one thing at a time. When you're doing something, don't worry about anything else. You can't answer two phones at once. You can't draft two documents at the same time. Do one thing. Finish it. Move onto the next.

Perspective

15–14 You need to keep a sense of perspective. If you try to accomplish too many tasks at once, it leads to what is termed "overwhelm" (feelings of stress) which—in turn—causes diminished performance. That's why you should always try and do one thing at a time. Your brain may try and tell you to do more, but you've only got two hands, one keyboard and one phone.

Keep in mind that the sun won't fall out of the sky if you fail to complete that last task of the day, or if you hold it over until the following morning, especially if it's part of a well thought out prioritisation strategy. Getting an early night, so that you're fit for work the next day, can be a much better option than meeting a self-imposed deadline.

Dithering

15–15 Dithering or procrastination is a significant challenge. Do you find yourself doing anything other than a task you just can't be bothered with? Is it a case of, "I'll do it tomorrow, there's still plenty of time"? Procrastination is defined as, "to put off till some future time, to defer" (Chambers English Dictionary). This rather suggests that dithering, in reality, has little correlation with the relative difficulty (or even pleasantness) of a task.

If you use a priority matrix, it's actually entirely reasonable to plan certain tasks to be completed at a later time. Here, however, you've made a decision that they're neither sufficiently urgent nor important. This isn't dithering; this is planning (to help get more important tasks completed first). However, if a job is considered to be both urgent and important, and you keep putting it off, then you're dithering. Why might this be? We'll tell you after a short coffee break. We might even walk our dogs for half an hour. Hang on, now we're dithering . . .

The classic reasons are:

- a task seems unpleasant;
- you might not know where to start;
- you're a perfectionist. People who tend towards perfectionism often feel they just don't have enough time to complete a task perfectly and, if they can't do it perfectly, they prefer to put it off until such time as they can.

There are, however, some practical strategies that you can implement, to help minimise your procrastination:

Invert the process

15–16 Do a task you don't want to do first and then reward yourself with something you do want to do.

Timing

If you're a morning person, cover off your tough tasks in the morning, when you're fresh. If you're an evening person, do it last, so that you know it's done before you go home. **15–17**

Write it down

It's much harder to ignore a task once you have written it on a "to-do" list (especially if it's a list of things to do that day). **15–18**

Involve others

Do unpleasant jobs with colleagues. People tend to complete jobs when working collaboratively, to avoid letting colleagues down. **15–19**

Question

Ask yourself: "will things get better if I put this job off?" The answer 99% of the time will be a resounding "no". This is a good way of persuading yourself to do small (but unpleasant) jobs, like sorting your desk out. **15–20**

Post-task satisfaction

Think about how good it'll feel when you've completed a job; the simple joy of ticking it off your "to-do" list; and that feeling of job satisfaction. The key is to focus on the end goal, not on the task needed to accomplish it. **15–21**

Break it down

Carve up large tasks into smaller bite-sized chunks. This makes even the most complex tasks seem more manageable. **15–22**

The two-minute test

If you have natural down time during the day (for example, between meetings) then make a list of the small jobs that will take you less than two minutes, and get them covered off. **15–23**

Reverse psychology

Think about the pain of not doing something. Just as people are motivated by reward, they can be motivated by a fear of loss. **15–24**

Controlling your environment

The third aspect of good time management is to learn how to control your environment, so as to minimise distractions and eradicate time-wasters. Let's look at some key environmental factors and the practical strategies to control them. **15–25**

Phone

If you're busy, turn your phone off or switch it to silent. You should use voicemail (with a message you update each morning) and set aside a time in the day to return your missed calls. **15–26**

When you're on the phone, always be polite (clearly) but avoid excessive small talk, to keep calls as short as possible. Try taking your calls standing up. Strangely, people who stand when on the phone tend more to keep their conversations brief and to the point (possibly to avoid lower back pain—the end result is the same).

Email

15–27 This is a difficult one. All your instincts tell you it's wrong, but only check your emails a couple of times a day. Close email when it's not being used, because new messages flashing up are a real distraction. Alternatively, switch off notifications so that you only see new emails when you check them.

Everyone tends to check emails constantly. However, if checking-in a few times a day is just too much for you (and it is for Iain Sim and Andrew Todd, too), you can set up preferences to filter your mail. You should delete your spam and any irrelevant emails immediately (including general emails that don't actually relate to you). If appropriate, forward emails to colleagues who can provide a better response. Once you open up a message, we suggest that you handle it once: read, respond, file. In other words, deal with it. Don't have your inbox cluttered with "read" messages. Finally, be wary of emails marked "urgent" or "high priority". They may be important to the person who sent it, but that doesn't necessarily mean that they are to you. Some people just mark all their emails urgent, even when they're not.

Tidy desk

15–28 Keep your desk tidy. Clutter is a distraction and, actually, is quite depressing. Allied to that, the act of tidying your desk improves your sense of motivation. You'll find it easier to stay on top of your work. This could be one of your two-minute procrastination busters?

Mail

15–29 You should open your mail near a bin and get rid of what you can, immediately. Again, aim to handle each piece of mail just the once. It's the same process as per email: read, process and reply (or action).

We suggest that you keep three piles: keep, give away and throw away.

- Keep—when you need something for your records, or you need to act on it.
- Give away—when it's work that can and/or should be delegated.
- Throw away—when the mail has no value to you or anyone else.

Meetings

15–30 You should only attend meetings that are relevant to you. If you get an invite, ask yourself, "is this necessary?" and "does it have a specific purpose?" Arrive on time (neither early nor late). You should know the purpose of each meeting you go to, by getting an agenda in advance. We suggest that you always use a timed agenda (especially for longer meetings, or where the chairperson is less effective). Don't be afraid to leave early, if your meeting is only partially of relevance. We know though this can be difficult when you're the most junior person at the table. As you gain experience, however, you can speak up and say if you don't have anything else to add. And, if you're planning to do this, let everyone know before the meeting too, so it doesn't come as a surprise.

Visitors

Schedule blocks of time when you can meet with clients and/or colleagues. Our advice is to refer to these as "appointments". This is just a little more formal, so that the person coming to see you then is more likely to stay focused. **15–31**

You might also want to try to limit your appointments to 10 or 15 minutes. You find that many people schedule all their meetings for one hour. If so, the meetings tend to last one hour. This states that people use up all the time they're given to undertake a task. A good tip is to schedule a meeting for 30 minutes. It'll tend to last that long and you'll cover off just as much. Make sure to book your meeting room for one hour. That way, if it does overrun, you won't have someone knocking on the door asking to use the room.

As you gain experience, you need to learn to say "no" if a meeting serves no purpose. As a trainee, every meeting is a chance to learn from colleagues. However, when you're 10 years qualified, you may have more useful things to do with that time. Lastly, if a colleague comes to see you at a time when you're pressured, don't be afraid to re-schedule.

Stress

When you're busy, you're more likely to have a quicker temper than usual. Stress and anger will both eat into your time, because you'll be spending wasted minutes here and there calming yourself down and trying to regain focus. Our advice is that you try to stay as calm as possible. It's actually worth letting your colleagues know that you're busy and that you need some quiet time to complete your work. **15–32**

Other

Our final pieces of advice are: **15–33**

- turn off instant messaging applications;
- close documents when you have finished (and file them away);
- close webpages after you have finished with them;
- log-out of social media at work and ensure personal phones are not nearby your workspace to prevent distractions.

Summary

Managing your time is more than just scheduling your day and setting out a list of tasks. It's about changing your priorities as emails arrive, colleagues ask for help and the phone rings. Controlling your environment helps ensure that you won't have needless distractions, so you can concentrate on your work. Avoiding dithering will help you work faster and smarter. **15–34**

CHAPTER 16

HOW TO DELEGATE WORK

Introduction

16–1 *Nine months after you qualify you're starting to see the light. You work quickly and efficiently and, most days, you get to go home at a regular time. It almost feels like you have a life again.*

Your partner tells you that one of your colleagues is leaving and it will be six months before they're replaced. As you've shown how good you are with the files you're currently working on, he now wants you to take responsibility for half of your colleague's files.

You know this means that you will now have at least 30 extra files to contend with. You have no idea how you'll find the time to deal with them. You're already working at capacity. What do you do?

16–2 There are 24 hours in a day, and only one of you. There's a finite amount that you can accomplish, however hard you work. When you're good at your job your colleagues and clients naturally want more and more from you (and of you). It's actually quite flattering, but it can have the effect of you becoming overloaded with work. In turn, this can make you feel pressured and stressed—feelings of being overwhelmed.

When you're overwhelmed, you end up not being able to do everything that everyone wants, and this leaves you feeling that you're letting people down. If you're extremely overloaded, it may well be that you're letting down colleagues and clients. And, that could lead to complaints to your firm, and even to the SLCC.

You need to learn to delegate. Quite simply, delegation is a skill whereby another person works for you. Normally, delegation is vertical (manager to subordinate, such as partner to assistant), but it also can be horizontal (peer to peer, such as assistant to assistant). It's important from the off, however, that you understand and appreciate that when you delegate any work, you remain accountable and responsible for the outcomes. Delegation simply empowers someone else in your team to make decisions and take action. It is *only* a shift of decision-making authority. It's not the same as abrogation or abdication. If you ask a trainee to complete a contract, it's up to you to make sure they do it right. You're responsible if they get it wrong. Delegation is a key skill for all new lawyers, because it's only through delegation that you can control all your files. If you master it, you really can be in two places at once.

Outcome

16–3 In this chapter we examine the 12 rules of effective delegation so that both you, and the person you delegate work to, gain from the process. We then examine what happens if you don't delegate effectively and you end up micromanaging work.

Delegation skills

How to delegate

If you work on your own, there's only a limited amount that you can do, however hard you work. We know that two hands are better than one, and four hands are better than two, but how often do we put that into practice by asking other people to help us? This is a particular problem for lawyers, because we tend to work on "our files" for "our clients". We don't like to delegate because we feel the need to deal with our files and clients ourselves. **16–4**

However, there are simply times when you can't do everything. You need to delegate either because you're running out of time or because it's cheaper (and/or faster) for someone else to do the work. There may only be 24 hours in the day, but that's 48 hours for two people and 72 hours for three people. You can't magically make more time, but you can do an awful lot more in the time you have if you delegate.

12 rules of delegation

There are 12 golden rules to effective delegation: **16–5**

Benefit

Delegation is a two-way street. It's meant to benefit you and your colleagues. You need to consider what you want to delegate, and why. Are you delegating simply to get rid of work you loathe, or are you trying to help a junior colleague develop? **16–6**

Use of a matrix

To answer this, use a delegation matrix. You'll see a simple one below. A basic delegation matrix has four quadrants and two scales. They're easy to use. **16–7**

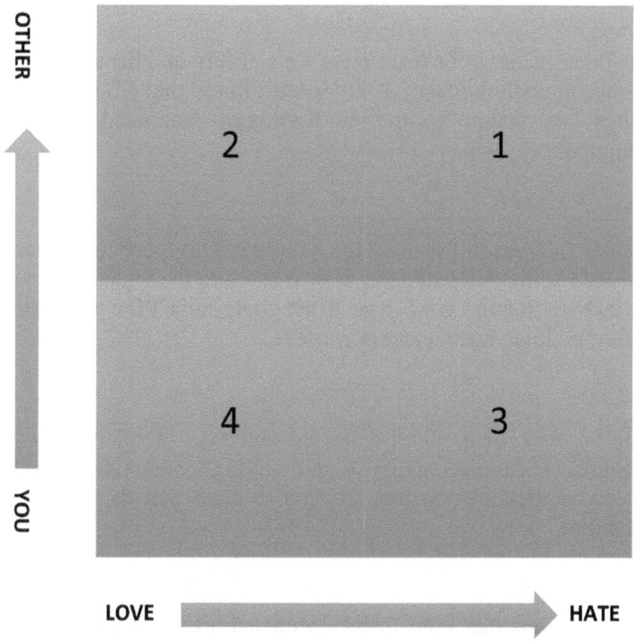

You simply place the pieces of work you're thinking of delegating into the appropriate quadrant. You can even take it further by adding numeric scales (1–10) and placing work tasks even more precisely within the quadrants. Ultimately, however, the point is that—at a glance—you can see the work you need to keep doing, and the work you definitely can/want to delegate first.

Suitability

16–8 Make sure that any work you intend to delegate is, in fact, suitable to be delegated. There are certain things only you should do (for example, anti-money laundering risk assessments (though larger firms will have separate teams for this, you should still know your own clients as we discussed in Ch.6 (how to open files))): there's no point in delegating one of these tasks.

Clarity

16–9 Be clear about what you're asking your team member to do. If you can't be clear, they won't be clear; that's a recipe for disappointment. Poor delegation is to say: "I want you to take this file and finish it off." Good delegation is to say: "I want you to take this file for the lease of a shop and finish it off by completing the LBTT return. You'll find the information you need to complete the form in this document. Can you prepare everything in draft then show it to me? Once I've checked it, we'll then arrange for payment. I'll explain then what you need to do."

Selection

16–10 Select who should take on a task, but make sure you can answer the question: "what are they going to get out of it?" If the work you delegate is obviously a task that will help a team member to develop, you get more buy in.

Ability

16–11 Make sure you consider your team member's ability and his training needs. Can he actually accomplish the task? If he doesn't know that LBTT stands for Land and Buildings Transaction Tax then he'll struggle. You need to ensure that any gaps are plugged.

Explanation

16–12 Explain clearly the reason for the work you're asking your team member to do. Explain why it's being delegated and how it fits into the wider legal project. This is linked to goal setting in Ch.17 (how to set goals and CPD); people like to know that what they're doing has a clear purpose.

Expectation

16–13 You need to be clear, also, about expected outcomes. Explain how you plan to measure progress (again, this is basic goal setting). Sometimes it's good to ask them to recap in their own words, so you're clear that there hasn't been any misunderstanding.

Resource

16–14 Discuss the resources that your team member thinks will be required (whether they relate to location, time, equipment, materials and money etc.).

Timescales

Agree a deadline. Make sure you include a means to monitor and measure progress. **16–15**

Inform others

Update any stakeholders (for example, your client, other staff/teams etc.) so that they also know that you're delegating certain pieces of work. This helps to avoid situations where colleagues also delegate work, leading to the team member becoming overwhelmed. **16–16**

Feedback

Provide feedback. It's important that you let people know how they're doing and that they're achieving the goals that you've set. **16–17**

Levels of delegation

There are different levels of freedom that you can confer on a team member. The more experienced and reliable your assistant is, the more you can safely delegate. It's good to explore with your colleague the level of authority they actually feel comfortable being given. Some people are confident, others less so. Since you're retaining accountability for work, it's your responsibility to delegate at an appropriate level. But why guess? Involving your colleague in establishing their comfort zone is an essential part of your "contract" with them. **16–18**

The following statements help to illustrate the different levels of delegation. These are simplified, obviously, for clarity. In reality you would use more expansive language. These also are not exhaustive. There are shades of grey. As you read through the list, you'll appreciate that each statement progressively offers your colleague more and more delegated freedom. Level one is the lowest level of delegation, level 10 is the highest level (and rarely found in law firms).

The 10 levels of delegation

1. "Do exactly what I say." This is an instruction, with no delegated freedom. **16–19**
2. "Look into this and tell me the situation. I'll decide." This is asking for investigation and analysis, but no recommendation. The person delegating will assess the options and make the decision.
3. "Look into this and tell me the situation. We'll decide together." This is subtly different to number two, with the decision being a shared process (which can be helpful when you're trying to develop people).
4. "Tell me the situation and what help you need from me in assessing and dealing with it. Then we'll decide." This opens the possibility of greater freedom for analysis and decision-making.
5. "Give me your analysis of the situation (reasons and options) and a recommendation. I'll let you know whether you can go ahead." This seeks analysis and recommendation, but the manager still will check the reasoning and make the final decision.
6. "Decide, but wait for my go-ahead." The other person is trusted enough to assess the situation and make a decision in principle. However, for reasons of task importance, the boss prefers to keep control of timing ("wait for my go-ahead"). This level of delegation can be rather

frustrating for people, if used too often. The reason for controlling the timing needs to be explained.

7. "Decide and go ahead unless I say not to." Now, the less senior person is starting to control the action. This subtle increase in responsibility will save the manager the time of making a decision. The default is positive, rather than negative.
8. "Decide and let me know what you did (and what happened)." This, as with each notch up the scale, saves even more time. This level of delegation also enables a degree of follow-up by the manager as to the effectiveness of execution of the delegated responsibility.
9. "Decide and act. You don't need to check back with me." This is the greatest freedom that can be given, while the manager still retains overall responsibility. A high level of confidence, clearly, is necessary.
10. "Decide where action needs to be taken and manage the situation. It's your responsibility now." This is generally not used without a formal change of the other person's job role. This basically amounts to assigning part of your job. You'd use this highest level of delegation when, for example, you're developing your successor as part of an agreed exit strategy (for example, retirement).

Micromanagement

16–20 A micromanager is someone who's the polar opposite of a delegator. They provide too much direction. In so far as they ever delegate, it tends to be done in only a limited way and—even then—they can't help interfering. The Merriam-Webster dictionary defines micromanagement as: "management . . . with excessive control or attention on details". Encarta defines it as: "attention to small details in management: control [of] a person or a situation by paying extreme attention to small details". Either way you want to be a good delegator and not a micromanager. Here are the signs to watch out for:

Key makers of a micromanager

16–21 The classic signs that you might be becoming a micromanager are (in no particular order):

- you monitor minutiae, to the exclusion of the big picture;
- you get annoyed when someone in your team makes a decision without consulting you, even if it's actually within his or her authority;
- you demand frequent, detailed reports;
- you are constantly nitpicking your team's performance, instead of stepping back and reviewing their overall results;
- you accept inefficiencies within your team (usually caused by you) because they're less important than you retaining total control;
- delegation is limited and is, itself, micromanaged.

This last point is interesting. Why would a micromanager interfere with the work they delegate? It lets them claim credit for positive outcomes, while transferring the blame for any negative outcomes. That is to say, they delegate accountability for failure, albeit they can't bring themselves to delegate the unfettered authority that actually might bring success (or at least mitigate problems that might arise).

In some ways, extreme micromanagement resembles addiction. Micromanagers become dependent on their control over others, yet fail to recognise and acknowledge it (even when everyone around them sees it). They exhibit "denial", which again is a trait found in addictive behaviour (as articulated in the work of Elisabeth Kübler-Ross).[1] Instead, they rebuff concerns by offering a competing view of their style, usually saying things like, "I am structured" or "I am a perfectionist."

Barriers to delegation

From you

There are some factors that might discourage you from delegating. **16–22**

- A fear of failure. In reality everyone makes mistakes and you need to view these as learning opportunities, to improve your performance in the future.
- Envy of your talented assistant, whose ability shines through. The solution is to let that talented assistant do the work. The truth is they'll make you look like a leader who can use the talents of his or her staff effectively.
- A feeling that you can do the job much better yourself. This is almost certainly true. After all, your technical ability is partly why your firm is successful. It's why you're rising through the ranks. The question to ask yourself, however, is: "should I be doing this work myself or is it better for me (and the firm) to delegate it to someone else?" If you fall into the trap of doing someone else's work, remember you're engaging in suboptimal management.
- You don't want to give up something you actually enjoy. There are aspects of every job that are more enjoyable than others. The question here is the same as above, should you be doing it?
- A fear of losing control. Don't fall into the trap of becoming a micromanager, with all of its downsides. By all means, establish check-in points so you can monitor progress. However, don't over-monitor your team (particularly your superstars) or you'll end up causing frustration.

Overcoming these inner obstacles is critical. If you can't delegate work effectively, your own partner might criticise your perceived inability to use your team members effectively. That, in turn, can exclude you from further promotion opportunities. On the other hand, if you do delegate effectively, senior colleagues will note your ability to get the best out of your people. You're then earmarked as a leader, deserving of even higher levels of responsibility.

From partners or management

These flow from our earlier discussion about the 12 golden rules of effective delegation. **16–23**

- A lack of clarity—your assistant has to take his best guess, which may not necessarily be what you want. If you ask him to fetch you a coffee, do you let him guess whether you want milk and sugar?

---

1 E. Kubler-Ross, *On Death & Dying: What the Dying Have to Teach Doctors, Nurses, Clergy & Their Own Families*, reprint edition (New York: Scribner, 2014).

- Lack of record keeping—you need to keep track of all the work that you've delegated. If you don't do this, things fall between the cracks.
- Bad choice—this is where you pick someone to do a job irrespective of their skills and/or proven aptitude.

From colleagues

16–24

- Unwillingness to accept a task—your team member may not share your enthusiasm about doing a particular piece of work. Perhaps, more reasonably, they may already have too many other tasks to complete and simply not have the time to take on additional work. Delegation, however, isn't a substitute for discipline. Ultimately, if your team member is being difficult it becomes a matter for HR.
- Inability to complete work—your assistant takes on a task for which he/she lacks the expertise or training. This is frequently the case where they hope to impress you, in an attempt to get a good quarterly review.
- Uncertainty about peer-to-peer delegation—quite simply, you might be a little uncertain of when and how to delegate horizontally. You might feel like it's being dictatorial to a colleague. Actually, it's not, and you'll know from this section how to best go about it.

Giving feedback

16–25 An essential element of delegating work is to give feedback to people after they've worked for you. If you don't give feedback how will they know if they've done a good job—or if they need to improve? It's always a pleasure to do this when the going is good and targets are being met. In fact, in that circumstance it arguably is an easy job.

However, when someone is underperforming, the process needs to be handled with care. We'll look at this skill through that particular lens: the feedback you give a colleague either can be *constructive*, or what's called *praise and criticism*.

What is constructive feedback?

16–26 Constructive feedback is information-specific and based on observations. This method is objective and, as such, has to be the preferred method.

What is praise and criticism?

16–27 Praise and criticism, on the other hand, are simply your own personal judgments about someone else's performance. The information is general and vague, and is based on your opinions or feelings. The process is highly subjective and may even be coloured by your own personal prejudices (that is to say, whether you even "like" or "dislike" the person you're talking to). This method should be avoided.

How to give constructive feedback?

16–28

- Be direct. Whether good or bad, feedback should be given in a straightforward manner.
- Avoid "need to" phrases, which send out an implied message that something didn't go well. These sorts of phrases don't actually tell the recipient what happened. Clarity, after all, is the aim of your feedback.

- Avoid mixed messages. These are sometimes called "yes, but" statements. For example, "Sarah, you've worked hard on this, but . . ." What then follows usually is negative, and yet is the intended point of the message. The word "but", along with its distant relatives "however" and "although", create contradictions. You're telling your colleagues "don't believe a thing I said before."
- In positive feedback situations, certainly you can (and should) express appreciation. Appreciation alone is merely praise, and should be tied to constructive feedback.
- With negative feedback, you should try and convey concern. An empathetic tone communicates a sense of caring. Anger, disappointment and sarcasm, on the other hand, simply convert your (objective) constructive feedback to (subjective) criticism. Ultimately, the purpose of negative feedback is to create an awareness that then will lead to improvements in your colleague's performance.
- Give all your feedback in person (not by email). The nature of constructive feedback is that it's given verbally and informally.
- Your feedback should be given as close as possible to when performance occurs so that events are fresh in everyone's minds. Delays lessen the value of any feedback.
- Finally, try and give your colleagues constructive feedback, regularly. Even a simple "you did that well—the report was very concise with everything the client needs to read in the first paragraph" helps reinforce good habits.

Summary

At first sight, delegation can feel like more hassle than it's worth, however by **16–29**
delegating effectively, you can expand the amount of work that you can deliver. To delegate effectively, choose the right tasks to delegate, identify the right people to delegate to, and delegate in the right way. There's a lot to this, but you'll achieve much more once you're delegating effectively.

CHAPTER 17

HOW TO CHOOSE GOALS AND CPD

Introduction

17–1 *It's almost a year since you qualified. The last three months have been hard. You're working late. Your desk is covered in papers that really should have been filed weeks ago, but you've just not had the time to attend to them. You feel like you're always behind and chasing your tail to catch up. Now, it's time for your annual review and you wonder what your partner might have to say about it.*

Your partner is in a good mood. He asks you to think about the goals you want to achieve in the year ahead, so he can track your progress. You say you want to get better at time management and delegation. So far so good, but how do you turn these aspirations into goals that your partner can understand (and measure)?

17–2 Everyone needs goals. Imagine, for a minute, setting off on a journey across an ocean, but without a set destination in mind. You might have a sense of the general direction you want to go in but, if you have no specific route, how will you know when you reach the end? As the late baseball legend Yogi Berra once said: "if you don't know where you're going, you might end up someplace else". Not having goals, whether at work or at home, is just like embarking on this imaginary journey, with no destination in mind and no compass to guide you. If you like, you can simulate it by trying to drive across East Kilbride without a Sat Nav. How far did you get? How long did it take? And, after the umpteenth roundabout, did you find yourself back exactly where you started?

The Law Society recognises that you need clear goals as part of your on-going professional development, also. Goal setting actually is an essential part of providing a good service to clients. That's why the Law Society has a system of annual Continuing Professional Development (CPD), to help you set goals that develop your awareness of:

- law;
- legal procedure;
- practice management;
- professional skills;
- ethics, attitudes and values; and
- other skills and knowledge required for a particular career milestone, such as becoming a partner.

The Law Society's system helps you to frame well thought out goals, so that you can plan where you're going, see what you have accomplished and acknowledge how you've developed. This last point is particularly relevant when you're a new solicitor, perhaps lacking in professional confidence. Appreciating what you've accomplished gives you an insight in to what you're capable of, going forward, which is likely to be much more than you think.

Your firm, too, wants to ensure that you have enhanced knowledge and skills, both for its own benefit and that of its clients. Most firms have an appraisal system. This can be as simple as a regular catch up with your partner, or it can involve forms, an HR team and systematic grading. Whatever form it takes, it starts with you setting goals and ends with a measurement of your progress.

Outcomes

By the end of this chapter you'll understand how setting goals can help your career. You'll know how to set appropriate goals and avoid unrealistic ones. You'll learn how to apply this knowledge to your CPD requirements. **17–3**

What is goal setting?

Before we look at specific Law Society rules regarding CPD, let's look at goal setting in general, so that you understand the principles that apply and the benefits they bring. **17–4**

Why do we set goals?

There are five key reasons for setting goals: **17–5**

Goals are motivational

Let's return for a second to sailing on the ocean. Visualise yourself on your boat, in the middle of that vast ocean. Do you have a clear idea about the purpose of your trip, your direction or where you're going? Without any additional information, we'd expect the answer to be "no". **17–6**

Imagine that someone asks you to sail to Canada, within 90 days, to deliver a treasure chest. What's the difference? You have a clear sense of purpose (to deliver a treasure chest) and a clear direction (to sail to Canada). This is more likely to encourage action. In other words, well-stated goals provide a sense of meaning, purpose and direction; they motivate you.

Let's think how this translates to your firm. After reading Ch.15 (how to manage your time), you might make your goal for the next six months to be to improve your time management. This gives you a purpose. However, it's not yet a fully developed goal, because goals also need to set clear expectations.

Goals should have clear expectations

Let's go back to our example. You've told your partner that you want to improve your time management. However, this is rather vague. You need to be more specific. Exactly how will you improve your time management? You might decide that you need to stop dithering and also reduce the number of distractions around you. Your developed goal might be to improve your time management by: updating your email settings so that notifications are switched off; using filters to identify important emails; and checking email only once an hour. Your goal is much more specific (and easier to implement). You not only have a purpose (to improve your time management), you know what actions you need to take to realise it. **17–7**

Goals drive performance

17–8 When your goals are clear and measurable, they invigorate you. You're able to check if you're meeting your goals, or falling short. In our example, in one month's time you can look back and check. Did you update your email settings? Are you only checking your email every hour? Or, are you still stuck in bad habits?

Goals enable teams to work towards a common purpose

17–9 Your goals are not just for you. If you share your goals with your team (even if it's just you and a secretary), they'll better understand what you're trying to achieve and why. This reduces the likelihood of team members being pulled in different directions, working on irrelevant activities, or getting into disputes. In our example, if you tell your secretary that your goal is to improve your time management and so, unless it's urgent, you don't want any calls before 10am, she can help you meet that goal.

Goals support a firm's culture

17–10 Lastly, it's not just you who sets goals. Your firm (via partners and senior lawyers) sets firm wide goals, as part of the appraisal process. As a trainee, that means meeting the Law Society's standards. It's also an opportunity for your firm to strengthen its work place culture. For example, if teamwork is particularly important to your firm, then goals that are designed to encourage and facilitate this can support this ethos, by driving appropriate behaviours.

Goals to avoid

17–11 Are there goals you should avoid? The answer is most certainly "yes". Everyone wants to make a meaningful contribution. If your goals either are not essential to your strategy (or your firm's strategy), a project or a piece of work, don't set them. Nothing is more frustrating than working on something that lacks purpose. Let's look at common mistakes in goal setting.

Setting unrealistic goals

17–12 Make sure that your goals are realistic, and that you actually can achieve each goal in the time frame you've set. For example, a realistic personal goal might be to lose one stone in a month. It would be unrealistic to try to lose that weight in two weeks. Equally, setting yourself a goal to finish all your work before you go home is likely never going to be achieved; you'll have too many interruptions. Instead, finishing all essential work is a better, more realistic goal.

Underestimating completion time

17–13 How often has a task taken longer than you thought? Probably more times than you can count. If you don't estimate completion times accurately, it can be discouraging when things take longer than you expect. This can sometimes even cause you to give up.

Always build in time for unexpected delays. You'll feel less pressure and you're more likely to achieve your goals by your target date. Plan a few hours each week for the unexpected. If you have a file that you think will take eight hours to finish, plan to have it done in two days. That gives you four hours on the first day, with extra time to deal with calls, emails, interruptions and urgent tasks that you hadn't anticipated. It also gives you four hours the next day with, again, time for the unexpected. You might not know what the additional time will be spent on, but you know something is likely to arise. The important thing is that you build in a sensible buffer.

Not appreciating failure

No matter how hard you work, almost certainly you'll fail to achieve some goals from time to time. We've all been there. However, failures ultimately shape your character more than anything else. They teach you lessons, if you're minded (or indeed open minded) to learn from them. In other words, don't be upset if you fail to achieve a goal. Instead, take note of where you went wrong and then use that insight to reach your goal the next time. Always remember that failure doesn't have to be the opposite of success; rather, failure is part of success. It is—if you like—deferred success. **17–14**

Perhaps you checked your email every 30 minutes, because waiting an hour made you anxious. If so, adjust your goal. Checking it every 30 minutes is still better than checking it every five minutes.

Not reviewing progress

It takes time to accomplish any goal and, sometimes, you might feel that you haven't made progress. That's why it's important to take stock on a regular basis (for example, monthly). You need to set staging posts and make a point of celebrating your successes. It doesn't have to be champagne but, if it's worth celebrating, then celebrate. Regular reviews also help you to analyse what you need to do to keep moving forward. Goals are never set in stone, so don't be afraid to change them. **17–15**

Setting "negative" goals

How you think about your goals influences how you feel about them. For instance, have you ever set yourself the goal of losing weight? This sort of goal actually has a negative connotation; it's focused on what you don't want (i.e. your weight). A positive way to reframe this goal would be to say that you want to "get healthy". That way your weight-loss becomes part of a more positive goal. **17–16**

Negative goals are emotionally unattractive, which makes it harder for you to focus on them. Reframe all your negative goals so that they're positive. Don't make your goal, for example, to stop dithering. Instead, set goals that help you become faster and more efficient.

Setting too many goals

You've got a fixed amount of time and energy. If you try to focus on too many goals all at once, you won't be able to give each individual one the attention it deserves and—indeed—requires. Instead, use a "quality, not quantity" rule when goal setting. Work out the relative importance of everything that you want to accomplish. After you've done that, pick no more than, say, three goals to focus on, at any one time. **17–17**

How should you choose the right goals?

When it comes to appraisals and setting goals, it pays to be S.M.A.R.T. A SMART goal is specific, measurable, attainable, realistic and timely (thus the acronym). **17–18**

Specific

17–19 You have a greater chance of accomplishing a specific goal than a general goal. To set a specific goal you need to answer the six "W" questions.

- "Who" needs to be involved, to help you achieve your goal?
- "What" do you want to accomplish?
- "Where" are you going to carry out all the required actions?
- "When" will you achieve your goal by (time-frame)?
- "Which" requirements do you have to succeed (plus constraints)?
- "Why" do you want to accomplish the goal (benefits)?

Example

An example of a general goal would be to "record time". However, a more specific goal would be to record time at the end of each working day.

Measurable

17–20 As you know, you need to measure your progress towards the attainment of every goal you set. When you measure your progress you tend more to stay on track and achieve your target dates. In turn, you experience a sense of achievement that motivates you to keep going to reach your ultimate goal. Ever heard of the self-fulfilling prophecy? If your goal is measurable, it answers the "how" questions.

- "How" much?
- "How" many?
- "How" will I know it has been achieved?

Attainable

17–21 You can attain almost any goal you set for yourself. You're the only one, however, who can decide just how high your targets will be. The sky's not the limit; you are. Interestingly, an ambitious goal often is easier to attain than an unambitious one. Why? A lower goal exerts only a low motivational force. Some of your biggest accomplishments, in retrospect, may seem easy, but that's precisely because they motivated you in some way. As you become more successful, goals that previously had seemed out of reach suddenly become attainable, when viewed with fresh eyes, not because they have become diluted in some way, but because you have developed to match them.

That being said, however, the concept of attainability is exactly the principle we looked at, earlier, whereby you should not set yourself unrealistic goals. One way to work out if your goals are realistic is to reflect on whether you've accomplished anything similar in the past.

Relevant

17–22 Your goals should be relevant both to you and your firm. A relevant goal is one in respect of which you can answer in the affirmative, the following questions:

- Is your goal worthwhile?
- Are you the best person to be trying to achieve the goal?
- Is the timing right?
- Does your goal align with your own needs and those of your firm?

Time

Your goals need to be bounded by a time frame. Without it, you have no sense of urgency. For example, if you want to lose 14lbs, you need to work out when you want to lose it by. Simply saying "someday" doesn't work. If you set a time frame, however (for example, a specific date) then your subconscious mind tends to encourage you to take action. **17–23**

SMART goal setting exercise

It's now time to do a bit more work. It's a simple enough exercise, and it won't take you too long. You can use the grids provided in Pt 3 of the Appendix to help you. **17–24**

Here's how you do it:

- choose a current piece of work (conveyance/estate/criminal work/trust etc.);
- undertake a SMART analysis and create some key goals;
- answer the "what" questions;
- answer the "how" questions;
- assess:
  - — attainability;
  - — relevance; and
  - — time-frames;
- using SMART analysis, identify any obstacles that might impede your progress;
- develop a simple action plan to achieve your goals; and
- identify the people who you can turn to for advice and support.

CPD goals

The Law Society expects you to provide clients with a competent and professional service. The standards of conduct require you to have, "the relevant legal knowledge and skills" to provide that service. **17–25**

This means you need to:

- meet the necessary educational requirements to become a solicitor, as we saw in Ch.11 (how to be professional) and Ch.12 (how to avoid complaints); and
- continue to keep your knowledge and skills up to date.

This is known as continuing professional development (CPD), and is defined as: "relevant education and study by a solicitor to develop his or her professional knowledge, skills, and abilities."[1] It's up to you to decide what training you need (goal setting), to complete the training and then record how it has helped you.

---

[1] The Law Society of Scotland, "CPD Requirements and guidance". Available at *http://www.lawscot.org.uk/media/596317/CPD-Requirements-and-guidance.pdf* [Accessed 19 April 2016].

How much CPD do you need?

17–26 You're required by the Law Society to undertake a minimum of 20 hours CPD annually. We emphasise that this is a bare minimum, and many solicitors in fact choose to complete more as they may have other targets. For example, solicitors accredited by the Society of Writers to Her Majesty's Signet (the WS Society) are required to complete at least 30 hours annually.

For example, between them, the authors completed more than 100 hours of CPD, last year. You may think that's a long time to spend in seminars and lectures. That's actually the first CPD myth we want to dispel. CPD doesn't just mean sitting in classes. It covers many forms of professional development (and more on that, later).

What is CPD?

Verifiable CPD (minimum of 15 hours)

17–27 At least 15 hours of CPD must be what's called "verifiable CPD". This is defined by the Law Society as an activity that:

- has clear aims and outcomes;
- provides interaction and/or the opportunity for feedback;
- can be evidenced;
- isn't part of a solicitor's daily work.

If you go to a seminar, it counts as verifiable CPD if it: has a clear aim (for example, to discuss a new law); has a clear outcome (for example, to improve your knowledge of that new area of law); has a signing sheet to record who gave the seminar, who attended it and how long it lasted; and is not part of your normal work.

Given that the criteria are broad, it's not just seminars that can be classed as verifiable CPD. It also covers online learning, structured coaching, distance learning or one-to-one mentoring.

It also means that you don't just get CPD for being a delegate. If you provide the training, you can claim the time it takes you to prepare along with up to four hours of presenting. This means, for four lectures in October 2015, Andrew accumulated over 20 hours of CPD (covering preparation time and delivery). Equally, Iain prepared an executive training module for one of Scotland's largest Plc. He could record all of his preparation time to his verifiable CPD.

Writing articles and books (like this one) also can count towards CPD. Sadly, however, there is a 10-hour cap for each article or book. We say "sadly" because, after writing this particular book for over 12 months, we were hoping to have completed all the CPD required for the rest of our natural lives.

Private study (up to five hours)

17–28 Reading articles and books can count towards CPD, too. That's because up to five hours of CPD can be private study. This includes relevant periodicals (*Journal of the Law Society of Scotland*), trade magazines (*Property Week*), academic journals (*Scots Law Times*) and books (what you're doing now).

How do you carry out CPD?

17–29 The CPD training year runs from 1 November to 31 October, each year.

If you work for a large firm, you're probably covered by a formal training programme, administered in-house by a training team or by professional support lawyers. This programme probably includes regular update meetings (where your team shares knowledge), seminars and workshops from colleagues (or external presenters) and skills workshops that are appropriate to the different stages of your career (for example, financial skills training when you start as a qualified solicitor, so you understand fees and billing).

This doesn't mean, though, that you should forget everything we covered at the start of this chapter. Just because your firm has a training regime, it doesn't follow that it's going to be right for you. After all, we've already said that other people formulating your goals can lead to undesirable goals being set.

You're in charge of your own career. While your firm might think you should have 10 hours of training on the topic of legal privilege, you're best placed to know whether that time would be better spent learning how to draft commercial contracts. Think about your diploma in legal practice. Some courses are compulsory; some you choose. Which courses did you learn more from? We hope you'll say the ones you selected yourself. Even if you have a training programme designed and delivered by your firm, you should still carry out the process of goal setting and pick the right goals for you and your career. Once you've identified what you need, speak to your Personal Support Lawyer (PSL) (or training partner) so they can help you.

What is the Law Society process?

The Law Society requires you to: **17–30**

- plan your annual training;
- record it; and
- justify it.

Let's look at each in turn.

Planning

The Law Society expects you to plan your training goals each year so that your CPD is relevant to your professional development. It suggests a four stage planning process[2]: **17–31**

Stage 1

Consider your current (and likely future) role. Don't consider only what you do (e.g. corporate finance, litigation, criminal defence) but also your non-legal roles: training supervisor; cash-room partner; department lead on tender processes etc. **17–32**

Stage 2

Consider the sorts of CPD activity that will assist your professional development. Reflecting on the following questions might help. **17–33**

---

2 The Law Society of Scotland, "Continuing Professional Development Handbook" (2011). Available at *http://www.lawscot.org.uk/media/227799/cpd%20handbook.pdf* [Accessed 19 April 2016].

- Have there been, or are there likely to be, updates in the area(s) of law in which you practice?
- Do you wish to expand into new areas of law?
- Are there events that you attend on an annual basis to keep you up to date (e.g. Crofting Law Conference, Legal Aid Conference etc.)?
- Do you need an update on:
    - — financial and business management;
    - — budget control;
    - — computer/IT skills;
    - — interview techniques;
    - — personnel management;
    - — training skills;
    - — setting priorities;
    - — time management?
- Are there any legal skills that you need to hone (for example, drafting, negotiation, interviewing, presentation, communication skills etc.)?
- Do you need an update on client care skills (for example, how to deal with complaints)?
- Given your role, do you require any updates on:
    - — professional ethics and standards;
    - — practice management;
    - — anti-money laundering;
    - — regulatory matters?
- Do you need a risk management update (for example, on fraud prevention and detection; information security; risk registers etc.)?
- Do you need to improve your commercial awareness (for example, in business development and marketing)?
- Do you have any other development needs?

Stage 3

17–34 Consider your favoured learning style (course, webinar, conference, online etc.) and the learning style that you feel is most appropriate for your development needs.

Stage 4

17–35 Identify CPD courses, over the course of the year, which assist in meeting these needs. You should then record your plan. The Law Society doesn't require you to use a prescribed form (though there is one available in the members' section of the Society's website, if you wish).

Example

Below is a plan that Andrew created for his own CPD: **17–36**

What are your training goals? For example, what knowledge, skill, attitude or value do you want to develop?	What time frame do you want to achieve this within?	Do you have a preferred approach to training?	Why have you chosen this training?
Developing my commercial awareness.	Within the next twelve months.	Writing a textbook on this subject.	As an in-house lawyer, I need to understand the business impact of legal advice. Developing my commercial awareness will help me provide more relevant and direct advice.
To learn about the new property tax, Land and Buildings Transaction Tax (LBTT).	Within the next year.	Course.	LBTT affects nearly all conveyancing transactions. I know the basics of it but want to know more about how the tax works and how it applies to complex property work.
To keep up to date with developments in property law.	Within the next year.	Private study.	I need to comply with my professional standards, and keeping my legal knowledge up to date will help me achieve that.
To learn more about balance sheets and financial accounting.	Within the next three months.	Coaching.	The house building industry has many financial reports and forecasts. Increasing my knowledge of how they link together will make me more effective as an in-house solicitor.

Record your training

Once you've planned your training, you need to carry out your plan, record it and then justify it. **17–37**

It's worth mentioning that your plan is flexible. You can change it at any time, and, in fact, you may need to do just that, as the law changes or your role develops, over the course of a training year. For example, Andrew moved from private practice to being in-house in May 2014 (almost half way through the CPD year). This meant that he needed to revisit his CPD goals, to ensure he had knowledge and skills about corporate governance, in-house regulation and house building and planning.

Again, the Law Society doesn't have a prescribed form for recording your CPD, though it does allow you to do this via its website. The key thing is that at least 15 hours of your training must be verifiable. In other words, it can be checked, independently. If you attend a seminar, the organiser should provide a sheet to confirm you have attended (or a certificate to confirm you have completed the course). If you write an article that's published, clearly this can be checked. If you provide training, again you'll have a note of who attends. If any training you undertake isn't verified, it can't count towards your minimum requirement. It can still count towards your five hours of private study, however.

Justify your training

17–38 This is the final (and arguably most important) step. This is where you reflect on what you've done. Have you increased your knowledge and/or skills? Did you achieve what you set out to do? Were your CPD goals SMART? Again, you confirm what you have learnt as part of your training record.

Worked example

What are your CPD goals? For example, what knowledge, skill, attitude or value do want to develop?	Do you have a preferred approach to CPD?	Why have you chosen this CPD?	What did you learn from this CPD?
Developing my commercial awareness.	Writing a textbook on this subject.	As an in-house lawyer I need to understand the business impact of legal advice. Developing my commercial awareness will help me provide more relevant and direct advice.	Commercial awareness is a big topic covering many different areas. I have learnt how those areas are connected and the importance of professional standards as a link between them.
To learn about the new property tax, LBTT.	Course.	LBTT affects nearly all conveyancing transactions. I know the basics of it but want to know more about how the tax works and how it applies to complex property work.	LBTT has different rules to its predecessor, Stamp Duty Land Tax (SDLT), and it's important to go back to the legislation and not to rely on knowledge of SDLT, as the rules may be different.
To keep up to date with developments in property law.	Private study.	I need to comply with my professional standards, and keeping my legal knowledge up to date will help me achieve that.	Changes in property law have affected our business—in particular in changes to factoring and common areas—and if I hadn't kept up to date I would have provided the wrong advice.
To learn more about balance sheets and financial accounting.	Coaching.	The house building industry has many financial reports and forecasts. Increasing my knowledge of how they link together will make me more effective as an in-house solicitor.	I understand how individual house sales impact balance sheets and profit and loss accounts.

17–39

What happens if you don't follow the Law Society's process?

17–40 If you fail to complete your CPD, it could be regarded as professional misconduct. To that end, the Law Society audits at least 5% of solicitors each year, and checks for evidence that their CPD was planned, recorded, justified and verifiable.

Are there any exemptions from CPD?

17–41 Yes. There are exemptions for illness and parental leave. If you believe you might be unable to complete all of your CPD, you should speak to the Law Society as soon as possible.

Summary

17–42 We started this chapter by saying that you need goals. We concluded by saying that you need SMART goals. Now, when setting off on your journey across that ocean (i.e. completing an appraisal, or complying with the Law Society's CPD regulations) you'll have a set destination, a specific route to follow, and, to misquote Yogi Berra: "you'll end up *exactly* where you want to be."

CHAPTER 18

HOW TO BE A LEGAL PROJECT MANAGER

Introduction

You've just had your first review. Your partner is pleased at what you've done and is impressed that you've decided to focus on time management and delegation as "those are really important skills to develop as a new lawyer—but I think you can do more. I want you to set yourself the goal of becoming a legal project manager. I want you to start thinking about not just how you can work smarter and faster but also how the whole team can work smarter and faster." **18–1**

Usain Bolt is the fastest man in the world at 100 metres and 200 metres, but when he runs in a relay, it doesn't matter how fast he runs, he won't win a gold medal unless everyone in his team runs fast too. A relay team is only as fast as its slowest member. The same is true for law firms. You might be in full control of your time, working efficiently and smartly, but, if you delegate work to a trainee and they take 40 hours on a 30 minute task, then you've lost all the time that you thought you'd saved—and even worse, they charge your file for all of those hours and your £1,000 file has £4,000 of time recorded on it. **18–2**

As a new lawyer, you're more likely to work on your own files or as a team member for others. However, as you become more senior, you'll take on more responsibility and you'll delegate more work to others. Ultimately, you'll have your own clients and those clients may have lots of different legal needs. A small business may need advice to take out a loan, buy a property, licence a product and sue a supplier. It doesn't necessarily expect you to deal with all of this work, but if you're their lawyer, it'll expect you to lead and manage a team who will. That means, as you gain responsibility you also need to spend more time managing others than doing the work yourself.

Equally, as you become more senior, your work will become more complex. Even a single instruction, such as raising an employment claim against an employer, might involve a number of people, from secretaries to trainees and assistants, all of whom need to be managed and led. That's why, as time management and delegation have grown in importance for individual lawyers, project management has also grown in importance so that lawyers can manage everything that a project will need, including scoping it correctly, allocating the right people to it, picking the right fee for it, and completing the work efficiently and smartly.

In this chapter we'll examine what it takes to become a legal project manager. This may sound complicated but, at its heart, a legal project manager is simply someone who thinks about the firm first rather than themselves. The skills and knowledge we'll cover in this chapter will help you think about your work in a different way.

Outcome

18–3 In this chapter we're going to examine how you can manage legal work (projects), whether a whole file or part of it, so that you're in full control of it. This is partly about time management, both for yourself and others, but also about managing people, managing budgets and managing clients (and their expectations). It's starting to pull together all the skills and knowledge we've covered so far.

Before we go any further though, you need to understand that mastering the art of project management requires you to invest some time and effort. You need to be a planner before you can be a "do-er".

Secondly, you'll need the backing and commitment of your firm. In other words, your firm must value good project management skills. In order to manage projects effectively you'll need the support of partners and others to back the changes you need. If not, people will just do the same things they've always done. That's not project management, that's inertia.

Thirdly, you need to become like Robert the Bruce and be willing to try, try and try again. Project management is a skill and like all skills it improves with practice.

What is a project?

18–4 This is a sensible first question. Projects are unique, with specific objectives and are usually never repeated in the same way. For this reason, you're arguably as much a project manager as anyone else already. How so? Every client's file has its own unique factors, whether it's a personal injury claim, a conveyance or an executory. What's more, because of these unique factors, it's unlikely that any transaction you're involved with will be repeated in exactly the same way.

Think of two semi-detached houses side by side on the same street. They're both for sale and you act for both sellers. While the process will be the same—you'll negotiate a missive, discuss title and prepare for settlement—the day to day details will change. One purchaser may accept a missive with minimal changes. The other may argue over every clause. One purchaser may be happy with the title, the other wants you to confirm various burdens within it don't apply to them. One file takes 10 hours. The other 30 hours. Both transactions are the same, but they're not repeated in exactly the same way.

Every file could be a project.

What is project management?

18–5 Traditionally, lawyers would think about themselves first. Not in a selfish way, don't get us wrong, rather they would think that because the client had asked them for help, then they should be the one to provide that help. If you go to see your GP you wouldn't expect her to call in the practice nurse or, worse, the receptionist, to speak to you. You would expect to just deal with the GP. It's the same attitude for lawyers. A client asks you for help then it's you they want, not the rest of the firm.

Modern lawyers realise that clients are not asking specifically for you and that when a client asks for help then you might not be the best person to deal with all or parts of your response—and that when a client asks for help, the whole firm can help, not just you. Project management is about changing your thinking from thinking about yourself first, to thinking about the firm first.

What skills and knowledge does a legal project manager need?

Project management is about *all* the skills and knowledge you and your firm need to move a specific task, event or duty toward completion. In the above example, the aim of your "project" is to sell a home. If your client was raising an employment tribunal then the aim of your project will be to reach a settlement or favourable decision from a tribunal. Your aim should match what your client is trying to achieve. **18–6**

Legal project managers need to master a mix of hard skills and soft skills. The hard skills include the use of tools and techniques such as the use of Gantt charts, work breakdown structures, resource allocation and risk management (the last of which we look at in Ch.24 (how to manage risks)).

Soft skills include managing teams, negotiating with clients and external parties, and juggling multiple projects (time and personal management). We have already looked at these in the preceding chapters.

The overriding aim of acquiring and using these skills is to help you:

- achieve the desired aim (sell the house, reach a settlement etc); and
- be efficient and use the best value resources.

Or, that is to say, your files (your projects) should be delivered on time, on budget (if you've quoted for the work) and in a way that always meets (or exceeds) your clients' needs.

Because, in the end, you never want to give a client the impression that his or her transaction has been completed successfully only because you worked a huge amount of overtime and, in so doing, became so stressed that you drank 12 cups of coffee a day and forgot to feed your cat. Instead, if you look at client matters from a project management perspective, it doesn't mean that you'll never experience problems. However, it'll help you manage and control any unforeseen eventualities—it's the difference between planning and managing, on the one hand, and fire-fighting and reacting, on the other.

How do you plan and manage a legal project?

Overview

Every project has a lifecycle, certain steps that recur in every project. There are striking similarities between generic project lifecycles and legal transactional lifecycles. A typical cycle might follow this path: **18–7**

Step one: management (conceptual)

There has to be a management decision to appoint you as the fee earner to lead on a file (i.e. your appointment as a legal project manager). This could be as simple as your partner passing you a file and telling you that it's yours. Or, it could be as complex as being appointed as an "official" legal project manager for a large deal involving many different teams and offices. **18–8**

Step two: scoping

The work that's required by your client has to be scoped and an appropriate engagement letter issued. This scoping exercise should be as thorough as you need it to be for the project you're dealing with, so that you can identify the **18–9** outcome your client wants. Are they looking to buy a house? Sell a company? Sue their employer? Go to tribunal or reach a negotiated settlement? The scope provides the final aim of your project.

It'll be possible to have different aims. You don't need to just have one. Your client may want you to go to an employment tribunal and, if so, to win. But they may also accept that if compensation was offered they would want you to negotiate the right to work for a competitor company.

Step three: basic planning

18–10 Once you know your destination, you need to work out how you'll get there. You need to do some basic planning. At this stage you would break up large projects into manageable chunks (this involves you applying your goal-setting knowledge), and start to set key diary dates. If you know you need to sell a home on the 1 March then you know you'll need to have drafted, agreed and arranged for a disposition to be signed in advance. You estimate it'll take you one day to draft the disposition and you need at least a week to ensure your client signs it and returns it to you. That means your plan could show you sending the disposition to your client by 22 February.

Step four: review resources

18–11 This is where you start thinking about the firm. You need to assess whether you have the people, resources and IT systems for the job in hand. This could include things like access to online resources (for example, Westlaw). If your firm doesn't have the necessary subscriptions to let you research the latest position on a highly specific point, good project management would suggest that either these be put in place or you withdraw (rather than carry on and risk a Scottish Legal Complaints Commission (SLCC) complaint, or worse).

Step five: detailed planning

18–12 This is where you consult all relevant people and develop a full understanding of your client's requirements. For example, at this stage, this may just involve the client, and you could have a lengthy, detailed client meeting. However, you could also consult with your partner and start to build your project team (for example, pulling in a trainee to draft the disposition as you already have many other tasks to do the week that will be required).

Step six: execution

18–13 You then undertake the client's work, keeping him or her fully informed and updated.

Step seven: review

18–14 You need to constantly review your work so that you avoid "scope creep". This is where clients ask for more work beyond that originally agreed. If you're not a good project manager, you might not recognise and identify scope creep when it arises, so your work becomes less profitable.

Step eight: evaluation

18–15 Projects, ultimately, are meant to bring about a good outcome for your clients (and your firm). The benefits of the work you've just completed need to be measured. You also need to evaluate the benefits you've derived against the investment of your time and your firm's resources. This could be as simple as sitting down with your boss, after your fee invoice has been sent out, and assessing how profitable the project has been.

We'll look at each of the stages in more detail.

Step one: management (conceptual)

Files that need a project manager typically fall into two types: one, volume work, **18–16** and two, complex work.

Volume work files are files that are similar and recur frequently. For example, a personal injury firm may receive a lot of claims for slips and trips. A conveyancing firm in Glasgow will receive a lot of instructions to sell tenement flats. A high street firm may receive a lot of instructions for simple wills from husbands and wives leaving everything to their spouse. The work required by these files may not be complex but, in their sheer volume, they may require someone to project manage them to make sure they're all completed on time and on budget.

The second example of work, complex work, requires a project manager to help ensure it's dealt with in the best way possible for the client and your firm. A surgeon wouldn't start an operation without knowing what they'll do and what people they'll need with them at the operating table. You shouldn't start any complex legal work without knowing what you'll do and who you'll need before you start. By planning what you'll do in advance you can plan what to do so that, just like a surgeon, you can act without making any unnecessary mistakes.

The first step in project management is to identify the need for a project manager. This may be something that you suggest or it may come from your partner. And, while it could be formal, it could equally just be a thought in your head that you need to approach a new piece of work with your project manager hat on. And you may find that you approach all new work like that. Either way, you've identified a need to use your project management skills, so what next?

Steps two and three: scoping and planning

Scoping and planning both cover a similar thought—do you know what you'll do **18–17** for your client before you start working for them? This is a thought you should cover in your engagement letter but, as project manager, it's one that you should examine further. An engagement letter will tell your client *what* you'll do, but it doesn't tend to tell them in detail *how* you'll do it. A client is not interested in whether you're using a template for your contract or drafting it from start. Nor is a client interested in knowing which particular trainee or assistant may help you in the background. However, a project manager will care how the work is done and will plan for it.

Let's examine a house sale to show the difference between what you might write in an engagement letter and what you'll cover in your planning. In your engagement letter you may explain to the client that you'll "negotiate and conclude a contract (known as a missive) on their behalf." However, your plan may show: "a trainee will draft a purchase offer in the firm's style. You'll review it before it is sent to the seller's solicitor. You'll review any changes required by the seller. You'll conclude the contract." You're describing what you'll do and how you'll do it.

At this stage you may also start working out how long the work will take and how much you can charge for it. For example, your plan might say: "a trainee will draft a purchase offer in the firm's style (two hours at £100 per hour). You'll review it before it is sent to the seller's solicitor (one hour at £150 per hour). You'll review any changes required by the seller (two to four hours at £150 per hour). You'll conclude the contract (30 minutes at £150 per hour)." Your plan is telling you that if you follow this plan then it'll take a trainee two hours of time and £200 and it'll take you up to six and half hours of time at £825 to draft and conclude a missive. This doesn't include the time it'll take to review titles or settle the sale. And you know your fee is £500. What do you do?

Step four: review resources

18–18 Your next step is to consider if you have the resources to carry out your plan. In practice, this would form part of your planning as you would be thinking of resources at the same time as you scope and plan the work. You wouldn't think of using a trainee if you didn't have one (though you might think of hiring one if there was a good reason for it). When you review resources you're testing your plan and considering alternatives. In the example of our house sale your initial plan shows that you'll make a loss on the sale. You'll spend more time on the sale than you'll recover in a fee. You need to reduce the time you'll charge to the file.

If this is volume work, you might think it would be good to spend time creating a template offer and to use document automation software to help tailor clauses quickly. While the time spent creating the template may take a long time, let's say 40 hours of time, it'll save almost two hours in every transaction because the offer can be produced in five minutes rather than two hours. You're saving almost two hours for every file after that initial work.

Alternatively, you might consider whether you should negotiate the offer. Your trainee is smart, they know what to do and although they're not as fast as you, you think they would still only take five hours at most to complete the negotiation. Your cost of negotiating the offer is £500 at most, instead of £600. You've saved £100.

Step five: detailed planning

18–19 This is where you start to finalise your plan and go into detail into exactly what you'll do. You may start to speak to your partner to check that you can use the trainee to help you. You'll speak to the client to explain that you're using a new template, which will help speed up the sale, and you're getting their feedback.

Your partner may tell you that the trainee will be on holiday when you need them. The client may want you to handle all of their work and they don't want anyone else dealing with it. If so, you'll need to change your plans again.

Step six: execution

18–20 You and your team do the work. Though that doesn't mean blindly following your plan, as you'll need to review it.

Step seven: review

18–21 Things change. Your client may give you new instructions. The other lawyers may raise points you've not considered in your plan. Even the simplest house sale can turn into the most complex property deal when you find out the title is missing an access right, the extension has no planning permission and the seller needs to implement a tax saving scheme to help reduce its land and buildings transaction tax liability.

When you review your plan that means going back to step two and thinking through again what you need to do, who needs to do it, what resources you have for it and who do you need to speak to in order to agree it. This review also includes effective supervision. Are your team performing as expected? If not, do you need to speak to them or, ultimately, change them to make sure you get the result you need?

This review is a vital step, as remember from our discussion about engagement letters in Ch.7 that the client is following your roadmap as set out in the engagement letter. If you need to take a different course you need to tell them, just as a pilot would tell you if your flight changed direction. You're the pilot, the client is your passenger and you need to let them know what's happening—especially if you plan to change your fee later.

If your legal projects go over budget (as they can easily do), your clients will not consider them to be unbridled successes (even if they're delivered on time and, in fact, meet or exceed their needs). That's why you need to manage your budgets particularly for large projects. Here are four strategies that will help you to avoid cost overruns.

- Continually forecast your legal project's budget—frequent checks prevent budgets getting too far out of hand. How much time has your team incurred? Does that figure change your view as to how much time you need to complete your project?
- Regularly forecast your human resources needs—just as a budget needs to be revisited to keep it on track, you need to do the same for your human resources, since the people working on your legal project clearly add to its cost. Do you need an extra trainee or Newly Qualified (NQ) support, or is there a team member who is surplus to requirements? The former will add to your budget; the latter will help you bring your legal project home under budget (cue a happy client).
- Keep your team informed about your budget forecast at weekly team meetings. An informed team is an empowered team that then takes ownership of a legal project. They'll have more of an incentive to watch their time and think twice about any client disbursements.
- Manage your scope of work carefully. Scope creep is perhaps the number one cause of project overruns. Unplanned work means billable hours are racked up, and your budget goes out the window. Some clients will always try and push their luck. In the face of client pressure, you need to be firm, and make sure that you issue change orders for any work that isn't covered by the initial scope. These new instructions (signed off by the client) give you a new, elevated budget to work to.

Step eight: evaluation

Once complete you want to review what you've done to see if there's anything you **18–22**
can repeat for similar transactions (or avoid). This is particularly important for volume work as five minutes saved in one file could be hours and days saved across all files if repeated. A proper evaluation will take place as soon as possible after the work has completed and will ask: "what worked well?", "where could we improve?" and "what lessons, documents or process can be shared or replicated?"

Choosing a team

We've looked at the steps you should take as a project manager. In a law firm, one **18–23**
of the most important steps is choosing your team. People are the most important element of legal work, as we saw in the first section, so having the right people is

the most important part of your project. However, building a team for the first time might seem rather daunting.

What is a team?

18–24 Your team is a group of people organised to work together to accomplish a set of objectives that you otherwise can't achieve alone. Even in small firms, you can't function without your secretary. In this example, your team is just you and your secretary. It's also important to realise that you can have different teams for different client projects; your teams won't be the same each time. In management there is a general move away from traditional, hierarchical structures i.e. where the partner passes work to an associate who passes work down to an assistant, etc. There are good reasons for this: about 40% of any business's gross spend is on overheads. Of that, the greatest component is staffing. Management has come under a lot of scrutiny, with many businesses trying to flatten traditional "command and control" structures in order to cut costs.

What's more, there is a body of opinion that these flattened structures actually compete more effectively (and can offer better client care), in a competitive market place. Hammer and Champy were the first to promote the idea of "boundaryless organisations".[1] The principle then was tested by the US company General Electric which (in its 1993 Annual Report) said: "the challenge . . . is to strip and break down walls that cramp people, inhibit creativity and waste time". In Japan, the concept developed into something called "Kaizen", where businesses pursue improvements (be they efficiencies, design enhancements or better service delivery) at source.[2] Having embraced this idea, Toyota Motor Company is reputed to have found that in one car plant alone, a staff of 4,000 would implement between 20,000 and 40,000 improvements each year.

When you're building your own teams, keep in mind that a hierarchical structure might not necessarily be the best strategy in this modern era.

Choosing your team

18–25 How do you set up your team? There are thought to be three attributes required in order to be a great team member:

- business or commercial skills (professional orientation);
- time and cost awareness (goal orientation); and
- the ability to work with different types of people (team orientation).

Dr Meredith Belbin is a pioneer of "team-role" research. In 1993, he published his theory that a good team player is someone who has a propensity to cooperate and interrelate with others in a particular way.[3] He suggested that there are four (connected) principles that can help you design and build a good team.

1. There has to be a good balance in the team roles you designate, and their corresponding functional duties/responsibilities.

---

[1] M. Hammer and J. Champy, *Reengineering the Corporation: A Manifesto for Business Revolution*? (New York: Harper Business, 1993).

[2] We can readily see that kaizen is part of the culture at Toyota by viewing the company's websites, such as *http://www.toyota-forklifts.co.uk/EN/company/Toyota-Production-System/Kaizen/Pages/default.aspx*, for example [Accessed: 15 June 2016].

[3] R. M. Belbin, *Team Roles at Work*, 2nd edn (Abingdon, Oxon.; New York: Routledge, 2010).

2. Your team members need to be able to adjust to relative strengths within the team, both in expertise and also in the ability to engage in specific team roles.
3. You need to understand that personal qualities fit some team roles while limiting the chance of success in others.
4. Your team can only use its resources to the best advantage when it has the right breadth and range of team roles. In other words, you need to plan to ensure that your team is properly equipped from a human resources perspective.

Another common question is whether people in teams all need to get along. Do your team members need to be Facebook friends? Do they need to go to the pub on a Friday and then play golf at the weekends? Do they need to "like" each other?

Surprisingly, the answer appears to be in the negative. In 1993, Jon Katzenbach suggested that teams don't need to work together happily in order to be effective.[4] Instead, effectiveness comes from striving towards a common vision or a common purpose.

Gantt charts

While we have said that project management is a way of thinking, it also has its own tools that can help you organise your thoughts. This section is for those looking for advanced skills and knowledge. The first tool, and one that many project managers use is a Gantt chart. This is a form of advanced diary management. Gantt charts are incredibly useful in showing planned, essential activities (i.e. your project's various tasks and events) as against a timeline. **18–26**

There are many free templates available online, in Excel format, and we have also included an example of one in Pt 6 of the Appendix. If you haven't seen a Gantt chart before then take a minute to review it.

Format

The format of Gantt charts is pretty much standardised, regardless of the template you use. Usually on the left of the chart (the vertical) is a list of all the actions that are needed in order to complete your legal project. Along the top (the horizontal) is a time line. Each activity (or event) is represented on the chart by a bar. The position and length of the bar reflects the start date, the duration and the end date of each activity. Taken together, this graphical interface allows you to see at a glance: **18–27**

- what all your various activities involve;
- when each needs to begin (and end);
- how long each is scheduled to last;
- if any activities actually overlap with others (and if so, by how much);
- the start and end date of your entire legal project.

[4] See Chapters 3, 4, 6 and 8 in J. Katzenbach, *The Wisdom of Teams: Creating the High-Performance Organization* (Boston, Massachusetts: Harvard Business School Press, 1993).

Your Gantt chart will show you what has to be done (your activities) and when (your schedule). Nowadays, since they usually come in Excel format, Gantt charts can be created and then updated easily.

Project plan

18–28 How do you go about even starting to make a Gantt chart for a legal project? It's simple.

The first thing you need to do (before you even open your Gantt chart file) is to complete a detailed project plan. Your project plan simply is your list of the all the tasks that you think will need to be performed, and in which order they need to be completed. For example, let's say you're moving into a new office. You can't start re-designing your office space before your lease has even been signed. In this example, your project plan would be: sign lease, re-design office space, move equipment in, and so on.

The next point to keep in mind is that your project plan should have a start date that matches the starting point of your first task (e.g. signing your lease—seems sensible) and an end date that corresponds to the completion of your last task (e.g. moving into your new office).

One trick when creating your project plan is to use what is called a work breakdown structure. This is a simple technique for splitting big tasks into smaller subtasks, and creating a task hierarchy (i.e. an order of what is most important, second most important, third, fourth, and so on). Good Gantt chart apps generally will let you reflect your project hierarchy in the task list, on the left hand side.

Data entry

18–29 Once your project plan is complete, you simply enter all the data from the plan into your Gantt app. A sensible method for inputting the data would be:

- Set your start date and end date. The default scheduling method usually is forwards from your project start date. In this mode your tasks are scheduled to start as soon as possible, which means that your whole legal project will finish at the earliest possible date.
- Define your project calendar. This is where you specify the number of working days in the week (and the number of working hours in each day) that you'll work on your legal project.
- Enter all your tasks (and their durations).
- Set up a resources list and then assign resources to tasks. Although you can often define your resources as and when you need them, it's usually much quicker to start by setting up a global list from which you can then select your resources.
- Create links to specify any dependencies between project tasks (i.e. task three might depend on task two being completed and—in turn—task one might depend on task two being completed).
- Set constraints on your tasks, as necessary (and we'll look at these in more detail just shortly).
- Make any final tweaks and adjustments to your legal project plan.

Your app will then automatically create a graphical Gantt chart for you, freeing up enough time for you to make yourself that second coffee of the day (and it's not yet 8am). To help you get started, some Gantt apps include various ready-made project plans for common activities (for example, organising a tradeshow, producing a publication, launching a product etc.), freeing up yet more time.

Timings

Any change that you make to the timing of a task will affect all the tasks that are dependent on it. If a task runs ahead of schedule, your Gantt application will automatically recalculate the dates of the other tasks that are dependent on it, in order to take advantage of the time gained. Conversely, if a task is delayed, all the tasks that depend on it will automatically be pushed back, which may or may not—depending how well you pad your timelines—affect the end date of your legal project. **18–30**

As you go along, you can easily add or remove tasks, adjust the duration of tasks (i.e. the length of the bars), link tasks (for example to make one task follow immediately after another) and add constraints (for example, to specify that a task must end "no later" than a given date).

Constraints

By default, your tasks usually will be linked from "finish to start". This means that the first task you select (the so-called "predecessor task") must end before the next task you select (the so-called "successor task") can start, and so on. This typically will be shown on your Gantt chart by lines with little arrowheads, joining each task to its successor. The arrowhead simply indicates the direction of the link (predecessor to successor). **18–31**

Constraints are handy. They define the degree of flexibility available to your Gantt app when scheduling (or rescheduling) tasks, by imposing restrictions on start dates and end dates. Two "constraints" are so flexible that they're generally not regarded as constraints at all.

- As soon as possible (ASAP)
    a. This is generally the default when you schedule a project from its start date, as is normally the case. To make life simple (and we like simple), try to keep this default whenever possible, as it gives your software the most flexibility.
    b. If you apply this "constraint" to an unlinked task, that task will be scheduled to start at the project start date. If you apply it to a linked task, however, it'll start as soon as its predecessor task is finished.
- As late as possible (ALAP)
    a. Generally, this is the default when you schedule your project back to front (i.e. from its end date).
    b. If you apply this to an unlinked task, that task will be scheduled so that its end date coincides with the end date of your overall project. If you apply it to a linked task, however, it'll be scheduled to end when the successor task needs to start.
    c. On the whole, try to avoid this option. It doesn't give you any extra slack time to deal with problems that might arise. And problems often do, in the most unexpected ways.

There are other, more sophisticated constraints that you can use within your Gantt app. When you're just starting out and getting comfy with Gantt charts, however, it's best to keep their use to a minimum.

- Start no earlier than
  - A task (whether linked or not) can't start before a date you specify. However, your Gantt app has the flexibility to start it later.
- Start no later than
  - A task (whether linked or not) can't start later than a date you specify. However, your app has the flexibility to start it earlier.
- Finish no earlier than
  - A task (whether linked or not) can't end before a given date. However, your app has the flexibility to end it later.
- Finish no later than
  - A task (whether linked or not) can't end later than a given date. However, your app has the flexibility to end it earlier.
- Must start on
  - This rigid constraint means that a task (whether linked or not) must start on a specific date. Even if its immediately preceding task is completed earlier, your app will not bring forward the task to take advantage of the time gained.
- Must finish on
  - This is another rigid constraint. A task (whether linked or not) must end on a specific date. As above, even if its immediately preceding task is completed earlier, your app will not bring forward the task to take advantage of the time gained.

If you do decide to apply any constraints to your tasks, it's a good idea to add a brief comment to your Excel to explain why. If a constraint causes scheduling conflicts later on, as your legal project evolves, you'll be able to refer to your notes to decide whether to: keep a constraint in place, change it to a different constraint, or remove it completely.

Summary

18–32 Project management is a process, a way of thinking, to help you think about how you deliver legal services using all of your firm's people and resources. You may ask if project management is just a way of making legal services cheaper so that firms may make more money. That is true, if your sole goal is to reduce costs then project management will help you identify where savings can be made. However, as a solicitor your ultimate aim is provide effective legal advice following professional standards. That doesn't always mean providing a service at the lowest cost. Instead, we want you to also think about using project management to provide a better service to clients. The next chapter will introduce another way of thinking to help you use your project management skills to identify the parts of your service that will provide the maximum benefit to clients.

CHAPTER 19

HOW TO IMPROVE CLIENT SERVICE

Introduction

You're two-years qualified. It's been a busy couple of years, but you've become a confident and trusted solicitor. For the last six months you've spent much of your time working on another unfair dismissal claim. It's turned out to be more complicated than you first thought. You've had to speak to fifteen other employees, and consult counsel and expert witnesses. **19–1**

You have a pile of paperwork that is threatening to break your desk. You're proud at how you've dealt with both your legal work and the project management of your caseload. Your partner has congratulated you on doing a good job. You've used your skills to keep costs under control and you've hit your fee targets.

Then, out of the blue, your client complains. He says that nothing is happening and he doesn't know what he is paying you for. Before responding, your partner asks you to talk him through what exactly you've done. Something has gone wrong, but what? How do you make sure it doesn't happen again?

If you're reading this and thinking that two years qualified seems a long time away, then don't think about it yet. Skip this chapter and come back to it in a couple of years. As a trainee or new qualified solicitor, it's enough to know that you're doing what your partner and senior colleagues tell you. You've got more than enough to deal with already. However, once you've worked as a lawyer for a few years you'll start to wonder if there are ways to improve the way you work to make it easier for clients to deal with you and to improve your workflow (both so that you can make more money). When you start thinking these thoughts, this chapter is for you. **19–2**

Let's start with an analogy. Think about a magician pulling a rabbit from a hat. A magician reaches into a hat and pulls out a rabbit. Were you impressed when you saw it? Or has the trick become so clichéd that it barely registers? You know exactly what's going to happen. It's like hearing the punch line of a joke you've heard a million times before. There's no surprise, and no sense of wonder. While it may take the poor magician two months to train his rabbit to stay still and not jump out of the hat, and another two months to practise pulling it out of the hat without revealing the secret compartment inside, you just shrug your shoulders and demand something more impressive: "Make the Forth Road bridge disappear! Pull an elephant out of the hat!"

Repetition has rendered the extraordinary mundane, but that's not the only reason for your lack of interest. Without appreciating the effort required to perform the trick, you—the audience—are unable to recognise the skill required to control the rabbit and make it appear flawlessly. Is it any wonder, then, that magicians swap rabbits for much easier, inanimate objects (such as flowers or flags) and pull these out of their hats instead?

There is a similar dilemma with legal services. Clients don't recognise the hard work you do. They turn round at the end of a transaction and shrug their shoulders. They don't understand why they're paying for hundreds of hours of work when all they saw were a couple of emails. Yet, from your perspective, you remember the late nights and weekends working on files. You know you could have charged more for the many, many hours that you put in. This conflict of the work you actually do and the service your client believes he/she has received can be avoided if you understand exactly what a client sees, hears and feels when you advise them.

Outcomes

19–3 We will examine a way of thinking that can help you understand the difference between what you do and what a client experiences. If you understand this difference, you can help your clients understand what you're doing, and why.

The client experience

19–4 Clients don't sit beside you when you work. They don't listen to your phone calls. They won't read most of the emails that you send, and they may not even read the contracts and papers you write. Instead, they judge you only on the conversations you have with them and the documents that they actually see. Depending on the particular task, this may only be a small fraction of the work you *actually* do for them.

It may take you half a day to prepare questions to interview a witness, a full day to speak to them and, finally, another to ensure you have all the relevant information you need. If you multiply this by 15 witnesses, you've spent more than a month on just this one task. Yet, your client knows little about it. When you tell them that you spoke to 15 people they probably imagine that took you only a day. Perhaps they even think you phoned them, one after another, and it only took a couple of hours. No wonder they complain if they don't hear from you for a month. You might be busy working for them, but they don't know that unless (and until) you tell them.

That's why (in Ch.6) we emphasised the importance of specifying what you will (and won't) do in an engagement letter. However, that's only your best guess at the start of a piece of work as to what will happen next. Things change and, as they do, you should update your client so that they always have an accurate picture. If you're vigilant and highlight what you're doing, from first instruction to the moment they pay their final bill, a client always feels more in control. They won't complain about your work or your bill, and they're far more likely to use you again (and indeed to recommend you). You should place yourself in your clients' shoes and identify what works, what doesn't and what needs to change. By doing so, you can provide your clients with the best service. How do you put yourself in your clients' shoes? How do you identify when it's appropriate to advise them of any changes?

We believe that you do this by preparing a simple "roadmap" of the work you intend to do. You then identify the steps that you propose to take and decide which of these will be visible to your client. Much like a magician, you work out what is going to happen backstage (behind the red curtain) and what is going to be visible onstage. We'll look at two examples below to show how to achieve this.

Background information

The idea of separating work into backstage and onstage actions was conceived some 30 years ago by Lynn Shostack, in an article published in *The Harvard Business Review*.[1] She put forward the idea of a "blueprint"; a document that sets out in visual form how a customer (client) and service provider (law firm) interact. Broadly, a blueprint helps you identify what clients actually experience when they instruct you. **19–5**

- Starting onstage by identifying all the events the client experiences (for example, when they receive documents from you, when they give you instructions, the documents they see etc.).
- Then moving backstage and identifying what you need to do to ensure these onstage events occur. For example, if a document is produced, how is it produced? Is the person who sends it out the same person who drafted it? Was your library involved in the research? Were precedents used or was the document drafted from scratch?

First example: using a blueprint to improve a magic trick

Step one: identify what the client will see, hear or experience

Let's return to our example of the magician pulling a rabbit from a hat. How might we visualise this? We can sketch out the steps required to perform the trick. We've included an example of this in Pt 5 of the Appendix. **19–6**

- As you can see, steps one to five represent the onstage action (what the audience sees).
- Backstage, you can see the steps required to perform the trick in public (whether it's finding a venue, buying supplies, training your rabbit or practicing the trick).

Sketching out the actions isn't the end of the process, however. Once you know what your client sees, you can work out how to improve the experience for them.

Step two: identify how you can improve what they see, hear or experience

Fail points

After identifying what occurs onstage and backstage, you can isolate the fail points. These are the parts of the process where events might go awry. If you can predict what the fail points are, you can build in preventive measures to prevent service failings, later. **19–7**

Timing

The process can be given approximate timings. Improvements can then focus on those parts of the process that might reduce the time required to complete a **19–8**

[1] G. L. Shostack, "Designing services that deliver", Harvard Business Review, January 1984, No.62. Available at: *https://hbr.org/1984/01/designing-services-that-deliver* [Accessed: 10 June 2016].

transaction. For example, if you have an audience that is impressed regardless of what comes out of your hat, you could decide that the time spent training your rabbit is unnecessary when you could use a plastic flower instead. Alternatively, you might seek to innovate and restore the wonder of the trick by replacing your rabbit with something more implausible, so that audiences once again gasp: "how did they do that?!"

Visible innovation

19–9 By identifying what your client sees (and the work required to achieve it) you can consider improvements to those parts of the process that are of the greatest visual value to your client. For example, buying better carrots to feed your rabbit won't improve how your audience perceives the trick. It's the focus on your client as the reason for innovation that gives blueprinting its greatest value. Let's look at an example, as applied to legal work.

Second example: using a blueprint to improve legal contracts

Step one: identify what the client will see, hear or experience

19–10 Let's examine part of a typical transaction e.g. negotiating and concluding a simple contract. How can you visualise this as a blueprint again? Remember, you sketch out the steps required.

- Again, steps one to five represent the onstage action (what your client actually sees).
- Backstage, you see the internal actions required to conclude the contract.

Step two: innovation and legal services

19–11 If you review the blueprint, you can identify the fail points, timings and visible innovations that can provide tangible benefits to your client.

Fail points

19–12 You can clearly appreciate, in steps one to five, that your client might only see a small number of documents during the transaction (perhaps a first draft, a summary of any changes and then a final draft). In order to improve your client's experience, many partners insist that they review your documents before you send them out. In particular, when you're a trainee, senior lawyers will check your work. Equally, larger firms are adopting quality assurance programmes to ensure that documents are reviewed to reduce the chance of mistakes creeping in. For example, spelling a client's name incorrectly is one of the most basic (but also most noticeable) errors that you can make.

Timing

19–13 Your client might be under pressure of time to complete a contract swiftly. It's important that you're able to support them. By examining how long it takes to produce a draft, you can start to see that there are things you could introduce to produce a first draft more expeditiously. For example, you might set up a template for future adaptation (to save drafting from scratch).

Visible innovation

Let's stay on the example of using a template. If you don't tell your client that you have created templates, he/she won't ever know the time saving mechanism you have introduced for their benefit. You might say to them at your first meeting, "we can deal with this quickly because we have templates that can easily be tailored for you. This will save you money." **19–14**

It's important to mention, at this junction, that service blueprinting doesn't advocate pulling back the curtain *completely* to reveal everything that you do backstage. Clients won't thank you for showing them every due diligence bundle and every internal email.

Service blueprints do, however, highlight those parts of a transaction that could be mentioned onstage, so that your client is fully aware of the work involved (and what their fees are paying for). If you don't tell them about the complexities of titles before producing a report on them, and if you don't share the nightmare due diligence bundles you have received, your client's perception of your service is then biased. You can understand why he or she might say, "all I got was an email". Conflict, then, becomes inevitable. By placing yourself in your clients' shoes, you can consider how much of the curtain you want to draw back so that your service (and value) can be appropriately recognised.

Benefits of blueprinting

A blueprint basically identifies the things you do that your clients actually experience. It helps you, in turn, highlight to your clients the actions that matter to them. By identifying what actions are taken "onstage" and what are not, you can appreciate the importance of communicating to your clients exactly what is required of you to perform the services that they're paying for. **19–15**

As discussed in Ch.6 (how to write an engagement letter), how often do clients complain about mistakes in your work, compared to how you communicated with them? It's communication (or lack of it) that leads to the greatest number of complaints. However, if you consider transactions from your clients' perspective, you realise that what they *see* of a transaction is entirely down to what you choose to reveal, or keep hidden.

Summary

The art of the magician is the art of visual manipulation. In card tricks, a magician diverts your attention so that cards can be palmed, decks stacked and coins dropped. For the magician, each pass of the hand, flick of a wrist and tap of a wand is choreographed so as to provide the maximum value to an audience. **19–16**

Equally, when designing legal services, if you want to maximise the tangible value of your services, the secret lies in what to reveal. When you start working as a lawyer, you may not be able to sketch out a transaction fully; you may not have sufficient technical and practical knowledge. However, as you gain experience, you'll be able to identify when you should be onstage and when you should pull back the curtain to reveal what happens backstage. No matter what level you're at, you should always try to think of the client's point of view.

PART 4

Running a Business—Finance

CHAPTER 20

HOW TO SPEAK TO CLIENTS ABOUT FINANCE

Introduction

You're three-years qualified. You've paid off your student debts and you've started to think about buying a flat, taking out a pension and perhaps saving some money each month. But where do you start? Should you speak to a financial advisor? **20–1**

Financial advice can appear complicated. It's filled with jargon and acronyms. Should you take out an ISA? Should your mortgage be capped, fixed or tracked? It can be difficult to know where to start and you may feel that you need to speak to an expert. The only problem is that many clients think that *you're* that expert when they seek financial advice. That's why we started this chapter with an example of how you approach your own financial decisions. You need to be confident in your own ability to understand finances before you can speak confidently to clients. **20–2**

And clients will ask for your advice. If clients buy a house they may ask you for advice about taking out a mortgage; when they invest money in a trust they may assume that you'll tell them if it's a good idea; when corporate clients take out a loan they'll expect you to understand what they're doing and that you'll keep them right. That's why you need to know how money works. You should understand the basics behind giving financial advice, as well as some of the main products such as shares, pensions, loans and insurance. We'll cover everything you need to know in this chapter and the way that we'll do that is by looking at how finance affects you.

Outcomes

To help you understand finance, we've addressed this chapter to you first. If you don't understand how your own finances work then you'll struggle to translate that to clients. Everything we talk about in this chapter, though, applies equally to clients. We start by examining the concepts behind financial advice. These concepts are simple and, once you know them, you'll be able to understand how one financial product differs from another. We'll examine the main financial products used by individuals and companies and the differences between them. We'll examine how governments help protect financial decisions—and how you can protect them through using insurance. We finish by looking at how these products are then bought and sold in the "financial market". **20–3**

The basics of finance

The money in your pocket

20–4 All financial decisions can be viewed in two ways. Either you're moving money from the present into the future, or you're moving money from the future into the present. In short, finance is about time travel. You don't create money from thin air, you move it through time to when you need it.

Imagine you have £100 in your pocket. What can you buy with it? Perhaps you can buy a new coat, or an expensive meal? In fact, you can buy anything up to the value of £100. Could you buy a MacBook Air (£1,000)? No. Could you buy a Fiat 500 (£10,000)? No. Could you buy a flat (£100,000)? No. You have only £100, and once you've spent it, it's gone.

Let's imagine that you've started work and you earn a salary of £24,000 a year. Let's forget about taxes and assume that every month you receive £2,000. Each month, you have £2,000 in your pocket. Could you buy that MacBook Air? Yes, it's only £1,000 and you have enough cash in your pocket to pay for it. Could you buy the Fiat 500? No. It's £10,000, which is still £8,000 more than you have. However, you know that in five months you'll have £10,000 (five months' salary of £2,000 a month). If you could only send that money back from the future, you'd be able to buy that car today.

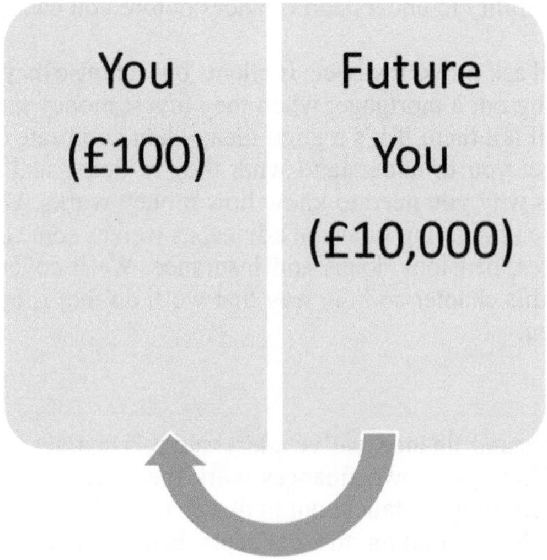

It's the same for the flat. In four years and two months you'll have £100,000 (50 × £2,000). If you want to buy it today, again you need to send that money back from the future. Either that, or you have to wait for 50 months.

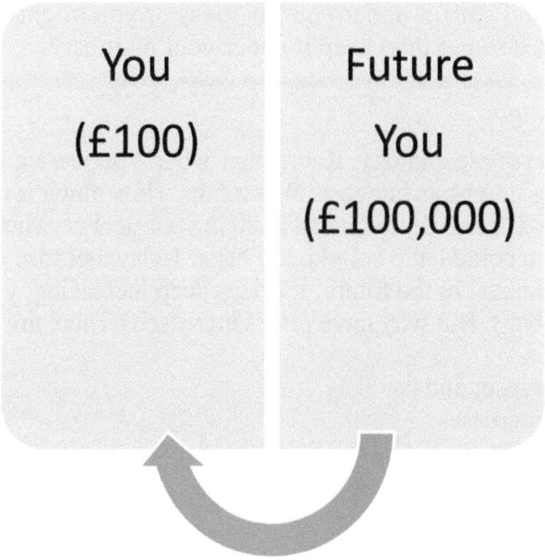

Many financial products are just time machines. Think about a pension. You might be earning £2,000 a month today but, when you retire, you'll be earning nothing. Future you would love to have £2,000 a month to spend after they retire. So, present you invests in a pension—a way to move your money from today to the future, to help future you when you retire.

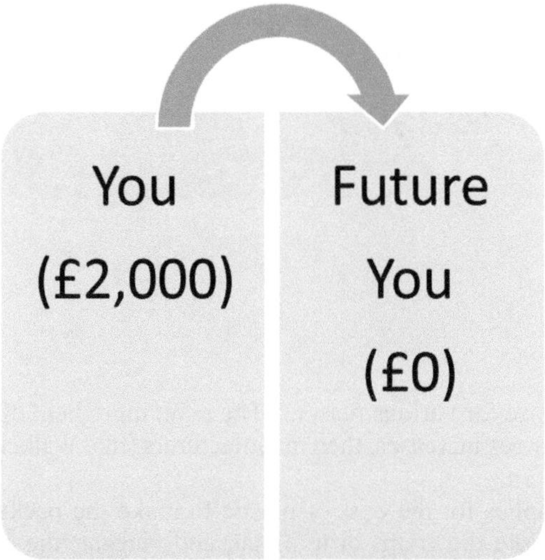

You're a time traveller again. Most *investments* work like this. *Loans* work in the opposite direction. A bank will give you a mortgage to buy a house. It calculates that you can pay it back from everything you earn in the next 25 years. When you take out a mortgage you're moving that money back to the present. Loans and investments are money time machines, and we look at how they work in the next section.

Investments: inflation and interest rates

20–5 You have £100 in your pocket and £2,000 in your bank account, from your first salary. After paying your rent, buying food, going out for drinks and buying some new clothes you have £1,000 left. You decide to be sensible and keep it. You have a choice. You could stuff it under your mattress or you might invest it. But why would you invest it rather than keep it under your mattress?

Introducing inflation

20–6 Let's start with a simple analogy. Remember when you were a child? How much did a bag of crisps or a Mars bar cost? Was it 50p? How much is it today? 75p? The price has increased. Imagine if you had £100 in your pocket, when the bag of crisps cost only 50p. You could have bought 200 bags. Today, because crisps are 75p you can only buy 150 bags. In the future, if prices keep increasing, your £100 will buy fewer and fewer bags. But why have prices increased? There are two main factors:

- costs increase; and
- demand increases.

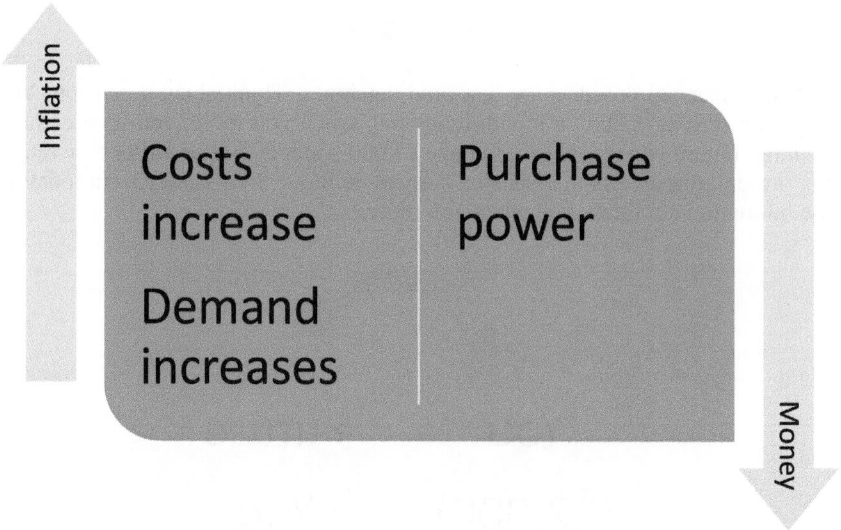

Cost increase

20–7 Costs can increase for various reasons. The main ingredient of crisps is potato. If the price of potatoes increases, then manufacturers (like Walkers) have to increase their prices in turn.

The same applies to: the cost of plastic to make the packets; the cost of the flavouring to make the crisps taste of salt and vinegar; the electricity to power the factory; taxes to pay the government; even Gary Lineker's salary to star in the latest advert. As any cost increases, the price of the end product may need to increase.

Demand increases

There are a finite number of potatoes in the world. In turn, there's a finite amount of crisps. The scarcer something is, the more people are prepared to pay for it. So, as demand increases (or as the supply of goods decreases), the price increases. **20–8**

Let's assume there are 10 people in your office who love crisps. Let's assume your local corner shop has 1,000 bags of crisps. If only 10 people want those 1,000 bags, the shop may need to drop its price. Fast forward a week and the crisps are half price; 500 people want the crisps. However, if it's just one bag of crisps (and 10 people want it) the shopkeeper can raise the price. These changes in supply and demand lead to price increases and decreases.

The housing market is a good example of supply and demand. The UK is an island. There is only a limited amount of land and a limited number of homes. House prices rise as the number of people looking for homes increase. House prices fall as the number of people looking for homes decrease.

What is inflation?

Inflation is simply the percentage increase in prices each year. It's measured monthly and it tracks price increases over a 12-month period. Inflation can be measured in a number of different ways. The most frequently quoted (and most significant) are the Consumer Prices Index (CPI) and the Retail Prices Index (RPI). Each looks at the prices of hundreds of items we commonly buy (including bread, cinema tickets, pints of beer and bags of crisps) and tracks how they've changed over time. The inflation rates are expressed as percentages. If CPI is 4%, this means that on average, the price of products and services bought is 4% higher than a year earlier. Or, in other words, you'd need to spend 4% more to buy the same things you bought 12 months ago. **20–9**

Can prices go down?

Yes. This is known as deflation. If prices are not going up, then economists assume people are scared to buy things. This is bad for the economy. If people are not buying, then companies are not getting paid. In turn, companies may become insolvent and employees made redundant (with a rise in unemployment). Inflation is a sign of a healthy economy; deflation is the sign of a poor economy (though too much inflation can also be unhealthy). **20–10**

Why is inflation important for investment?

If we didn't have inflation then you could stuff your money under your mattress, take it out in 40 years and buy exactly the same things you can buy, for the same price. However, inflation means prices increase. Your money, over time, becomes worth less, until it's worthless. **20–11**

To avoid this scenario, you need to invest your money in a way that it increases in value by *more* than inflation. If, for example, inflation is 3% per year, you need your money to increase by at least 3% so that it retains its value. The more you can increase the value of your money, the better your investment.

The following example shows how this would look if you had £100 in your pocket and inflation is 3%:

Year	To keep up with inflation (3%) you'll need	If investment returns 2%	If investment returns 4%
One	£103	£102	£104
Two	£106	£104	£108
Three	£109	£106	£112
Five	£116	£110	£122
Ten	£138	£122	£148

After 10 years, to keep up with inflation your £100 needs to become £138. If your investment increased by 2% you end up losing £16 after 10 years. If it increased by 4% you gain £10.

Introducing interest rates

20–12 We've looked at inflation. We know that it changes the value of the pound in your pocket over time. However, what we need to know, is how do you "beat" inflation? As we showed you above, you need to invest your money. The simplest way to invest is to invest it in a bank. A bank will pay interest and you want this interest rate to be greater than inflation.

How are interest rates set?

20–13 Every month the Bank of England sets a base rate. Banks and building societies use this base rate when calculating their interest rates. These rates are the rate of interest you get each year if you invest your money with them. So, if the interest rate were 3% (assuming inflation is also 3%), your money would be safe—it would neither increase nor decrease in value. If the interest rate were 4%, your money would increase in value. On the other hand, if the interest rate was 2% (with inflation at 3%) your money would decrease in value.

Interest rates are also used for loans, and we look at this in more detail later.

Why does the Bank of England set interest rates?

20–14 The Bank of England is the UK's central bank. A central bank is a public institution that manages the currency of a country (or group of countries) and controls the money supply (literally, the amount of money in circulation). The central bank of the EU is the European Central Bank. The Federal Reserve is the central bank of the US. One of a central bank's functions is to ensure that economies are stable. In the UK, one of the main ways the Bank of England tries to achieve this is to ensure that inflation doesn't increase by more than 2% each year.

The bank can control inflation by increasing or decreasing interest rates. When interest rates are low, people are less likely to save money because they can make more money spending it or saving it elsewhere. When rates are high, people are more likely to save as they know the bank will give them a good return. This is a constant balancing act as the more people spend, the more inflation is likely to rise—the central bank has increased demand. The less people spend and the more they save, the more likely it is that inflation will fall—the central bank has decreased demand.

This balance between interest rates and inflation is one that is debated each month by the Bank of England's monetary policy committee, leading to an announcement about the interest rates.

Introducing investments

Assuming you or your client want to save their money, and move it from today to a future date, how do they go about doing this? You have a number of options. You could save it in a bank or building society; you could save it with the government; you could buy a bond; or you could invest it in shares, property or other assets. **20–15**

Investments: save it in a bank or building society

Think of a deposit as a safe that you put your money in, which you'll open in the future. When you open it, you want the money inside to be worth as much as when you put it in, and, hopefully, even more. However, because your money is in a safe, it's not doing anything. And, because it's not doing anything, it's harder for it to grow in value. Would someone pay you if you put your feet up all day? No. So, why should your money be any different? It's not doing anything in the safe. That's why we have different types of deposit, or different types of safe. These are current accounts and savings accounts. **20–16**

Current accounts

This is the most common type of deposit. Most people have a current account. A current account is a deposit account designed for everyday transactions. You access it most days to pay in your salary, to set up direct debits for bills and, importantly, to take out cash from ATM machines. These accounts usually yield only a low rate of interest (if indeed any) on the money deposited (also known as your *capital*), because you can withdraw the money at any time. The money always has to be in your "safe", because you may need it at any time. **20–17**

Saving accounts

If you want a higher interest rate, you need to let the bank use your money. A savings account is an account that is harder to access. You may not get a debit card and you may even need to give the bank notice before you can take your money out. 60 to 90 days' notice is quite normal. Since the bank doesn't need to give you your money instantly, it can take the money from your "safe" and invest it itself. It then returns that money to you with a higher rate of interest as a "thank you" for letting them use it. Notice accounts are also referred to as term deposit accounts. **20–18**

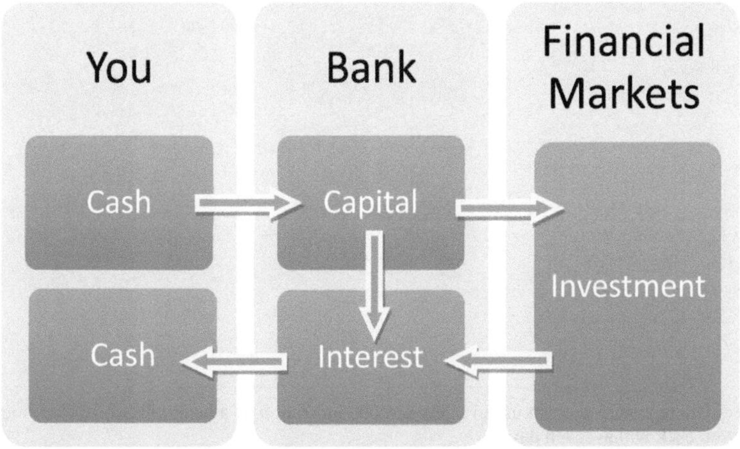

Investments: save it with the government

20–19 When you place your money in a "safe" you want that safe to be secure. You don't want to give your money to someone who might run off with it, who won't return it to you, or won't invest it wisely. Banks and building societies are authorised by the Government to deal with money. You know they're safe because the Government stands behind them.[1] You may, however, wish to invest in the government directly, particularly after the banking crisis that started in 2008. You may believe that the Government represents the safest place to keep your money. The interest rates offered usually are lower than those of a bank of building society, but your money is more secure.

National Saving and Investment

20–20 The UK Government provides deposits through National Saving and Investment (NS & I), an executive agency of the Chancellor of the Exchequer. NS & I provides the following options:

Current account

20–21 The NS & I Investment Account is an instant access account offering varying rates of interest, depending on how much money is invested. The product offers higher returns for larger investments, with a maximum investment of £1,000,000.

Saving account

20–22 The Direct Saver is a savings account which pays a variable rate of interest. The Direct Saver account pays interest gross. This is, in turn, taxable and must be declared to HMRC.

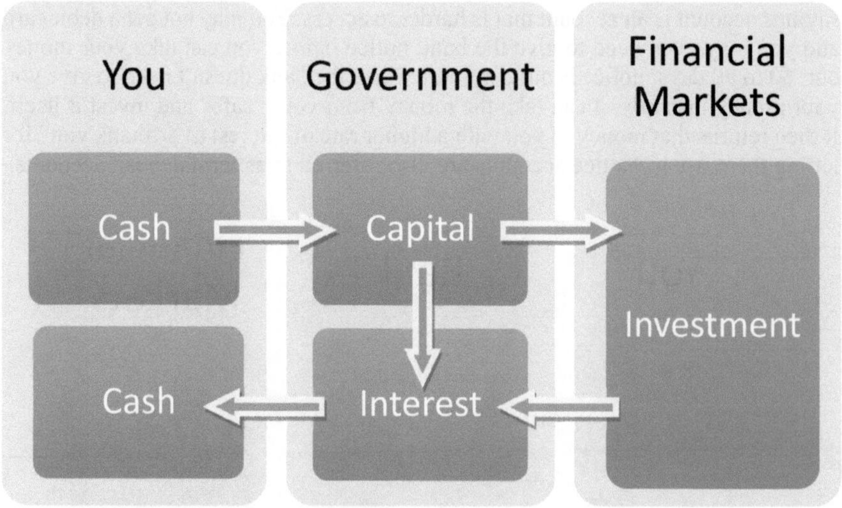

[1] Every UK regulated account usually gets £75,000 protection. If a bank fails, the Government will pay you back within seven days.

Pensions

Strictly speaking a pension is no different to any other investment. You're taking cash you have today and sending it to future you, to use when you retire. You could do the same thing by converting your cash into a deposit, you could buy shares or you could buy assets. So why have pensions at all? We didn't always have pensions. Either you worked until you died or your family would step in and care for you. The Government wouldn't help. In fact, it created laws to make begging a crime and forced the poor into workhouses. That changed at the turn of the 20th century. **20–23**

In 1908, David Lloyd George, in a Liberal government led by Herbert Asquith, determined to take action to "lift the shadow of the workhouse from the homes of the poor".[2] He believed the best way of doing this was to guarantee an income to people who were too old to work. In 1908, he introduced the Old Age Pensions Act and created the pension, worth about £23 a week today. In the years since, to encourage people to take charge of their own pension arrangements, successive governments have created tax breaks and incentives to encourage companies to offer workplace pensions.

There are two types of pension. There is the state pension, which is provided by the UK Government and paid for through your National Insurance contributions (NICs). There are also private pensions, which are arranged by you or your employer. We'll look at private pensions later in the chapter. **20–24**

State pension

The basic state pension is a regular payment from the Government that you get when you reach the state pension age (65 for a man, 63 for a woman) on or after 6 April 2016. In 2016, you get a state pension if you're eligible and either you're:

- a man born on or after 6 April 1951; or
- a woman born on or after 6 April 1953.

To get the pension you must have paid (or been credited with) NICs.

The most you can receive is £115.95 per week. The actual total is based on how much you have contributed through national insurance. The basic state pension increases every year by at least 2.5% or, if higher, the highest of: **20–25**

- earnings—the average percentage growth in wages (in Great Britain); and
- prices—the percentage growth in prices in the UK as measured by the CPI (to beat inflation, as we discussed).

---

[2] Quoted in the biography of David Lloyd George at *http://www.historic-uk.com/historyuk/historyofbritain/lloyd-george* [Accessed: 13 June 2016].

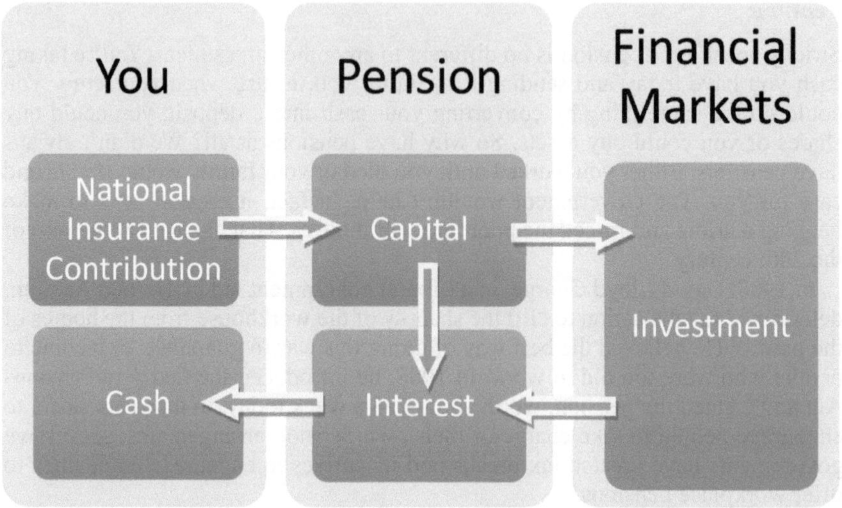

Investments: buy a bond

20–26 Instead of investing your money in a "safe" by saving it, you may want to make your money work by lending it to someone else to use. In return you get an IOU. This IOU promises to return your money at a certain time, and it promises to pay you a set rate of interest each year. This type of arrangement is known as a bond. In some ways, it follows the same principle as a savings account. However, instead of a bank, you're letting someone else use your money, when you don't need it. The main differences are that instead of having to give notice to get your money back, you agree a date upfront for when it'll be returned. Secondly, you can sell the bond to other people as the IOU is valuable. How valuable depends on who has granted it.

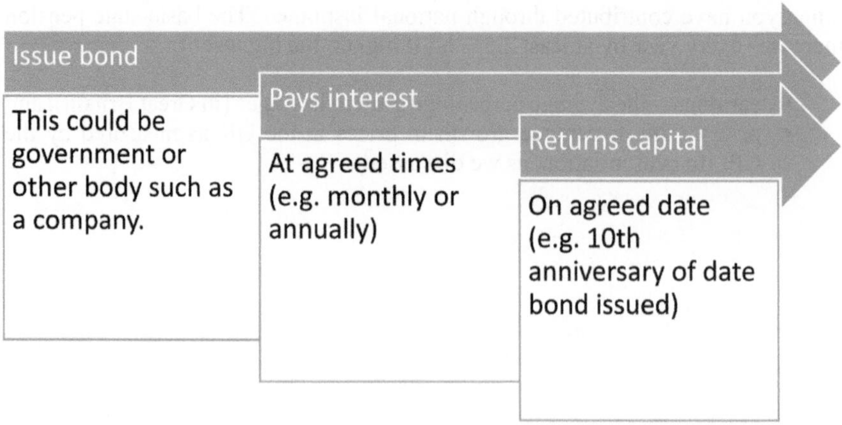

If a government issues the bond, you know it's safe. If a bank issues a bond, it should be safe. If a company set up last week issues a bond, you may never see your money again. Would you accept an IOU from someone you didn't know? However, for a high rate of interest you might be willing to take that risk.

Bonds take a number of forms. The most common forms are:

Gilts

If the government issues a bond it's known as gilt-edged securities or "gilts", because originally the security had a gilded (or gilt) edge. Gilts can be bought in two ways. Firstly, the Treasury issues gilts to raise money for the Government. Since 1993, this has been done by way of an auction, whereby potential investors bid for gilts. Secondly, gilts can be bought and sold on the London Stock Exchange. Investors simply instruct a broker to buy and sell at a particular price, and settlement happens the following day. **20–27**

Corporate bonds

Also known as "stocks", corporate bonds are fixed interest securities. They're similar to gilts, but issued by companies. As such, they're riskier than gilts and offer a higher interest rate, to attract buyers. Corporate bonds offered by blue chip company trading on the FTSE 1000 should be safe and will offer a lower interest rate than a bond offered by a company formed last week. **20–28**

Income Bonds offered by NS & I

Income Bonds, as their name suggests, provide a monthly income from the underlying capital. The minimum investment is £500 and the maximum is £1,000,000. The interest rate varies. Interest is paid monthly, without deduction of income tax, but is still taxable (and so must be declared to HMRC). Capital may be withdrawn without notice. Anyone over 16 can open an account and an investment can be made in trust for someone else. **20–29**

Savings Certificates offered by NS & I

Savings Certificates either are fixed rate or index linked and provide a guaranteed return at the end of the term. They're issued for periods of three or five years. However, if they're cashed in before the end of the term, a penalty might be applied. The return is tax-free. There are no new Certificates currently on general sale, but existing Certificates can be renewed at maturity either for the same (or a different) term. **20–30**

Children's Bonds offered by NS & I

These provide a tax-free return for children under 16 (even if the child becomes a taxpayer in the meantime). There is a guaranteed return for each period of five years, until a child reaches 21. The maximum investment is £3,000 per issue, per child (with a minimum investment of £25). Parents, legal guardians and grandparents can invest on behalf of a child. They can be cashed in early, with a penalty equivalent to 90 days' interest. **20–31**

Premium Bonds offered by NS & I

Bonds can be bought in multiples of £100. They allow an investor to be entered into a draw, every month, to win up to £1,000,000. There are 1,500,000 prizes awarded every month, all of which are tax-free. Interest is not paid on these bonds, **20–32** as such, and the initial investment can be withdrawn at any time. The maximum investment is £50,000 (for 2015–16).

Investments: buy shares

Ordinary shares

20–33 Companies, to raise money, issue ordinary shares. Shares carry with them ownership and a right to participate in any profits the company makes (usually by the company paying a dividend). Larger companies may choose to trade their shares on the stock market and become public companies. These companies are referred to as *quoted companies*, as opposed to companies that choose to trade their shares privately (*unquoted companies*). Unquoted shares can't be bought and sold on the stock market, making them harder to sell (or less "liquid") than quoted shares.

Larger firms with good track records often have little problem finding people to buy their shares. Companies like these are called "blue chip companies" and would include most of the large Plcs such as banks, industry leaders such as BT Plc, and major corporates such as Tesco Plc or Next Plc. Their shares are traded on the London Stock Exchange (we look at exchanges later in the chapter).

The London Stock Exchange is not the only place to buy and sell share. Shares can also be bought through the Alternative Investment Market (AIM). Companies on the AIM don't have to meet the same requirements as the London Stock Exchange. If London Stock Exchange is eBay with strict rules about selling, then AIM is Gumtree, where anyone can post with little checks. Another advantage of AIM is that it costs less to use it. This makes it more attractive for smaller companies to raise money on AIM rather than the London Stock Exchange.

The performance of shares in the UK is measured using various indices like the FTSE 100. The FTSE 100 is an index of the leading 100 companies in the UK. As well as the FTSE 100, there is also the FTSE 250 and the FTSE all-share index. The FTSE 250 is an index of the 250 shares below the top 100 and the all-shares index is an index of the leading 850 companies in the UK.

Every country has its own indices for measuring the performance of its stock market. These include the NASDAQ and Dow Jones, in the USA, the Hang Seng in Hong Kong, the Nikkei in Japan, the DAX in Germany and the CAC in France.

There are two big advantages to buying shares. Some shares are known for paying large dividends. Investors may choose these if they're looking to provide themselves with extra income. The second advantage of shares is the scope for the share to increase in value. As a company grows in reputation and stature, there should be an increase in the number of people wanting to buy shares, which then pushes up the market price. Another example of how demand can increase price.

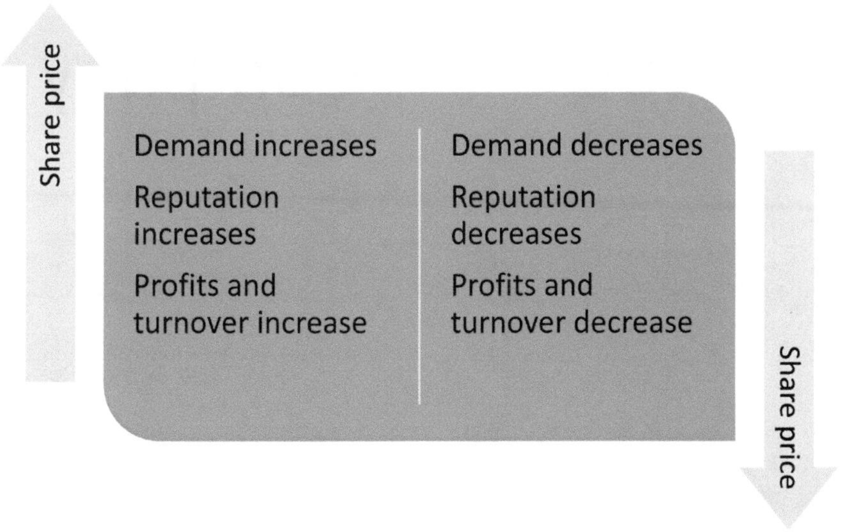

As share prices change over time, based on the company's reputation and financial performance, most shares are considered to be a long-term investment. Companies don't make money overnight. They grow gradually and it's rare for a company to suddenly make money. It takes time for sale and reputations to grow.

Preference shares

Other kinds of shares, such as preference shares, are appropriate for particular clients. Preference shares pay out a fixed rate of dividend, which is declared before any dividend to ordinary shareholders. There are several kinds of preference share. Some are cumulative, meaning that if a company doesn't have enough profit to pay a dividend in one year, it's rolled into the following year. Non-cumulative preference shares, however, often lose the dividend right altogether, if a company simply can't afford to pay. An investor must be wary about which kind of shares he or she is purchasing. **20–34**

Ordinary shares offer potential for high growth and a big return, but you must always bear in mind that the opposite can be true. Dividends might not be paid for a long time and a company can fail completely. Individuals with limited capital (and those who can't afford to lose their initial investment) should not invest directly in the stock market. Preference shares are less of a gamble and the reward from them is usually less.

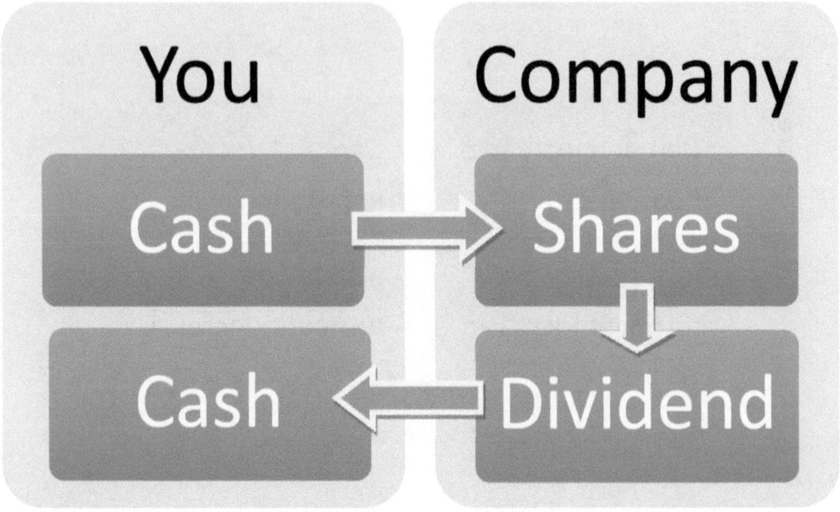

Investments: buy property or other assets

20–35 When you buy something (like a bag of crisps) you haven't lost your cash. You've just converted it to something else. You can convert it back, if someone will buy the bag of crisps from you. Instead of investing your cash by depositing it with a bank or building society, or buying a bond from the government, you could instead buy an asset in the hope that when you need cash in the future, you can sell the asset at a profit. Perhaps the most common asset is property. For example, you buy a house for £100,000 and, 10 years later when you want to move, you sell it for £150,000. You can also invest in gold and other metals, oil and even in wine and whisky. The principle is the same; you're buying something in the hope that it'll be worth more when you sell it in the future.

Also, assets may give you an income. Think of a flat. If you buy a flat, you can rent it out to a tenant. You've not only gained an asset, which can increase in value, you've also gained a monthly rent. This type of asset is known as an income asset.

We look more closely at property when we discuss loans (and mortgages).

Investments: invest in a private pension

20–36 There are two main types of private pension: defined benefit (also known as a final salary pension, for reasons which will become apparent) and defined contribution.

Defined benefit

20–37 A final salary pension is one that promises to pay out an income when you retire, based on how much you earn. For example, if you're paid £20,000 a year (as at your retirement date) your pension will pay £20,000 a year, until you die. This type of pension is the easiest to understand. Your employer automatically deducts part of your salary to pay your pension. When you retire, it then continues to pay you your final salary.

Defined contribution

Defined contribution schemes pay an accumulated sum when you retire, which you can use to secure a pension income (by buying a product called an annuity or by income drawdown). You can also take the lot as a lump sum, but may face a hefty tax bill. Your employer can arrange either type of pension (a workplace pension) or you can make arrangements directly with a provider. Your pension provider invests the money you put in. The value of your pension pot can go up or down, depending on how these investments perform. **20–38**

Private pension—how much will you receive?

A final salary pension is easy to work out. When you retire, you're paid your final salary.[3] A defined contribution scheme is harder to work out. It's an investment, like any other, and what you get depends on how much you've paid in, how well your investments have performed, and how you choose to be paid. You can choose to be paid regular sums, a lump sum or even smaller sums. You usually get 25% of your pension pot tax-free. **20–39**

Private pension—when can you receive payments?

The state pension starts when you're 63 or 65, depending if you're male or female. A private pension is not linked to the state pension age. Instead, you get paid based on your scheme's rules. This may allow you to be paid earlier (though rarely less than 55) or it may be linked to other conditions. **20–40**

Private pension—what happens if my employer no longer exists when I need my pension?

Although your employer might run your pension scheme, your funds don't form any part of your employer's finances. Instead, funds are managed by a pension trust or pension provider, on behalf of the company. **20–41**

Why would you use a pension instead of another investment?

A pension is a tax efficient way to invest for your retirement. A pension lets you take up to 25% of your investments out tax-free. This is a big saving, compared to direct investments. **20–42**

We've looked at investments and what happens when you want to send money into the future. We turn to what happens when you want future you to send money back to you.

---

[3] This is not strictly your final salary as shown on your last payslip. If it were, an unscrupulous employer could reduce your final wages. Instead, it's calculated using an average so that you receive a fair figure for your final salary.

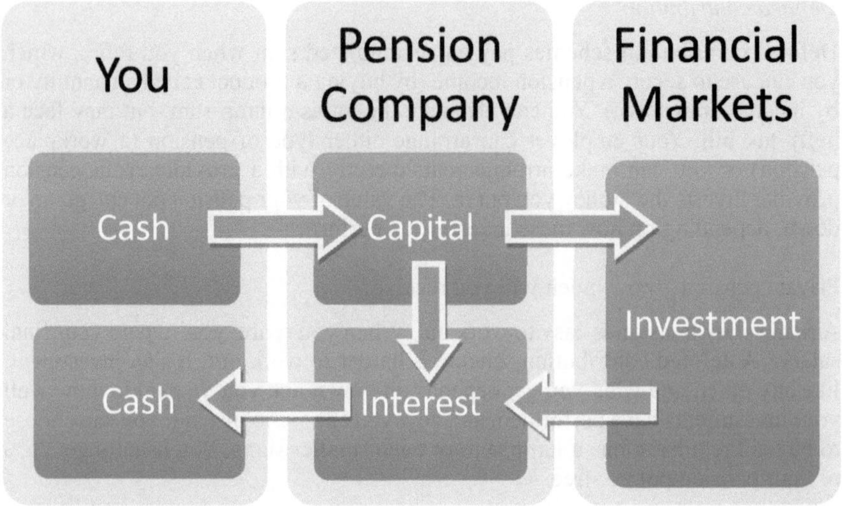

Introducing loans

20–43 A loan is the opposite of an investment. Instead of sending your money from the present to the future, you're sending money from the future back to the present. Think about your student loans. These are based on the idea that once you graduate you will earn a salary that'll help you pay them off. Future employed you is sending money back to student you.

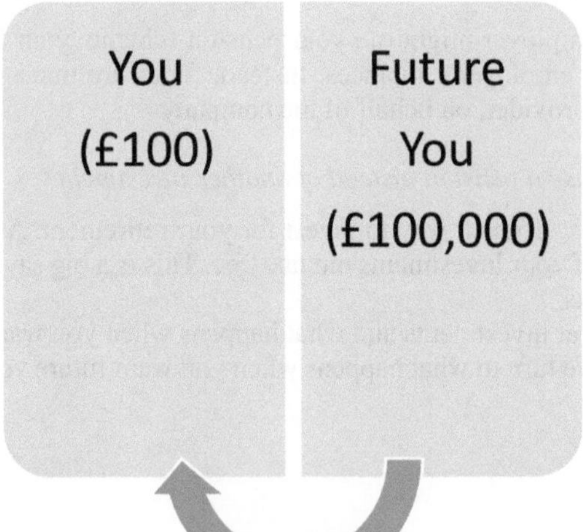

Loans take many different forms. In this section we look at two of the most common loans: personal loans and mortgages.

Loans—personal loans

20–44 A personal loan from a bank, building society, company or individual usually consists of four things:

1. the amount loaned (let's say £1,000);
2. the interest rates (let's say it's 10%);
3. when it needs to be repaid (let's say in 10 months' time); and
4. how it is to be repaid (monthly at £110 per month).

A lender needs certain pieces of information. They may want to know future you will have at least £110 per month, to pay off the loan. They may want evidence that you have a job, that your salary will cover the repayments and that you don't already have any other debts. Using this information, a lender can build up a picture of what future you will be like and—on that basis—they can decide to lend.

A personal loan is a risk for any lender. It's giving you money now, on the understanding that future you will pay it back. However, future you could take ill, lose your job, you might stop paying or you could die. There are all sorts of things that could stop a lender from getting repaid. That's why personal loans tend to be for smaller amounts (perhaps £1,000 to £10,000) and the interest rates are higher.

If you need more money (for example to buy a house) you would apply for a mortgage. This is a form of personal loan. It has the same four elements (set out above). The main difference is that your bank will ask for a security over your property. If you can't pay back your loan, it can use that security to sell your property and recoup its money that way.

Loans—mortgage

For most of us, mortgages are necessary if you want to buy your own home. **20–45**
Homes are expensive, the average price in the UK is more than £200,000, and it would take years, if not decades, to save enough money to buy one. Without mortgages, we would not be able to afford to buy a home.

How do you arrange a mortgage?

A mortgage is just a type of loan. As with a personal loan, the lender (a bank or **20–46**
building society) will want to know that you can pay it back. They'll consider your borrowing capability and examine income, liabilities, employment and whether you have any money to pay a deposit or part of the price already. They also consider how much the home is worth as, ultimately, they could sell it to recoup their loan.

Traditionally, when working out how much you can pay, lenders applied income multiples when deciding how much to lend. This is a simple calculation. The lender asks how much you earn and then multiplies it by a set figure to let you know how much you can borrow. Before 2008, this could be as much a five times your salary, for one person applying for a mortgage; while, in the case of joint incomes, a lender might take the higher salary and apply the appropriate multiple and then add the lower salary. When lenders calculate income they're looking at guaranteed income, such as your basic annual salary, while excluding things like bonuses, which could be discretionary. Proof of income is necessary; pay slips are usually required for at least three months. If you're self-employed (which you may be if a partner in a law firm), your accounts for the previous three years will be needed. As well as your income, the lender may also want to know how much you owe. The lender may ask for details of any credit cards, hire purchase agreements or overdrafts.

Your credit score is also relevant. In extreme cases a low credit score might prevent a mortgage lender even considering lending to you. Alternatively, a low score might mean that a lender applies a lower multiple.

However, these rules have changed and many lenders only use income multiples as an indicator now to show the maximum they'll lend. This is in light of new rules for mortgage lending that came into force as a result of the Mortgage Market Review—a comprehensive review following the property crash in 2008—on 26 April 2014. These impose an obligation on a lender to also conduct an "affordability test" for every mortgage application.

Affordability test

20–47 A lender must verify your income and demonstrate that a mortgage is affordable. It does this by checking your income (such as your salary), your costs (such as credit cards), personal loans, hire purchase, but also other costs such as basic household expenditure (food, utilities, insurance, clothes and household goods). The lender is checking whether, after you spend your salary each month, you have enough money left to pay your mortgage.

Interest rate stress test

20–48 Along with checking your income and costs, the lender must also take into account the impact on mortgage payments of future interest rate increases (over a minimum of the following five years). You might be able to afford a mortgage today, but could you afford it if interest rates increase and your monthly payments increase? This test is to check that the mortgage remains affordable.

How much will the lender lend?

20–49 While the maximum a lender will lend may still be lined to a multiple of your salary, there's also another important check that the lender will carry out. It wants to know that the property is worth more than what they're lending you to pay for it. This test is known as the loan to value (LTV) and is simple to calculate. A surveyor will value the property (let's say they value it £200,000) and the lender will compare that with the amount you have asked as a loan to give a percentage value. If you ask for £150,000 then the LTV would be 75%. If you ask for £100,000 the LTV would be 50%. Lenders always specify an upper LTV limit for each of their products, and its rare now for any lender to lend any more than 95%. This doesn't mean that they'll always lend this amount. That depends on a borrower's credit score, income and outgoings.

The lower the LTV the more likely it is that you will receive a lower interest rate. LTV shows the lenders risk if property prices fell. If a lender has an LTV of 95% then if prices fell by more than 5% it wouldn't be able to recover all of its loan by selling the property. However, if a lender has a LTV of 50% then the price would need to fall by 50%, which is unlikely, before it was at risk of not being able to recover all of its loan by selling the property.

Repayment options

20–50 Various kinds of mortgages are available:

Capital and interest repayment

20–51 A sum of money is borrowed for a fixed period. Let's say £200,000 again and you agree to pay it back over 25 years. Monthly repayments are scheduled to pay back the £200,000 plus interest. By the end of 25 years, if payments have been kept up to date, the mortgage is paid back in full.

Interest only mortgage

With this kind of mortgage, the loan capital is not paid back until the end of a fixed period. If you borrow £200,000 then you would only pay the interest and, at the end of 25 years, you would still need to pay £200,000 back. This means you need to take out some other form of investment to cover this final payment. An interest only mortgage is risky. You're assuming that you will be able to invest money to pay the capital at the end of the term. If you don't have the money to pay the capital, the lender could sell the property and you could be left with nothing. **20–52**

Flexible mortgage

This is a hybrid of the two kinds described above. Repayments can be larger than first contracted, so that a mortgage can be repaid more quickly. It may be possible to have "holidays" during which no repayments are made, and the term extended so that final repayment is deferred. **20–53**

Interest rate options

The type of interest rate selected at the outset of a mortgage has a large effect on the subsequent repayments. The choice depends on your risk profile and whether you need certainty about how much the repayments will be, over the term of the loan. The most common are: **20–54**

Tracker: As the interest rate of the Bank of England changes, so the interest rate of the loan changes (over the term). Trackers are available for different terms (most commonly two or five years). You can get term trackers (for the life of the loan). The rates for trackers tend to be lower than fixed rate deals. The danger is that interest rates rise quickly and that monthly repayments increase substantially.

Fixed rate: The rate of interest is fixed for a set period of time (typically one to five years). For that period, the borrower pays the same amount each month, regardless of what happens to the Bank of England rates. For some, this helps with budgeting. Once the fixed rate period is over, the rate reverts to the lender's variable rate. It's common for an agreement to stipulate that the borrower is tied into the variable rate for a fixed period too.

A potential problem is that interest rates might fall and the borrower is stuck paying much higher rates of interest.

Discount: Trackers aren't the only variable mortgage. Discount mortgages are linked to the lender's standard variable rate (SVR). The SVR can change even if there is no change in the Bank of England base rate. Discount mortgages are available over different terms (usually one to five years).

Offset: This is a more complicated mortgage. It links the borrower's savings to the mortgage debt. Interest on savings is offset against the loan, so the borrower pays less interest on the debt. There is the flexibility of keeping monthly payments constant (even when savings are rising) with the consequence that the mortgage is paid off more quickly and a substantial amount of interest saved.

In addition to the potential interest saving, there is also a tax benefit. Ordinarily, income tax is paid on interest earned on savings. With an offset mortgage, you don't earn interest so there is no income tax to pay. An offset can be particularly attractive for people in the higher or top rate tax brackets. The disadvantage with offset mortgages is that the rates tend to be higher.

Corporate finance

20–55 So far we've just looked at individuals. We've asked how you can manage your money and, indirectly, demonstrated how you can help clients in similar situations. However, many of your clients will be companies, partnerships, public bodies and other corporate entities. We need to consider how those entities can raise money.

Corporate investment

20–56 The principles are the same as per individuals. Just like an individual, a company needs to beat inflation by choosing the best investment options. This means it might also look at depositing cash in current and saving accounts. The options are, in general, no different to an individual (though some specific options may not be open to it, like premium bonds).

Corporate loans

20–57 Most corporate bodies are financed by their owners or by loans from banks (or other institutions).

Financed by owners

20–58 When a company is formed it issues shares. Every subscriber owns a share of the business. If a company issues 100 shares, equally, to two subscribers, each is a 50% owner. As a company grows, however, it may need cash. To leverage new investment, it might ask its original owners to purchase more shares, via a rights issue. A rights issue gives a company's owners the right to buy new shares, to the extent of their existing holding (to keep the relative percentages the same).

For example, if our company wants to issue 1,000 shares, it must offer 500 shares to each of its two original owners. This maintains the balance; they each would have 550 shares (500 + original 50) of 1,100 shares (1,000 + original 100). If they decline to buy the new shares these can then be sold to others.

In practice, the Companies Acts 2006 gives directors the right to impose rules on how shares are allotted, so our simple scenario might end up being more complicated. For example, The Rangers Football Club Limited, has a prohibition on issuing new shares to anyone other than existing shareholders—even if they decline—without prior approval.

Can you see a potential problem with rights issues? There's no guarantee a company's owners will have the cash to increase their investment. Equally, they may not want new people owning shares. Imagine you're a shareholder in your family business; every share is owned by a family member. Even if you're penniless, do you really want to invite non-family members to effectively co-own your family business?

Further, if you're asked to invest, you may need to buy a certain percentage of shares to ensure that you have a say in what the company does. If you own the company, then presumably you'll want to be able to decide what it does. That means you may need to own at least 25% of the shares (to have any real influence).

Financed by lenders

20–59 The alternative is that a company seeks a loan from a bank or third party (such as a private equity house). Once again, these can include loans for property, or loans direct to the company. As for individuals, a bank or other lender will attach conditions and almost certainly seek securities, for protection. This might be in the form of a personal guarantee from a director, a security over heritable property, a floating charge over moveable property and/or insurance.

Investment risk

Some people are more adventurous in their investing, and other people prefer a more cautious approach. There's no right or wrong way—just the way that's right for you or your client. This balance between risk and reward is managed by investing across a range of investments and across a range of assets within those investments to build up a portfolio that will strike the right balance between risk and return to help you achieve your financial goals. Just as you wouldn't put all eggs in one basket, so you shouldn't put all your nest eggs into one investment. **20–60**

For example, if you want to save money for your retirement you might invest in a pension which is low risk as it's backed by the UK Government. However, as it's low reward, you may also invest in some shares in new or risky companies which are higher risk but promise high rewards if the companies are successful. Finding the right balance is an essential part of your own personal investment and the advice you may give a client.

Tax

Two things are certain in life: death and taxes. While we can help little about the former, there are many highly paid accountants who will try and help you with the latter. Just ask singer Gary Barlow, comedian Jimmy Carr or Google. People and companies will try and do everything they can to reduce the tax they pay through lawful means (tax planning or tax avoidance) or unlawful means (tax evasion). As a lawyer, you'll find you'll be asked to advise clients who'll be following (or even want you to suggest) ways to help them reduce their tax. It should go without saying that you should never be involved in tax avoidance, however, you may be asked to advise on tax planning. This could involve suggesting ways to invest money in a trust, to setting up companies or following certain courses of action which attract lower taxes than others. It's important that you know your way round the various taxes that can apply to you and your clients. This section will examine the main taxes and what they do. **20–61**

A full discussion of tax is beyond the scope of this book and we always recommend that you either read the most recent textbook that you can or, better yet, read the law and guidance set out on the HMRC and Revenue Scotland websites before you advise anyone on tax. Tax laws and guidance change frequently and you should make sure you're always up to date. As Gary Barlow, Jimmy Carr and Google have found, the taxman may come back for more money (or worse) if he doesn't think he's been paid correctly.

Direct tax

Direct taxes are directly paid to the government by the taxpayer. It's a tax applied on individuals and organisations directly by the government. The most common direct taxes are: **20–62**

Income tax

20–63 As an individual, you're responsible for paying taxes on any income that you earn in each tax year (from 6 April to the 5 April the following year). Income includes not just your salary and is calculated based on:

- how much of your taxable income is above your personal allowance (the amount you can earn as income before you're taxed); and
- how much of your taxable income falls within each tax band above your personal allowance.

The personal allowances and tax bands for 2016–2018 (with 2015/2016 for comparison) are as follows:

	2015/16	2016/17	2017/18
Personal allowance	£10,600	£11,000	£11,500
Basic rate band	£31,785	£32,000	£33,500
Higher rate threshold	£42,385	£43,000	£45,000

The personal allowance and rates bands are the same across the UK. The rates paid, however, are set independently by the UK Government for England, Wales and Northern Ireland and the Scottish Government for Scotland.

In Scotland, the Scottish Rate of Income Tax (SRIT) is set at 10% for all bands. The Scottish Government can then vary the UK rate. Any change affects all bands equally, so a 10% rise in basic rate from the UK rate would also need a 10% rise in higher rate and 10% rise in additional rate. As you'll see from the table below, a 10% rise means Scottish tax payers pay the same as the rest of the UK. This is the current rate for 2015/16.

UK rate for England, Wales and Northern Ireland	Income band	UK rate paid in Scotland	Scottish rate	Total rate for Scottish taxpayers
Basic rate 20%	£11,001–£43,000	10%	10%	20%
Higher rate 40%	£43,001–£150,000	30%	10%	40%
Additional rate 45%	Over £150,000	35%	10%	45%

However, if the SRIT is set at 9%, the income tax rates for Scottish taxpayers would be:

- basic rate—19%;
- higher rate—39%; and
- additional rate—44%.

Corporation tax

Corporation tax is like an income tax for companies. The UK Government taxes companies on the money they make and this is calculated based on their world-wide profits (for UK companies) or for their trading profits in the UK (for non-UK companies). In simple terms, Google and Starbucks seem to pay little tax because they argue they only make a small profit in the UK and, instead, their profits are generated in other countries, such as Ireland. **20–64**

The main rate of corporation tax is currently 20%. This rate will fall to 19% for the year beginning 1 April 2017, and to 18% for the year beginning 1 April 2020.

National Insurance

NICs are payable by employees at rates of 12% on weekly income between £155 and £815, and 2% on income above this limit. Employers also pay NICs on employees' earnings above £155 per week (at 13.8%). This includes benefits in kind. Your NICs help pay for your state pensions as discussed above. **20–65**

Capital gains tax (CGT)

CGT is a type of tax on capital gains incurred by individuals and companies. Capital gains are the profits that you make when you sell a capital asset for a price that is higher than the purchase price. For example, if you buy a flat as an investment for £100,000 and you sell it for £200,000 you have made a profit of £100,000. That profit would be subject to CGT. **20–66**

CGT is charged at two rates. Those who pay basic rate income tax pay CGT at **18%**, but higher rate taxpayers are charged CGT at **28%**. Lower rates (and reliefs) are available to support entrepreneurial and business activity.

The annual exempt amount (currently £10,900) and the exemption for your main home (which is why we used the example of a second home above), ensures that most people don't, in fact, pay CGT.

Stamp taxes

Stamp taxes apply to transfers of property. There are four types: **20–67**

Stamp duty: this applies to shares and securities sold using a stock transfer form. It is charged at 0.5%.

Stamp Duty Reserve Tax (SDRT): this applies to shares and securities sold electronically. It is charged at 0.5%.

Stamp Duty Land Tax (SDLT): this is a tax on property sold or leased in England and Wales.

Land and Buildings Transaction Tax (LBTT): this is a tax on property sold or leased in Scotland. While the rules are similar to SDLT in England and Wales, and may lead you to think they're connected, there are enough differences that you should not rely on any SDLT guidance when reviewing LBTT.

Other business taxes

There are local property taxes that are paid on non-residential properties. These are called business rates or non-domestic rates. These are set by the UK Government for England and Wales and the Scottish Government for Scotland. The rates are collected by local authorities, to pay for local services. The rate depends on the value of the property that is used for business purposes. **20–68**

Indirect taxes

20–69 Someone other than the Government collects indirect taxes before it's passed on to the Government. The main indirect tax is VAT and we'll examine how it's collected below.

What is VAT?

20–70 Value Added Tax (VAT) applies in all countries in the EU. VAT is added to most goods or services sold by businesses as a 20% charge (subject to certain exception) on the price of goods or services sold by them.

How does VAT work?

20–71 VAT is collected on behalf of HMRC by companies. A company pays VAT to HMRC by calculating the amount of VAT charged to customers (its output VAT) minus any VAT it has paid on its own purchases (its input VAT). Every quarter, a company will pay HMRC the difference between its input VAT minus its output VAT. If it has paid more in input VAT on its own purchases than it received from selling goods or services to customers from output VAT, it can ask HMRC to reimburse it.

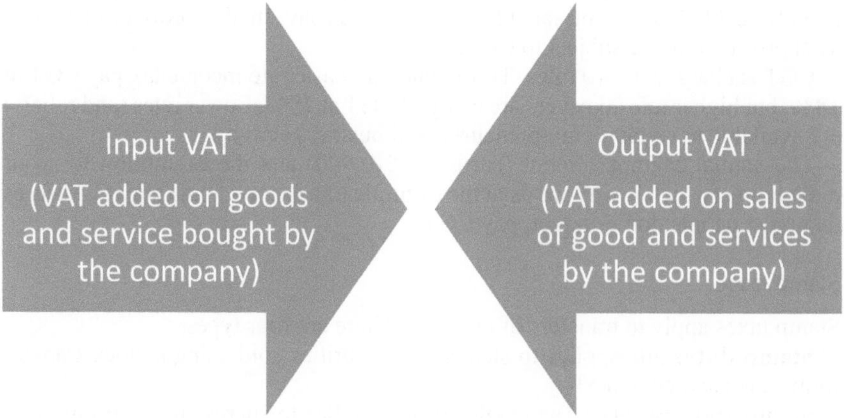

Does VAT apply to all goods and services?

20–72 Certain goods and services are exempt from VAT (i.e. there is no VAT on the supply, but also no refund of VAT incurred on the costs of supply), while others are charged at a reduced rate (5%). Uniquely, the UK also has a broad range of zero-rated supplies, including books, newspapers, magazines and children's clothes, which means VAT on the supply is 0%, but input tax may be reclaimed.

How does VAT affect businesses?

20–73 As a general rule it should not affect any business that sells goods or services. It can recover any VAT incurred in making these supplies. VAT only becomes an issue if it sells goods or services which are exempt as it can't then recover any VAT it was charged to make those goods or services.

Who protects the financial system?

Governments and regulators

If you carry £100 in your pocket, you always know where it is. You can keep it safe. However, as soon as you give that £100 to someone else, it might not be quite so secure. If you give it to the Government, there's nothing to stop it investing in an MP's duck house. If you give it to a bank, it could be spent on a chief executive's scallop kitchen. If you give it to a company, it might become part of the chairman's bonus. The next thing you know, the government changes, the banks collapse or the company is liquidated. Your money is gone. To build confidence in the financial system, the Government has created laws and appointed regulators to ensure the system works correctly. The most important regulators are the Financial Conduct Authority (FCA) and the Prudential Regulation Authority (PRA), discussed below. **20–74**

Legal system

The UK is regarded as having a stable legal system in which rights are enforced, debts settled and contracts honoured. That makes the UK a good place to do business. Increasingly (particularly in relation to financial matters) there is a push for greater standardisation of law across various countries. This means that some principles (such anti-money laundering—as we saw in Ch.6 (how to open files) will be the same regardless of the country you're in. However, even with harmonisation there are some countries which are more stable, more reliable, and better to do business in than others. **20–75**

Regulators

If you have laws and rules you need the means to enforce them. This means you need an effective court system and government bodies and independent regulators who will ensure any laws and rules are enforced. **20–76**

The Financial Services Act 2012 came into force on 1 April 2013. The Act created a new regulatory system which:

- gave the Bank of England (through a new Financial Policy Committee) responsibility for oversight of the UK financial system as a whole—it has powers to monitor and respond to risks;
- set up a new regulator of safety and soundness in the financial services sector, the PRA, working under the Bank of England, to supervise all firms that manage significant risks as part of their business—banks and other deposit takers, insurance companies, and large investment banks; and
- established a new business regulator for financial services, the FCA, that protects consumers and supervises all firms to ensure that business across financial services and markets is conducted fairly.

Together these regulators "police" the financial markets.

Insurance

Every investment is a risk. Share prices may go down as well as up. If you buy a home, it could burn down before you pay off the mortgage that helped you buy it. Running a business also involves risk. Whether it's the risk of fire, the risk of damage to goods or the risk of natural disasters, all these incidents may have a financial impact on your business. **20–77**

If you want to reduce the risk of your home or office burning down, you could install smoke alarms and sprinkler systems to reduce the damage caused by fire. However, you may also want to protect yourself against the financial impact of a fire—e.g. the cost of repairing or rebuilding. Most financial risks can be protected by insurance. Insurance is the transfer of risk from themselves and on to someone else. You cannot avoid all risks but you can protect yourself against them by transferring those risks to someone else. This transfer of risk is the principle behind insurance.

How does insurance work?

20–78 An insurer is someone who agrees to take on risks on behalf of a company or individual, in exchange for a fee. It does this by providing the business or individual concerned with an insurance contract, sometimes called a "policy". This policy covers a person or business for many of the costs they have to meet as a result of a risk occurring, and provides the policyholder with some security should the worst happen.

How is the insurer paid?

20–79 The insurer is paid an insurance premium. This is the sum of money paid by you in return for the insurer giving you a policy. The sum depends on how much the policy will pay out and how likely the insurer will need to pay out. The greater the likelihood of a pay out the more the premium will be.

Think about car insurance. It'll pay to replace your car if it's stolen. If you have a second hand Mini worth £1,000 then the cost of replacing it is small. If you have a Porsche worth £100,000 then the cost of replacing it is high. Because the Porsche is faster and more desirable, it's more likely to be stolen. So that increases the premium too. It's a riskier car to own. Every time you take out insurance the insurer calculates the risk of paying out. That's why it asks hundreds of questions when you apply. It's trying to work out how risky the policy is based on statistics.

Who are the main insurers?

20–80 There are three main types.

- Insurance companies—mostly owned by shareholders, but "mutual" insurance companies are owned by policyholders i.e. when you take out a policy you're also becoming an owner in the business itself. "Specialists" offer one type of business, (e.g. life insurance), while "composites" offer a range of insurance products.
- Lloyd's of London—not an insurer itself, but an organisation providing a building (the Lloyd's building in London) and facilities for its underwriting members to do business.
- Reinsurers—for large risks, insurers may insure some of it, then seek cover for the remainder—called reinsurance—from other insurers.

What are the main types of personal insurance?

20–81 Insurance can cover anything. John Schnatter, owner of Pizza chain, Papa John's Pizza, has insured his hands for $15 million,[4] Sebastian Michaelis, a tea blender

---

[4] A. Victor, "Papa John's pizza founder has his hands insured for $15 MILLION . . . putting him in the same league as Heidi Klum's legs and Madonna's breasts' (8 July 2015), *Dailymail.co.uk*, *http://www.dailymail.co.uk/femail/food/article-3153322/Founder-Papa-John-s-pizza-hands-insured-staggering-10-MILLION.html* [Accessed 19 April 2016].

for Tetley, has insured his taste buds for £1 million,[5] while super model Heidi Klum has insured her legs for £1.2 million.[6] However, these are extremes. The most common types of insurance are:

Life insurance: Life insurance pays out if you die (or, for some policies, if you also suffer a terminal illness). This ensures that you can help partners or relatives if you were to die unexpectedly. For example, if you own a home with a partner, you may take out a life insurance policy so that you know that they'll have money to pay the mortgage if you die. The two basic types of life insurance are *traditional whole life* and *term life*. Simply explained, whole life is a policy you pay on until you die and term life is a policy for a set amount of time. Life insurance will increase in price as you get older or if you suffer from any illnesses or disabilities which could reduce your life expectancy.

Health insurance: Health insurance will pay to cover any medical treatments you require.

Home insurance/contents insurance/car insurance: These all cover things that you own: your house; your furniture, television, jewellery, laptops, bikes etc.; and your car.

Travel insurance: This will pay for health cover, cancellations and theft while you're abroad.

What are the main types of business insurance?

A business can insure against the decisions it makes, the products it produces, the advice it gives and the possibility that an employee or other person could sue them. **20–82**

Key person insurance: Many businesses rely on one or more people to be successful. For many years former Apple chief executive Steve Jobs was the face of the company. He was seen as instrumental in creating the iPhone and iPad. When he died, Apple were seen to have lost a vital part of their success. Without Steve Jobs' vision, Apple's shares fell by 5%.[7] The company lost billions. To protect against this risk, many businesses will take out key person insurance to cover them against losing key people. In a small business, this is usually the owner, the founders or perhaps a key employee or two. These are the people who are crucial to a business—the ones whose absence would sink the company.

Directors' and officers' liability insurance: Directors' and officers' liability insurance—also known as D & O insurance—covers the cost of compensation claims made against a business's directors and key managers (officers) for alleged wrongful acts. Wrongful acts include: breach of trust; breach of duty; neglect; error; misleading statements; and wrongful trading. If directors did not have insurance they might refuse to act as directors. The insurance helps protect them against the risk that someone may accuse them of a wrongful act by covering their legal costs to defend any claim and by paying for compensation if any claim is successful.

---

5 L. Hyslop, "Tetley insures tea blender's taste buds for £1m' (26 November 2016), *Telegraph.co.uk*, *http://www.telegraph.co.uk/foodanddrink/foodanddrinknews/11252789/Tetley-insures-tea-blenders-tastebuds-for-1m.html* [Accessed 19 April 2016].

6 L. Milligan, "Heidi's Legs" (20 September 2011), *Vogue.co.uk*, *http://www.vogue.co.uk/news/2011/09/20/heidi-klum—-legs-insured-not-worth-the-same-amount* [Accessed 19 April 2016].

7 J. Kollewe, "Apple stock price falls on news of Steve Jobs's death" (6 October 2011), *TheGuardian.com*, *http://www.theguardian.com/technology/2011/oct/06/apple-stock-steve-jobs* [Accessed 19 April 2016].

Employers liability: Employers' liability insurance covers the cost of compensating employees who are injured at or become ill through work.

Public liability: Public liability insurance covers the cost of claims made by members of the public for incidents that occur in connection with your business activities. Public liability insurance covers the cost of compensation for: personal injuries; loss of or damage to property; and death.

Product liability: Product liability insurance covers the cost of compensating anyone who is injured by a faulty product that your business designs, manufactures or supplies.

Professional indemnity: Professional indemnity insurance covers the cost of compensating clients for loss or damage resulting from negligent services or advice provided by a business or an individual.

How do you know insurance companies will pay out?

20–83 Insurance companies make money in two ways. Firstly, they pool all of the premiums paid by everyone taking out insurance policies. For example, if you take out travel insurance for £40 to go travelling this summer, the insurance company will add that £40 to everyone else who has also taken out travel insurance from them. If 100,000 people take out travel insurance, then the insurance company has £4 million. However, not everyone will make a claim under that policy. The insurance company is calculating that if 100,000 take out travel insurance for £4 million, only a few will actually raise a claim—and those few will be paid less than £4 million. The difference between the insurance premiums collected and the policies paid out is how the insurer makes money.

The second way the insurer makes money is by using the money it's collected to invest. As you know from earlier in the chapter, if you don't invest your money it'll start to lose value because of interest rates. Insurance companies will use part of the money it collects and it'll invest it to make more. This return is known as "the float".

Provided the insurer has calculated its risk correctly, it should always have more money than it pays out, as the pool (the total of money collected) should be greater than the potential claims (the total of money paid out), and the float (investment return) should ensure that the pool doesn't lose value over time.

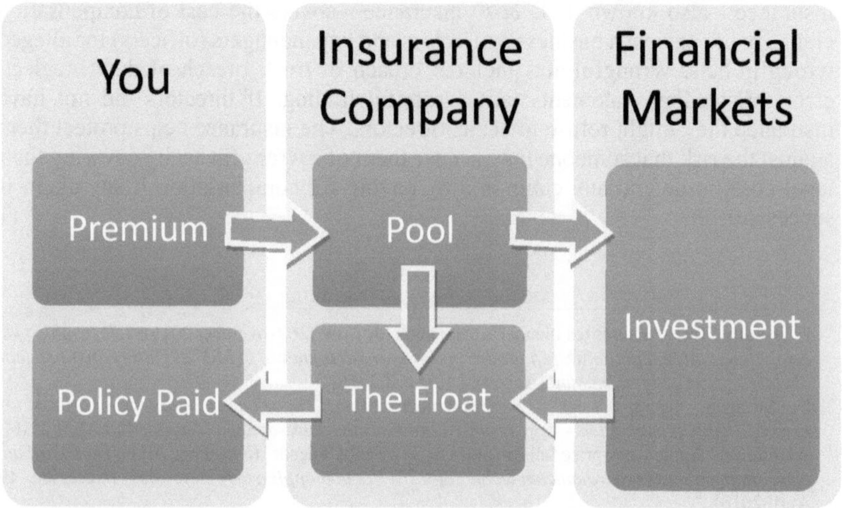

The financial markets

Before we end this chapter its worth spending some time reviewing how financial markets work. How do banks, building societies, pension or insurance companies make money? They don't just keep your money safe, they use that money to make more money on "the market". **20–84**

What is "the market"?

In general, the market refers to the financial markets. A cattle market sells cattle and livestock. A farmer's market sells meat and vegetables from local farmers. The market refers to a market that buys and sells financial products. The main markets are: **20–85**

The capital and money markets

This is where people buy and sell investments such as shares and bonds. The capital market deals with long term investments, including shares. The money markets deal with short term investments, typically bonds which have less than 12 months before they're paid back. If you've ever bought shares in a company you've participated in the capital and money markets. **20–86**

The foreign exchange market

This is where people buy and sell currency such as the dollar and the euro. When you change money before going on holiday you're participating in a money market, albeit on a much smaller scale. If you're travelling to Paris, you offer to buy euro at the rate of, for example, 75p for every euro. When you return, you offer to sell the euro back to the travel agent for £1. You're buying and selling currency—and, depending on the price, you can make a profit or a loss when the price changes. If, when you return, the travel agent will accept £1.10 then you will have made 10%. If, and more likely for a travel agent, they only offer to buy it back at 90p, you've lost an additional 10p. The secret of the money market is to buy currency that will increase in value so you can then sell it for a profit. **20–87**

The debt capital market

This is where people buy and sell debt. If a company owes money, then this debt can be sold by the person who is owed it. **20–88**

The commodities market

This is where people buy and sell assets, mainly raw material such as steel, minerals, gold and oil, and agricultural products such as a wheat, coffee and sugar. **20–89**

How do the markets work?

The markets operate through exchanges. Exchanges were originally physical places where buyers and sellers could meet to trade. The London Stock Exchange was founded in 1801 at Paternoster Square close to Saint Paul's Cathedral in London. Today there are more than a hundred exchanges throughout the world including the New York Stock Exchange and the NASDAQ stock exchange (both based in America, and the two largest exchanges in the world). **20–90**

Exchanges are more than physical locations. They set the rules that govern trading including centralising all information about trades so that no one receives information before anyone else. That way, everyone has the same opportunity to buy and sell on the exchange. Think of it like eBay. If you ask a question on eBay any answer will be published on eBay for all to read. An exchange ensures everyone can see all information at the same time.

How do you buy and sell on an exchange?

20–91 As part of controlling information, an exchange centralises the communication of bid and offer prices so that everyone can see who is selling and what they're selling. You can then respond by buying at one of the prices quoted or by replying with a different quote. Depending on the exchange, you can respond by voice, hand signal, a discrete electronic message, or computer-generated electronic commands. When a buyer and seller reach agreement, the price is then communicated throughout the market. The result is a level playing field that allows anyone to buy as low or sell as high as anyone else, as long as the trader follows exchange rules.

Do you need to be in the exchange to take part in trades?

20–92 No. Electronic trading has meant that many traditional trading floors are closing, and all communication takes place electronically. The London Stock Exchange is completely electronic.

What is "the City"?

20–93 The City refers to the City of London, an area of London which is also known as "The Square Mile" because it is 1.12 square miles in area. The City of London is the traditional home to the UK's trading and financial services industries, including the London Stock Exchange. When people refer to "the City" they're using it as shorthand to refer to the UK's main financial services industry.

What does "how will the City/the market react" mean?

20–94 Every day market traders try to interpret news and events to work out how to make money. When commentators refer to the reaction of the City or the market they're principally looking at whether people are buying or selling. If more people buy, prices tend to increase and this shows confidence. If more people sell, then this shows less confidence as people try and recover their money. When you see the Chancellor, George Osborne, announce a "sugar tax" as part of his budget statement in April 2016, the markets instantly reacted by selling shares in soft drink manufacturers such as AG Barr, the makers of Irn-Bru. Commentators would say the market reacted badly, because it started to sell as many shares as it could in companies affected by the sugar tax.

How does the market link to you and your clients?

20–95 Every time you or your clients invest money with a bank, building society, pension or insurance company, you give money for that bank, building society, pension or insurance company to invest in the market. In this way, the money in your pocket is directly linked to how the market performs. If the market does well, and you have invested in it, then you will do well too. If the market turns, as we saw in 2008 with the financial crash, then you will lose money too.

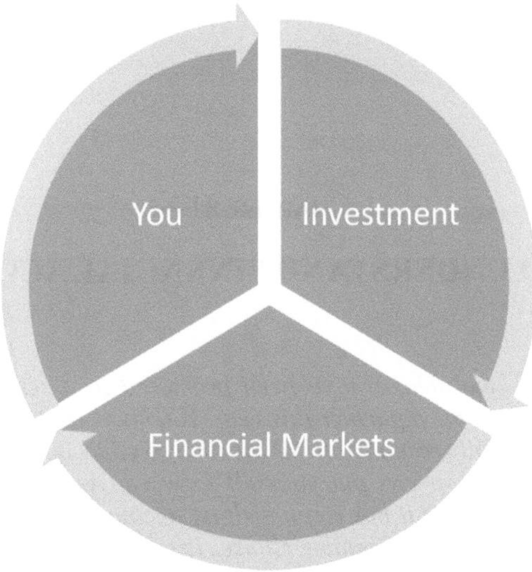

Summary

Time travel is not real (clearly). However, financial advice is perhaps the closest **20–96**
you get to it, because you're trying to move money from the present to the future, and from a possible future to the present.

We can't predict the future, so we need to protect our money. The government can do this by putting in place laws to protect individuals and companies. It can appoint regulators to oversee these laws, and it can enforce them so that no one ignores them. However, even with all these protections, you can still do more by, for example, taking out insurance. Together, you can move money to when it's needed and protect you and your clients from the financial impact of any wrong decisions. And, when you move money you're giving it to companies either directly or indirectly to invest in the financial markets.

Chapter 21

HOW TO UNDERSTAND FINANCIAL ACCOUNTS

Introduction

21–1 *You're eight-years qualified. You've been promoted to a senior associate and you're on track to become a partner this year. You know that becoming a partner will make you financially responsible for the firm so you want to know more about the firm's finances before you put yourself forward. As your firm is a limited liability partnership (LLP) it has to publish its account annually. You download last year's accounts from Companies House. It contains a profit and loss statement, balance sheet and cash flow statement. It's filled with numbers. Where do you start your review?*

21–2 Every number tells a story. If you have £100 in your pocket today and £5 in your pocket tomorrow, then you may ask what happened to £95? Did you spend it? Did you lose it? Did someone steal it from you? Whatever happened, those two numbers are the start of a series of questions that eventually tell you a story about what happened to the £95.

In this chapter we look at how you turn numbers into information. This requires you to understand the following points.

- Accounts are based on *assumptions*. You need to know the assumptions first before you start looking at the numbers.
- Accounts have a set format. We look at two formats in this chapter (*profit and loss and balance sheet*) and one other format in the next chapter (*cash flow*). Between them, these tell you the main things you need to know.
- You need to know how to ask the right questions. These can take the form of calculations (also known as ratios). We look at how you use ratios later in this chapter.

You may ask why people keep accounts. Most people don't keep accounts for fun. So, why do it? There are four good reasons. The first three are regulatory. You have to do it because others demand it.

1. The Law Society of Scotland (Consolidated Practice Rules 2011) compels you to keep accounts for your firm.
2. HMRC needs to see a partnership tax return each year (albeit your firm doesn't pay "partnership tax").
3. Companies House requires accounts to be lodged (if your firm is a limited company or an LLP).

The fourth reason is equally as important.

4. Your accounting documents are your "friends". Good quality accounts tell a story and they'll help you predict the future. They'll tell you if your firm is making money, they'll warn you if you're losing money. They can even point out where you can improve your business. You just need to know how to translate the numbers into the information you need.

We can't deny that understanding financial accounts will involve a calculator and some work on your part. However, once cracked, you'll be able to run your business confident in the knowledge that you know exactly what it's doing and whether you'll make money.

Outcome

In this chapter we'll review the basic assumptions that apply to accounting, we'll **21–3** introduce you to profit and loss and balance sheets, and we'll look at how you can use ratios to ask questions of financial information.

Assumptions

Imagine a house. What do you see? Does it have four walls and windows? Does **21–4** it have a roof and a front door? Imagine your parents' home. Do you see the same house? What about the Queen's home, Buckingham Palace, and the White House? Further afield, what about an igloo? While these are completely different, they're all recognisable as a type of house.

Accounting is no different. Accounts may change, they may look different but, because they're based on common standards and assumptions, they're all recognisably the same. That's why, before we start looking at any numbers, we should start by looking at the assumptions that apply to accounts. These provide the conceptual framework of accounting. Just as you would expect a house to have a doorway, so you expect accounts to show certain things too. There are a number of assumptions and the main ones are:

True and fair

"True and fair" is not defined in statute, but accountants take it to mean that your **21–5** financial statements should be drafted in accordance both with Generally Accepted Accounting Principles (GAAP) and their professional judgment. GAAP is a common set of accounting principles, standards and procedures that companies use to compile their financial statements. This means that accounts should be the same around the world provided they all follow GAAP.

Materiality

How accurate do your firm's financial statements need to be before they give a **21–6** "true and fair" view? An amount less than 5% of the result before tax is considered unlikely to impact on their reliability.

Consistency

Your accounts should be consistent both internally and also with your accounts **21–7** from previous years.

Prudence

21–8 Profits should not be recognised until your firm is confident that they'll arise; losses, conversely, should be accounted for as soon as anticipated.

Matching

21–9 Your income and expenditure should be matched to the period to which they both relate.

Going concern

21–10 Your accounts should be drawn up on the basis that your firm will be trading for the foreseeable future.

Know the terminology

21–11 It's always good to know some lingo. Not only will it help you understand what follows in the rest of the chapter, it'll make you look rather erudite the next time you're talking to an accountant.

Fixed and current assets

21–12 A *fixed asset* is something acquired by your firm for use within the business, with a view to earning profits (i.e. not acquired for resale). It includes things like computers, printers and furniture. Your *current assets* are the opposite, and include cash in your bank accounts. Any sums of money (i.e. debts) that your clients owe also are treated as current assets. Fixed and current assets can also be divided further. They can be divided into *tangible* or *intangible* assets. Tangible assets are obvious; you can touch them. Intangibles are items you can't touch, and include things like your firm's intellectual property.

Liabilities

21–13 Liabilities are sums of money that your firm owes; they either are short-term (current) liabilities or long-term (non-current) liabilities. They include so-called accruals. Accruals are liabilities that exist, but for which no invoice has been received (for example, you use electricity in the final month of a trading period, but don't receive your bill till the following month).

Values

21–14 The values of your firm's assets and liabilities are obtained from its books and records, as at the "balance sheet date". We look at balance sheets a little later. The basis on which your assets are valued is usually "at cost" (i.e. the amount your firm paid for them), with depreciation ("wear and tear") over their estimated useful life factored in.

What is capital?

21–15 Your firm's capital is the residual claim on the business by its partners. When solicitors start a firm, the capital they introduce is the total value that they've committed to the business. It's important that any contribution is quantified in monetary terms, to establish his or her true capital input. If a partner removes an asset for private use (e.g. a computer), or withdraws cash, then their capital is reduced by the relevant amount.

Clearly, a net profit has the effect of increasing your firm's overall capital. Conversely, a loss reduces that capital.

Double-entry bookkeeping

You don't need to worry too much about this. However, this is the system that underpins the creation of your final set of profit and loss accounts. Basically, an account is created for each item (or group of items) of assets, liabilities, capital, income and expenditure that you have. Each account records changes (whether an increase or decrease) in the monetary value of each item concerned. **21–16**

Trial balance

A trial balance allows you to check the accuracy of your individual accounting records (T-Accounts). Once a month each account is balanced-off and then the full trial balance is created. It's a summary of all of your balances. **21–17**

Profit and loss account

At the least, your firm needs to have access to its most recent set of annual accounts, comprising a: **21–18**

1. profit and loss account (P & L account); and
2. balance sheet.

Your P & L account gives you the overall picture of your firm's profitability. It's a summary of income and expenditure, over a financial period (usually a year). Income is accounted for only if earned (irrespective of whether it has been received) and so is expenditure. In other words, if you render an invoice and it's not been paid, you still need to add it to your income for the period.

This is an important distinction and can be summed up as profit doesn't equal cash. Cash flow (which we examine in the next chapter) is the lifeblood of any business. A business can survive for a period of time without profit but it can't survive without cash. Like it or not, cash is how a business keeps afloat. If you don't have enough cash on hand, you can't pay your suppliers, your employees, or the bank. Without cash, you'll go out of business.

Cash flow is the flow of money in and out of your business. You may have acted for lots of clients and have a heap of invoices to show for it, but you can't spend those invoices. Paying staff and suppliers requires cash. Those invoices are profit, but they're not cash.

The following table will give you an example of a P & L account for a fictional law firm Sim & Todd.

Sim & Todd LLP

Summary Profit and Loss Accounts for the Periods from 2014 to 2016

Income	**2014**		**2015**		**2016**	
	£	£		£		£
Fees Rendered		1,500,000		1,350,000		1,250,000
Commission		125,000		95,000		68,000
Bank Interest		8,125		7,225		6,950
Add: Increase in WIP		100,000				40,000
Less: Decrease in WIP				–20,000		
		1,733,125		**1,432,225**		**1,364,950**
Less: Expenses						
Wages and salaries	725,000		805,000		875,000	
Office rent and rates	66,000		78,000		78,000	
Heating and lighting	35,250		38,925		41,135	
Telephone	9,995		11,995		12,495	
Post and stationery	20,475		18,775		16,985	
Insurance	5,205		8,875		11,750	
Professional subscriptions	3,750		4,425		4,995	
Travelling expenses	11,200		15,475		19,960	
Bank charges	22,195		24,295		25,295	
Motor car running costs	22,450		25,650		28,230	
Bad debts w/o	35,000		48,000		56,000	
Equipment repairs	1,500		1,750		1,680	
General expenses	4,800		3,760		5,245	
Depreciation charges:						
Motor car	2,500		1,875		1,406	
PCs	2,000		1,500			
Less: Sundry Expenses						
Loss on sale of PCs					2,500	
	967,320	**-967,320**	*1,088,300*	**-1,088,300**	*1,180,676*	**-1,180,676**
		765,805		**343,925**		**184,274**

Geography

You're probably wondering what all the numbers mean, so it's time for a short geography lesson. Along the top (the horizontal, or left to right) you have a time line. Our time line runs from 2014 until 2016. This is a technique used by lots of accountants to let users see patterns really easily. You can spot incoming going down, or expenses going up, easily, if the numbers are side by side. **21–19**

On the left hand side (the vertical, up and down) you have a:

- list of all your income (your money coming in);
- list of all your expenses (your money going out); and
- total (income minus all expenses).

Your income figure includes everything you've earned, including fees, commission and bank interest. It also includes any increase or decrease in work in progress (and we look at that a little later).

The expenses column lists all your outgoings, like wages, heating and lighting, telephone and postage etc. It also includes an allowance for bad debts, depreciation and any gain or loss on the disposal of an asset (keep reading to find out what we mean by this).

Accounting adjustments

So far it's been just a case of simple arithmetic i.e. deducting the sub-total of your expenses from the sub-total of your income. However, you can't leave it there. There are five accounting adjustments you need to be aware of: **21–20**

1. depreciation;
2. the disposal of assets (leading to a gain or loss being incurred);
3. bad debts;
4. accrued and pre-paid expenses; and
5. work in progress.

Depreciation

Depreciation is the measure of the wearing out, consumption or other loss of value of your fixed assets, whether arising from their use, the passing of time or good old obsolescence. It's worked out using either the straight line or reducing balance method. **21–21**

Straight-line method

Formula: **21–22**

Original cost of asset—[residual value/useful life]

Worked example

21–23 A car costs £12,000 and has an estimated residual value of £2,000. Its useful life is four years. The workings are:

Workings:

(£12,000 – £2,000) ÷ 4 = £2,500

The annual depreciation charge (from years one to four) is £2,500.

Reducing balance method

21–24 The more commonly used method is called "reducing balance". This assumes that the cost of owning an asset is actually loaded towards the earlier years of its life. This leads to a higher depreciation charge in the early years, with a lower charge in the later years.

Formula:

Carrying value of asset × percentage (%) charge

Worked example

21–25 A car costs £10,000 and the firm decides it should be written down at 25% per year (using reducing balance):

Workings:

Year 1 £10,000 × 25% = £2,500

Year 2 £7,500 × 25% = £1,875

Year 3 £5,625 × 25% = £1,406

Year 4 £4,219 × 25% = £1,055

The P & L account will look like this:

Sim & Todd LLP

Depreciation: Summary Profit and Loss Accounts for the Periods from 2014 to 2016

Income	**2014**		**2015**		**2016**	
	£	£		£		£
Fees Rendered		1,500,000		1,350,000		1,250,000
Commission		125,000		95,000		68,000
Bank Interest		8,125		7,225		6,950
Add: Increase in WIP		100,000				40,000
Less: Decrease in WIP				–20,000		
		1,733,125		**1,432,225**		**1,364,950**
Less: Expenses						
Wages and salaries	725,000		805,000		875,000	
Office rent and rates	66,000		78,000		78,000	
Heating and lighting	35,250		38,925		41,135	
Telephone	9,995		11,995		12,495	
Post and stationery	20,475		18,775		16,985	
Insurance	5,205		8,875		11,750	
Professional subscriptions	3,750		4,425		4,995	
Travelling expenses	11,200		15,475		19,960	
Bank charges	22,195		24,295		25,295	
Motor car running costs	22,450		25,650		28,230	
Bad debts w/o	35,000		48,000		56,000	
Equipment repairs	1,500		1,750		1,680	
General expenses	4,800		3,760		5,245	
Depreciation charges:						
Motor car	**2,500**		**1,875**		**1,406**	
PCs	**2,000**		**1,500**			
Less: Sundry Expenses						
Loss on sale of PCs					2,500	
	967,320	**-967,320**	*1,088,300*	**-1,088,300**	*1,180,676*	**-1,180,676**
		765,805		**343,925**		**184,274**

Disposal

21–26 When one of your firm's assets is sold, the accuracy of its depreciation charge can be assessed. If the charge that has been applied over the years matches the disposal proceeds, no further action is required. However, if the two figures don't match then some further work needs to be done. Either you've not depreciated the asset enough, or you've claimed back too much.

Formula:

A gain on disposal is shown as income in the P & L

A loss on disposal is shown as an expense in the P & L

Worked example

21–27 Four computers cost £8,000. They're sold at the end of year three for £5,000. Accumulated depreciation is £3,500.

Workings:

Total proceeds = £5,000 + £3,500 = £8,500

Cost = £8,000

Gain = £500

This is shown as *income* in the P & L account

Let's say your computers sold at the end of year three made £2,000, but the accumulated depreciation is still £3,500.

Workings:

Total proceeds = £2,000 + £3,500 = £5,500

Cost = £8,000

Loss = £2,500

This is shown as an *expense* in the P & L account

The P & L account will look like this:

Sim & Todd LLP

Disposal: Summary Profit and Loss Accounts for the Periods from 2014 to 2016

Income	**2014**	**2015**	**2016**			
	£	£		£		£
Fees Rendered		1,500,000		1,350,000		1,250,000
Commission		125,000		95,000		68,000
Bank Interest		8,125		7,225		6,950
Add: Increase in WIP		100,000				40,000
Less: Decrease in WIP				–20,000		
		1,733,125		**1,432,225**		**1,364,950**
Less: Expenses						
Wages and salaries	725,000		805,000		875,000	
Office rent and rates	66,000		78,000		78,000	
Heating and lighting	35,250		38,925		41,135	
Telephone	9,995		11,995		12,495	
Post and stationery	20,475		18,775		16,985	
Insurance	5,205		8,875		11,750	
Professional subscriptions	3,750		4,425		4,995	
Travelling expenses	11,200		15,475		19,960	
Bank charges	22,195		24,295		25,295	
Motor car running costs	22,450		25,650		28,230	
Bad debts w/o	35,000		48,000		56,000	
Equipment repairs	1,500		1,750		1,680	
General expenses	4,800		3,760		5,245	
Depreciation charges:						
Motor car	2,500		1,875		1,406	
PCs	2,000		1,500			
Less: Sundry Expenses						
Loss on sale of PCs					**2,500**	
	967,320	**-967,320**	*1,088,300*	**-1,088,300**	*1,180,676*	**-1,180,676**
		765,805		**343,925**		**184,274**

Bad debts

21–28 This one's easy. If it becomes apparent that one of your clients simply isn't going to pay his or her invoice(s) and all reasonable steps have been taken to recover the outstanding amounts, the fee can be written off as a bad debt and then charged as an expense to your P & L account.

As a summary of P & L accounts, this looks like:

Sim & Todd LLP
Bad debts: Summary Profit and Loss Accounts for the Periods from 2014 to 2016

Income	**2014**		**2015**		**2016**	
	£	£		£		£
Fees Rendered		1,500,000		1,350,000		1,250,000
Commission		125,000		95,000		68,000
Bank Interest		8,125		7,225		6,950
Add: Increase in WIP		100,000				40,000
Less: Decrease in WIP				–20,000		
		1,733,125		**1,432,225**		**1,364,950**
Less: Expenses						
Wages and salaries	725,000		805,000		875,000	
Office rent and rates	66,000		78,000		78,000	
Heating and lighting	35,250		38,925		41,135	
Telephone	9,995		11,995		12,495	
Post and stationery	20,475		18,775		16,985	
Insurance	5,205		8,875		11,750	
Professional subscriptions	3,750		4,425		4,995	
Travelling expenses	11,200		15,475		19,960	
Bank charges	22,195		24,295		25,295	
Motor car running costs	22,450		25,650		28,230	
Bad debts w/o	**35,000**		**48,000**		**56,000**	
Equipment repairs	1,500		1,750		1,680	
General expenses	4,800		3,760		5,245	
Depreciation charges:						
Motor car	2,500		1,875		1,406	
PCs	2,000		1,500			
Less: Sundry Expenses						
Loss on sale of PCs					2,500	
	967,320	**-967,320**	*1,088,300*	**-1,088,300**	*1,180,676*	**-1,180,676**
		765,805		**343,925**		**184,274**

Pre-paid expenses

21–29 Clearly some expenses are going to be pre-paid. For example, it may be that your rent is paid quarterly, in advance. Let's say your rent for the period from 6 April to 5 May is paid in March, then that payment shouldn't be included in your P & L account to 6 April. Even though the money is paid in March, it relates to the *following* tax year and—to apply the principle of matching—it has to be applied to that year. If not, it would increase your rent figure artificially and the effect of that would be to reduce your profit figure (and decrease your tax liability) for the previous financial year.

Accrued expenses

21–30 Accrued expenses are the opposite. An accrued expense is an amount relating to something in a financial period that remains *unpaid* at the end of that period.

Let's say your telephone bill for the period from 6 March to 5 April is paid in May, then that payment *should* be included in your P & L account to 5 April. Even though the money is paid in May, it relates to the *previous* tax year and—to apply the principle of matching—it has to be applied to that year. If not, it would decrease your telephone figure artificially and the effect of that would be to increase your profit figure (and increase your tax liability) for the previous financial year. Both are shown on your balance sheet (and more on balance sheets, later).

Work in progress (WIP)

21–31 WIP is the value of the work you carry out prior to a fee invoice being raised. Complex transactions can run for weeks, months or even years, with ever increasing WIP. Until you can convert this to cash (by rendering an invoice) it's your firm that has to bear the cost of the WIP (including the overheads referable to it). For the purposes of P & L accounts, where your firm has previously included a figure for WIP, then any increase experienced over a financial period is added to the fees section, with any reduction being deducted.

The P & L accounts will look like this:

Sim & Todd LLP

Work in Progress: Summary Profit and Loss Accounts for the Periods from 2014 to 2016

Income	**2014**		**2015**		**2016**	
	£	£		£		£
Fees Rendered		1,500,000		1,350,000		1,250,000
Commission		125,000		95,000		68,000
Bank Interest		8,125		7,225		6,950
Add: Increase in WIP		**100,000**				**40,000**
Less: Decrease in WIP				**-20,000**		
		1,733,125		**1,432,225**		**1,364,950**
Less: Expenses						
Wages and salaries	725,000		805,000		875,000	
Office rent and rates	66,000		78,000		78,000	
Heating and lighting	35,250		38,925		41,135	
Telephone	9,995		11,995		12,495	
Post and stationery	20,475		18,775		16,985	
Insurance	5,205		8,875		11,750	
Professional subscriptions	3,750		4,425		4,995	
Travelling expenses	11,200		15,475		19,960	
Bank charges	22,195		24,295		25,295	
Motor car running costs	22,450		25,650		28,230	
Bad debts w/o	35,000		48,000		56,000	
Equipment repairs	1,500		1,750		1,680	
General expenses	4,800		3,760		5,245	
Depreciation charges:						
Motor car	2,500		1,875		1,406	
PCs	2,000		1,500			
Less: Sundry Expenses						
Loss on sale of PCs					2,500	
	967,320	**-967,320**	*1,088,300*	**-1,088,300**	*1,180,676*	**-1,180,676**
		765,805		**343,925**		**184,274**

Balance sheet

What is a balance sheet?

21–32 The balance sheet shows you exactly what things of value a company controls (it's *assets*) and who owns those assets: is it someone else (*liabilities*) or is it the business owners or partners (*owner's equity*)?

Why is the balance sheet called a balance sheet?

21–33 The balance sheet is so named because the two sides of the balance sheet ALWAYS add up to the same amount. The balance sheet is separated with assets on one side and liabilities and owner's equity on the other. At first, this rule can be really confusing. But think of it this way. All the assets owned by your firm fall into one of two categories: they're either owned by a creditor (you had to take a loan to get them) or they're owned by your firm (your firm paid for them in full). That's pretty much all the rule is saying.

How does a balance sheet differ from a P & L account?

21–34 The balance sheet shows the financial position of your firm at a given date, for example, 1 January 2016. This date could be monthly, quarterly and/or the end of an accounting period such as the final day the tax year (4 April each year) or the final day of your firm's financial year (Pinsent Masons and CMS both use 30 April as the final day of their financial year). Think of a balance sheet as a snap-shot, a frozen moment in time. It will tell you everything the firm owns and who owns it, but only for that moment. This is different from a P & L account, which shows your financial position over a set period of time, usually a year.

What does the balance sheet show?

21–35 A balance sheet explains, in relatively simple terms, what form all your assets, liabilities and owner's equity take. That means you can regularly check, for example on a monthly basis, four crucial numbers—how much cash you have in the bank, the value of your WIP, the value of all outstanding fees and how much your firm owes to other people.

What is an asset?

21–36 An asset is anything the business owns that has monetary value. These are further divided on a balance sheet into current and fixed assets. A current asset is anything that can be easily converted into cash within one calendar year. This includes cash, money held in current accounts, WIP which can be fee'd to clients to pay, and invoices issued but not yet paid. Fixed assets include land, buildings such as an office, any machinery or equipment (such as IT systems or photocopiers), and vehicles that are used in connection with the business.

What is a liability?

21–37 Liabilities are also divided into current and long-term liabilities. They include everything the firm owes, including, critically, the money originally invested to start the business. For companies this may take the form of shares and for partner-ships it could take the form of money invested by each of the partners (the owners' equity or, more commonly, *partners' capital* in law firm accounts). Current liabilities would include all bills that have not been paid and which are due to be paid within one calendar year. It would also cover any loan payments from, for example, a bank, that are due to be paid back within a calendar year. Long term liabilities are any debts or obligations owed by the business that are due more than one year out from the current date. For example, your firm may have paid off five years of a 20-year mortgage, of which the remaining 15 years, not counting the current year (which would be shown as a current liability), would be shown on the balance sheet as a long-term liability.

What is a balance sheet used for?

In simple terms, the balance sheet can show you how much money you have and **21–38**
how that's made up—cash, bank accounts, outstanding debts etc. You want to have as much money in the bank as possible (as we'll see in the next chapter on cash flow) and you want to collect outstanding fees as quickly as possible.

Additionally, you need to keep control of any money you owe so that you're in a position to pay debts as they become due. If you know you have a large payment to make to the bank this year then you'll want to ensure you have as much cash as possible to pay it (or you've made alternative arrangements, such as another loan, in sufficient time to pay the debt).

Does the balance sheet have any other uses?

Yes. Along with helping you manage your cash and debts it also shows how your **21–39**
business is financed. The liabilities will reveal how much your partners have invested in the business (this is shown as partners' capital), how much (if any) your firm has borrowed from a bank (bank borrowing), and how much money is being reinvested each year from the profits your firm is making (retained profit).

What the balance sheet will tell you is how your firm has approached its finance by how it has drawn from all three sources. It's important to get this mix right. If partners' capital is too high, there may be a problem with paying that out to a retiring partner. If retained profits are too high, partners may have a problem with financing their tax payments (as tax is paid on retained profits regardless of whether it is paid out to partners), and if bank borrowing is too high, interest payments are likely to be high too, and your firm will be required to make regular payments to the bank.

There is no right or wrong mix—it depends on the firms, the work they do and how their partners approach the business. A cash rich business may be happy to pay regular high interest payments because it knows it will have the cash to pay it. A cash poor business may need to rely more on its partners who will cover costs while knowing they'll be paid back later.

Example of balance sheet

21–40 **Sim & Todd LLP**
Balance Sheet – 05.04.17

Fixed Assets	(£)	(£)
Land and Buildings	200,000.00	
Motor Vehicles	30,000.00	
Computers	10,000.00	
Furniture	50,000.00	
Total Fixed Assets		290,000.00
Current assets		
Bank Account – Current	50,000.00	
Prepayments	2,500.00	
Debtors	80,000.00	
Total Current Assets		132,500.00
Less Current Liabilities		
Accounts Payable	120,000.00	
Loan	20,000.00	
Accruals	8,000.00	
Total Current Liabilities		(148,000.00)
Net Assets		**274,500.00**
Capital and Reserves		
Drawings	200,000.00	
Profit and loss account	74,500.00	
Total Equity		**274,500.00**

A warning about P & L account and balance sheets

21–41 Though useful, there are disadvantages in relying solely on the P & L account and balance sheets.

- They're historic documents reflecting the position of the firm "as was".
- They're not forward looking (or predictive).
- They do not yield certain additional information that a modern firm needs.

Management accounting

21–42 Earlier we said that accounts also give you some useful management information, and it's to that we turn our attention.

Fees

21–43 Your P & L account doesn't show you whether the fees you have rendered in the current year compare favourably with results from previous years. This can be resolved by taking the simple step of making a comparison with your previous figures.

Management accounting also enables more detailed information to be obtained, including:

1. fees generated by each partner/fee earner;
2. fees generated by each category of work that your firm undertakes; and
3. fees generated by each department (or branch) of your firm.

Time?

Another really useful piece of information to have is your cost of time. Your firm's profit equates to its gross (total) fees less its total costs. It's possible to break the costs of time down for particular fee earners and/or types of work etc. By using this analysis your firm's management can work out the true cost of a particular piece of work, or a type of work. **21–44**

To calculate the hourly cost of a fee earner, take the total cost of running the business and divide this by that fee earner's chargeable hours for the period. Costs include staffing (salary, National Insurance contributions, pensions etc.) and property costs (rent, lighting, heating) etc. The resulting hourly cost rate varies from firm to firm and depends on a number of factors, including your firm's size and location etc. It also varies across different grades of fee earners; senior partners tend to have the highest hourly cost rate, trainees usually have the lowest. ?If the rates you charge clients equal your firm's cost rates then, assuming all your fee earners meet their chargeable hour targets, the costs of running your firm will be recovered. Conversely, if targets are not met then your firm will operate at a loss—at least for a while.

What we've just talked about only gets you into the position of breaking even. But that's not good enough if you want to make money. We want profit. For your firm to be profitable, the fees paid by your clients have to exceed the total costs of running the business. Working out your cost of time requires an appropriate time recording system to be in place. In smaller firms you might simply make a hand written note on a file. In larger firms, however, usually sophisticated computer based systems are used (see Ch.15 (how to manage your time)).

The information from any time recording system helps a firm highlight areas of fee-earner inefficiency and also helps create accurate and reliable data on which to base your client fees.

WIP

The higher the level of WIP your firm carries, the greater the business risk should a client subsequently default. Your firm should draft its terms of business to enable interim (e.g. monthly) fees. And, each fee earner should have his or her WIP reviewed on a regular basis. **21–45**

Control of expenses

Good control of your expenses is essential. It's good practice to collate expense analysis reports showing details of the different expenses your firm has incurred. Again, this can be tabulated with comparative data from previous years, to illustrate any trends in costs. **21–46**

Client debtors

21–47 Clients defaulting on payments require a firm hand. Sadly, this is quite common and, if uncontrolled, impacts adversely on your firm. An analysis can be made of your debtor figures in the balance sheet, at the end of any financial year, to see if it's reasonable relative to your total fees rendered. Again, a comparison can be made with previous years to see if you're getting better (or worse) at controlling client default rates. The aim is to minimise your debtor levels. If the situation is under constant review, cash flow is better protected and the risk of bad debts accumulating is reduced. A debtors ageing schedule can be prepared, showing the length of time your clients' debts have remained unpaid, with reference to the fee earner/partner responsible.

Client outlays

21–48 The same guidance applies, here, as per WIP. You firm should avoid accumulating a large balance of otherwise recoverable outlays. Outlays should be monitored and recovered regularly. Why subsidise your clients?

Trend analysis

21–49 Trend analysis is where your results from several periods are converted to a common statistical base, compared in terms of the changes that have occurred in each item from the current to the earliest year (the so-called "base year"), and then expressed as a percentage.

Percentage changes show, at a glance, the levels of change in a digestible way. The formula, which can be applied to anything (fees, commission, expenses etc.) is:

Formula:

[(this year – last year) ÷ (last year)] × (100 ÷ 1)

Ratios

21–50 Ratios are useful for summarising large amounts of financial information, particularly the results of different accounting periods. They emphasise changes that have occurred between financial periods. Trends become readily apparent, weaknesses can be identified easily and, in turn, appropriate future plans can be made. Ratios reduce the large number of accounting figures that can be produced into small sets of readily understood and meaningful indicators for financial planning. Let's look at the key ratios you need to be aware of. We'll use the numbers from our example P & L account.

Ratio one: Return on Capital Employed (ROCE)

21–51 This measures the return earned by the providers of long-term finance to a firm (i.e. your firm's partners). The formula is calculated by dividing your firm's net operating profit by its employed capital. Let's have a shot using Sim & Todd's 2016 figures. Let's assume Sim & Todd's total employed capital (i.e. all of its assets less all of its liabilities) stands at £80,000.

Formula:

ROCE = (net operating profit ÷ capital employed)

ROCE = (£184,274 ÷ £80,000)

ROCE = 2.3:1

For every pound of Sim & Todd's capital, £2.30 is returned. When interpreting the results, the higher the ratio the better (2:1 is better than 1.5:1, and 4:1 is twice as good as 2:1).

Ratio two: Net Profit Percentage (NPP) (or profit margin)

This looks at net profit earned per £1 of fee (and other) income (i.e. your profit margin). Note that you can use an after-tax profit figure, if you wish. This is one of the best measures of your overall financial performance. Let's again use Sim & Todd's 2016 figures to illustrate it. **21–52**

Formula:

NPP = (net profit/net sales) × 100

NPP = (£184,274 ÷ £1,364,950) × 100

NPP = 13.5%

Whether 13.5% is healthy, must be measured against industry averages.

Ratio three: Average Fees Per Partner (AFPP)

This simple ratio is worked out by dividing the total fees rendered by the number of partners. How is Sim & Todd doing? **21–53**

Formula:

AFPP = (total fees/partners)

AFPP = (£1,250,000 ÷ 2)

AFPP = £625,000

Ratio four: Average Fees Per Fee Earner (AFPF) (including partners)

21–54 This simple ratio is worked out by dividing the fees rendered figure by the number of fee earners. Sim & Todd clearly have staff; they spend £875,000 on wages after all! Let's assume (to keep it simple) that they have two salaried partners, three associates, four senior solicitors, five Newly Qualifieds (NQs) and four trainees (with the rest of the wages being spent on admin staff).

Formula:

AFPF = (total fees/fee earners)

AFPF = (£1,250,000 ÷ 14)

AFPF = £89,286

Ratio five: expenses as % of turnover ratio

21–55 This considers your firm's expenses, per £1 of fees. This ratio can be applied to individual expenses (e.g. staffing costs, rent etc.) if more detail is needed. It's calculated by dividing a particular expense (or group of expenses) by your net fees. Let's review Sim & Todd's figures, and see what we get. We've excluded both depreciation and the loss on the sale of the PCs, from our net expenses calculation (to give a slightly lower expenses figure of £1,176,770).

Formula:

Expenses ratio = (particular expense(s)/fees) × 100

Expenses ratio = (£1,176,770 ÷ £1,250,000) × 100

Expenses ratio = 94%

The ratio shows what percentage of your fee income is used up by an individual expense (or a group of expenses). A lower ratio means more profitability; a higher ratio means less profitability. It's a helpful tool in controlling and estimating future expenses.

Ratio six: gross (turnover) and Net Profit per Employee (NPE)

21–56 These ratios measure staff productivity. They can be tweaked to show just fee earners or all staff (including partners). You can use either your firm's gross turnover, or you can use its net profit. In addition to having two salaried partners, three associates, four senior solicitors, five NQs and four trainees, let's assume that Sim & Todd also has five admin staff. Let's have a look at a worked example, based on gross turnover.

Formula:

NPE = gross/net ÷ number of employees

PPE = £1,364,950 ÷ 23

PPE = £59,345

Ratio seven: current ratio

This measures the ability of your firm to meet its short-term liabilities (e.g. creditors, bank overdrafts etc.) without having to resort to selling off its capital assets. Since current assets should become liquid within 12 months, this should correspond with the current liabilities, which will fall due for payment over the same period. **21–57**

Let's assume that Sim & Todd's cash in bank is its net profit (£184,274), it's owed £10,000 by its debtors (clients who haven't paid) and has £10,000 of WIP. It, in turn, owes £120,000 to its creditors.

Formula:

Current ratio = current assets ÷ current liabilities

Current ratio = £204,274 ÷ £120,000

Current ratio = 1.7:1

A result greater than one implies that the firm is liquid; the higher the figure, the better the liquidity.

Ratio eight: liquid ratio (acid test ratio)

This removes WIP from the current ratio calculation, on the basis that it can't readily be turned into cash. Let's have a look at how that changes the scenario. In this case, we need to strip out £10,000 (being the WIP figure). **21–58**

Formula:

Liquid ratio = current assets (less WIP) ÷ current liabilities

Liquid ratio = £194,274 ÷ £120,000

Liquid ratio = 1.6:1

You can readily appreciate that the liquid ratio will always tend to give a more pessimistic (but perhaps realistic) outlook.

Ratio nine: debtor payment period (debtor days)

21–59 This measures the average amount of time taken by your firm to collect payment from its debtors. This is vitally important for your cash flow. The time taken to pay should equal (or be less than) the time given to pay.

The formula requires you to know the amount owed to your firm that is outstanding at the end of a financial year. Let's change our Sim & Todd scenario and let's say that it's owed £250,000 at financial year-end.

Formula:

Debtor days = (amount outstanding ÷ annual fees) × 365

Debtor days = (£250,000 ÷ £1,250,000) × 365

Debtor days = 73 days

So, in this scenario, the average time to pay is 73 days. If credit terms are 30 days, then clearly that is a significant issue for Sim & Todd, because (on average) clients are taking twice as long as they should to pay. Sim & Todd should revisit its credit control procedures.

Ratio 10: Longer Term Solvency (LTS) (cash cover)

21–60 Longer-term viability is analysed using this formula, which examines your firm's cash cover i.e. can its cash flow meet its short term and long term liabilities? Going back to Sim & Todd, we earlier said that it owed £120,000 to its creditors. Let's add on, say, £50,000 of long-term debt, to make a grand total of £170,000. Remember, these are purely made-up figures, to illustrate how the formula works.

Formula:

LTS = (net income + depreciation) ÷ (short + long term liabilities)

LTS = (£1,179,270 + £1,406) ÷ (£120,000 + £50,000)

LTS = 6.9:1

This is a healthy enough ratio. However, the lower your firm's solvency ratio, the greater the chance it'll default on its debt.

User considerations

Ratios come with a health warning. You need to make sure that you choose appropriate ratios. Information needs to be collated regularly (and accurately). Be aware that ratios don't give the full picture. Other information is needed and an in-depth knowledge of your business is required. A ratio relevant to one firm may be irrelevant to another. You must compare like with like. Figures and calculations must be consistent. Avoid information overload. It's best to select appropriate ratios for the purpose. Lastly, critically review the information i.e. what has caused the result; what has changed within your firm; what should your firm do? Ratios are pieces of a jigsaw and shouldn't be looked at in isolation. Comparative analysis with ratios from earlier periods, or indeed other competitors add value and perspective. **21–61**

Summary

Accounts can tell you a story and help you predict the future. The balance sheet and P & L account can show you how your business has spent its money and whether it'll be profitable. They don't however tell the whole story. Profits are not cash, and cash is the lifeblood of a business as we'll see in the next chapter. **21–62**

CHAPTER 22

HOW TO MANAGE CASH

Introduction

22–1 *Your partner is looking worried at your monthly management meeting. You don't know why. You've never been busier. You've had 10 new instructions this week. You're working on good projects and the clients have all agreed to pay big fees. Yet your partner is still worried. "I don't know if we'll be able to pay salaries this month—we just don't have any cash coming in." How could a seemingly successful firm be struggling so badly?*

22–2 Even the biggest law firms can go out of business. You might wonder how an otherwise seemingly lucrative business could ever go to the wall. Yet, as we saw in Ch.3 (what are law firms?) the evidence is clear, with several major names such as Ross Harper, McClure Naismith and Semple Fraser extinguished in recent years. How exactly can a profitable business go bust? Let's look at another illustration. In 2014, Tods Murray (founded in 1856) was ranked 14th in the Scottish legal league table, with a turnover of £12.4 million. That year it reported that it had grown its pre-tax profits to £2.5 million (in the year to 31 March 2013), from £2.3 million the year before. However, on 3 October 2014 this venerable firm went into administration. Tom MacLennan (one of its administrators) said:

> "Tods Murray had exhausted every option to turn the business around, and was faced with an unsustainable gap between high fixed costs and income. Administration was the only alternative for the firm".[1]

There is a simple answer to this question. Tods Murray managed to get itself into the position whereby its cash (money in) wasn't enough to cover its high fixed costs (money out). It was that basic: Tods Murray had to spend more cash than it received.

Often, solicitors confuse profit with cash. Be under no illusion, cash is the money available to your firm and includes coins, notes, money in an account and any unused overdraft facility. Profit, on the other hand, is what is left once all the costs of running your firm are paid.

---

[1] Quoted in "Shepherd & Wedderburn acquires Tods Murray on administration" (4 October 2014), The Journal of the Law Society of Scotland, *Jounralonline.co.uk*, *http://www.journalonline.co.uk/News/1014536.aspx#.Vvo6ZeIrJD8* [Accessed 19 April 2016].

Outcomes

In the last chapter we looked at profit and loss statements and balance sheets, two of the three main financial reports. In this chapter we'll examine the third—the cash flow statement. You will learn how to read and understand a cash flow statement and how to ask questions of it so that you get meaningful information. 22–3

A simple cash flow statement

Let's start examining cash flow by looking at a simple worked example. Sim & Todd is a boutique Glasgow based law firm. Its cash flow statement to 31 January 2017 looks something like this: 22–4

SIM & TODD **DATE: 31.01.17**						
£	**NOV** ***Actual***	**DEC** ***Actual***	**JAN** ***Actual***	**FEB** ***Estimate***	**MAR** ***Estimate***	**APR** ***Estimate***
Fees	10,000	10,000	0	10,000	0	60,000
Other income	1,000	1,000	2,000	1,000	500	1,000
Subtotal	**11,000**	**11,000**	**2,000**	**11,000**	**500**	**61,000**
Drawings	(–5,000)	(–9,000)	(–5,000)	(–5,000)	(–8,000)	(–5,000)
Rent	(–500)	(–500)	(–500)	(–500)	(–1000)	(–1000)
Heat and lighting	(–100)	(–100)	(–100)	(–100)	(–200)	(–200)
Travel	(–100)	(–100)	(–100)	(–100)	(–200)	(–200)
Subtotal	**(5,700)**	**(9,700)**	**(5,700)**	**(5,700)**	**(9,400)**	**(6,400)**
Monthly total	+5,300	+1,300	–3,700	+5,300	–8,900	+54,600
Running total	+5,300	+6,600	+2,900	+8,200	(700)	*+53,900*

Basics

What does this table show? 22–5

Horizontal

Firstly, look at the horizontal axis (i.e. left to right). This gives you the timeline. Notice that for November, December and January, Sim & Todd can record actual, known figures. That's because this statement is dated 31 January 2017 (the date at the top of the table). On 31 January 2017, Sim & Todd know what it has spent and what it has received. For February through to April, the firm can only record estimated figures (i.e. sensible "best guesses"). In January, the firm will not know what it'll actually receive or spend in February, March or April. It can only guess. That leads us to our first point; sometimes when you prepare 22–6 a cash flow statement is prepared actual, known numbers are included, but poor estimates for the future are made.

Ultimately, cash flow statements are only useful if you ask sensible questions about the data contained in it. Solicitors often don't ask sensible questions. They might not question why their income is falling, month on month, and instead still project a rise in fees. They might not question an evolving pattern of rising costs, and instead keep their cost projections fixed at existing levels. Later, we look at how to ask good questions to elicit valuable information.

Vertical

22–7 Next, look at the vertical axis (i.e. up and down). This shows you the firm's different streams—i.e. what the firm spends money on and who (or what) it receives money from—and also all of its expenses/costs.

Monthly total

22–8 At the bottom of the table you find the total for each month, which is calculated by deducting the expenses from the income, leaving either a net surplus (good) or a net deficit (bad) figure.

Running total

22–9 Finally, you have the running total. Again, this is easily calculated, by adding the monthly total of the first month to that of the next month, and so on. Because Sim & Todd's cash flow statement starts in November, the running total figure for November is the same as its monthly total. However, skip to December, and you have a second month's data. You can add the running total from November to the monthly total for December, to create the running total for December (£6,600). Going forward, you add the running total for December with the monthly total for January, and so on.

Summary

22–10 This short geography lesson is well worth your time, because all cash flow statements are similar in their layout and construction. Before we move on, there are two other general points to note. Firstly, in our example, the column for January is shaded light grey. This is to indicate that it's the current month under review. It's a good technique, when presenting any financial information to your team, to use colour shading to draw their attention to the month/period you need them to focus on. Secondly, the column for March is shaded dark grey, simply to draw your eye to this being the month in which it all goes wrong for Sim & Todd.

Analysing the cash flow statement

22–11 Let's look at the figures. These are fictitious and rather exaggerated; don't get caught up in them. The point of our example, as you'll recall, is to demonstrate how an otherwise profitable firm can run out of cash. However, as we go through the figures we'll make some observations and ask some relevant questions about the data. For example, why is fee income low; why does the partner drawings vary from month to month; and why is the rent going up?

You also can practice, by thinking of additional questions that you might ask. Remember, without good questions and solid analysis, there is little point in having the source data that a cash flow statement generates.

Here are our general observations (and questions) on the figures:

- Fee income in November is healthy, at £10,000. If this were replicated each month, this firm would gross £120,000 per year.
- Estimated fee income in April shoots up to an astonishing £60,000. A question, here, could be why such a large fee has arisen?
- Other income will include things like interest received and commission (for referring business to another firm). Sim & Todd is earning at least something each month that can be classed as "other income", which is a good bonus. A question you might ask is how this could be improved? For example, are all Sim & Todd's referrals yielding commission? If not, why not? You'd be surprised how many solicitors just give their business leads away.
- Drawings are the sums of money that partners of a firm take out of the business as earnings. You'll see that Sim & Todd doesn't seem to have any control over its monthly drawings, with the figure changing all the time. Ominously, even though the firm is anticipating zero income in March, Sim & Todd still intend to take money out of the firm as drawings, and they plan to increase what they're taking. Is this sensible?
- The firm's rent is due to double in March. In reality this would be almost impossible with a well-drafted commercial lease, but maybe Sim & Todd were not on the ball? A question you might ask is whether the firm could renegotiate a lower rent increase? Alternatively, could it give notice to quit and move to new, more cost effective premises?
- Heating and lighting costs are estimated to double, even though better spring and summer weather is coming. Perhaps the firm is being careless and leaving the lights on overnight? Perhaps it should consider energy efficiency measures, like installing LED lights?
- Travel costs are expected to increase substantially. Again, perhaps the partners are using first class travel, when standard class would suffice? However, don't be afraid to "question your questions". Perhaps standard class is inappropriate? Maybe Sim & Todd find they get more work done in first class as they have guaranteed access to a table for their laptops and a socket for power?

Going back to the key point of the example, if you look at the projected figures for April, the firm hits the jackpot with estimated fees of £60,000. This, in turn, is projected to put Sim & Todd, that month, in a net cash position of +£54,600, and a cumulative cash position of £53,900.

When measured over the period covered by the statement, Sim & Todd is a profitable firm. However, it's only going to be profitable if it can trade until the end of April. Why might it not? Look at March, when fee and other income are projected to be low, with estimated costs and drawings projected to be high. Taken together, the firm is due to enter a financial deficit. That means it's going to spend more than it earns.

If this transpires, and if the firm's creditors are unwilling to renegotiate credit terms and instead demand immediate payment, Sim and Todd could be in big trouble. It just needs one client to default on fee, or one unexpected bill to crop up, and the firm will run out of cash and be unable to trade to April. You might well be wondering why Sim & Todd would even contemplate taking out cash as drawings, given the fee income projection. You'd be right—a really good question. However, it assumes that Sim & Todd are preparing a regular cash flow forecast, on the one hand, and asking sensible questions about the data, on the other.

In reality, more complex variations on this simple theme have played out in the Scottish legal profession more often than you might think. There sadly are too many real-life examples where partners have failed to fee large jobs, have allowed costs to rise and yet have continued to take large drawings. Why do they do this? Partners are no different to anyone else. They still need paid each month to pay for mortgages, rent, car loans, bills, food etc. Could you go a month without a salary?

Conclusion

22–12 For the moment, just lock into your minds that profit is not the same as cash. Profit doesn't become cash until a fee note is rendered and paid by a client.

Cash flow forecasts

Get in the flow

22–13 Cash flow forecasts are the best tool to use to avoid ending up like Sim & Todd. Basically, they let a firm predict the peaks and troughs in its cash balance. We showed you a simple forecast in the last example. You're well on your way to understanding, firstly, what a typical statement looks like and, secondly, the importance of asking good questions about the data it contains.

In order to make a profit, you have to deliver services to clients before they get paid (unless a chunk of money can be negotiated as a front-end payment). It's essential in legal business to control cash flow, so your firm always has enough cash to pay staff and suppliers before receiving payment from clients. What's more, regular cash outflows will be made on fixed dates (e.g. rent, wages, VAT). You must always be in a position to meet these payments in order to avoid fines, penalty interest or a disgruntled workforce. This is called aligning your cash inflow (that is, cash coming in from fees and other sources) with your cash outflow (money going out on wages, rent, utilities etc.).

Once you're able to see if (and when) problem months are going to occur, you can plan for them, whether you simply reduce partner drawings or, perhaps, arrange a bank loan (if that is your preferred way of bridging shortfalls). We look at other strategies a little later. It's worth noting at this point, however, that many banks require forecasts before considering whether to lend.

Elements

22–14 A real-life cash flow forecast identifies all of the sources (and amounts) of cash coming into your firm, and the onward destinations (and amounts) of cash going out of your business, over a given period.

Cash inflows (i.e. the money coming in over the period) can include:

- fees from clients;
- receipt of a bank loan;

- bank interest on savings and investments; and
- commission (on referrals).

Cash outflows (the payments disbursed over the period) can include:

- purchase of materials (stationery etc.);
- staff wages and partner drawings;
- rent;
- gas and electrics;
- purchase of fixed assets (PCs, printers, furniture, cars etc.);
- loan repayments; and
- tax (income tax, corporation tax, VAT, National Insurance contributions for employees etc.).

In our earlier example, we kept it simple by using just one column. Often, however, you have two columns, one listing the forecast numbers and the other listing the actual numbers. A forecast is usually done for a year (or quarter) in advance and then updated monthly.

Note that your forecast figures should relate to sums that are due to be collected and sums that are due to be paid out, not invoices actually sent and payments actually received.

Commenting on a forecast

We've said this a lot. To reiterate, raw data is of no value unless it's subjected to **22–15** sensible analysis. At a basic level, if a forecast shows a steady net outflow of cash then this is an indicator of problems that need to be addressed quickly. Another easy thing to spot is a misalignment of cash inflow and cash outflow. Be aware of divergences of your projected figures and actual figures. When commenting on your forecast, you should be trying to identify the reason (or reasons) for any variances, and then developing or revising your strategy to combat these issues, going forward.

Here are some examples of the sorts of things that you might ask.

1. Fee income has/is projected to come down.
   a. Has a competitor moved in?
   b. Is it affecting all types of work, or specific areas?
   c. Is it referable to the loss of a high profile partner (who has taken his or her clients away)?
   d. Is it symptomatic of the post-recession economy or is a result of changes in the market (e.g. fixed fee conveyancing)?
   e. Is there a seasonal variation?
   f. Is it worth improving your marketing?
   g. Can you undercut your competitors?
   h. Is it better to stop one type of work completely and consolidate in other areas?
2. Commission income has/is projected to come down.
   a. Has the market shifted so that there is less commission work in general?
   b. Can the firm be appointed to other panels (e.g. for insurance work)?

3. Bank interest has/is projected to come down.
   a. Is it due to the base rate being fixed at 0.5%?
   b. Is there a more generous account from another provider, close to the firm?
   c. To get better interest will the firm need to tie up a chunk of its cash balance in notice accounts (e.g. 90-day notice accounts) and can it afford do this?
4. Gas and electricity costs have risen/are projected to rise.
   a. Is it part of a general market trend?
   b. Can the office switch off lights, appliances and heating on certain days (e.g. weekends)?
   c. Is it worth changing supplier?
5. Significant capital costs will push the firm into deficit.
   a. Can acquisitions or renewals be deferred?
   b. If they're necessary, can better payment terms be obtained?

Updates

22–16 Accurate forecasts are essential. This means you need to set aside a chunk of time each month to perform an update, by recording your actual (known) numbers. If you use a two-column model (one for projected figures and one for actual figures) you can easily tweak the following months' projections. For example, if fees are projected to be £10,000 a month and, over a three-month period you actually receive £8,000 a month, in the absence of any good reason that would tend to suggest an improvement in your fee income, it would be wise for you to reduce your projected future fees to £8,000 per month.

You have to also consider new factors such as the arrival of a new competitor on the market, and whether these changes need to be incorporated into the business plan or the forecast. When reviewing your forecast, you might choose to:

- keep your original forecast, but measure and understand any variances in the actual figures against the original budget; or
- use a rolling forecast; as each month's actual information is finalised, the forecast is updated to provide an additional month's data. This means that there is always a 12-month rolling projection.

Strategies

22–17 We turn to cash flow strategies. In particular, what can you do if you spot problem months, where your income won't cover expenditure?

Overdraft

22–18 One option is to negotiate an overdraft from your bank. Most business banking facilities offer an overdraft, but make you prove that you can trade in surplus for at least a year, and then charge you for the privilege of using it. In reality, an overdraft is not going to cover anything other than small shortfalls.

Borrow

The second option is to take a business loan. The issue here is that lenders nowadays require partners to have a good credit rating. Furthermore, the rate of interest usually is quite high (i.e. a high cost of borrowing). Finally, they often require the partners to give a personal guarantee of repayment. This means if the firm cannot pay, the bank can sue the partners direct. **22–19**

Partner loan

This is probably the cheapest way to borrow money. Quite simply, you and your partners lend your firm the money it needs to cover any lean periods. That way, you can choose not to charge your firm interest (whereas a bank always will). There are no issues with credit worthiness and also there are fewer problems if you want to write-off your loans (i.e. not demand repayment). **22–20**

Reduce drawings

If your firm routinely fails to hit its income target, it would be sensible to look at a new drawings policy. Are partners taking too much out? **22–21**

Credit terms

It's sometimes possible to renegotiate terms with your creditors. However, it might come at an unexpected cost. Clearly, your creditors could just refuse. Alternatively, if they accept they may wish to apply interest. It also can erode creditor confidence. Word can spread; a conversation with one creditor can lead to a loss of confidence across several suppliers. This, in turn, can cause a spiral effect, where your creditors all demand immediate payment. **22–22**

Other strategies

What else can you do to improve your cash flow, to try to avoid having to "plug the gaps"? Ultimately, your aim has to be to speed up inflow and slow down outflow. This helps you build up a positive cash balance that, in turn, helps iron out any short-term problems, as well as funding the future growth of your firm. You can: **22–23**

- draft better invoicing terms to get clients to pay sooner, or on an interim basis;
- charge a front-end fee;
- implement proper and robust credit controls to chase debts;
- defer certain items of capital expenditure (e.g. firm car, PCs etc.);
- negotiate extended credit terms at the outset (this is much better than trying to re-negotiate after the event); and
- take steps to increase fees and profitability, generally (e.g. better marketing, reduced costs etc.).

Problem clients

Before we examine a more complex cash flow forecast, let's look at some techniques to detect problem clients. If your firm has only a few clients and one **22–24** develops financial problems (and can't pay his or her fees), it can have a serious impact. The first piece of advice is that you should avoid relying on a small number of clients if possible, and be vigilant for signs that existing (or indeed potential) clients are in financial trouble. There are several signs that a client might be struggling—for example:

- a change for the worse in payment patterns;
- frequent mistakes on cheques (your client might be trying to buy time);
- your client refuses to talk to you;
- less frequent instructions; and
- your client unexpectedly seeks an extension to his or her credit.

It always pays to keep the ear to the ground and it's worth using a credit agency, like Experian or Equifax, to get access to databases with up-to-date financial information about individuals If your client is a company, or limited liability partnership (LLP), it's also worth accessing its accounts at Companies House.

Lastly, sometimes it's possible to help your problem clients by renegotiating their payment terms. This defers your firm's income, but it could also help you to retain that client in the future by supporting them during a difficult period.

Example

22–25 Let's look at a more complex example. Sim & Todd has started again. This time better sense has prevailed and the partners have decided to prepare a cash flow forecast and keep it up to date.

This first table shows just the financial projections of Sim & Todd for April and May 2017. June 2017 has still to be completed.

SIM & TODD
Forecast cash flow for the period from 1 April 2017 to 30 June 2017

	April	April	**May**	May	**June**	June
	Projected (£)	Actual (£)	**Projected (£)**	Actual (£)	**Projected (£)**	Actual (£)
CASH INFLOW						
Fees recovered	45,000		45,000			
Commission	2,000		2,000			
Bank interest	160		160			
Total cash inflow	**47,160**	**0**	**47,160**	**0**	**0**	
Less: CASH OUTFLOWS						
Wages and salaries	3,750		3,750			
Rent	800		800			
Gas and electricity	420		420			
Telephone	180		180			
Other office costs	275		275			
Transport	150		150			
Capital outlays*	0		12,000			
Cash outflows Subtotal	**5,575**	**0**	**17,575**	**0**	**0**	
TAXES						
Quarterly VAT	20,000		0			
National Insurance	450		500			

Cash outflows Subtotal	**26,025**	**0**	**18,075**	**0**	**0**	
NET CASH FLOW BEFORE	**21,135**		**29,085**			
DRAWINGS						
PARTNERS' DRAWINGS	10,000		10,000			
Less: partners' drawings						
NET CASH FLOW AFTER	**11,135**		**19,085**			
DRAWINGS						
CUMULATIVE CASH	5,000					
Opening bank/cash						
Net cash flow for month	11,135					
Closing bank/cash	16,135	0	0		0	

Below is the actual financial information recorded by Sim & Todd's accounts team.

APRIL	**£**	**MAY**	**£**
Fees received:	40,500	Fees received:	32,750
Commission:	875	Commission:	600
Bank interest:	114	Bank interest:	100
Wages and salaries:	3,750	Wages and salaries:	4,950
Rent:	800	Rent:	1,600
Gas and electricity:	580	Gas and electricity:	720
Telephone:	180	Telephone:	180
Other office costs:	415	Other office costs:	330
Transport costs:	180	Transport costs:	240
Capital outlays:	1,600	Capital outlays:	15.975
VAT:	20,000	VAT:	0
National Insurance:	450	National Insurance:	500
Drawings:	10,000	Drawings:	10,000

Instructions

Now you're going to do some work. **22–26**

(1) Review the cash flow forecast for Sim & Todd.
(2) Note that the forecast covers the period from April until June 2017.
(3) Note that projected figures are provided for April and May.
(4) Complete the "actual" columns for April and May, by plugging in the information provided above (you might want to photocopy the page first).
(5) Analyse the projected and actual figures and comment on them, on a sheet of blank A4
(6) Revise the projections for June and explain your revisions.
(7) Complete the cumulative cash position entries (at the foot of the forecast).

Once you've done that, read on as we've provided a suggested solution.

SIM & TODD
Forecast cash flow for the period from 1 April 2017 to 30 June 2017

	April	April	**May**	May	**June**	June
	Projected (£)	Actual (£)	**Projected (£)**	Actual (£)	**Projected (£)**	Actual (£)
CASH INFLOW						
Fees recovered	45,000	40,500	45,000	32,750	30,000	
Commission	2,000	875	2,000	600	500	
Bank interest	160	114	160	100	80	
Total cash Inflow	**47,160**	**41,489**	**47,160**	**33,450**	**30,580**	
Less: CASH OUTFLOWS						
Wages and salaries	3,750	3,750	3,750	4,950	4,950	
Rent	800	800	800	1,600	1,600	
Gas and electricity	420	580	420	720	720	
Telephone	180	180	180	180	180	
Other office costs	275	415	275	330	300	
Transport	150	180	150	240	240	
Capital outlays*	0	1,600	12,000	15,975	0	
Cash outflows Subtotal	**5,575**	**7,505**	**17,575**	**23,995**	**7,990**	
TAXES						
Quarterly VAT	20,000	20,000	0	0	0	
National Insurance	450	450	500	500	500	

Cash outflows Subtotal	**26,025**	**27,955**	**18,075**	**24,495**	**8,490**	
NET CASH-FLOW BEFORE DRAWINGS	**21,135**	**13,534**	**29,085**	**8,955**	**22,090**	
PARTNERS' DRAWINGS	10,000	10,000	10,000	10,000	10,000	
Less: partners' drawings						
NET CASH-FLOW AFTER DRAWINGS	**11,135**	**3,534**	**19,085**	**–1,045**	**12,090**	
CUMULATIVE CASH	5,000	5,000	8,534	8,534	7,489	
Opening bank/cash						
Net cash flow for month	11,135	3,534	19,085	**–1,045**	12,090	
Closing bank/cash	16,135	8,534	27,619	7,489	19,579	

Analysis

22–27 Below are our observations, together with potential reasons (and/or issues to consider) and a range of possible solutions. This is not a prescriptive list. You should analyse the information and come up with your own additional observations, reasons, issues and solutions.

OBSERVATION	REASON(S)/ISSUES	SOLUTION(S)
Fee income projection is higher than actual fees.	• Has a competitor moved in? • Has a high profile partner left, taking clients? • Due to a sluggish post-recession economy? • Due to market shift (e.g. Alternative Business Structures (ABS)/ removal of reserved status etc.)? • Due to a small client pool? • Seasonal variation? • Is it affecting all types of work or just some?	• Undercut competitors. • Improve marketing (targeted strategy and integrated social media). • Can the firm adopt new business models e.g. fixed fee conveyancing?
Commission income is below projected levels.	• Review the above (certain points apply, here). • Has there been a market shift such that there is less commission work generally?	• Can the firm seek out other panels (or similar) for insurance work? • Can the firm partner with other firms (including accountants) to cross-sell?
Bank interest is flat-lining.	• Is this due to a factor outwith the firm's control (e.g. the Bank of England has kept the base rate at 0.5%)?	• Can the firm change to a more generous account from the same/another provider? • To get better interest, can the firm tie up its cash in notice accounts (e.g. 30 days)?
Wages and salaries are rising.	• Has the firm taken on new staff? • Are the increases in line with inflation? • Do the increases relate to bonuses?	• Review recruitment. • Consider redundancies. • Consider pay-freeze. • Consider moratorium on bonuses.
Rent is rising considerably.	• Why have the partners not taken avoiding action in good time? • Does the increase fall within the terms of the lease?	• Can the firm sub-let unused space? • Can the firm re-negotiate terms? • Is it viable to move premises?

Gas and electricity costs are rising significantly.	• Is this part of a market trend? • Is the office inefficient e.g. does it use too much electricity?	• Can the firm better use its power (e.g. switch-off appliances at night/ weekends)? • Does the firm have an energy policy? • Is it worth changing supplier?
Telephone costs showing no change.	• This is clearly good.	• Can the firm use online technologies for cheaper calls (e.g. Viber)? • Are there yet still more cost efficient providers?
Transport costs rising.	• Is this part of a market trend?	• Where possible any tickets should be booked in advance (e.g. through *trainline.com*) • Switch from first to standard class.
Other office costs fluctuating.	• What comprises the other costs? • Is the fluctuation within acceptable parameters?	• Can prices be fixed with suppliers?
Capital outlays.	• What comprises the capital outlays? • Are the outlays necessary?	• Can the acquisitions or renewals be deferred? • If not, can better payment terms be negotiated? • Does the firm need such an expensive car? • Is it better to lease an asset as opposed to buying it?
VAT.	• Compliance issue. • Critical it is paid to avoid fines.	• Does the firm have a tax account, with a sensible reserve to meet VAT?
National Insurance (NI).	• Compliance issue.	• Does the firm have a tax account, with a sensible reserve to meet NI?
Partners' drawings steady, but high.	• Drawings are usually the single biggest drain on cash flow.	• Partners might consider reducing their take from the firm, for a period.

Projections

For your revised projections for June, you should have slotted in some sensible numbers. There is no right or wrong answer, but the following suggestions should keep you in the right ballpark. **22–28**

ITEM	PROJECTION / REASON
Fees	Revise down to the actual fee figure for May.
Commission	Revise down to a more realistic level.
Bank interest	Revise down to reflect reduced fees and commission.
Wages and salaries	Use actual figure for May (pending staffing review).
Rent	Use actual figure for May (pending negotiation with landlord).
Gas/electricity	Use actual figure for May (pending change of supplier).
Telephone	Use actual figure for May (pending change of supplier).
Other office costs	Prudent to revise up slightly (as they're fluctuating).
Capital outlays	Zero—no outlays anticipated.
VAT	Zero—VAT is paid quarterly.
NI	Revise up—slight increase to reflect increased wages.
Drawings	Revise down—sensible to help ensure a return to surplus.

Other key questions

22–29 To conclude, we leave you with some more general questions. These are the sorts of "big picture" questions you might ask in a financial analysis session.

- Has Sim & Todd been sensible, overall, in its financial projections?
  - — Yes—it has actually created a cash flow forecast.
  - — No—it has over-estimated key income figures significantly.
- Does the firm have a healthy cash balance?
  - — No—in May it's in a cash negative position.
  - — No—the margin in April was not significant, and a range of common occurrences was always likely to tip the firm in to a cash-negative situation e.g. loss of a major client; increase in overheads etc.
- Why are there heavier cash demands in certain months?
  - — Some outlays (e.g. VAT) are incurred on a fixed, quarterly basis.
  - — During the winter, gas and electricity costs, clearly, will be higher.
- What can Sim & Todd do to improve its cash flow and cash balance?
  - — Draft better invoicing terms (interim fees).
  - — Implement robust credit control.
  - — Seek better credit terms.
  - — Generally, seek to increase fees (increase hourly rates, widen the breadth of work the firm does, improve targeted marketing, maintain a current client database and cross-sell services to existing clients, improve social networking and firm branding, seek appointment to public authority and insurance panels etc.).

  - — Generally, cut costs (review staffing, re-allocate work so that partners do not undertake cost in-efficient work more appropriately handled by an assistant, switch to using cheaper paralegals, more efficient use of office materials and utilities).

- What might the impact be of excessive partnership debts?
  - — If not an LLP, Sim & Todd will have joint and several liability for the debts.
  - — The partnership might be forced out of business, if creditors call in debts.
  - — Firm then reliant on: overdraft; a bridging loan; or partners injecting their own capital. These do not address underlying problems and the first two options are expensive ways to raise money.
  - — Partners might struggle to find a buyer (or complete a merger) on good terms.
  - — If the financial problems become known more widely, suppliers may impose more robust credit terms and clients may leave.

Summary

Cash is the life-blood of any business. If you start losing cash then you won't be **22–30**
able to pay salaries, rent, suppliers and others. Without cash you can't run a business. The cash flow statement helps you track cash so that you can quickly and easily spot problems and deal with them.

PART 5

Running a Business—Management

CHAPTER 23

HOW TO START A LAW FIRM

Introduction

Ten years post-qualification, and you're restless. You like your job; you've risen to become a senior associate. Yet, you hunger for more. You want more responsibility for your clients and for your firm. You've got friends who are now partners or who are setting up their own firms. You wonder if you should push your partners for promotion, too, or whether you should become your own boss. **23–1**

However, what does it mean to be a partner of a partnership, or a limited liability partnership (LLP)? You've heard that your house might be at risk if your firm fails and that you'd be safer if your firm were a company? You promise yourself to look into the options, as you ponder the next big step in your career.

A business vehicle is the structure (or legal model) you use to create a business. **23–2** This could be, for example, a partnership, limited company or a limited liability company. It's important to know the difference between each vehicle: there are advantages and disadvantages to each. This helps you for three reasons:

1. If you choose to set up your own firm, you'll know which vehicle to use.
2. If you move into the management of your existing firm, you'll understand how the business works.
3. You may want to set up your own non-legal business, whether as a side project or a change of career, and—while you might start small (e.g. a sole trader)—you almost certainly will transition to different vehicles as you grow.

This isn't just about your own future business plans. To be commercially aware, you also need to understand your clients' business structures, so to be better placed to advise them. You need to understand the business landscape in which you (and they) operate. As we discussed in Ch.2 (who are your clients?), when you act for a business you need to know how it's structured so that you understand the challenges it faces and the powers it has. Understanding the different business vehicles means you can better understand your clients.

On a similar thread, you need this knowledge to hone your financial advice; each vehicle has different tax structures. You should read Ch.20, if you've not already done so, before reading this chapter. Start thinking about how each vehicle can raise (and invest) money.

Outcomes

23–3 In this chapter we look at the four most common business vehicles: sole traders, partnerships, LLPs and limited companies. For each vehicle, we look at the formation process, factors to consider before you start, on-going compliance and an overview of tax issues (bearing in mind we look at tax in much more detail elsewhere). Some information is repeated, but we thought it was easier to repeat information in full rather than direct you to previous pages, so that you have all information in one place.

Sole traders

The basics

23–4 The sole trader is the most basic business vehicle that there is. It's also one of the most popular. Sole traders are at the forefront of business growth in the UK, with almost 200,000 start-ups in 2014, according to the UK Government's business population statistics.[1] At the start of 2014 there were 5.2 million private sector businesses (330,000 more than in the previous year). Of those 330,000 new businesses, 197,000 were sole traders, according to the report. In the Scottish legal market, there are more than 600 sole practitioners.

The term "sole trader" (or sole proprietor) describes any business that is owned and controlled by just one person. In other words, if you decide to be a sole trader you'll trade in your own right. This is the case even if you employ workers. For example, if the owner of a 24/7 store employs an assistant, the owner is still regarded legally as a sole trader.

As a sole trader you're flying solo. You've to manage every aspect of your firm: advertising for new clients, creating a marketing plan (using your knowledge of clients from Chs 2 and 4), cash flow and financial management, client relationships (including issuing your business terms), client files, hiring staff, delegating to staff, compliance with Law Society rules, and so on.

Business planning

23–5 Business planning is critically important for sole traders. See Chs 4 and 5 for advice on marketing, and Chs 21 and 22 for a guide to accounts and basic financial awareness. It's worth making sure that you avail yourself of the support offered by the Business Gateway organisation. You can access their website at *www.bgateway.com*.

Formation

23–6 There aren't any special rules if you want to be a sole trader. It's easy to get started. You don't need to go through Companies House and there's no formal paperwork to fill in. The only thing you must do is to notify HMRC that you're trading as a self-employed person, because that has tax implications (as we'll see).

Business name

23–7 One consideration when starting out is your business name. You can trade under your own personal name, or you can use a non-personal name i.e. a business name.

---

1 See: *https://www.gov.uk/government/statistics/business-population-estimates-2014* (26 November 2014) [Accessed: 15 June 2016].

If you do decide to use a business name, your personal details must be disclosed to your clients and suppliers, so that they know with who they're doing business. The information you need to disclose is:

- your full name; and
- an address at which your business can be contacted and have any legal documents formally served.

What's more, this information has to be:

- displayed in a prominent position in all business premises to which your clients and suppliers have access; and
- included legibly on all your business documents, including:
  - letters
  - orders for goods or services;
  - invoices and receipts; and
  - demands for payment.

Also, it has to be displayed prominently on your website[2] and provided immediately in writing to any client or supplier who requests it.

Unlike companies, you don't need to satisfy a registrar that your name isn't already being used. However, you still might run into legal issues if you're not careful. In particular, you need to bear in mind the old common law of "passing off". This is where you can be sued for having a name that is identical (or similar) to that of an existing business, such that it could cause confusion in the market place. We look in detail at passing off in Ch.23.

Key features

If you become a sole trader you won't have a legal existence separate to that of **23–8**
your business. Let's take a quick refresher on the concept of separate legal existence (otherwise called "separate legal personality"). Every person has what's termed "natural legal personality". Your legal personality is what makes you a valid person in the eyes of the law. It's the thing that lets you own property, enter into contracts, sue people, and so on.

In 1897 it was established, in the famous case of *Salomon v Salomon & Co Ltd*, that companies (as opposed to sole traders) have their own, separate, legal personality.[3] The judge in that case, Lord Macnaghten, formulated the classic definition:

> "The company is at law a different person altogether from the **subscribers to the memorandum**; and, though it may be that after incorporation the business is precisely the same as before, and the **same persons are managers** and the same hands receive the profits, the company is not in law the agent of the shareholders or a trustee for them. Nor are the subscribers as members liable, in any shape or form, except to the extent and in the manner provided by the Act." [Emphasis added.]

---

2 The Electronic Commerce (EC Directive) Regulations 2002 (SI 2002/2013) reg. 6.

3 *Salomon v Salomon & Co Ltd* [1896] UKHL 1.

What does this all mean? A company's owners (its shareholders) are regarded as being separate from their company. In other words, a company is just like a newly born child; it is its own person. Consequently, if something goes wrong with a company then its shareholders (generally, but not always) will have no personal liability for any of the consequences (like legal actions, financial losses etc.).

Let's go back to you as a brand new sole trader. Sole traders are not companies. They (you) are normal human beings with natural legal personality. Another way of looking at it is that you and your business are actually one and the same person. In consequence, as a sole trader you're personally liable for all your business obligations (contracts etc.) and all your debts. You need to pay your debts out of your own pocket, with no cap or limit on what you potentially might have to shell out. This is called unlimited liability, and it can sometimes force sole traders into personal bankruptcy.

Let's look at some other key benefits of sole traders.

1. Generally, only a small amount of capital is required to start-up (usually provided by you).
2. Your wage bill is low because there are few (or no) employees.
3. Your business is easy to control, because you've hands-on control and can make decisions quickly, without having to consult anyone else.
4. The ease of decision making makes it a nimble vehicle, quick to respond to business opportunities and market changes.
5. No public filing of accounts is required, so you can keep all your key financial information private from your competitors.

There are some disadvantages.

1. You've no one to share the responsibility of running your business—you're on your own.
2. You can end up working long hours, and also you might find it difficult to take time off.
3. Growth potential is limited by the amount of capital available. As—by definition—there aren't any shares that can be offered to potential investors, any growth has to be funded by a bank or family loan (the former which, almost certainly, you would need to guarantee personally) or from your own private funds.
4. Unlimited liability means you technically can be forced to sell your personal assets to cover your debts.

Compliance

23–9 There aren't any special rules for ongoing compliance, bar a requirement to prepare a set of annual accounts for HMRC and to pay whatever personal tax you owe. As regards the Law Society, you need to hold a full practising certificate, have personal indemnity insurance and must pay into the master policy. You also need to fulfil the various regulatory roles required by the Law Society (which we look at in Ch.1 (what will you do?)) and deal with all ongoing continuing professional development (CPD) requirements yourself.

Tax

23–10 As a sole trader you pay personal income tax on the net profit from your self-employed income. This is what's known as Schedule D tax. You must fill in a self-assessment tax return each year, detailing all your income (fees, commission and bank interest) and expenses. You also need to register as self-employed with HMRC as soon as you start to trade. If you don't do this within the first three full months of becoming self-employed, you face a penalty of £100.

The current rates of personal income tax are set out in Ch.20 (how to speak to clients about finance). If you've (or expect to have) a turnover exceeding £83,000 per year, you also need to apply for a VAT number, and then charge VAT to your clients, complete VAT returns and send VAT payments to HMRC. You also can voluntarily register for VAT. This has the merit of enabling you to reclaim all the VAT you pay out (input tax) against the VAT you charge your clients (output tax). Some business commentators argue that being VAT registered can help to make you look more professional in the eyes of your clients (the assumption being that you're doing really well and must be effective).

Finally, as a sole trader you've to make National Insurance contributions (so-called NICs). There are two categories of NICs: Class 2 and Class 4. As of financial year 2016/17, Class 2 NICs are collected along with your personal income tax (in your January self-assessment payment). For financial year 2016/17, the charge is £2.80 per week. If your net profits are under the small profit threshold (£5,965 for financial year 2016/17), you don't have to pay any Class 2 NICs. However, you might still elect to pay them, in order to preserve your entitlement to your state pension (and other state benefits). If your net profit is above £8,060 (financial year 2016/17) you also have to pay Class 4 NICs, at the rate of 9% (falling to 2% on any excess over £43,000). Again, you pay these together with your personal income tax (in your January self-assessment payment). From April 2018, Class 2 NICs will be abolished.

Other

For certain types of work a sole trader might need a licence from a local authority. **23–11**
Restaurants and taxi drivers, for example, need to have a local authority licence. In addition, your qualifications and business premises may be inspected to ensure you comply with certain regulations.

Advantages and disadvantages

Advantages

- No regulatory hurdles for start-up. **23–12**
- Small amount of capital is required at inception.
- Low wage bills.
- Nimble response to opportunities and market changes.
- Limited on-going regulation.
- Privacy of financial information.
- You're your "own boss" and can work flexibly.

Disadvantages

- Day to day management rests on one set of shoulders. **23–13**
- Long working hours.
- Need to deal with Law Society regulation by yourself.
- Need to arrange CPD training by yourself.
- Personal liability for business obligations and debts.
- Lack the power and spend of established big players.
- Challenging to grow due to difficulty in leveraging investment.

Partnerships

The basics

23–14 This business vehicle has been around a long time. In fact, the UK has regulated partnerships since 1890 (via the Partnership Act of that year). Even today, in 2016, it's still a popular structure for a lot of law firms. The essence of a partnership is that a firm's partners (its owners) share with each other the profits (and losses) of the business, in which they've all invested. Partnerships often are chosen for tax reasons, because the vehicle does not incur any tax on its profits before they're distributed to its partners (i.e. there is no equivalent of corporation tax). Overall, a partnership is a relatively simple way for you, along with one or more others, to own and run a business together.

Business planning

23–15 The advice is the same as per sole traders (see above).

Formation

23–16 If you want to set up a partnership, there is no formal process of incorporation to follow and also no form filling to be done. Quite simply, you become a partner of a partnership when you, together with one or more people, come together and start to trade with a view to making a profit (we'll look at this in a little more detail shortly). You still need to know exactly when you start trading, however, because HMRC will need this information.

When does a partnership exist?

23–17 The essential elements of a legal partnership are that it must:

- have more than one person;
- carry on a business; and
- have a profit motive.

In other words, you can't have a partnership all by yourself (although nowadays, conversely, there is no upper limit to the number of partners that you can have). You also have to be working towards making a profit. A charity, thus, can't be a partnership.

There's no requirement to have a formal partnership agreement. However, unless an agreement is in place, it makes working out when exactly your partnership comes into existence rather difficult and, generally speaking, not having one is considered to be undesirable. Ultimately, whether there is a partnership is established by reference to the legal test set down in s.2 of the Partnership Act 1890.

1. An interest (either joint or common) in property does not create a partnership (so, owning a flat with your partner, husband or wife) does not create a partnership).
2. Sharing gross returns doesn't create a partnership (you need to have made a profit).
3. Sharing of net profits is evidence of partnership (subject to some exceptions).

Or, if you share your net profit with one or other people, this is evidence of the existence of a partnership.

Before you start

If you're thinking of going into business with someone, then you need to think things over carefully. You won't be a sole trader making all your own decisions and controlling your own destiny. As we saw in Ch.4, a rogue partner can bring down a global business. It pays dividends to research your proposed business partner(s). For example, you might instruct a search via Experian or Equifax, to see if they've good credit. It's also worth a general internet search, as this can throw up a wealth of information. If your proposed partner also is (or has been) a company director, search Companies House and download their latest company accounts. How well are they doing in their other ventures? Ask around also; it's amazing what your friends and colleagues might know. In other words, go into any partnership with your eyes (and ears) open. **23–18**

Business name

You need to choose a sensible name for your partnership, and the general advice is the same as for sole traders. There is no central register of partnership names and no requirement to register your name. However, it's still a good idea to check the internet, domain name registries, phone books, trade journals and the trademarks registry to see if any other business is already using your proposed name. **23–19**

While company names can be checked at Companies House with ease, it's much more difficult to check on partnerships, so the sorts of searches suggested are essential. If your preferred name appears to be available, you should lodge details with a solicitor to establish the date from which you commenced using it, in case this is challenged at a later date. Your trading name can be a combination of your partners' surnames, or you can use a non-personal name (i.e. a business name). Once again, if you do decide to use a business name, you and your partners' personal details nonetheless must be disclosed to your clients and suppliers (in the same way as per sole traders). This rule also applies if your firm's name includes your surname and your partners' surnames, but also with other words (for example, "Sim and Todd Legal Services").

In the interests of practicality, however, the requirement does not apply if your firm has more than 20 partners, subject to:

- a list of the names of your partners being maintained at your principal place of business;
- none of your partners' names appearing in documents (except in the text or as signatories);
- all your documents state clearly your principal business address (and that the list of your partners' names can be inspected there); and
- the list being available for inspection during office hours.

If your firm uses a business name (i.e. it does not trade under the names of the partners), it must also conform to Pt 41 of the Companies Act 2006. This says that you can't use a business name if:

- its use would be a criminal offence;
- it includes words and abbreviations that denote a particular type of business, if the business is not in fact of that type—this include things like

"limited", "public limited company" and so on (clearly your firm cannot be a limited company or a Plc);
- it suggests a connection with the Scottish or UK Governments;
- it suggests a connection with a local authority or a specified public authority;
- it includes a sensitive word or expression (without the approval of the Secretary of State).[4]

Finally, the common law rule of passing off applies to partnership names, in exactly the same way as for sole traders (see Ch.25 (how to manage your firm's intellectual property) for more on passing off).

Key features

23–20 To an extent, a partnership is recognised as being independent. Unlike you as a sole trader, it has what is termed "quasi" separate personality. As such, your firm can:

- enter into contracts;
- sue or be sued;
- be declared bankrupt;
- own property in its own name.

Unlike a company's shareholders, you and your fellow partners are still liable for all the debts of your partnership, jointly and severally. This means that if one partner can't contribute to expunging your firm's debts, you and your other partners must bear his or her share. Once again, your liability is unlimited.

Let's look at some of the other key features of partnerships.

- Your business is easy to start—you simply commence trading.
- Your partners bring a variety of skills and ideas to the table.
- Decision making can be easier, with more people to work to solve problems.
- You share responsibilities and duties, so the burden does not rest on just your shoulders.
- With a division of labour, your working hours should be less (and holidays easier to arrange).
- Pooled resources give you a marketing clout that rivals established big players.
- Growth potential is better because equity (in the form of a partnership share) can be offered to potential investors.
- Law Society regulatory matters are dealt with by a bigger team.
- There is no need to deal with CPD training by yourself.
- No public filing of accounts is required, so you can keep all your key financial information private from your competitors.

In other words, partnerships retain a lot of what is good about being a sole trader, but also deal with some of the negatives that come with that vehicle. There are some other disadvantages.

[4] See ss.54 and 1194 of the Companies Act 2006.

- Unlimited liability means you technically can be forced to sell your personal assets to cover the partnership's debts.
- There is greater scope for management disputes to arise, among partners, which clearly can lead to problems.
- Growth options are not as flexible as with limited companies.
- There is no continuity of existence; your partnership actually dissolves if one partner dies, resigns or becomes bankrupt (unless you've a partnership agreement in place that specifically exempts you from this rule).

Partnership agreement

Before starting up, it's clearly advisable that you and your new business partners should sign a comprehensive partnership agreement. A typical agreement contains the following: **23–21**

1. names of all your partners;
2. commencement date;
3. duration of the partnership;
4. business to be carried out (exactly what your firm will do);
5. firm name (and importantly who owns that name);
6. initial investments (how much each partner will invest);
7. division of profits and losses (what proportion of the profits each partner will receive, and the proportion of the losses each partner will bear); and
8. provisions regarding the winding up of the business.

As regards point seven, the normal starting point is that all profits and losses are divided equally. However, that might not be fair, if some partners contribute more capital than others. Any inequity can be dealt with easily. One option is to have different grades of partner (equity and non-equity/salaried), with only your equity partners sharing the net profit.

As regards point eight, the usual options are: assets are converted to cash and divided among the partners (in proportion); one partner purchases the others' shares at value; or the assets are not sold, but simply divided among the partners.

Your partnership agreement is also a useful way of dealing with what can be major disagreements, namely how new partners are assumed and how existing partners might be removed (e.g. if they under perform, or are guilty of some misdemeanour). In addition, it also sets out what should happen if one of your partners simply wishes to leave, and move on to pastures new. In this scenario, a well-drafted agreement might contain a so-called restrictive covenant clause. This has the effect of preventing your departing partner from participating in a similar business, within a certain geographical proximity and for a particular period. You've got to tread with care, however, because although these clauses are enforceable, if the terms are too onerous they can be struck down as anti-competitive.

Compliance

As per sole traders, there are no special rules for ongoing compliance, bar the requirement to prepare annual accounts for HMRC and to pay whatever personal tax you owe (but see further, below). As regards the Law Society, you and your partners need to hold full practising certificates, there needs to be personal **23–22** indemnity insurance in place and your firm needs to pay into the master policy. Once again, you all need to fulfil certain regulatory roles and deal with your ongoing CPD requirements.

Tax

23–23 As a partner of a partnership you pay personal income tax on your share of the partnership's net profit (your so-called drawings). In other words, you're treated as if you're self-employed, and so you pay Schedule D tax.

You must fill in a self-assessment tax return each year, detailing your income (which in this case is your share of the net profit) and any expenses that are incurred in running the business. You still need to register as self-employed with HMRC as soon as you start to trade, and the same penalty rule applies as for sole traders. The current rates of personal income tax are set out in Ch.20 (how to speak to clients about finance).

In addition to paying your own personal tax, you need to register your partnership with HMRC and submit a partnership tax return. This is the case even though your firm (unlike limited companies) doesn't actually pay any "partnership tax". In fact, it's really a way for HMRC to understand who the partners of your firm are, what your firm earns and what each partner draws from the business. In turn, it knows what to anticipate in your fellow partners' personal income tax returns. You need to appoint a nominated partner whose job it is to manage your firm's relationship with HMRC. That partner also must send HMRC your partnership return.

If your firm has (or expects to have) a turnover exceeding £83,000 per year, you also need to apply for a VAT number, and then charge VAT to your clients, complete VAT returns and send VAT payments to HMRC. As per sole traders, you also can voluntarily register for VAT. Remember, this has the merit of enabling you to reclaim all the VAT you pay out (input tax) against the VAT you charge your clients (output tax), and it can help make you look more professional in the eyes of your clients.

The same rules that apply to sole traders as regards NICs (both Classes 2 and 4) apply equally to all the partners of your firm. The same rates and thresholds apply also.

Other

23–24 The need to be aware of the requirement for local authority licences applies to partnerships as much as it does to sole traders.

Summary advantages and disadvantages

Advantages

23–25
- No regulatory hurdles for start-up.
- Still able to be nimble in response to opportunities and market changes (but perhaps depending on size).
- Multiple partners bring greater skills and knowledge base.
- Shared responsibilities and duties.
- Decision making can be easier.
- Growth potential is better, making it easier to expand.
- More economic strength.
- Division of labour can mean shorter hours.

- Little ongoing regulation apart from annual tax returns.
- Easier to deal with Law Society and CPD requirements.
- Privacy from competitors as accounts are not published on public registers.

Disadvantages

- Greater amount of capital is required to start-up (when compared to sole traders). **23–26**
- Disagreements among partners can lead to problems.
- Unlimited personal liability for business obligations and debts.
- Still not as flexible as limited companies in terms of growth options.
- No continuity of existence (unless provided for in partnership agreement).

Limited liability partnerships (LLPs)

The basics

Over time (and with some hard work), the number of partners in your firm will increase. That indicates real growth. However, it also comes with associated risk; can you trust each and every partner not to make a mistake that could cost you a lot of money via joint and several liabilities? One solution is to set up an LLP, or to convert your existing ordinary partnership to an LLP. **23–27**

The LLP is a relatively new vehicle in the UK, first introduced in 2000 by the Limited Liability Partnerships Act of that year. It's an entirely separate legal entity. If you choose this vehicle, your firm can:

- enter into contracts;
- sue or be sued;
- be declared bankrupt; and
- own property in its own name.

However, unlike ordinary partnerships, this is no "halfway house"; LLPs have full separate legal personality and you, as its owners, enjoy limited liability. This limited liability protects you from losing your personal assets if your firm goes under.

Business planning

The advice is the same as per sole traders (see above). **23–28**

Formation

If you want to set up an LLP, there is a formal process of incorporation that you must follow (we'll look at this in a little more detail shortly). With this vehicle, things are a little more involved, however, compared with the sole trader and ordinary partnership vehicles. **23–29**

Essential elements

Section 2(1)(a) of the Limited Liability Partnerships Act 2000 says an LLP must have ". . . two or more persons associated for carrying on lawful business with a view to profit". **23–30**

In other words, you can't have an LLP by yourself (though there is no upper limit to the number of partners that you can have) and, once again, the requirement to have a profit motive would exclude a charity from using the vehicle. In addition, your LLP can't be set up and then just left dormant, as this would—by definition—be incompatible with the requirement to "carry on lawful business with a view to profit". This doesn't mean, however, that your LLP can't be dormant for a short while (e.g. due to the retirement of older partners and an influx of new partners).

Before you start

23–31 The same guidance applies, as for ordinary partnerships.

Business name

23–32 As always, you need to choose a good name, and the general advice is the same as for sole traders and ordinary partnerships. However, for LLPs there is also the central registry held at Companies House, and the requirement to register your name. Your LLP can't have a name to conflict with an existing entry on the register. Beyond that, you're largely free to choose as you please. However, the registrar will not register any name which is offensive or which would constitute a criminal offence.

Just as with partnerships, if your proposed name implies a connection with government or if it contains a so-called "controlled word", it can only be registered with the approval of the Secretary of State. Controlled words are words that are deemed sensitive by the Secretary of State. The Secretary of State also can order your LLP to change its name within 12 months of registration, either if an objection is made by an existing LLP (or a company) or, if in his opinion, it's too similar to a name already on the index. That being said, the registrar is unlikely to take proactive steps unless some sort of objection is received. As always, it's open to any business to raise a "passing off" action against your firm, if it feels that its rights are infringed.

Before filing in your application to start your LLP, it's vital to search the Companies House register of names. It's also a good idea to check the internet, domain name registries, phone books, trade journals and the trademarks registry to see if any other business is already using your proposed name.

Members

23–33 You must have at least two so-called "designated members", at all times. They have extra responsibilities, including keeping the firm's accounts. You can have any number of ordinary members, however.

Forms

23–34 To get going, you need to fill in Form LL IN01. LL IN01 contains details about your members (i.e. your partners) and your firm's registered office. Under s.2 of the Limited Liability Partnerships Act 2000, a registration agent then submits all your incorporation documents to Companies House.

Companies House is the body responsible for: incorporation, re-registration, striking-off, and the registration of all documents required to be delivered under the Act. Registration is complete only when Companies House issues a Certificate of Incorporation. This is basically your LLP's birth certificate and bears the name of your firm, the date of incorporation and its registration number. Once your LLP is incorporated it's normal practice for your registration agent then to supply (in addition to the Certificate of Incorporation) a set of books including statutory and non-statutory registers, which are:

- Register of Members (not statutory).
- Register of Debenture Holders.
- Register of Charges Minute Book.

These registers are used to record information about the names and addresses of your members, and details of any and all capital contributions made.

Your statutory books must be kept up to date. Your company registration agent or an accountant, solicitor or professional advisor may take on this responsibility, on your behalf. Financial penalties can be imposed on you and your fellow partners for non-compliance. Keep in mind it's the members of an LLP who are penalised for non-compliance; you can't blame your accountant, solicitor or professional advisor.

The conversion of an ordinary partnership into an LLP is also a relatively easy process, with the assets owned by you and your partners simply being transferred to a new LLP, with you then becoming members of that firm.

Key features

LLPs enjoy all the general advantages of ordinary partnerships, so we won't list them again. The vehicle also addresses most of the downsides of operating either as a sole trader or an ordinary partnership. In particular, you and your fellow partners are not liable for the debts of your firm. In other words, you enjoy limited liability (to an agreed amount). The other key point is that because your LLP has full legal personality, it has what's termed "perpetual succession". In other words, it doesn't dissolve upon the death or bankruptcy of any partner. **23–35**

Let's look at some of the other key features of LLPs.

1. Decision making can be easier, with more people to work to solve problems but also with the pressure of unlimited liability lifted from your shoulders.
2. Generally greater resources can give you even more marketing clout than ordinary partnerships and sole traders.
3. Growth potential is arguably better than for ordinary partnerships (due to limited liability and perpetual succession).

There are some other disadvantages.

1. Your business is a little more complicated to start—you've to go through a registration process with Companies House.
2. There is still scope for management disputes to arise, among partners, which clearly can lead to problems.
3. Growth options are arguably still not as flexible as with limited companies.
4. Public filing of accounts is required, so you unfortunately cannot keep your key financial information private from your competitors.

LLP agreement

23–36 Before starting, it's again clearly advisable that you and your new business partners sign a comprehensive partnership agreement. A typical LLP agreement sets out the powers of the LLP and also all the rules regulating its members' actions.

Your agreement (which incidentally isn't mandatory) should contain:

1. the name of your LLP (and who owns that name);
2. the names of all your partners (members);
3. the minimum and maximum number of members;
4. duties of members;
5. the address of your registered office;
6. the business activities of your LLP;
7. a procedure for appointing new members;
8. a procedure to remove problem members;
9. a procedure to deal with partners who die (including returning their capital);
10. the initial investments (how much each partner will invest);
11. the distribution of profit;
12. the contributions to the debts of the LLP on winding up;
13. a date for commencement of the agreement;
14. restrictions on members regarding competition and confidentiality;
15. provisions about insurance and pensions;
16. a procedure for issuing notices to members;
17. procedures at meetings; and
18. detail of partners' voting rights.

As regards profits and losses, the usual starting point is equal sharing. However, once again, any imbalance can be dealt with by having equity and non-equity/salaried partners, with only your equity partners sharing the net profit (and contributing to any losses on winding up). Again, your agreement is the best way to deal with: the assumption of new partners; determining how existing partners might be removed; and the distribution of assets (and division of any losses) upon winding up. In addition, it can set out what happens if one of your partners simply wishes to leave (including a well-drafted restrictive covenant clause, which we discussed earlier).

If you don't have a partnership agreement, the Limited Liability Partnerships Act 2000 acts in a similar way to the Partnership Act 1890 (for ordinary partnerships) and various default provisions apply, which may not be suitable to your firm.

Rule D5

23–37 Rule D5.2 of the Law Society's Consolidated Practice Rules 2011,[5] imposes some additional restrictions you need to be aware of. If you intend to trade as a body corporate (that is to say, an LLP), your firm must be recognised by the

[5] The Law Society of Scotland Practice Rules 2011 r.D5: Incorporated Practices. Available at *http://www.lawscot.org.uk/rules-and-guidance/section-d-requirements-of-and-restrictions-on-practice/rule-d5-incorporated-practices/rules/d5-incorporated-practices/* [Accessed 19 April 2016].

Council of the Law Society as an "incorporated practice". Control (and membership) of your firm must be exclusively limited to solicitors, firms of solicitors, registered European lawyers, registered foreign lawyers or other incorporated practices. Your registered office must be situated in Scotland. To form an incorporated practice you must (at least one month prior to starting business as such) submit:

- the names, designations and business addresses of your members;
- your proposed firm name;
- the address of your registered office;
- application form and fee;
- a draft of your LLP incorporation document; and
- an undertaking to the Council (in prescribed form).

Compliance

As per sole traders and ordinary partnerships, you're required to prepare annual **23–38** accounts for HMRC and to pay whatever personal tax you owe (see further below).

As regards the Law Society, you and your partners again need to hold full practising certificates, there needs to be personal indemnity insurance in place, and your firm needs to pay into the master policy. And you all need to fulfil certain regulatory roles and deal with your ongoing CPD requirements.

Compliance for an LLP, however, is a little more involved. Every year, your firm must prepare and submit to Companies House a summary of its current members (together with a filing fee). Your first so-called "Annual Return" normally will be due on the anniversary of your firm's incorporation. Companies House does send a reminder, which contains information taken from the public record. This must be checked for accuracy, signed by a member of the LLP and returned to Companies House within 28 days of the date of the return.

Tax

An LLP is transparent for tax purposes and no corporation tax is payable. **23–39**

As a partner of an LLP, you pay personal income tax on your share of the partnership's net profit (your drawings). In other words, you're treated like partners of ordinary partnerships and you pay Schedule D tax. Once again, you've to fill in a self-assessment tax return each year, detailing your income (your share of the net profit) and the expenses that are incurred in running the business. You still need to register as self-employed with HMRC as soon as you start to trade, as the same penalty rule applies. The current rates of personal income tax are set out in Ch.20 (how to speak to clients about finance).

In addition to paying your own personal tax, your firm needs to submit a tax return. This is the case even though your firm (unlike limited companies) doesn't actually pay any "LLP tax". You also have an obligation to publish your accounts via Companies House. However, if your LLP is small, it can file abbreviated accounts (which don't contain a full balance sheet and profit and loss account). The same rules about VAT apply, as they do to ordinary partnerships. Finally, the same rules that apply to sole traders and ordinary partners as regards NICs (both Classes 2 and 4) apply equally to all the partners of your LLP. The same rates and thresholds apply also.

Other

23–40 The need to be aware of the requirement for local authority licences applies to your LLP as much as it does to sole traders and ordinary partnerships.

Advantages and disadvantages

Advantages

23–41
- Full separate legal personality (with limited liability for members).
- Perpetual succession.
- Decision making can be easier, with more people to work to solve problems but also with the pressure of unlimited liability lifted from your shoulders.
- Multiple partners bring greater skills and knowledge base.
- Growth potential is better (arguably) than ordinary partnerships.
- More economic strength (arguably) than ordinary partnerships.

Disadvantages

23–42
- Formal process of incorporation.
- Greater ongoing compliance (with Annual Return).
- Greater amount of capital is required to start up (when compared to ordinary partnerships).
- Still scope for management disputes to arise.
- Still not as flexible as limited companies in terms of growth options.
- No privacy of key financial information from your competitors.

Limited companies

The basics

23–43 The final vehicle we're going to look at is the limited company. At the start of 2013, there were 1.4 million limited companies in the UK, with about 56% employing staff. This means that there are around 600,000 "one-man-band" limited companies in the UK.[6] It's worth noting that a proportion of these 600,000 companies may be in a dormant state (i.e. not actively trading). Limited companies are regulated under the Companies Act 2006. A limited company is also an entirely separate legal entity. If you choose this vehicle, your company can:

- enter into contracts;
- sue or be sued;
- be declared bankrupt;
- own property in its own name.

With full separate legal personality again comes limited liability for you and your fellow owners (shareholders), this time capped at the amount unpaid on your shares.

---

[6] Figure comes from evidence lead before the House of Lords: "Select Committee on Personal Service Companies Oral and Written Evidence" *https://www.parliament.uk/documents/lords-committees/Personal-Service-Companies/personalservicecompaniesevvolume.pdf* (at p. 170) (30 December 2013) [Accessed: 15 June 2016].

Business planning

The advice is the same as per all the other vehicles we've looked at (see above). **23–44**

Formation

Before you start

The same considerations apply. If you're going to go into business with someone then you need to think carefully. It pays dividends (literally, in the case of a company) to do research on your proposed new business partners. We gave you some suggestions as to how you might do this in the section on ordinary partnerships. **23–45**

Promoters

To set up your limited company you need a promoter. This is the person who carries out all the preliminary activities. There is no legal definition, but there is common law guidance. A promoter is: **23–46**

> ". . . One who undertakes to form a company with reference to a given project and get it going, and who undertakes the necessary steps to accomplish that purpose".[7]

Promoters owe fiduciary duties (good faith duties) to your new company and any profit they make (or interest they might have in a transaction e.g. commission deals) must be disclosed.[8]

Pre-incorporation contracts

What happens if your promoter tries to enter into contracts before your company is fully incorporated? They might, for example, want to make sure certain practical and logistical matters are bottomed out, so that your company can "hit the ground running". For example, they might try and conclude a lease, enter a utilities agreement, and so on. If your company isn't incorporated, however, it has no capacity to contract. In this scenario, your promoter is personally liable on the contract.[9] What's the work-around? **23–47**

There are three solutions. Your promoter can:

1. prepare a draft contract for your company to enter into, after incorporation;
2. enter into a binding contract and then change ("novate") that contract, after incorporation, with the consent of the third party, such that a new contract (on the same terms) is entered into between that third party and your company; or
3. enter into a binding contract and then transfer only the benefit to the company, in exchange for the company's agreement to indemnify the promoter in respect of his or her liability to the third party.

---

[7] *Twycross v Grant* (1877) 2 C.P.D. 469.
[8] *Gluckstein v Barnes* [1900] A.C. 240.
[9] Companies Act 2006 s.51.

Registration

23–48 What is the process by which your company becomes incorporated? First, your promoter has to submit several documents to Companies House.

1. Memorandum of Association.
2. Articles of Association.
3. A statement of compliance with formalities.
4. The registrar's fee.

The Memorandum of Association is simply a document (in prescribed form) that states that those who subscribe it seek to form a company. It has to include five things:

1. your company's name;
2. your registered address (to determine domicile);
3. your business objects;
4. whether your company is private limited or a Plc; and
5. details of its share capital.

The Articles of Association, quite simply, is your company's constitution, and regulates its day-to-day operations. If you don't submit articles, Companies House will give you model articles (which may—or may not—be suitable for your company).[10] The registrar must be satisfied that your company has complied with all the provisions of the Companies Act 2006. The objects clause must demonstrate that your company is being formed for a lawful purpose. If not, your registration may be refused.[11] Upon registration, a Certificate of Incorporation is issued and—at that point—those who signed the Memorandum are members of a "... body corporate ... capable of exercising all the functions of the incorporated company".[12] Your Certificate of Incorporation is conclusive evidence of compliance with the Companies Act 2006 during the incorporation process.[13]

Business name

23–49 The same general advice (provided elsewhere in this chapter) applies equally to companies. There is—largely—freedom of choice, but you can't have the same name as an existing registered company. Some names are barred by the Companies Act 2006, and the Secretary of State has the right to demand that you change your company's name if it is misleading, too similar, is offensive or amounts to a criminal offence. You're not allowed to choose a name that suggests a connection with government and (as with LLPs) certain names require the permission of the Secretary of State. Finally, the rules of "passing off" apply to companies.

Members

23–50 Your new company needs at least one member (i.e. one shareholder) and at least one director (an individual) to run it. Directors must be aged 16 years or over, but

---

[10] The Companies (Model Articles) Regulations 2008 (SI 2008/3229) Schs 1 to 3.
[11] *Attorney General v Lindi St Clair (Personal Services) Ltd* (1981) 2 Co Law Rev 69.
[12] Companies Act 2006 s.16.
[13] Companies Act 2006 s.15(4).

there is no upper age limit. Neither undischarged bankrupts nor disqualified persons can act as a director. It's normal practice to have a director's service agreement (a contract) between your company and each person who serves as a director.

Forms

To set up your limited company, you need to fill in Form IN01. IN01 contains, among many other things (over 18 pages): **23–51**

- your proposed company name (including a declaration on sensitive words);
- the location of your registered office;
- a choice of three options for your articles (model, model with amendments, bespoke);
- details of your proposed officers (including directors);
- a statement of capital;
- the initial shareholdings;
- a statement of compliance.

Registration is complete only when Companies House issues a Certificate of Incorporation (bearing its name, date of incorporation and registration number).

Key features

Limited companies arguably enjoy all the tactical and human resource benefits of LLPs. As you know, they also have separate legal personality and you and your fellow shareholders enjoy limited liability (to the extent of the amount unpaid on your shares). **23–52**

Let's look at some of the other key features of limited companies.

1. Your company has perpetual succession.
2. Your business is a little more complicated to start—you've to go through a registration process with Companies House.
3. Decision making can be easier, with more people to work to solve problems but also with the pressure of unlimited liability lifted from your shoulders.
4. Generally greater resources can give you even more marketing clout than ordinary partnerships and sole traders.
5. Growth potential is arguably the best of all vehicles, with investors able to take shares (while not taking on any operational responsibilities as a director).

There are some other disadvantages.

1. There is still scope for management disputes to arise, which can lead to problems (especially if the directors are not the same persons as the shareholders).
2. There is more complicated ongoing compliance.
3. Public filing of accounts is required, so you unfortunately can't keep your key financial information private from your competitors.

Rule D5

23–53 Rule D5 of the Law Society's Consolidated Practice Rules 2011, again imposes additional restrictions you need to be aware of. If you intend to trade as a body corporate (that is to say, a company, in this instance) your firm must be recognised by the Council of the Law Society as an "incorporated practice". The same criteria and approach, as per LLPs, apply (and these are covered earlier in this chapter).

Compliance

23–54 As per sole traders, ordinary partnerships and LLPs, you're required to prepare your own annual accounts for HMRC and to pay whatever personal income tax you owe (see further below). As regards the Law Society, you and your partners —as directors—again need to hold full practising certificates, there needs to be personal indemnity insurance in place and your firm needs to pay into the master policy. And you all need to fulfil certain regulatory roles and deal with your ongoing CPD requirements.

Every year, your limited company must prepare and submit to Companies House a summary of its current members (together with a filing fee), called an Annual Return. Your first return normally will be due on the anniversary of incorporation. Companies House does send a reminder, which contains information taken from the public record. This must be checked for accuracy, signed by a director and returned to Companies House within 28 days of the date of the return. It can be completed online.

Tax

23–55 Your company is taxed under a separate tax structure called corporation tax. In addition, all your shareholders are charged tax on dividends (the amounts paid to them from the company's net distributable profits). For this reason (the "double charge" to tax), limited companies are not considered to be tax transparent. The current rate of corporation tax is set out in Ch.20 (how to speak to clients about finance).

As regards dividends, as of April 2016 a £5,000 tax-free dividend allowance was introduced. Dividends above this level are taxed at 7.5% (basic rate), 32.5% (higher rate) and 38.1% (additional rate). To declare your dividends, you have to fill in a self-assessment tax return each year.

Directors also are usually paid a salary. This is paid under the PAYE (Schedule E) scheme. Any such salary is liable for personal income tax (deducted at source). You also pay Class 1 NI (if you earn more than £155 per week) at a rate of 12%. The company also has to pay Employers' NI, at a rate of 13.8%. The same rules about VAT apply to limited companies. The guidance we've given, earlier, thus remains the same. Lastly, your company's accounts must be filed at Companies House; thus there is no privacy of information.

Other

23–56 The need to be aware of the requirement for local authority licences applies to your company as much as it does to sole traders and ordinary partnerships.

Summary advantages and disadvantages

Advantages

- Full separate legal personality (with limited liability for members). **23–57**
- Perpetual succession.
- Decision making can be easier, with more people to work to solve problems (but also with the pressure of unlimited liability lifted).
- Multiple members/directors bring greater skills and knowledge base.
- Growth potential is arguably the best of all the vehicles.

Disadvantages

- Formal process of incorporation. **23–58**
- Greater ongoing compliance (with Annual Return).
- Greater amount of capital is required to start up (when compared to partnerships).
- Still scope for management disputes to arise.
- You can't keep your key financial information private from your competitors.

Summary

Knowing the differences between different business vehicles and the advantages **23–59** and disadvantages of each will help you decide how to run and manage your own business. It'll also help you understand how your clients run their businesses as they'll be faced with similar choices. Should they set up as a sole trader? Do the need the protection of a limited company? The choice you and they make will help shape what you and they can do and how they can do it.

CHAPTER 24

HOW TO MANAGE RISKS

Introduction

24–1 *Ten years qualified. You've missed your alarm and you've slept in by a whole hour. You tumble out of bed and rush to the shower. You don't check the temperature of the water before you jump in. You might not realise it, but actually you've just taken a risk.*

Fifteen minutes later, you're running to catch the train but arrive at the station to see it disappearing into the distance. You decide to drive instead.

You know that you're going to struggle to make it through the rush hour traffic in time for your 8.30am team meeting, so you text your colleague (all the while doing 45mph in a 30mph zone); more risk.

You get to the office. It's still only 8.15am—you've made it. However, you've been lucky. You could have had an accident. You could have been caught by the police and charged with speeding or using a phone while driving. You could have lost your licence or—worse still—your liberty. You swear you won't ever do any of these things again. You should know better. You're a senior lawyer. However, even as you promise you're going to change, you know this will happen again. Doesn't everyone check their phone or breach the speed limit now and again?

24–2 This chapter is all about risk management. Already, from this simple scenario, you can appreciate that your personal life is full of risk. Some are inherent (for example, the risk of scalding as you jump in the shower); others are man-made (for example, driving over the speed limit). However, risk doesn't stop there. It also affects your professional life in a number of ways. You're exposed all the time to the risks that flow from dealing with new clients and new retainers (for example, money laundering). Going back to our scenario, your personal actions can expose you to ethical risk (for example, a driving conviction could be a matter for the Discipline Tribunal). Your firm, also, is exposed to risk (for example, the risk of flood damage, data loss and staffing issues).

In all cases, risks can be identified, assessed and mitigated. This becomes more important as you rise through the ranks. As a trainee (or new lawyer), you're heavily supervised. As you gain experience, however, you become the supervisor. Ultimately, you could manage your own teams, departments or even the entire firm. You need to understand the risks that you and your team face, so that you can plan ahead. Imagine, for a second, you're the partner of the lawyer in our scenario. Imagine your senior associate hasn't come to work that morning and let's say that lawyer had been due to attend court. What do you do? Risk management is all about assessing what might happen, so that you can plan ahead.

Outcomes

In this chapter we examine what we mean by "risk". We review different ways to identify risks and manage them appropriately. We then look at a number of management theories, illustrated by examples of common legal risks. **24–3**

What is risk and risk management?

Let's start with some theory. **24–4**

What is risk?

Broadly speaking, risk is the possibility that something bad or unpleasant (such as injury or loss) will occur. If you advise a client to sue a competitor, there's a risk they might lose and have to pay costs. If you review a title deed and your client then buys the property based on your advice, there is a risk that you could be wrong and they might complain to the Scottish Legal Complaints Commission (SLCC). If you leave the house in the morning, there's a risk that a car might hit you. Risks are all around you; you can't avoid them. Instead, what matters is that you understand how to identify risks, how to measure them (the likelihood that a particular risk will materialise), how to estimate their impact on you (and your firm), and how to develop appropriate responses. For example, you can tell a client that court actions aren't always successful. You have professional indemnity insurance to cover you if you make a mistake. You have the Highway Code and the police to protect you when you walk down the street. Risks can be managed. **24–5**

What is risk management?

Risk management is defined as "[t]he identification, analysis, assessment, control and avoidance, minimisation or elimination of unacceptable risks."[1] Note that this definition refers to *unacceptable* risks. There are then, by definition, acceptable risks. You take acceptable risks every day. Every time you write an email to a client giving them advice, for example, you're taking a risk. However, you tend not to think about it in that context, because it's just part of your job. **24–6**

However, sometimes you might draft an email, acutely aware that the advice within is going to have a huge impact on your client. You swither about pressing "send", and so you seek a second opinion from a colleague. In other words, an everyday acceptable risk has become unacceptable. However, by speaking to others and getting that second opinion, you've managed the risk and it falls within the parameters of what is acceptable. You can go ahead and send it.

You can always avoid an unacceptable risk simply by not doing something. As you will appreciate from Ch.6 (how to open files) there might be circumstances in which this would be a perfectly acceptable strategy. For instance, you might assess that a particular client (or matter) that you're asked to accept is replete with risks that can't be mitigated to an acceptable degree. For example, you might decide that a politically exposed person asking you to deal with a complex corporate structure in a non-European Economic Area jurisdiction is just too risky, and decline the instruction. However, if you were to adopt that approach to every risk,

---

1 Definition from *Businessdictionary.com, http://www.businessdictionary.com/definition/risk-management.html* [Accessed 19 April 2016].

your firm would cease to trade. You'd never send an email. You'd never speak to a client. You would do nothing. How do you manage risks effectively? How do you mitigate unacceptable risks so that they become acceptable?

Effective management

24–7 Let's consider some theory again. Effective risk management involves ". . . risk assumption, risk avoidance, risk retention, risk transfer, or any other strategy (or combination of strategies) in proper management of future events."[2] We look at risk assumption, avoidance, retention and transfer later on. However, these all pre-suppose that you have some sort of strategy. The International Organisation for Standardisation (ISO) has identified a number of principles[3] that underpin every good risk management strategy:

Create value

24–8 The value principle says that the resources you invest in dealing with a risk ought to be less than the consequences that would flow from inaction. In other words, the gain should exceed the pain. A famous example is the RMS Titanic. When the Titanic was built, her designers decided that to save deck space they would forego lifeboats for all the passengers. Since the ship had a double hull, the White Star Line proclaimed her "unsinkable". In this case, the consequences transpired to far outweigh the cost of installing enough lifeboats. With the benefit of 20/20 hind-sight, a different decision would have been taken.

Organisational ethos

24–9 The ethos principle says that your strategy needs to be part of your firm's culture. Since your partners are the biggest influencers of a firm's ethos, by definition the strategy must be implemented at the top and then cascaded down. That's hard, because if you think about it, most firms are pyramid shaped, with a few partners at the top and more and more (increasingly junior) solicitors beneath them. The minority has to influence the vast majority.

A famous example is the sinking, in Zeebrugge 1987, of the Herald of Free Enterprise. Sir Barry Sheen, who conducted the subsequent public enquiry, concluded that the company had a "disease of sloppiness". Indeed, a request to put an indicator on the ship's bridge that would have shown the position of its bow doors had been rejected by management on the basis that it would be wasteful to spend money on equipment that effectively would show that employees had failed to do their job properly.

Integrated to decision making

24–10 Certain personalities (particularly narcissistic ones) tend to push boundaries and cut corners. Your firm's culture can also influence staff. For example, if there is enormous pressure of time (for instance, due to high billing targets), staff might tend not to assess risks as rigorously and diligently as otherwise they might.

---

2 Definition from *Businessdictionary.com, http://www.businessdictionary.com/definition/risk-management.html* [Accessed 19 April 2016].

3 ISO 31000:2009, *Risk management – Principles and guidelines*. Available at: *http://www.iso.org/iso/home/standards/iso31000.htm* [Accessed: 15 June 2016].

External factors can have the same effect. Financial downturns are the classic example, where staff become fixated on billing to the exclusion of all else.

Your risk assessment strategy needs to be integrated into your firm's internal processes, so that assessments are—in effect—compelled. For example, you might use an anti-money laundering (AML) system that won't let you record time against a client matter unless and until "red flags" are lifted by a central registrar. These only would be lifted upon verifying that all AML checks had, in fact, been completed.

Uncertainty and assumptions

You need to be clear about the assumptions (if any) that you apply to your risk **24–11** assessments. Are there any factors that you consider might make your assessments inherently uncertain? Alternatively, are you satisfied that your assessments are reasonably robust and accurate?

Systematic and structured

This is intuitive. Your risk assessment system needs to be structured in such a way **24–12** that anyone in your team can use it with ease. In addition, a structured system helps to ensure that the results it generates are (as far as possible) standardised, regardless of who is using it.

Best available information

Again, this is self-explanatory. You need to use the best information that you can lay **24–13** your hands on to make any risk assessment you undertake as accurate as it can be. Turning again to AML, there is a sound rationale for the old chestnut "know your client". If you know a client's personal and business circumstances, the retainer that he or she is asking you to accept easily can be assessed. If you don't know them at all, that assessment is—by definition—not based on as high quality information.

Customised

This is another intuitive point. Whatever system you choose must be able to be **24–14** customised to suit the particular circumstances of your assessments.

Human factors

Your system must take into account human factors. It shouldn't be susceptible to **24–15** short cuts. As we've mentioned already, some people are risk takers. If you know you've got someone who might push boundaries, your system needs to be designed to manage that personality.

Transparency

The transparency principle says that your system should be manifestly obvious. **24–16** Why? If something is manifestly obvious, you get the most buy-in from your team. Teams tend to be more reluctant to engage with something they regard as pointless red tape.

Responsive to change

This says that your system must be able to move with the times. For example, the **24–17** risk a particular client poses (or that a transaction poses) can evolve over time.

Something might start innocuously, but may change and give you cause for concern. Your system needs to be able to detect emerging risks.

Continual improvement

24–18 This is a straightforward, aspirational principle. You can't rest on your laurels.

Periodically re-assessed

24–19 Quite simply, the world (and the legal market) is ever changing. So, too, are the range and nature of possible risks. For example, with the web, the ways criminals can scam you are growing. Similarly, the risks of hacking (with its implications for client confidentiality and data loss) are rising. Finally, with each winter the risk of flooding seems to increase. Flooding can affect your firm's records, equipment and its ability to trade. Your risk assessments have to be reviewed so as to remain fit for purpose.

How do you identify risks?

24–20 Let's consider how risks can be identified. Risks, basically, are potential events that, if they happen, will cause you and your firm problems. Hindsight is no use (just ask the captain of the Titanic). Instead, you're trying to look into the future. There are two types of risk identification that can help you: source analysis and problem analysis.

Source analysis

24–21 With source analysis, you're looking at a bigger picture. You're looking at potential sources of risk, whether internal or external. An internal source of risk could be your employees, or even your clients. An external source might be the economy. With source analysis you're not identifying specific risks or specific problems. Instead, you're identifying the root of potential problems. As such, it's quite general.

Problem analysis

24–22 With problem analysis, you're taking out your microscope and examining particular problems that might arise. Again, these can be internal or external. However, they'll be much more specific than the broader brush of source analysis. Examples include a breach of confidentiality or an infraction of the AML regulations.

Outcome

24–23 Once the sources of risks are identified, the events that any particular source might trigger can be investigated. Similarly, once specific problems are highlighted, the events that can lead to a particular problem being precipitated can be examined.

Step 1: identify types of risks

24–24 Once you've chosen your general approach (whether source or problem analysis) you need to select a more specific formula to hone in on—and identify—risks. The formula you choose largely depends on your firm's corporate culture and prevailing industry norms. However, there are a number of common methods (all of which can be standardised by the use of templates). Let's look at some, before you do an exercise.

Objectives-based risk identification

This is where any events that endanger achieving your objectives are classed as risks. For example, your firm might have an objective of improving its fee income. Any event that might impede that (whether partially or completely, internally or externally) would be classed as a risk. An example might be clients not paying their fees; clearly that's an impediment to improving fee income. **24–25**

Scenario-based risk identification

In scenario analysis, different scenarios are envisioned. These are your alternative ways of achieving your objectives. Any event that triggers an alternative to your desired scenarios is classed as a risk. **24–26**

Taxonomy-based risk identification

Taxonomy-based risk identification is a breakdown of possible risk sources (a form of detailed source analysis). It's based on knowledge of best practices within an industry or profession. Using that knowledge, a questionnaire is compiled, and then your answers to those questions help you detect and uncover risks. **24–27**

Common-risk checking

Some industries (for instance, chemical engineering) have lists with known risks already available (developed in the light of experience). Each risk in the list can be checked for whether it might apply to a particular situation. **24–28**

Risk charting

This combines the above approaches, and displays risks graphically on a risk matrix. It's a hybrid of risk identification and risk assessment. We look at a risk matrix in just a short while. **24–29**

Risk identification exercise

What we want you to do is a simple exercise. This is about getting comfortable with the ISO principles and, secondly, having a go at some basic risk identification. **24–30**

When you're completing the exercise, reflect on the degree of risk management that you think might be commensurate with the risks that you identify. In other words, at one end of the spectrum will you use a sledgehammer to crack a nut, or (at the other) will you readily accept risks (even if they're identified by a rigorous process)?

Reflect, also, on your own appetite towards risk and give yourself a risk-score, out of 10 (with one meaning you're extremely risk averse and—at the opposite end—10 meaning that you're extremely relaxed about risk).

The "4 Cs" task

The task is called "4 Cs". You're going to do it in the context of planning a short trip away. Most people can relate to planning a trip. It's easy to do. **24–31**

1. Identify everything that you might want to pack for a two-mile walk in the Scottish country, on a warm day. Write your list on a post-it note.
2. Then consider:

    a. Costs—what will it cost you to take each item? Write this down on a separate post-it note.
    b. Consequences—what might the consequence be to you of not taking each item? Again, jot this down on a post-it.
    c. Context—keep in mind the context of the exercise (in this case a two-mile walk in the country). This is important; risk identification depends heavily on context. Relating that back to your work, a small rural firm might identify something as a risk that a large city firm might not.
    d. Choice—make your final choice as to what you will pack, based on an informed balance of cost versus consequences. Create a final, edited list on a post-it.

After you've completed the exercise, repeat it by changing the parameters (you could make it a 10-mile hike or a week-long trip to the mountains, in winter). What you find is that your lists get longer as you prepare for more and more eventualities.

One fascinating aspect relates to your personal risk-score. In a recent continuing professional development (CPD) training session, a group of five solicitors undertook this exercise. Each participant reflected on his/her appetite for risk and selected a personal risk-score. On the day, each of the cohort gave themselves either a "five" or "six". Yet, in the plenary, it transpired that each had made quite different choices about what he/she would pack. This illustrates how difficult it is to calibrate risk assessments.

Step 2: assess risks

Common legal risks

24–32 According to Marsh, who until 2016 were the insurers for the Law Society's master policy, the leading causes of claims include:

1. communication failures;
2. the failure to examine and/or report on documents;
3. delayed or missed time limits;
4. errors and/or omissions in drafting;
5. errors in law or incorrect advice;
6. fraud; and
7. a failure to generally identify risk for clients.

Other commonly reported issues include: reading confidential documents (or having conversations) in public places; using portable devices in such a way others can see your data; and losing documents.

Risk assessment

24–33 Once you've identified risks (such as those above) you then need to assess them as to the potential severity of their impact (generally negative, such as damage or loss) and also the probability of them actually occurring. If you take the example of an AML risk assessment, risk assessment is what you do once you've ingathered all the relevant information from your client, on a customer due diligence questionnaire. You're analysing that information and making an assessment of risk.

The potential severity of impact of any risk either can be easy to measure (for instance, the value of your firm's building if it's destroyed by fire) or it can be impossible to know, especially in cases where there is a low probability of occurrence (after all, if something has never happened, it's difficult to judge what its effect might be were it to arise in the future). There can be a real difficulty in determining occurrence, because statistical information is often not available for past incidents. After all, why would a business publicise things that have gone wrong? Best-educated opinions likely will be your primary sources of information. When trying to assess risk, a useful tool is the "risk magnitude" formula.

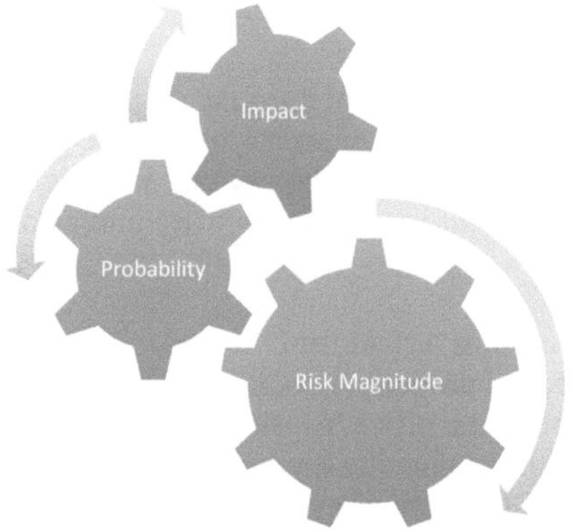

This gives you a magnitude score for each risk that you identify. You work it out by multiplying the rate (probability) of occurrence of an event, by its impact.

Probability is assessed on a scale from one to five, where one represents a low probability of the risk actually occurring, while five represents a high probability. Impact, likewise, is assessed on a scale of one to five, where one and five represent the minimum and maximum possible impact.

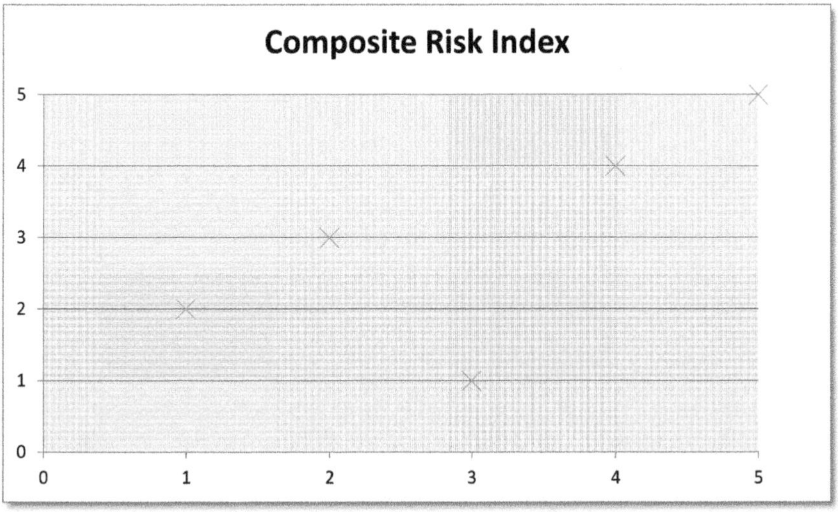

Once you've got a whole raft of risk magnitude scores, you can plot them on a chart called a composite risk index, which looks a bit like this:
As we've mentioned, impact can be impossible to predict if the rate of occurrence historically has been low. Probability, also, can be difficult to estimate, since historic data often is not readily available.

Keep in mind that your magnitude scores can change. For example, you might change a score because of the way a retainer evolves, or because of changes in the external business environment. This is why it's necessary to periodically re-assess your risk assessments and then either intensify or relax your mitigation measures, as necessary. If you think again, for a second, about AML, this is why you're asked to re-do your risk assessment of a client after a certain period and/or if your client is asking you to undertake intermittent transactions.

Risk assessment exercise

24–34 It's time for you to complete a second exercise. This time, you're going to assess impact and probability for a range of scenarios. You're going to plot them on the blank composite risk index (below). The exercise is designed to make you aware about the breadth of different risks that can arise and also to get you to start to assess risks.

1. A major client joins a rival firm.
2. Your commercial property associate is headhunted.
3. There is a fire in the office, causing it to burn to the ground.
4. A client file turns up on the train and the press find out.
5. A Law Society inspection reveals a £100,000 client account shortfall.
6. You're sued for £1 million due to registration issues in your conveyancing department.
7. Your server malfunctions and goes offline for two days.
8. A local property company defaults on a substantial fee owed to your firm.

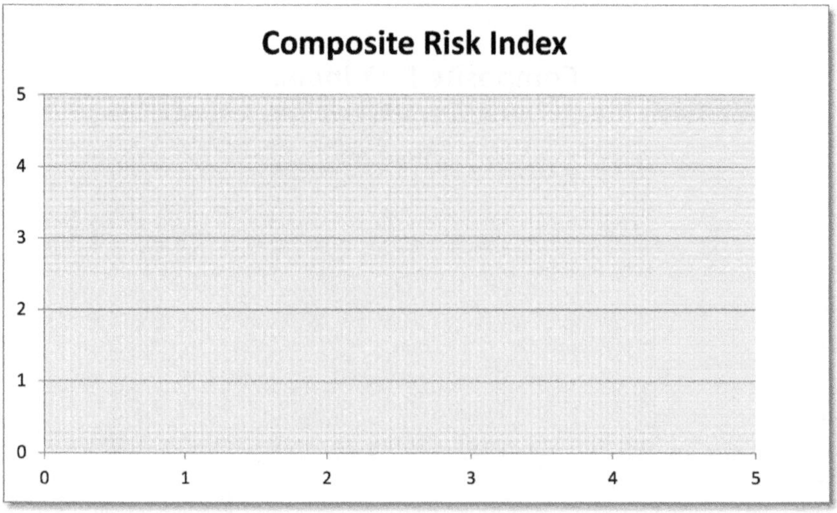

9. Your trainee is arrested for drink driving.
10. Your court assistant has posted offensive material on social media.

Step 3: deal with risks

Risk management options

The next thing you need to do is to work out how to manage the risks you identify and—then—whether you apply these management measures immediately, or above some sort of threshold. **24–35**

Risk management measures are usually formulated according to one or more of the following options:

- avoidance (withdraw from or don't become involved);
- reduction (mitigate);
- sharing (transfer); and
- retention (accept).

The ideal—or optimum—use of any of these strategies might not be possible. Some of them may involve trade-offs that simply are unacceptable to you or your firm. Let's look at each in turn.

Avoidance

This involves not performing an activity that could carry risk. An example would be not buying a property so as not to take on any legal liability that might come with it. Another example would be not to fly, in order not to take the risk that your plane might crash. **24–36**

Avoidance can seem the answer to all risks, but avoiding risks also means losing out on the potential gains that accepting (or retaining) risks may yield. To re-iterate an earlier point, it is not possible to avoid all business risks unless you're going to shut up shop. That's why we say that the optimum use of each strategy might not be possible. The following puts this into context.

- A study by the Virginia Tech Transportation Institute (VTTI) reported that a driver's risk of collision is 3 times greater if they text. A risk avoidance strategy would stop you driving. Risk reduction, however, means you'd still drive but would, instead, simply not text.[4]
- According to the Centre for Disease Control, falling out of bed accounts for 1.8 million accident and emergency visits in the USA, each year. A risk avoidance strategy would stop you sleeping in your bed and, instead, have you sleep on your floor.[5]
- Every year, in Russia, about 100 people die or are injured by falling icicles. A risk avoidance strategy would have you cancelling all your travel plans to Russia, between the months of December and March.
- Every year vending machines topple and kill approximately 13 people. A risk avoidance strategy would stop you buying any sweets from a vending machine.

---

4 "New VTTI study results continue to highlight the dangers of distracted driving" (29 May 2013) Available at: *http://www.vtti.vt.edu/featured/?p=193* [Accessed: 15 June 2016].

5 See: *http://www.disabled-world.com/artman/publish/bedfalls.shtml* [Accessed: 15 June 2016].

- There has never been a recorded death, in Scotland, from a shark attack. A risk avoidance strategy, however, still would keep you out of the water, even though the risk has never before materialised. Risk avoidance can go too far.

Reduction

24–37 Risk reduction involves accepting a risk, but then reducing either the severity and/or likelihood of loss. For example, sprinkler systems are designed to put out a fire, thus reducing the risk of total loss. Outsourcing is an example of risk reduction, also, if the outsourcer can demonstrate a higher capability at managing or reducing risks. For example, a business might outsource its customer service delivery to another company. This way, it can concentrate on its core activities without having to worry about managing a call centre team.

Sharing

24–38 The term "risk transfer" is often used in place of risk sharing, in the mistaken belief that you can transfer a risk to a third party through insurance or outsourcing. In practice, if an insurance company or a contractor becomes bankrupt, the original risk is likely to revert to you.

Retention

24–39 Retention is where you accept the loss caused by a risk crystallising. This is a viable strategy for small risks, where the cost of insuring against them would be greater than the total losses that would be incurred were they to arise. It also covers risks so large that they just can't be insured against, such as war. Insurance companies won't cover you for losses incurred during a war. These have to be retained by you. Any risks that are not avoided or transferred are—by default—retained, albeit they might be controlled (i.e. risk reduction measures are put in place).

Create a risk management plan

24–40 Creating your risk management plan involves selecting appropriate measures to contain the risks that you identify. It needs to be approved by the appropriate level of firm management (following on from our point about ethos earlier). For instance, a plan to deal with the risk of money laundering needs to have all of your firm's partners backing it. However, a plan that addresses the risks that might flow from a firm's marketing might only require the approval of the marketing partner.

A good plan should contain a schedule for implementation and it should also identify the staff responsible for any actions that are required.

This leads to a related point—when should your controls kick in? This depends on your appetite for risk, ultimately. A way of dealing with this relates back to risk magnitude scores. Let's use the example of AML, one last time. What you could do is set a threshold above which you automatically reject an instruction, or a new client. For example, let's say you score a particular risk as five for impact and five for probability. Multiplied, that gives you an overall score of 25. Your control could be that such a score requires all fee earners to walk away (i.e. avoid the risk).

Alternatively, you could make it more sophisticated by selecting multiple thresholds. For example, for risk scores between 15 and 20, fee earners could be required to seek approval from a partner. A weakness, though, is that those who tend to push their luck might undertake a fresh risk assessment and massage their magnitude scores so as to artificially keep them below the threshold that requires partner scrutiny. Finally, experience (sometimes bitter) necessitates changes. Your plans should be reviewed regularly.

Summary

We take risks every day. When you walk across the road you take a risk. When **24–41**
you give advice to clients you take a risk. When you stand on one leg on a chair, while trying to reach a file at the top of the cabinet, you take a risk. Managing risks allows you to take risks, in greater safety. It helps you prepare for what might happen so that you have a back-up plan for the unexpected. The more senior you become the more you need to plan ahead. This means thinking about not just the good things you'd like to happen but also the possibility that something bad or unpleasant will happen.

The key thing, however, is that good risk management helps you manage risks and prevent (or at least reduce) undesirable outcomes. It helps you, also, change something that you otherwise might avoid (an unacceptable risk) into something you can manage and control.

CHAPTER 25

HOW TO MANAGE YOUR FIRM'S INTELLECTUAL PROPERTY

Introduction

25–1 *You've made the break. You've started a new firm. For the last two years you've worked hard to win clients, attract staff and develop your own reputation. Then, on the same street, a new firm opens. They're using a similar name; they have a logo that's almost identical to yours; they've ripped off your corporate brochure and client newsletters; they've even tried to claim credit for some of your work. What can you do?*

25–2 It takes a huge amount of effort to build a successful business. Thankfully the law protects you just as much as it does your physical property. It doesn't just apply when you become a partner or manage your own business. You should also know the basics of intellectual property (IP) as a new lawyer. When you change firm you may think that you can take documents with you. You may want templates or know-how that you find useful. You may even think you own them as you wrote them. However, any documents you take are as just as much the property of your firm as their chairs in their boardroom. You don't want to break the law, even accidently, so a basic knowledge of IP will protect you.

Outcomes

25–3 This chapter provides a summary of basic IP rights protection for passing off, defamation, trademarks, copyright and confidential information.

Passing off

25–4 The common law of passing off protects your firm from losing fee income and/or suffering reputational damage if a competitor tries to sell their services in a manner that it appears to the general public that these are—in some way—associated with you. In other words, it stops them "piggy backing" on your good reputation. There's competition, and then there's unfair competition. Quite simply, competitors can't use your hard earned goodwill for their own benefit.

How does it work?

25–5 You need to demonstrate that your firm has some sort of goodwill, that there is misrepresentation (which has caused—or is likely to cause—confusion with the general public) and, finally, that you have suffered loss as a result.

What is goodwill?

Goodwill is the: "... benefit and advantage of the good name, reputation and connection of a business. It is the attractive force which brings in custom".[1] Though incorporeal, goodwill is regarded as an asset of every successful business. If your firm is sold, in the future, your purchaser will want to acquire not only your business, but also the goodwill you've built up. Goodwill can be found in your firm's name, its logo and its address. It's established and developed through, for example, the use of trademarks and advertising campaigns. **25–6**

What passing off protects is the abuse of that goodwill. There's a distinction, however, between goodwill and reputation: "... damage to reputation without damage to goodwill is not sufficient to support an action for passing off".[2] To be successful with any passing off action, your firm's goodwill must exist in the location where you suffer the alleged infringement.[3] You can't argue an infringement if, for example, your goodwill demonstrably is in the Glasgow area, but the firm you're trying to sue is based in Madrid.

The period of time over which your goodwill has to exist within an area, however, isn't a determining factor; only its presence needs to be demonstrated.[4] Furthermore, as long as you can show that you have the requisite goodwill, it also doesn't matter how long your firm has been trading for, overall.

What is misrepresentation?

Misrepresentation is a material falsehood—a significant false statement. Your competitor's motive is irrelevant (albeit he or she probably knows what they're about) and the falsehood either can be express or implied (the latter, for example, by their conduct).[5] Typically, misrepresentation involves your competitor: **25–7**

1. using a name similar to that of your firm (thus suggesting that their business and its services somehow are linked to you);
2. imitating the appearance of your advertising (especially if it's distinctive)[6];
3. claiming your work as their own[7];
4. suggesting that you endorse their work[8];
5. using "your" domain name and pointing it at their website.

The misrepresentation has to cause confusion (or be likely to cause confusion) in the minds of the general public.

Loss

You must suffer actual loss, or demonstrate a reasonable likelihood of loss. The latter is sufficient (and a bit easier to prove). The former is more difficult to prove because, in all probability, it'll involve inspecting your competitor's accounts. **25–8**

---

[1] *Inland Revenue Commissioners v Muller & Co's Margarine* Ltd [1901] A.C. 217.
[2] *Harrods v Harrodian School* [1996] R.P.C. 697.
[3] *Sheraton Corp of America v Sheraton Motels Ltd* [1964] R.P.C. 202.
[4] *Starbucks (HK) Ltd v British Sky Broadcasting Group Plc* [2015] UKSC 31.
[5] For example, see *Reckitt & Colman Products Ltd v Borden Inc* [1990] 1 All E.R. 873.
[6] *White Hudson & Company Ltd v Asian Organisation Ltd* [1964] 1 W.L.R. 1466.
[7] *Bristol Conservatories Ltd v Conservatories Custom Built Ltd* [1989] R.P.C. 455.
[8] *Associated Newspaper Holdings v Insert Media Ltd* [1988] 1 W.L.R. 509; [1988] 2 All E.R. 420.

Geographical limitations

25–9 In addition to examining the likelihood of confusion, a court also looks at the geographical area in which you and your competitor trade. Goodwill often (but not always) is restricted to just this area. However, if you have a large company with a huge amount of goodwill attached to the business, that goodwill might extend to places even where you don't trade. For example, Arnold Clark probably would be regarded as having goodwill extending throughout the whole of Scotland, despite not having a place of business in every single town or city. Unfortunately, goodwill associated with a small firm is often restricted just to its local area of trading, which makes it difficult to establish passing off in respect of competitors that are benefiting from your goodwill, but perhaps in another city.

Exceptions

25–10 Do keep in mind that it's still possible for another person or firm to use your name, if it's done in a way that is not tantamount to deceiving the public. An example of this might be where someone uses your name but makes it unambiguously clear that the goods or services supplied are not connected in any way to your firm.

Web domains

25–11 Courts have accepted that passing off can be used in respect of domain name disputes. In the *One in a Million* case, the defenders registered various domains using names of famous companies like BT.[9] BT sued for passing off. Taking account of the extent of BT's reputation, the court granted an injunction (an interdict) to stop them. Scottish courts also have been willing to grant interim interdicts in domain name disputes, on the same basis.

What does a court look for if your firm needs to stop a competitor using a domain? In *EasyJet Airline Co Ltd v Tim Dainty* [2001] E.B.L.R. 104, the court looked at the actual content of the website to which a domain name ("easyRealestate") pointed. Other courts are likely to do something similar, so it follows that a website might state (or otherwise make it obvious) that no connection exists between the operators of the site and the firm whose name has been used. In that scenario, it might be quite hard to establish passing off.

A difficulty you might face when trying to sort out a domain name dispute is identifying who the defender is. An offending website might not actually disclose the person's identity. In the case of co.uk domain names, you can use the WHOIS search facility on Nominet (*www.nominet.uk*) to determine the identity of the registrant. In other cases, you can search Better Whois (*www.betterwhois.com*).

Another complex issue is actually working out what form the misrepresentation takes. Is the allegedly infringing webpage accessed by keying in your own trading name, with visitors simply redirected to a site built on another domain name? Does that site contain your trading name? Consider how any loss might be proven. Have your clients phoned the wrong firm, in confusion? Has traffic to your own website reduced? Have you experienced a drop-off in the number of instructions received?

---

[9] *British Telecommunications Plc v One in a Million Ltd* [1999] 1 W.L.R. 903.

Defamation

"Sticks and stones may break your bones . . .". This may be true in the playground, but it provides little assistance to your firm if it finds itself in a position where a competitor makes a defamatory statement. **25–12**

Reputation management

Reputation management is a key consideration in today's world. You and your firm—quite rightly—should guard its reputation. In doing so, you can rely on the law of defamation for protection. However, you do need to be aware that a hurtful statement might not necessarily be defamatory, as it may fall into another category of merely vulgar words (which are not actionable). **25–13**

False

To be defamatory, your competitor's statement has to both be false and lower your firm in the estimation of the general public (i.e. damage its reputation). A court applies the "standards of the day" when looking at an offending statement; a statement that would have been defamatory in 1916 might not be so, when applying the societal standards of 2016. **25–14**

Communication

Your competitor has to communicate his or her statement, in some way. The traditional forms of communication are publication in print, or verbally. However, new forms of communication (for example: email, blogs, Twitter, LinkedIn, Facebook, TripAdvisor, and so on) are also valid forms of communication, for the purposes of the law of defamation. The rule of thumb is that the wider the circulation of the defamatory statement, the greater the sum of damages likely to be awarded by a court. In passing, this is why (historically) people who have been wronged in Scotland have generally been counseled to wait until the statement is repeated in the London press (with its much wider circulation). **25–15**

Who can you sue?

Clearly you can take your competitor to task, as the person (or firm) who made the statement, originally. In addition, you also can take action against all those who repeat the statement (e.g. by forwarding a defamatory email). **25–16**

Defences

Your competitor might try and mount some sort of defence. The main defence is that his or her statement is true (this is known as *veritas*); that would be uncomfortable for you, were a court to agree. There are other defences. For example, "fair comment" allows freedom of speech and protects an inherent public interest in being able to express opinions about public figures (especially politicians, some might argue). An alleged defamer also can offer to make an apology in a reasonable way (as well as offer to pay compensation) and this will provide a defence as long as he or she did not know (or have reason to believe) that the statement was false. **25–17**

Trade marks

Distinguishing features help you stand out from the crowd, and ensure that your firm's services are immediately recognisable by potential clients (for example, **25–18** you might have a distinctive logo). The good news is that the Trade Marks Act 1994 lets you register distinguishing features in various ways. If one of your competitors then markets a similar service, in a similar way, he or she may well be infringing your registered mark.

Registration also creates a right of ownership over the trade mark in question. This can be disposed of in the same way as any other property, when you sell your firm. In other words, as a form of intellectual property, trade marks can add real value to your balance sheet.

What can you register?

25–19 The 1994 Act defines a trade mark as any sign that can be "represented graphically", and which is capable of distinguishing your services from those of another firm.[10] The words "represented graphically" mean that the thing you're trying to protect has to be capable of being put in to a form of pictures, words or numbers. As well as letters and numbers, it's possible to register the shapes of goods, and their packaging. Moving images also fall within the definition, as do advertising jingles (since these—by definition—can be represented graphically by their notation). In short, trade marks can cover many different things.

A mark of distinction

25–20 All sounds great, doesn't it? However, before you rush out to try and register a trade mark, you need to remember that your proposed mark must be distinctive. Your mark can be in a verbal or non-verbal and form. Verbal marks include the following.

1. Names of people—these can be protected, but have to be represented in a way that make them immediately recognisable as being that of one business, alone. An example would be the use of a signature (like Walt Disney) or a distinctive style of lettering (like Marks & Spencer).
2. Names of products—these can't just relate to the character, quality, or geographical origin of a product or service. For example, "wholemeal flour" can't be registered. This is to prevent your competitors from being unreasonably restricted in advertising their own services. In other words, it's to prevent you monopolising the use of ordinary words.

Non-verbal marks include things like symbols, pictorial representations and combinations of letters and numbers. As noted, this enables advertising jingles to be trademarked (by using their notation). It also means your firm name could become a trade mark, using a combination of its letters.

Restrictions

25–21 Let's assume you decide try to register your firm name. You won't succeed if it is:

1. insufficiently distinctive[11];
2. against the public interest, or is morally offensive[12];

---

[10] Trade Marks Act 1994 s.1.
[11] *Philips Electronics NV v Remington Consumer Products* [1998] E.T.M.R. 124; [1998] R.P.C. 283.
[12] Trade Marks Act 1994 s.3.

3. identical or too similar to existing trade marks (and applied to the same, or similar, goods and services).[13]

Registration process

An application has to be made to the UK's Trade Mark Registry. Your application must include a representation of your proposed mark and also needs to specify the product or service it might apply to. There is a fee for this service.[14] Once everything is received, the Registrar assesses whether your proposed mark is sufficiently distinctive and proceeds to carry out various searches.[15] If your application is accepted, the Registrar then publishes a notice so that all interested parties might have the opportunity to lodge objections.[16] Provided no objections are received, your mark then is entered into the Register (for use in relation to a particular class of goods or services).[17] Your registration lasts for 10 years and, at expiry, is able to be renewed. **25–22**

Infringements

Infringements can only be committed in the course of a competitor's trade.[18] If an infringement is perpetrated outwith the course of business and, as such, you're unable to litigate for that (or indeed any other) reason, you can of course still raise an action for passing off. **25–23**

Copyright

The basics

Your firm has copyright over its original literary works, by virtue of the Copyright, Designs and Patents Act 1988.[19] Literary works can include all templates, know-how and client documents such as contracts. It can also include your client newsletters, brochures and even your client lists. Again, copyright is a form of property that has value when it comes to selling your firm (and its assets). **25–24**

Requirements

The main requirement is that each literary work you wish to be covered by copyright is "original".[20] This means that it should not be a straight copy, rather than being completely unique. Originality relates to how a concept is expressed, rather than the idea itself. In other words, your copyright extends to copy (the form of words used) as opposed to the information conveyed by these words. **25–25**

The term "literary" includes anything written, so long as it's recorded in a tangible form. As noted, it can include client newsletters, brochures and client lists. It also can include: the reports and business plans your firm prepares, the design of your website, and even the content of your website.

---

[13] Trade Marks Act 1994 s.5 and see *Berlei (UK) Ltd v Bali Brassiere Co* (1970) R.P.C. 87 (16): 469–480.

[14] Trade Marks Act 1994 s.32.

[15] Trade Marks Act 1994 s.37.

[16] Trade Marks Act 1994 s.38.

[17] Trade Marks Act 1994 s.40.

[18] Trade Marks Act 1994 s.10.

[19] Copyright, Designs and Patents Act 1988 s.1.

[20] Copyright, Designs and Patents Act 1988 s.2.

More than an idea

25–26 To be covered by copyright, something must be more than just an idea. It has to be in a tangible form (like a piece of writing). If you tell someone your idea (e.g. a competitor), you can't then sue for an infringement of copyright.

Process

25–27 There is no formal registration process. Copyright exists automatically at the point you put the words in your mind on to paper.[21] That's a different matter from proving exactly when you wrote the words. A competitor might simply claim that he or she wrote "your" words, but on an earlier date.

Duration

25–28 Copyright lasts for 70 years from the end of the calendar year in which the author dies.[22]

Employees

25–29 A common question pertains to the ownership of a literary work created by an employee, in the course of his or her employment. The general rule is that the owner of a work is its author. However, in an employment scenario, copyright belongs to the employer (i.e. your firm).[23] The phrase "in the course of employment" is interpreted widely, so a literary work created by one of your team in his spare time (and even without your express instruction) is still likely to belong to your firm if it's relevant to that employee's job.

Outcome

25–30 If you discover a competitor infringing your rights, you can sue for what is called "direct infringement".[24] It doesn't matter that they might not have made any profit out of their actions.

Confidential information

The basics

25–31 The final IP protection we're going to look at is confidential information. Basically, if you reveal any information to another person (friend or competitor), a legal duty can be created such that the information can't be passed to anyone else.

How it works

25–32 Either you tell someone specifically that the information you're giving them is confidential (and then it takes on that status), or it's apparent from the circumstances that the information must be private (and that it should remain so). It's possible to create a duty of confidentiality in a contract, by simply putting in a

---

[21] Copyright, Designs and Patents Act 1988 ss.154–158.
[22] Copyright, Designs and Patents Act 1988 ss.12–15.
[23] Copyright, Designs and Patents Act 1988 ss.9–11.
[24] Copyright, Designs and Patents Act 1988 ss.17–21.

non-disclosure condition. This is common in consultancy contracts and—indeed—any contract for the provision of services where sensitive information might be accessed.

Sometimes, a duty arises by the operation of law. A good example is the standards of conduct (as discussed in Ch.9 (how to be professional)), where you're bound not to reveal the information which clients give to you.

Why it's important

In a business environment, confidential information can include know-how and **25–33** also any ideas and information not yet protected by copyright. It can also include information that forms the basis of a competitive tender (prior to this submission), where a leak of that information might cause your firm to lose.[25]

Once it's out—it's out

Any information that is confidential ceases to be so once it's in the public **25–34** domain—be warned.

Summary

Lawyers and law firms rely on their reputation, knowledge and information to win **25–35** clients and provide advice. A firm's reputation is based on both its brand (as seen in Ch.4 (what do law firm's sell?)) but also on what people say about it (as seen in Ch.5 (how do you build your reputation?)). While its advice is recorded in contracts, emails and letters. IP rights help protect law firms from competitors attacking their reputation unfairly and it helps protect the advice.

---

[25] See *PSM International v Whitehouse & Willenhall Ltd* [1992] FSR 489.

PART 6

Commercial Awareness

CHAPTER 26

HOW TO SHOW COMMERCIAL AWARENESS

Introduction

Let's go back to the start. Job adverts want you to show it. Interviewers question you about it. Employers ask you to demonstrate you have it. After 25 chapters you know what "commercial awareness" means. **26–1**

But how will other people know that you have commercial awareness? Do you have to pass an exam? Write an essay? Will you have to demonstrate it? What exactly do you have to do next?

We've attempted to show you that commercial awareness has three meanings: **26–2**

- knowing what it means to be a lawyer;
- knowing your clients; and
- knowing how to run a business and make money.

We hope that after reading the book you understand that commercial awareness is at the heart of every modern, successful business. If a business doesn't listen to its clients (or customers), it won't make money, and, if a business doesn't make money, it won't last long. Just look at some of the big profile failures on the high street in the last few years. Blockbuster once had thousands of stores worldwide, renting and selling videos, DVDs and Blu-rays. Today it has none. It didn't understand that its customers no longer rented films; the internet had changed everything.

As a lawyer, the pace of change may be slower. There's been no legal equivalent of a Netflix type transformation yet, but it's still there. Firms have collapsed; others have merged. The Scottish legal market is almost unrecognisable from just a few years ago. Client demands have changed and you (and your firms) need to change with them. Modern firms know this. A 2013 study of 19 global firms, by King's College London, listed commercial awareness as one of the top three attributes they looked for in future lawyers.[1] Law firms want lawyers who know what it means to be a professional, and someone who understands what clients want and need. You can't be insular or exist in your own silo. You can't expect clients to just walk through your door, or email you out of the blue. That is not business reality and the law—nowadays—is very much a business. If you don't respond to those changes, you'll be as relevant as Blockbuster.

[1] King's College London, *King's College London Law Employability Research, in partnership with The Times* (2013). Available at *http://www.kcl.ac.uk/law/newsevents/newsrecords/Kings-Law-Employability-Research-2013.pdf* [Accessed 19 April 2016].

When you're asked to show that you're commercially aware, how do you do that? We've given you three definitions and we've covered what each of these means. That said, there's a big difference between *knowing* something and *showing* something. We said in Ch.1 (what will you do?) that while you might say that you know how to swim, that's not the same as jumping in the English Channel. "Knowing" is not "showing". In this final chapter we discuss how you can *show* others that you have commercial awareness.

Outcomes

26–3 If you want to show that you're commercially aware you need to behave (or perform) as if you're commercially aware. Behaviour is a combination of knowledge and skills. We start by exploring the difference between knowledge and skill before we look at how they can be combined in commercial awareness as a way for you to behave. We then look at two challenges you might face.

The difference between knowledge and skills

26–4 Can you drive? If so, you should know that driving consists of both the knowledge of how to drive together with the skill to actually drive your car. You need the knowledge set out in the Highway Code so that you know to drive on the right (left) side of the road and to identify road signs so that you can drive safely from A to B. Knowledge is something you acquire from books—you can memorise and learn. It's facts and figures; it's answers to questions on Mastermind or Pointless; it's answers in an exam for your LLB.

Skills are different. A skill is an act or action. It's turning a steering wheel; operating a clutch; slamming on brakes when someone pulls in front of you without signalling. It's not what you know—it's what you do. If someone asks if you can drive, how do you show him or her that indeed you can? You can explain that you know the difference between a single yellow line and a double yellow line, and you can point out the signs beside the road and tell them what they mean. Until they see you behind a wheel, however, you've not *actually* shown them that you can drive. Driving's a skill—an action. Equally, if someone sees you driving through Glasgow and you turn the wrong way down a one-way street, or drive at 60mph beside a primary school, or park on a double yellow line, you haven't demonstrated that you know how to drive. Driving's not just a skill: it's also your knowledge of the Highway Code. If you want to show someone you can drive you need to show that you have both the *knowledge* and *skill* to drive. It's the combination of the two that make you a driver.

Commercial awareness is no different. You need knowledge and skill. You can read this book and tell everyone you know how to delegate but, until you sit in a room with a colleague and try and pass them a file before you go on holiday, you're not actually delegating. You need both knowledge and skill: the knowledge of how to delegate and the skill to put that into practice with other people. You need both elements to demonstrate you have commercial awareness, just as you need both elements to show that you can drive. Think about commercial awareness (or driving) as a coat hanger for your suit. Your knowledge is the trousers. Your skill is the jacket. You can wear one without the other but, until you put them together, you're half dressed. When you want to show someone that you have commercial awareness, you want to put on that suit. This combination of knowledge and skill is your "behaviour", and it's your behaviour that others see and judge.

Commercial awareness as behaviour

What are commercial awareness behaviours?

When you learn to drive you learn how to react in different circumstances. You learn how to reverse the car, to turn it in tight spots, to spot dangers and to drive safely in traffic. All of these different skills—and the knowledge you need to use them—combine to show people how you behave when you drive. **26–5**

When you learn commercial awareness you're also demonstrating a variety of skills (and the knowledge underlying them) to show people how you behave. Take time management. It's not enough to say that you can delegate work to a trainee or your secretary because you know it saves time, you actually have to do it. You need to speak to them, pass over the file, and be responsible for what they do. Or take professionalism. If you want people to say that you're a good professional, then you need to know the relevant standards of conduct and practice rules so that you can spot professional issues (such as conflicts of interest) when they arise. Then you need to deal with them effectively, for example by speaking to clients and getting their consent to act or by refusing to act for one or more people. It's not enough to just spot a conflict, you need to act and deal with it to. You're using both your knowledge and your skill.

What knowledge do you need to be commercially aware?

When we discussed this chapter we hesitated before offering a comprehensive list, as any list runs the risk of being prescriptive and closed. Is that a problem? Yes. Commerciality is a concept in flux. Just as fashions change, so does the knowledge needed to show commercial awareness. The categories of what might be regarded as commercially aware continue to change in response to changes within the legal market, and also with technological advances. **26–6**

For example, 15 years ago you wouldn't have thought of social media as a possible lynchpin of your networking strategy to win new business. Nowadays, the opposite is true. If you were a lawyer during those 15 years your knowledge would have to change to remain relevant, and—yes—commercially aware.

If you need a starting point, the ones that are unlikely to change are three you already know.

- Commercial awareness means knowing what it means to be a lawyer.
- Commercial awareness means knowing the impact your advice has on your clients.
- Commercial awareness means knowing how to run a business and make money.

Let's look closer at each of these with a fresh perspective.

External and internal

When looking at what knowledge and skill you need you should make a distinction between internal and external behaviours. **26–7**

What is internal commercial awareness?

26–8 Internal commercial awareness behaviours are those that are inwardly focused (i.e. internal to your firm) and can include things like the cross selling of services, good financial control (e.g. financial leakage and time recording) and delegation. In other words, they're the behaviours you exhibit that are seen by your colleagues.

What is external commercial awareness?

26–9 External commercial awareness behaviours, in contrast, are outwardly focused (i.e. to your clients and third parties, even the court) and can include good business development and good transactional skills (in particular, good communication, professionalism and being able to conclude your transactional work without making mistakes).

Why make this distinction?

26–10 This distinction is important because you should be aware of how you're seen by others. If you're brilliant at speaking to clients at business events yet only grunt to colleagues in the office, you're going to find it difficult at your review to tell everyone that you're a great communicator.

Equally, if you're diligent at file opening but never remember to phone clients back, can you say that you're professional? Your colleagues might think so, but that's only until clients start phoning your client relationship manager to complain. We recommend that you always think how your behaviour is seen both internally and externally. That's why we included Ch.17 (how to improve client service). You need to know how others see you.

How do you turn knowledge and skills into behaviour?

26–11 Once you know how others see you. Let's start adding skills to your knowledge. A quick re-cap. Skills are not themselves knowledge, nor are they behaviours. You need both knowledge and skill. But what skills do you need? This book can help you, once again. Every chapter has attempted to show you the skills you need. For example, we've covered:

Project management

26–12 Your team is a group of people you organise to work together, to accomplish objectives that you can't achieve by yourself. Even in small firms, for example, you can't function without a secretary. Your team might be just you and your secretary. Of course, every law firm has a multitude of different teams. Recognised attributes needed for membership of a team are:

- business or commercial skills (professional orientation);
- time and cost consciousness (goal orientation); and
- an ability to work with different types of people (team orientation).

We looked at team building, in detail, in Ch.18.

Delegation

26–13 There are 24 hours in a day, and only one of you. When you're good at your job, clients want more from you (and of you). It can lead you to having work overload that, in turn, can leave you feeling overwhelmed. You end up not being able to do everything that everyone wants, leaving you feeling that you're letting people down. Indeed, if you have extreme work overload, it may well be that you are in fact letting clients down. That can lead to complaints.

Quite simply, delegation is the assignment of authority by you to someone in your team to carry out specific activities. Delegation empowers your team member to make decisions and to take action. It's a shift of decision-making authority from you—operating at a high organisational level—to someone less senior, operating at a lower organisational level. We looked at delegation, in detail, in Ch.16.

Time management

There's a compelling business case for you to improve your time management. Wasted time costs UK businesses £80 billion per year, equivalent to 7% of GDP.[2] Time management involves you understanding the difference between tasks that are urgent and those that are important. An urgent task requires immediate attention and action. However, whether you actually give it that immediate attention may (or may not) matter. An important task, however, is one that always matters. Not doing it will have adverse consequences for you and/or your firm. **26–14**

Good time management is influenced by various factors, including: the time of day at which you work best, multi-tasking, perspective and procrastination. We looked at time management in Ch.15 and showed you how you might use a range of tools (including a priority matrix) to improve.

Networking

It's not "who you know", but "who knows you". Networking is the skill of making contacts and then making use of your contacts (by nurturing and maintaining them). The aim of networking is to create a pool of people that will increase the quality of your services, lead to new clients, and help increase your knowledge. **26–15**

We looked at networking in Ch.5. Remember that it has a range of benefits, including knowledge exchange, connection building, increasing your profile and winning new business.

Goal setting

Not having work-place goals (and indeed personal goals) is just like to embarking on a journey with no particular destination in mind and no compass to guide you. By setting goals and then measuring their success, you can see where you're going (i.e. they give you a clear path), what you have accomplished and understand better what you're capable of. Goals have a range of benefits: they're motivational, provide clear expectations, drive your team's performance and reinforce your firm's culture. We looked at goal setting in Ch.17. **26–16**

Risk management

All your business activities have inherent uncertainty. Risks can include strategic failures, operational failures, financial failures, market disruptions, environmental disasters and regulatory violations. Risk management involves identifying the **26–17**

---

[2] Quoted from the "2007 Proudfoot Productivity Report", as reported in the news article on *http://www.reliableplant.com/Read/8753/cost-of-poor-productivity-in-uk-put-at-%C2%A380-billion* [Accessed 15 June 2016].

types of risk exposure within your firm (or in relation to a transaction), measuring these potential risks, proposing strategies to mitigate them and estimating their impact, if they materialise.

In Ch.22 we examined how risks can be identified. We looked at how you might assess the potential severity of impact and the probability of occurrence. Finally, we examined various strategic approaches, including avoidance, reduction, sharing and retention.

Negotiation

26–18 Negotiation is the process by which you seek to achieve agreement on a matter, or a number of matters. The agreement may favour you, the other party, or may favour neither. A successful negotiation is one that:

- generates the best possible deal in the circumstances;
- avoids litigation;
- achieves a workable, lasting agreement;
- establishes or maintains a client relationship; and
- maintains professional standards and ethics.

In Ch.10 we looked at the basic requirements for a good negotiation. And that's the start. Can you see that every chapter is not just about the knowledge you need, it also points you to the skills you need to acquire.

External

26–19
- You understand, follow and maybe even join the community of people who form the legal market and the markets your clients work in.
- How to open files correctly.
- Writing engagement letters that tell clients what you'll do, how you'll do it, what you'll charge and who'll do the work for them.
- You communicate clearly to everyone you deal with.
- You're professional and follow the standards of conduct and service.

Internal

26–20
- You manage your time to fee clients fairly.
- You work as a team and delegate work appropriately.
- You continue to learn by choosing and meeting goals (including continuing professional development (CPD)).
- You manage teams effectively.
- You always strive to improve your service to clients.
- You understand the business you work in (or run).
- You manage risk (including intellectual property (IP)).
- You manage your finances so that your firm makes money.

Challenges to showing behaviours

26–21 This sounds easy so far, doesn't it? You know the law from university. You've read this book, so have the knowledge to become commercially aware. You know what skills you need to demonstrate to show commercial awareness. You're ready to be a lawyer. What's stopping you?

You are stopping you

Not everyone can swim. Not everyone can drive. Some people can pick up new languages as quickly as picking up a new suit. Learning a skill is different for everyone. Some you will pick up easily, others you will struggle with and think you'll never learn. That's just life. You can expect a degree of difference in how well different people acquire and apply skills. For example, you might struggle with good financial management and yet be a natural at delegation; your colleague might tend towards micro-management and yet exercise the sort of budgetary control that George Osborne can only dream of. If so, don't worry about it—nobody is brilliant at everything. **26–22**

Instead recognise your strengths and weakness, and recognise that either it may take you longer to change or try and work in a team that complements you. Remember, ultimately, that's part of why we have partnerships; that's why we have teamwork. You don't need to do everything. You can rely on others. However . . .

Your firm might be stopping you

Your firm's management and culture can influence your commerciality. We say you can rely on your team but what if your partner or your colleagues resist you. What if they don't want to change? **26–23**

Take delegation. If your firm's management rewards lawyers based solely on how many hours they charge regardless of whether they're profitable, then you'll find people will keep work for themselves. They want the most hours so they get the most rewards. They're not rewarded for passing work to others in the firm. In other words, even though you have the knowledge and skill to delegate, to project manage, to manage your time, and produce a profit for your firm, others might not help you. You might be impeded by your firm's management culture.

If this culture persists, it's less likely that you'll go on to acquire new skills that might unlock further commercially aware behaviours. This sort of firm chokes the evolving commercial awareness of its staff. Either you need to change the firm, or you need to change to another firm that will support you. Remember, you, and only you, are in control of your career. You're in charge of what happens next.

Conclusion

It takes time to become commercially aware. You need knowledge and skill. No one learns to drive the first time they step in a car. You need to practice, and learn, and practice again (and again) until it becomes second nature. Commercial awareness is no different. It's a continuous process, and an enjoyable one. When you learn anything or gain any skill, you take pride in what you can do and what you can accomplish for both yourself and for your clients. You won't know what you're capable of until you start. And, while you may have a few bumps and scrapes along the way, in the end, your commercial awareness will help you become a modern lawyer who understands your clients, your business and your profession. This is just the start. **26–24**

APPENDIX

Part 1

STANDARDS OF CONDUCT

Rule B1.1: application

1.1 Save when and to the extent engaged in cross-border practice you shall comply with the standards of conduct set out in this rule 1.

Rule B1.2: trust and personal integrity

1.2 You must be trustworthy and act honestly at all times so that your personal integrity is beyond question. In particular, you must not behave, whether in a professional capacity or otherwise, in a way which is fraudulent or deceitful.

Rule B1.3: independence

1.3 You must give independent advice free from external influences or personal interests which are inconsistent with these standards. It is your duty not to allow your independence to be impaired irrespective of the nature of the matter in which you're acting.

Rule B1.4: the interests of the client

1.4.1 You must act in the best interests of your clients subject to preserving your independence and complying with the law, these rules and the principles of good professional conduct.

1.4.2 You must not permit your own personal interests or those of the legal profession in general to influence your advice to or actings on behalf of clients.

1.4.3 You must at all times do, and be seen to do, your best for your client and must be fearless in defending your client's interests, regardless of the consequences to yourself (including, if necessary, incurring the displeasure of the bench). But you must also remember that your client's best interests require you to give honest advice however unwelcome that advice may be to the client and that your duty to your client is only one of several duties which you must strive to reconcile.

Rule B1.5: proper instructions

1.5.1 You're the agent of your client and must have the authority of your client for your actings. You must not accept improper instructions, for example to assist a client in a matter which you know to be criminal or fraudulent, but you may properly advise on the legal consequences of a proposed course of action or on the scope or application of the law to particular circumstances.

1.5.2 You may decline to accept new instructions, whether from a new or established client, without giving a reason for doing so, provided the refusal to act is not motivated by discrimination in breach of rule 1.15.

Rule B1.6: confidentiality

1.6 You must maintain client confidentiality. This duty is not terminated by the passage of time. You must also supervise your employees to ensure that they keep client matters confidential. Only the client, Acts of the legislature, subordinate legislation or the court can waive or override the duty of confidentiality. The duty does not apply to information about any crime a client indicates they'll commit.

Rule B1.7: conflict of interest

1.7.1 You must not act for two or more clients in matters where there is a conflict of interest between the clients or for any client where there is a conflict between the interest of the client and your interest or that of your practice unit.

1.7.2 Even where there is only a potential conflict of interest you must exercise caution. Where the potential for conflict is significant, you must not act for both parties without the full knowledge and express consent of the clients.

Rule B1.8: disclosure of interest

1.8 Where you're consulted about a matter in which you have, or your practice unit has, a personal or a financial interest, the position must be made clear to the client as soon as possible. If the interest is such that you cannot reasonably give independent advice, you must decline to act and advise the client to seek appropriate advice elsewhere.

Rule B1.9: effective communication

1.9.1 You must communicate effectively with your clients and others. This includes providing clients with any relevant information which you have and which is necessary to allow informed decisions to be made by clients. It also includes accounting to clients for funds passing through your hands. Information must be clear and comprehensive and, where necessary or appropriate, confirmed in writing.

1.9.2 You must advise your clients of any significant development in relation to their case or transaction and explain matters to the extent reasonably necessary to permit informed decisions by clients regarding the instructions which require to be given by them. In particular you must advise clients in writing when it becomes known that the cost of work will materially exceed any estimate that has been given and must also advise the client in writing when the limit of the original estimate is being approached.

Rule B1.10: competence, diligence and appropriate skills

1.10 You must only act in those matters where you're competent to do so. You must only accept instructions where the matter can be carried out adequately and completely within a reasonable time. You must exercise the level of skill appropriate to the matter.

Rule B1.11: professional fees

1.11.1 The fees you charge must be fair and reasonable in all the circumstances.

1.11.2 When the work is to be charged at an hourly rate, you must inform the client what that hourly rate will be and of any change to the hourly rate.

Rule B1.12: withdrawing from acting if instructions are accepted

1.12 You must not cease to act for clients without just cause and without giving reasonable notice, or in a manner which would prejudice the course of justice. So far as possible, the client's interests should not be adversely affected, but you're entitled to exercise your rights in law to recover your justified fees and outlays.

Rule B1.13: relations with the courts

1.13.1 You must never knowingly give false or misleading information to the court. You must maintain due respect and courtesy towards the court while honourably pursuing the interests of your clients.

1.13.2 You must not do or say anything which could affect evidence or induce a witness, a party to an action, or an accused person to do otherwise than give in evidence a truthful and honest account of that person's recollection.

1.13.3 As far as reasonably practical, you must give reasonable notice to witnesses of court hearings and when questioning witnesses, treat them with appropriate respect and courtesy.

1.13.4 Where you appear against a person who represents him or herself, you must avoid taking unfair advantage of that person and must, consistently with your duty to your client, co-operate with the court in enabling that person's case to be fairly stated and justice to be done. However you must not sacrifice the interests of your client to those of the person representing him or herself.

1.13.5 In rule 1.13 references to the "court" include tribunals and other bodies or persons exercising judicial or determinative functions.

Rule B1.14: relations between regulated persons

1.14.1 You must act with other regulated persons in a manner consistent with persons having mutual trust and confidence in each other. You must not knowingly mislead other regulated persons or, where you have given your word, go back on it.

1.14.2 Other than as permitted by rule 3, you may only communicate with a person known or believed to be the client of another regulated person ("the other regulated person") if:

(a) the other regulated person has agreed to the communication;
(b) the other regulated person confirms that he or she is no longer acting;
(c) you're serving a court document or formal notice;
(d) you're sending a fee note (or a reminder letter with regard to a fee note which remains unpaid) to a former client;
(e) you have (i) warned the other regulated person in writing that a reply to correspondence is needed within a specified and reasonable length of time and that if no reply is received within that time, you will write direct to the other regulated person's client; and (ii) no reply has been received within that time; or
(f) you're not already acting for another party in the matter and the person has sought advice from you.

1.14.3 In respect of rules 1.14.1 and 1.14.2 references to regulated persons shall be deemed to include advocates, English/Welsh solicitors, Northern Ireland solicitors, Isle of Man advocates, Jersey solicitors and Guernsey, Alderney and Sark advocates.

Rule B1.15: diversity

1.15.1 You must not discriminate on the grounds of age, disability, gender reassignment, marriage and civil partnership, pregnancy and maternity, race, religion or belief, sex or sexual orientation in your professional dealings with other lawyers, clients, employees or others.

1.15.2 Where you act in a managerial capacity or supervise others you must ensure that:

(a) there is no unlawful discrimination in employment including recruitment, training, employment terms, promotion, advancement and termination of employment;
(b) those you manage or supervise do not discriminate unlawfully;
(c) you and those you manage or supervise, have appropriate awareness and understanding of the issues surrounding equal opportunities, unlawful discrimination, equality and diversity; and
(d) there is no unlawful discrimination in the provision of legal services, and that those to whom legal services are provided can access them in a manner most appropriate to their needs.

PART 2

STANDARD OF SERVICE

> "Lawyers help people at times of crisis and bereavement, they protect the rights of the vulnerable, and they support business and economic growth."[3]

Lawyers interact with a wide cross section of our society and fulfil a critical role in meeting the interests of that society. Their clients are entitled to expect a good level of professional service from their solicitor. This means the solicitor must demonstrate the appropriate legal knowledge and skill to address the needs of the client, must communicate effectively in a clear and understandable way with their clients and others, must do what they say they're going to do, and must treat their clients and all others with respect and courtesy at all times

At the same time, a solicitor is required to comply with rules of professional conduct and behaviour, recognising that their professional obligations are not only to their clients, but to the courts, the legal profession and the public. Amongst other things, these rules regulate:

- Confidentiality and legal professional privilege
- Trust and personal integrity
- The interest of the client
- Independence of the solicitor
- Disclosure of interest
- Relations with the Courts
- Conflict of Interest

Standards of service are based on broad principles recognising the range and variety of work which can be undertaken by a solicitor. The standards have equal application to an individual solicitor, whether as a partner in a firm or an employee, and to firms. The application of these standards requires the use of effective systems, good training and appropriate supervision.

At the heart of providing a legal service are the interests and needs of the client. The importance of those interests and needs means that solicitors must adhere to the following overriding principles:

- Competence
- Diligence
- Communication
- Respect

Competence

- Know and apply the relevant law
- Keep up-to-date
- Ensure that those to who work is delegated are properly trained and supervised

---

[3] Former Justice Secretary, Kenny MacAskill, speaking on 26 November 2007.

In deciding whether to agree to work for a client and in carrying out the work, a solicitor must consider the nature and complexity of the matter and must have the appropriate level of professional skills to do that work. This means that a solicitor must consider if he or she has the knowledge and experience needed. Given the range of specialised areas of legal work it's essential that a solicitor recognises the need to keep his/her knowledge up to date and to make an ongoing commitment to continuing professional development.

Where a solicitor delegates work, whether to another solicitor or solicitors or to paralegals or other members of staff, it's essential that such staff are properly trained and that there are in place systems to ensure that the delegated work is adequately supervised.

Diligence

- Deliver on commitments
- Act in the best interests of each client
- Maintain and review systems of work
- Prompt and transparent fee arrangements

It is expected that a solicitor will fulfil commitments made to the client, other solicitors and the court.

By way of example, this would include responding to letters, e-mails and telephone calls within an appropriate or agreed timescale.

A solicitor must only agree to work for a client where the work can be done within a reasonable timescale. Where a solicitor considers, for example, that the service to a client would be inadequate because they already have work to do that it would not be dealt with within a reasonable period of time, they should not agree to take on the work.

The solicitor will at all times seek to do his or her best for the client. This will include identifying the client's objectives in relation to the work to be done, giving the client a clear explanation of the issues involved and the options available to the client, and agreeing with the client the next steps to be taken.

In keeping the client informed, the solicitor must provide updates on progress.

With the increasing advancement of technology, it's expected that the solicitor will regularly look at ways in which technology can support client service. By way of example, this may include client reporting systems, file and data management systems and use of knowledge management systems.

At the conclusion of the work, or earlier if agreed, the solicitor will ensure that the fees to be charged are promptly notified to the client and that a clear explanation and breakdown is provided. If there is any variation from the fees previously discussed, the solicitor must explain the reasons for the variation. The solicitor must respond promptly to any clarification sought from the client.

Communication

- Use of clear language and explanation from the perspective of the client
- Agreement on the means and frequency of communication between client and solicitor
- Letters of engagement or their equivalent clearly explaining and defining the service to be carried out, how that work will be carried out, who is responsible and the cost associated with the service
- How complaints will be handled in the event of dissatisfaction

Whatever the nature of the work carried out by a solicitor, communicating effectively with the client is important. Solicitors must make sure that they communicate clearly, effectively and in plain understandable language with their clients and others. This includes keeping clients informed regularly about progress with the matter. The overriding aim is to ensure that the client can gain a proper understanding of what is being communicated. This necessarily requires the communication to be tailored to suit the audience, their needs and interests. Communication requires the solicitor to listen to the client and understand their objectives.

Solicitors must send a letter to their clients as soon as possible after the first instruction providing information about:

(a) the work to be carried out;
(b) what the fees and other costs will be, or the basis upon which such fees and costs will be charged including where appropriate the hourly rate to be charged. Where the client is receiving legal advice and assistance or legal aid, they should be told about any contribution that might be payable, the consequences of preserving or recovering property, and where appropriate their possible liability for the expenses of the other party;
(c) the name of the person or persons who will do the work; and
(d) the name of the person the client should speak to if they're unhappy about the work done.

Clients who use a solicitor or firm regularly to carry out the same type of work should be sent such a letter whenever there is any change in the terms previously agreed with them.

Solicitors should advise their clients of any significant development in relation to the matter they're working on for them and explain matters clearly in order to allow clients to make informed decisions.

Information should be clear, easy to understand and comprehensive and where necessary or appropriate confirmed in writing. In particular solicitors should advise clients in writing as soon as it becomes known that the cost of work will exceed any estimate previously provided.

The duty to communicate effectively includes the duty of solicitors to report to their clients at the appropriate time about all money related to their matter which is handled by the solicitor.

Respect

- Treat each person as an individual
- Recognise diversity, different cultures and values

The relationship between solicitor and client is a mutual one built upon trust and respect.

Relationships based on openness, trust and good communication enable the solicitor to work in partnership with the client to address their needs. Implicit within a good level of professional service provided by a solicitor is that each and every client will be treated respectfully and with courtesy, in recognition of their dignity and rights as individuals. The solicitor also has a responsibility to treat colleagues, other members of the legal profession and the public with similar politeness and respect.

This will require of the solicitor to listen to and understand the interests and needs of the client and to bring his or her knowledge and experience to the work.

The solicitor must treat clients fairly and in line with the law. The solicitor must not discriminate against clients because of their age, sex, race, ethnic origin, nationality, special needs or disability, sexuality, health, lifestyle, beliefs or any other relevant consideration.

PART 3

GOAL SETTING FORM

What is your goal:

Summary:
How is it SPECIFIC?
How will it be MEASURABLE?
Is it ATTAINABLE?
Is it RELEVANT?
What is your TIMELINE?

Action plan

Identify practical steps you need to take to achieve your goal.
1.
2.
3.

Obstacles

Identify any obstacles that might stand in the way of you achieving your goal. What is your strategy for dealing with them?
1.
2.
3.

Assistance

Identify any people who could help you achieve your goal.
1.
2.
3.

Identify any resources that you might use to help you achieve your goal.
1.
2.
3

PART 4

PRIORITY MATRIX

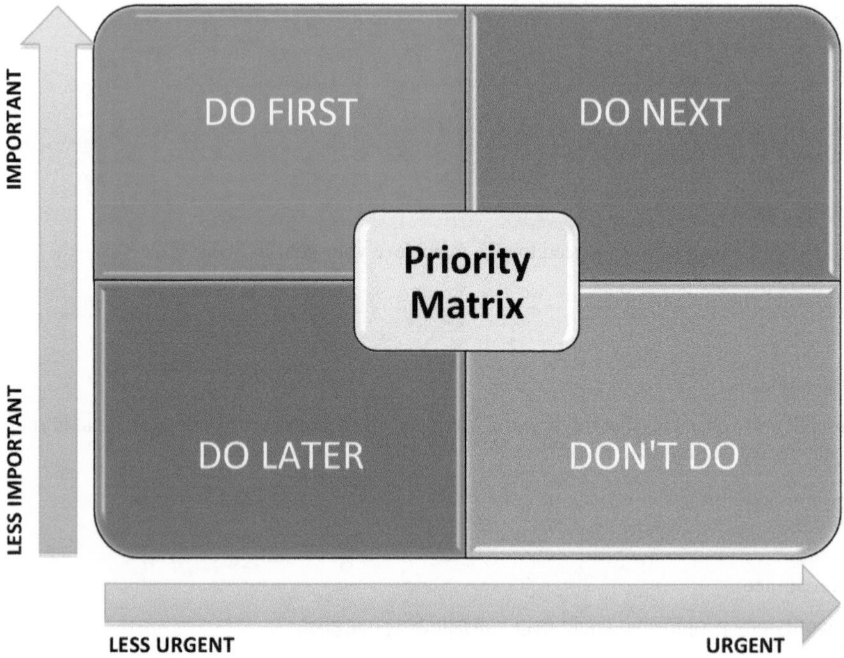

Part 5

BLUEPRINTS

Figure 1

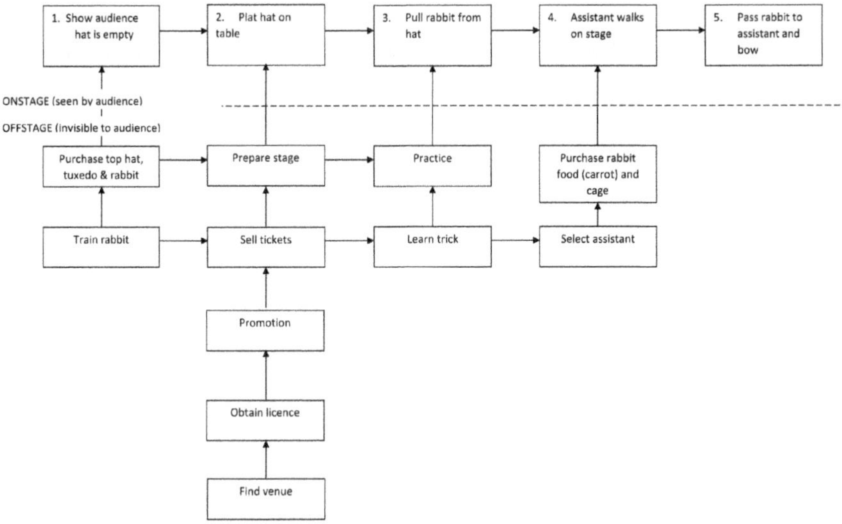

Figure 2

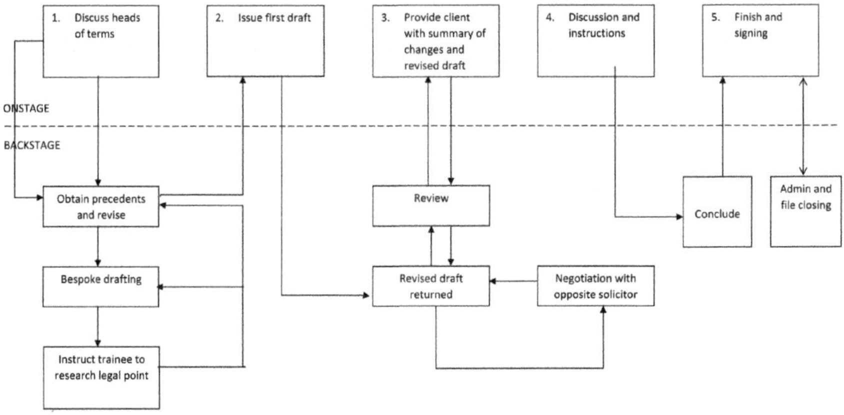

PART 6

GANTT CHART

IMPORTANT CLIENT - NEW WILL & PoA

SIM & TODD LLP

Project Lead: Andy Todd
Project Start Date: 09-Jan-17
Display Week: 1

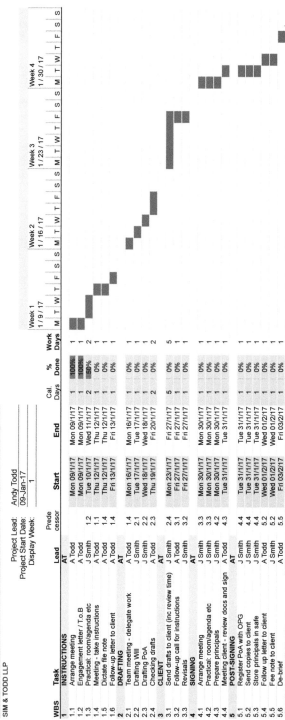

WBS	Task	Lead	Predecessor	Start	End	Cal. Days	% Done	Work Days
1	**INSTRUCTIONS**	**AT**						
1.1	Arrange meeting	A Todd		Mon 09/1/17	Mon 09/1/17	1	100%	1
1.2	Engagement letter / T.o.B	A Todd		Mon 09/1/17	Mon 09/1/17	1	100%	1
1.3	Practical: room/agenda etc	J Smith	1.2	Tue 10/1/17	Wed 11/1/17	2	50%	2
1.4	Meeting - take instructions	A Todd	1.1	Thu 12/1/17	Thu 12/1/17	1	0%	1
1.5	Dictate file note	A Todd	1.4	Thu 12/1/17	Thu 12/1/17	1	0%	1
1.6	Follow-up letter to client	A Todd	1.4	Fri 13/1/17	Fri 13/1/17	1	0%	1
2	**DRAFTING**	**AT**						
2.1	Team meeting - delegate work	A Todd	1.4	Mon 16/1/17	Mon 16/1/17	1	0%	1
2.2	Drafting Will	J Smith	2.1	Tue 17/1/17	Tue 17/1/17	1	0%	1
2.3	Drafting PoA	J Smith	2.2	Wed 18/1/17	Wed 18/1/17	1	0%	1
2.4	Checking drafts	A Todd	2.3	Thu 19/1/17	Fri 20/1/17	2	0%	2
3	**CLIENT**	**AT**						
3.1	Send drafts to client (inc review time)	J Smith	2.4	Mon 23/1/17	Fri 27/1/17	5	0%	5
3.2	Follow-up call for instructions	A Todd	3.1	Fri 27/1/17	Fri 27/1/17	1	0%	1
3.3	Revisals	J Smith	3.2	Fri 27/1/17	Fri 27/1/17	1	0%	1
4	**SIGNING**	**AT**						
4.1	Arrange meeting	J Smith	3.3	Mon 30/1/17	Mon 30/1/17	1	0%	1
4.2	Practical: room/agenda etc	J Smith	3.3	Mon 30/1/17	Mon 30/1/17	1	0%	1
4.3	Prepare principals	J Smith	4.2	Mon 30/1/17	Mon 30/1/17	1	0%	1
4.4	Meeting client - review docs and sign	A Todd	4.3	Tue 31/1/17	Tue 31/1/17	1	0%	1
5	**POST-SIGNING**	**AT**						
5.1	Register PoA with OPG	J Smith	4.4	Tue 31/1/17	Tue 31/1/17	1	0%	1
5.2	Send copies to client	J Smith	4.4	Tue 31/1/17	Tue 31/1/17	1	0%	1
5.3	Store principals in safe	J Smith	4.4	Tue 31/1/17	Tue 31/1/17	1	0%	1
5.4	Follow up letter to client	A Todd	5.2	Wed 01/2/17	Wed 01/2/17	1	0%	1
5.5	Fee note to client	J Smith	5.2	Wed 01/2/17	Wed 01/2/17	1	0%	1
5.6	De-brief	A Todd	5.5	Fri 03/2/17	Fri 03/2/17	1	0%	1

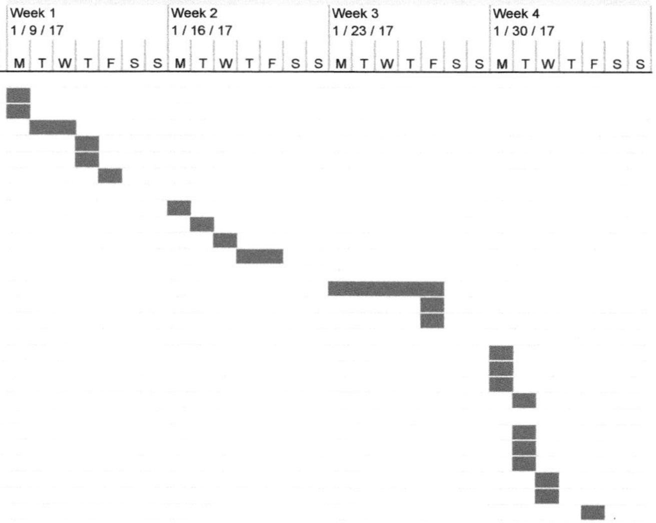

INDEX